Elmira Prisoner of War Camp
The North's Answer to Andersonville

By

Richard H. Triebe

First published by Smokey River Publishing

ISBN—13: 978-0-9798965-6-9

ISBN—10: 0-9798965-6-8

Cover photograph: This photograph shows 5,000 prisoners who were living in tents lined up for morning roll call. The photograph was taken in November or early December of 1864 as evidenced by the lack of leaves on the tree in the foreground. Note the hills, which had been heavily forested before the war, are now nearly devoid of trees. *Photograph courtesy of the North Carolina Museum of History.*

All photographs in this book are from the author's collection unless otherwise noted.

Other books by this author:

Confederate Fort Fisher, ISBN 1484032497

Fort Fisher to Elmira, ISBN 1530023238

On A Rising Tide, ISBN 1-4208-7849-2

Point Lookout Prison Camp and Hospital, ISBN 1495310140

Port Royal, ISBN 0-9798-9650-9

Smokey River Publishing

Printed in the United States of America

This book is printed on acid-free paper.

Table of Contents

__Introduction__

When I became interested in the American Civil War, I was full of questions. I guess that's why I became a writer of Civil War history. My interest in the war followed the usual progression in learning about the major battles, campaigns and the Northern blockade. Lastly, I became curious about what happened to the soldiers after they were captured. I soon discovered that the prisoner of war system gradually evolved from simple battlefield exchanges into something resembling World War II Nazi concentration or death camps. How did this happen?

When the Civil War began the Federal government instituted a Union blockade of all Southern ports. Certain items such as munitions, food, medicine and clothing were considered contraband of war and confiscated. As the war progressed many imported items were nearly impossible to obtain in the Confederacy.

As in all wars, battles are fought and soldiers are sometimes killed or taken prisoner. These captured soldiers were exchanged on the battlefield usually within ten days. These exchanges were halted by President Lincoln because he refused to recognize the Confederacy as a sovereign nation. The prisoners were then sent to prison camps and after a time the exchange was resumed. Yet due to an increase in tensions between the Federal government and the Confederate government the prisoner exchanges were suspended by the North in May of 1863. The prisons in the North and South became grossly overcrowded and conditions began to deteriorate which ultimately led to pollution, disease and thousands of deaths.

Because of the increased death toll, the Northern military accused the Confederacy of abusing Union prisoners by withholding food, and medicine. Although this was not the case. Many of the essential items a prisoner would need were extremely difficult to obtain in the South. This lack of essential supplies helped explain the high death rate in Confederate prisons. However, what could possibly cause so much disease and death in Union prison camps? After all, they had all the essential articles that the prisoners would need. This question led me to closely examine the Federal prison system. I studied the section of the Official Records of the Army that dealt with prisoners of war. After I had a thorough grasp of the situation it became apparent that the high death rate was because the Union military had reduced the amounts of essential supplies that were sent to the Northern prisons. Why were they doing this when it caused so much grief and suffering? Apparently, the Union felt justified in using retaliation against the Confederate prisoners.

In April and May of 1864 Major General Ulysses S. Grant's Overland Campaign in Virginia captured thousands of Confederate soldiers at the battles of the Wilderness, Spotsylvania and Cold Harbor. A new prison camp at Elmira, New York, was opened to relieve the overcrowding of the Federal prison at Point Lookout, Maryland. However, this prison was like no other. On the surface Elmira prisoner of war camp appeared to be very normal. Nevertheless, behind-the-scenes certain influential officials secretly planned to create a retaliatory prison to punish the Confederate prisoners for the suspected wrongs of Andersonville prison in Georgia.

My book, *Elmira Prisoner of War Camp,* explains how these things came about and were implemented to transform Elmira into what one prisoner says was "Hellmira."

A Note from the Author

Why do you write about Civil War prisons? I get asked that question a lot. I used to think the answer was fairly simple. It goes back to the time when I was doing research for another book. I went to the library one day to examine the microfilm of the Civil War Wilmington, North Carolina, newspaper. I was hoping to find some information that I could use in my book. Little did I know that I would uncover an article that would influence the type of books that I wrote.

While reading a paper from several days after the fall of Fort Fisher, I happened upon a note from a soldier who had been captured during the battle to his wife in Lumberton, North Carolina. The newspaper had printed this letter that was passed through Fort Fisher's lines under a flag of truce. This note caught my attention because it demonstrated how a husband and wife could be helplessly caught up in the throes of war. In it, Confederate soldier Benjamin Kinlaw assures his wife that he is well and will go north to prison in a short time. He tells her that she must do the best she can. With a writer's curiosity I investigated this man and found that he and his cousin were sent to Elmira prisoner-of-war camp in January of 1865. Both men would die from disease within two months. Why did two men in their early twenties die so quickly at Elmira? Then it hit me! I have a background in police work and love a good mystery! A prison camp with a high death rate is a lot like a murder mystery because you are searching for the truth about what caused the men to die so rapidly. One of the facts to emerge was the average death rate for Northern prisoner-of-war camps was 11% while Elmira prison camp had more than twice that rate. Why was it so high?

A Civil War prison with a high loss of life is a lot like a crime scene. What makes this story different is these men were captured fighting for their country and condemned to a life of misery, disease and possibly death. The punishment consisted of not being given adequate clothing and shelter for the harsh northern winter climate and being starved until disease and death overtook them. But this was just the tip of the iceberg. The prisoner's rations were also reduced by 30 percent causing the men to lose their ability to fight off deadly diseases. Unfortunately, this story only gets worse. As I dove deeper into the facts, I found Secretary of War Edwin M. Stanton halted the prisoner exchange in May of 1863. Gone was any hope of release from this nightmarish hell. The insidious part of halting the exchange now took effect. With no soldiers being released, Elmira prison camp became overcrowded and conditions deteriorated at a rapid pace. A body of water called Foster's Pond became so polluted that it prompted the chief surgeon to warn authorities numerous times about the danger it posed to the men's health. The vindictive nature of Stanton ignored these warnings because he wanted to punish the Confederate prisoners for their audacity to defy the United States Government.

Halting the prisoner's exchange was sacrificing not only Confederate lives, but also captured Union soldier's lives that languished in Southern prisons. The final insult, or nail in the men's coffins, was when a delegation of captured Union soldiers were allowed to go north to speak to the President about the horrible living conditions of the men at Andersonville prison camp in Georgia. Not only were they not allowed to see President Lincoln, but they were ushered in to see guess who? None other than Secretary of War Stanton! The answer they received? If you have any doubt about Stanton's answer, it went sort of like this, *Sorry, I can't help you! There is still a war going on and we cannot release thousands of the enemy soldiers to fight against us. You understand.* Stanton's argument does not hold water. These men came to see Lincoln in August of 1864. At this late date the war had less than a year to go and the Confederacy was on the ropes. In essence these men who did their patriotic duty fighting the enemy were told you no longer have the support of the United States government. You are on your own. These helpless men were left to die in prison because their release was not in the government's plan.

In the final analysis it is my sense of justice which prompts me to speak for these men. They have no other voice but historians who study the facts and expose the truth. If we as writers of history do not help them, we have also failed these patriots who gave their lives for their country.

Richard H. Triebe, June 2017

Chapter 1

The North Turns to Total War

The American Civil War has often been thought of as the first modern war. Certainly, it saw many warfare firsts: the first use of extensive trench warfare; the first use of rifled weapons; the first wartime use of modern inventions like the telegraph and the train for rapid troop movement; the first time mines and hand grenades were used; it also was the first time aerial observation of an enemy occurred.

Another first took place during this period that is often overlooked. What I am referring to is the mid-war change in strategy of the Northern military toward "Total War". The Federal authorities' attitude became increasingly harsh over time because of a widespread conviction that crushing the rebellion justified the severest action. No longer would the Union army only battle the Confederate army. This new concept began in earnest in 1864 and involved damaging the ability of people to supply the Confederate army with food, military information and aid. Many Northern officers felt the surest way to defeat the Confederate army was destroy the will of the Southern people. If the Union army could threaten the homes of southern civilians it was thought that Confederate soldiers would desert their posts and rush home to protect their families and property. Unfortunately, this new policy targeted innocent civilians whose only offense had been living south of the Mason-Dixon Line. Sherman was eager to teach the people of the South a lesson in the horrors of war. He wished to "make them so sick of war that generations would pass away before they would again appeal to it." This ruthless type of warfare left an indelible mark on Southern culture and forever stained the Federal military's conduct during the War Between the States.

As it will be shown in Chapter 2 this "Total War" policy was also applied to the prison system but for an entirely different reason.

Thaddeus S. Lowe's Civil War balloon *Intrepid* **observes the Confederate army, May 1862, Fair Oaks, Virginia.** *Picture courtesy Library of Congress.*

1

General Gillmore's Bombardment of Charleston

The war also saw the first bombardment of civilian areas like Atlanta, Ga., Charleston, S.C. and Vicksburg, Miss. A new type of incendiary shell was used in the siege of Charleston. The Union army fired explosive cannonballs into civilian areas filled with a substance known as Greek Fire. These shells contained a chemical similar to napalm that spread fire everywhere when the shell exploded. These flames were difficult to extinguish and produced volumes of noxious fumes.

Confederate Major-General Pierre G. T. Beauregard wrote a letter of protest to Union General Quincy A. Gillmore because only four hours notice had been given before the Union batteries opened fire on Charleston at 1:30 in the morning of August 22, 1864. Beauregard used the strongest terms to chastise General Gillmore for not allowing sufficient time for him to evacuate noncombatants from the city. I am including a portion of his letter here to show the reader the gravity of the situation involved and to illustrate Beauregard's indignation at this shameful act. It must be kept in mind that when General Gillmore gave notice of the bombardment it was during the night,

Union shells explode in Charleston, South Carolina. Photo appeared in *Illustrated London News*, August 1863.

at which time people were likely to be asleep. This is almost the same as not giving any warning before the Union batteries would open fire only a few hours later.

Charleston, S.C., August 22, 1863

Brig. Gen. Q. A. Gillmore,
Commanding U.S. Forces, Morris Island, S.C.:

SIR: Last night, at 15 minutes before 11 o'clock, during my absence on reconnaissance of my fortifications, a communication was received at these headquarters, dated headquarters Department of the South, Morris Island, S. C., August 21, 1863, demanding the "immediate evacuation of Morris Island and Fort Sumter by the Confederate forces." . . . . If this demand were "not complied with, or no replies thereto were received within four hours after it is delivered into the hands of your (my) subordinate commander at Fort Wagner for transmission," a fire would be opened on the city of Charleston "from batteries already established within easy and effective range of the heart of the city."

About half-past 1 AM this morning, one of your batteries did actually open and throw a number of heavy rifled shells into the city, the inhabitants of which, of course, were asleep and unarmed.

Among nations not barbarous the usages of war prescribe that when the city is about to be attacked timely notice shall be given by the attacking commander, in order that non-combatants may have an opportunity for withdrawing beyond its limits. Generally, the time allowed is from one to three days; that is, time for a withdrawal, in good faith, of at least the women and children. You, sir, give only four hours, knowing that your notice, under existing circumstances, could not reach me in less than two hours, and that not less than the same time would be required for an answer to be conveyed from this city to Battery Wagner. With this knowledge, you threaten to open fire on the city.

It would appear, sir, that despairing of reducing these works (Fort Sumter and the Confederate works on Morris Island), you now resort to the novel measure of turning your guns against the old men, the women and children, and the hospitals of the sleeping city, an act of inexcusable barbarity from your own confessed point of sight.

That you actually did open fire and throwing a number of the most destructive missiles ever used in war into the midst of the city taken unawares, and filled with sleeping women and children, will give you "a bad eminence" in history, even in the history of this war.

Since you have felt warranted in inaugurating this method of reducing batteries in your immediate front which were found otherwise impregnable, and the mode of warfare which I confidently declare to be atrocious and unworthy of any soldier, I now solemnly warn you that if you fire again on the city from your Morris Island batteries without granting a somewhat more reasonable time to remove non-combatants, I shall feel impelled to employ such stringent means of retaliation as may be available during the continuance of this attack.

General Beauregard reacts with surprise when shells containing Greek Fire explode in Charleston, SC.

Finally, I reply, that neither the works on Morris Island nor Fort Sumter will be evacuated on the demand you have been pleased to make. Already, however, I am taking measures to remove, with the utmost possible celerity, all non-combatants, who are now fully aware of and alive to what they may expect at your hands.

Respectfully, sir, your obedient servant,

G. T. Beauregard

Gen., Commanding[1]

Beauregard's letter of protest did nothing to deter Union General Gilmore from his course of action. In fact, the bombardment of Charleston increased.

Not to be outdone by the army, the Federal Navy in the western theater got into the act. Admiral David D. Porter ordered ten gross of incendiary rockets loaded with Greek Fire. Porter then distributed the rockets to gunboats of his fleet, so they could be fired into the city of Vicksburg, Mississippi. After the attack, Porter reported observing many fires raging in the city as a result.[2]

President Lincoln had a keen interest in new weapons of war. So-much-so, that he required a demonstration of new military hardware to see if they would meet the needs of the Government. Since the president needed to authorize the purchase of weapons containing Greek Fire it can be assumed this undertaking had his approval. Therefore, General Gilmore and Admiral Porter were not acting alone in their bombardment of civilian occupied cities. The Lieber Code was a set of rules concerning war that was instituted at the request of President Abraham Lincoln. It was published at the government printing office on April 24, 1863 as General Orders No. 100. The Code's Article 19 addresses the matter of bombardment of civilian areas. "Commanders, whenever admissible, inform the enemy of their intention to bombard a place, so that the noncombatants, and especially the women and children, may be removed before the bombardment commences."[3] This document shows the North knew it was legally and morally wrong not to give sufficient notice of an impending bombardment of civilians.

General Sheridan in the Shenandoah Valley

In early August of 1864 Lieutenant-General Ulysses S. Grant applied this "Total-War" strategy by placing Major-General Philip H. Sheridan in command of the Middle Military Division of the Army of the Shenandoah. Virginia's Shenandoah Valley had always been a thorn in the side of the Union because it was a vital resource to the Confederacy. Not only did the fertile valley serve as the "breadbasket" of the Confederacy, but it was an important route of march for Southern armies to move north without being observed. Their movement was hidden from Union eyes by the Blue Ridge Mountains to the east and the Allegheny Mountains to the west. A perfect example of this was when Confederate Lieutenant-

Major-General Sheridan employed a "scorched-earth" policy in the Shenandoah Valley. *Sketch by Alfred Waud, October 7, 1864.*

General Robert E. Lee used the Shenandoah Valley to conceal his army's march into Pennsylvania and ultimately to Gettysburg in June and July of 1863.[4]

On August 5, 1864, Lieutenant-General Grant issued the following order to Sheridan, "In pushing up the Shenandoah Valley it is desirable that nothing should be left to invite the enemy to return. Take all provisions, forage, and stock wanted for the use of your command; such as cannot be consumed, destroy. It is not desirable that the buildings should be destroyed—they should rather be protected; but the people should be informed that, so long as an (Confederate) army can subsist among them, recurrence of theses raids must be expected, and we are determined to stop them at all hazards."[5] Sheridan was further instructed by General Grant to "Do all the damage to railroads and crops you can. Carry off all stock of all descriptions, and Negros, so as to prevent further planting. If the war is to last another year, we want the Shenandoah Valley to remain a barren waste."[6]

In mid-August Sheridan's 40,000-man army began carrying out Grant's order in the northern end of the Shenandoah Valley by relentlessly burning all provisions and crops harvested and those still remaining in the field. Sheridan's cavalry, numbering approximately 5,000 horsemen, devastated the cities of Augusta, and Rockingham in Shenandoah, and Page counties in one of the war's most notorious examples of total-war. To this day residents of the Shenandoah Valley refer to this devastating time as "The Burning."

On October 3, 1864, as Union forces moved through Harrisonburg, Confederate scouts shot and killed Lieutenant John Meigs after he had severely wounded one of their men. Lieutenant Meigs was the son of Major-General Montgomery C. Meigs and Sheridan's favorite aide. Believing that local residents were responsible for the killing, an enraged Sheridan ordered the small village of Dayton, along with every house within a five-mile radius burned. This was contrary to General Grant's order that homes must not be destroyed. On the morning of October 4th, the men of the 116th Ohio learned to their dismay that it would be their job to burn the town of Dayton. People pleaded with them to stop, and Union soldiers often helped them carry belongings out of the house before setting fire to it. One Ohio Sergeant William T. Patterson wrote, "Such mourning, such lamentations, such crying and pleading for mercy. I never saw nor never want to see again, some were wild, crazy, mad, some crying for help while others would throw their arms around a Yankee soldier's neck and implore mercy."[7]

Lieutenant Colonel Thomas F. Wildes, who had once commanded the 116th Ohio, had reservations about retaliation toward civilians. He noted that the people of Dayton "were very kind to our men." Because of this, he wrote a letter to Sheridan in which he "urged and begged (him) to revoke the order in so far as Dayton was concerned." Although continuing to be upset about the killing of his favorite aide, Sheridan respected Wildes and was persuaded by his plea to spare the town. The order to burn the village was rescinded, although General Custer's 5th New York Cavalry was instructed to burn the homes in the surrounding area. However, this damage was not enough to satisfy Sheridan's anger. He also had all able-bodied men in the area arrested and held as prisoners of war. Whether it was intended or not, Sheridan's instructions extended well beyond the five mile radius.[8] A Pennsylvania cavalryman wrote home in mid-October: "We burnt some sixty houses and most of the barns, hay, grain and corn in the shocks for fifty miles (south of) Strasburg . . . . It was a hard-looking sight to see the women and children turned out of doors at this season of the year." An Ohio major wrote in his diary that the burning, "does not seem real soldierly work. We ought to enlist a force of scoundrels for such work."[9] The hard-hand of war had indeed come to the Shenandoah Valley.

Confederates Engage Sheridan in the Shenandoah Valley

The Confederates were not sitting idle while the Union army was burning and pillaging the valley. Lieutenant-General Jubal Early, commanding a 12,000-man army, was ordered into the Shenandoah to oppose the 40,000 soldiers of the Union army. On September 19th Union forces met the much smaller Confederate army at the battle of 3rd Winchester.

While Early's front was heavily engaged, Union General Crook's cavalry came around the Confederate's left flank and turned it causing a rout of the Southern force. To prevent annihilation, Early ordered a general retreat.

The armies battled again three days later at Fisher's Hill. This time the Confederate army held a strong position between the north branch of the Shenandoah River to Fisher's Hill. On the morning of the 22nd, General Crook's Corps commenced a flanking movement along the steep, timbered shoulder of North Mountain to outflank Early's forces. Early had considered defending against an attack from this quarter but thought this route was impassable. Unfortunately, he was mistaken. About 4 PM, Crook ordered his cavalry to charge into the Confederate left flank. The Union troopers rushed down the

President Lincoln's note saying General Sheridan has "the thanks of the nation" for burning the Shenandoah Valley!

side of the mountain scattering the outnumbered Confederate cavalry before them. The Confederate defense collapsed from west to east as Sheridan's other corps joined in the assault from the front. Early was utterly defeated once more.

Undaunted by the stronger Federal army, Jubal Early's soldiers carried out a daring night march. On the foggy morning of October 19, 1864, the Confederates surprised Union troops near Cedar Creek and drove first one, then another, then a third Union Corps from the field. Once an ally, the heavy fog now became a liability for the Confederate army. Early's troops became hopelessly jumbled during the heavy fighting. Also, the starving Confederates looted the abandoned Union camp where food and supplies were found.

As General Early paused to reorganize his victorious army, Union General Phil Sheridan arrived from headquarters in Winchester just in time to rally his troops and launch a crushing counterattack from which Early's force could not recover. Sheridan's victory at Cedar Creek extinguished any hope of further Confederate offensives in the Shenandoah Valley.

Sheridan continued the punitive operations of his mission, sending his cavalry as far south as Waynesboro to seize or destroy livestock and provisions, and to burn barns, mills, factories, and railroads. Sheridan's men pursued their work relentlessly, rendering over 400 miles uninhabitable. General Sheridan's destructive actions in the Shenandoah Valley proved to the Confederacy that the war had entered a new, harsh phase.

The Atlanta Campaign

With Northern presidential elections nearing, it was crucial for the Lincoln administration that Union armies make progress especially since the war in Virginia had bogged down. Seizing the city of Atlanta would severely weaken Southern morale and give confidence to Northern citizens who were tiring of the war. Capturing the city would be a major accomplishment since Atlanta was second to none as a Confederate war production center and railroad crossroads. Since Sherman's 100,000-man army heavily outnumbered Johnston's 40,000 Confederates the Atlanta campaign was characterized by a series of defensive battles and tactical retreats by the Confederate army, slowly drawing closer to Atlanta.

Anticipating that Sherman's army was headed to Atlanta, Confederate General Joe Johnston built a strong defensive position at Dalton, Georgia. When Sherman began advancing on this position, he avoided direct assaults on the Confederate defenses and instead began a series of flanking movements to force Johnston of out of his strong position. This wasn't easy since Johnston formidable defensive works allowed his troops to inflict more casualties than they received. Finally, the overwhelming Union attacks forced the Confederates to move from their works and meet Sherman's army in the open. Fierce but inconclusive fighting occurred on May 25, 1864, at New Hope Church. Again, Sherman refused a direct assault on the Confederate position choosing instead to attack Johnston flanks, trying to turn him away from Atlanta. Johnston was forced to make a tactical retreat to Pickett's Mill where Sherman again assaulted the Confederate flanks May 27. Johnston was forced to retire in the direction of Dallas where the Union army renewed their attacks on May 28. By June 1st, heavy rains turned the roads to quagmires and Sherman's troops marched to the nearest railroad to rest and resupply.

Johnston's new defensive position was established by June 4 northwest of Marietta, at long Lost Mountain, Pine Mountain, and Brush Mountain. On June 14, following eleven days of steady rain, Sherman was ready to move again. A group of Confederate officers were observed on Pine Mountain and Union artillery batteries opened fire. Lieutenant General Leonidas Polk was killed and Johnston withdrew his men from Pine Mountain, establishing a new arc-shaped defensive position from Kennesaw Mountain to Little Kennesaw Mountain.

Battle of Kennesaw Mountain

Hood's corps attempted an unsuccessful attack at the Battle of Kolb's Farm south of Little Kennesaw Mountain on June 22. Sherman was in a difficult position, stalled 15 miles north of Atlanta. He could not continue his strategy of moving around Johnston's flank because of the impassable roads, and his railroad supply line was dominated by Johnston's position on the top of Kennesaw Mountain.

Sherman wrote to Federal Army Chief of Staff Major-General Henry Halleck from his camp at Big Shanty, Georgia, on the 23rd of June.

"The whole country is one vast fort, and Johnston must have fifty miles of connected trenches, with abatis and finished batteries." "Our lines are now in close contact and the fighting incessant, with a good deal of artillery. As fast as we gain one position the enemy has another all ready, but I think he will soon have to let go Kennesaw, which is the key to the whole country."[12]

Sherman's path was blocked by imposing fortifications on Kennesaw Mountain, so he changed his tactics by ordering a large-scale frontal assault on June 27, 1864. Major General John A. Logan assaulted Pigeon Hill on its southwest corner while Major General George H. Thomas launched strong attacks against Cheatham Hill at the center of the Confederate line. Both attacks were repulsed with heavy losses, but an assault by Major General John M. Schofield achieved a strategic success by threatening the Confederate army's left flank, prompting yet another Confederate withdrawal toward Atlanta.

President Jefferson Davis was growing impatient with General Johnston's constant withdrawals because they looked like defeatism and were bad for moral. He demanded Johnson take offensive action since both armies were less than two days march north of Atlanta. As always, Johnston examined the ground and determined that the best place to attack Sherman's army was when it was separated and crossing Peachtree Creek. On July 17th Davis finally had enough and relieved Johnston of his command, replacing him with the aggressive Major General John Bell Hood.

Confederate Major-General John Bell Hood

Hood saw the value of his predecessor's plan and immediately went on the offensive by attacking General George Thomas after his army forded Peachtree Creek. The determined assault threatened to overrun the Federal troops at various locations, but eventually the Union held, and the Confederates fell back. In the fighting at Peachtree Creek, Hood suffered 2,500 killed and wounded while Thomas sustained around 1,900.

Quickly recovering, Hood began planning to strike at Sherman's other flank by sending some of his troops east. Hood attacked Sherman on July 22nd at the battle of Atlanta. The battle's name is somewhat of a misnomer since the fighting occurred several miles southeast of the city.

By the time Sherman's army marched to Atlanta, Hood's Confederates were entrenched in the outer line of defenses that ringed the city. The Union Army probed these trenches searching for a weakness. During the night of July 21st, Hood withdrew his main army from Atlanta's outer works to the inner line, enticing Sherman to follow. In the meantime, he sent General William Hardee with his corps on a fifteen-mile march to assault the unprotected Union left and rear, east of the city. The following morning General Benjamin Cheatham's corps was to attack the Union front. Hood miscalculated the time necessary to make the march, and Hardee was unable to attack until the afternoon. Union General James McPherson became concerned about his left flank and sent his reserves to that location. Two of Hoods divisions ran into the reserve force and were repulsed after heavy fighting.

The Confederate attack stalled on the Union rear, but began to roll up the left flank. About 4 PM Cheatham's Corps broke through the Union front, but massed artillery halted the Confederate assault. Union General John A. Logan's 15th corps then led a counterattack against Cheatham's troops and restored the Union line. The Union troops held and Hood suffered 5,499 casualties to the Union's 3,641. One of the greatest losses for the Federals was when Major General James B. McPherson was shot by a sniper when he rode out to observe the fighting.

The Siege of Atlanta

When Sherman's army marched from Decatur and began approaching Atlanta from the north he issued Special Field Order No. 39 to his commanders.

"The whole army will move on Atlanta by the most direct roads tomorrow, July 20, beginning at 5 a.m. Each army commander will accept battle on anything like fair terms, but if the army reach within cannon-range of the city without receiving artillery or musketry fire he will halt, form a strong line, with batteries in position, and await orders. If fired on from the forts or buildings of Atlanta no consideration must be paid to the fact that they are occupied by families, but the place must be cannonaded without the formality of a demand."[13]

So, it seems Sherman was going to cannonade the city without the usual formality of issuing a letter of warning to the citizens of Atlanta announcing his intentions. This surprise bombardment gave non-combatants no time whatsoever to prepare for this hostile action.

When Sherman's 65,000-man army marched to the outskirts of Atlanta he brought his artillery within a mile of the city and arrayed them in an arc around the east side of the city.

The shell damaged Ponder House in Atlanta, Ga. *Photo courtesy of Library of Congress.*

The Confederate Army had prepared Atlanta for such a reality. Under the supervision of military engineer Colonel L. P. Grant the city had been made the center of a circle of impenetrable forts and breast works. Thousands of Negroes had cut down every tree and shrub within a mile of the fortifications, so the Confederate guns had a clear field of fire.

The Federals brought in several long-range siege guns by train from Chattanooga to aid in the siege of Atlanta. Now with these heavy artillery pieces in place, he wired General Henry Halleck and boasted, "We can pick out almost any house in town." And then he added, "Whether we get inside of Atlanta or not, it will be a used up community when we are done with it."[14] Before we proceed any further I need to define the terms "Total War" and

"Hard War" to prevent any confusion. There is a distinct difference between these two expressions. "Total War" was a type of warfare that targeted Southern civilians who were suspected of giving aid, food and information to the enemy. "Hard War", on the other hand, treated all Southern civilians as the enemy.

This part of the campaign signaled a departure from Sherman's previous treatment of civilians. The siege of Atlanta is where Sherman truly begins his brand of "Hard War" against innocent civilians. He now viewed them as a part of the enemy that he was unable to fight. As a military officer, he overstepped his bounds by targeting a civilian population who were doing nothing to aid the enemy. They were not legitimate targets for a normal, commanding officer. Sherman left conventional military wisdom behind and fired his long-range cannon indiscriminately into residential areas populated by old men, women and children. Many of these innocent victims were gunned down unaware they were now considered targets by a Union General who had convinced himself that the people of the city were also his enemy.

This is what Article 44 of the Lieber Code said about this type of behavior: "*All wanton violence committed against persons in the invaded country, all destruction of property not commanded by the authorized officer, all robbery, all pillage or sacking, even after taking a place by main force, all rape, wounding, maiming, or killing of such inhabitants, are prohibited under the penalty of death, or such other severe punishment as may seem adequate for the gravity of the offense.*

A soldier, officer, or private, in the act of committing such violence, and disobeying a superior ordering him to abstain from it, may be lawfully killed on the spot by such superior."

The only difference between what the Lieber Code said, and Sherman's actions were that he authorized it. This undertaking is far removed from what the code intended. The Code was talking about a single incident, not widespread killing and destruction of civilians. This bombardment of civilian areas of the city made it clear that Sherman was putting himself above the law and making up the rules as he went along.

On August 9, 1864 Sherman unleased the full power of his artillery by bombarding Atlanta with 5,000 rounds of solid shot and shell. This proved to be the heaviest bombardment ever inflicted on an American city. This siege would continue wreaking extensive damage on Atlanta and its occupants through the month of August.

Wallace P. Reed wrote about some of the civilians who suffered the wrath of Sherman's bombardment of August 9th. Ironically one of the first people to be killed was a free Negro named Solomon Luckie. Solomon was a well-liked barber who stepped outside of his shop that morning to listen to the shelling of Atlanta. Suddenly a shell hit the street where it ricocheted up,

Negro Barber Solomon Luckie was killed by a cannonball fragment when a shell hit a gas lamp and exploded in front of his shop.

struck a lamppost then burst into deadly fragments. Several pieces of this jagged, red-hot iron ripped through Solomon's body. He was taken to Atlanta Medical College where his leg was amputated, but he died two hours later.

Captain E. C. Murphy of the first Volunteer Fire Department wrote about the shell that killed Luckie. "All of a sudden there came a moaning overhead and a shell cracked in the middle of Alabama Street. It ricocheted off the street and came straight at me. It hit a lamppost, and down I fell flat on my stomach. Right behind me was an old Negro man (Luckie), and the shell pieces went right over my head with a sucking noise and . . . to him. When I got up he was lying there covered with blood. Johnny McGee and I wrapped him up in a horse blanket and took him to the hospital."[15]

Nelson Warner and his six-year-old daughter lay asleep in their house at the corner of Elliott and Rhodes streets. A shell tore through the ceiling and ripped the girl's body in half. The same shell cut off both of Warner's legs at the thighs. Both the father and daughter bled to death.[16]

An unknown lady who was ironing some clothes in a house on North Pryor Street, between the Methodist Church and Wheat Street, was struck by a shell fragment and killed. In another incident, a woman and her son stood in front of their home on Forsyth Street, saying goodbye to a Confederate officer when a shell struck nearby. Both the officer and her son were struck by iron fragments and carried to a shady spot under some trees where they bled to death.

In another section of the city, a family of six scrambled into their shelter. It suffered a direct hit and all inside were killed. Near the railroad station a refugee from Rome, Georgia, was bending over to pick something up when shell fragments tore through his body killing him instantly.[17]

All of these fatalities happened on August 9th because of Sherman's refusal to attack Atlanta directly by using a coordinated assault by artillery and infantry. This was the traditional way a well defended city was attacked. The military fought the enemy's military and the citizens were not involved. No city during the Civil War was ever captured by artillery alone. So why did Sherman expect a different outcome? Apparently, he didn't. He was trying to intimidate the people and the Confederate army into leaving the city undefended. This was not the act of an honorable man. This was the act of a coward who brought shame to thousands of decent officers.

After several days of shelling by Union artillery nearly all able-bodied men dug a bomb shelter in the backyard for their family. This was done by digging a hole about twenty-five feet in length, eight feet in width and nine or ten feet deep. Then a framework of wooden timbers would be erected and the top and sides were covered with the dirt that was removed from the hole. A heavy door was then fashioned from wooden planks and attached to the doorframe.

Some of the soldiers guarding Atlanta were glad to give families a helping hand in building a bombproof. This not only got them out of the trenches for a while, but provided a chance to meet the fair sex and perhaps socialize with someone other than soldiers. A soldier, who was also a correspondent for the *Columbus Sun*, wrote that "every citizen has a bombproof in his yard." He went on to say that he assisted one family in the construction of their dugout "till my hands were well blistered but felt well-paid when dinner time came."

Diarist Sam Richards wrote, "For fear that (shells) should ever reach us I have done several days' hard work preparing a "pit" in our cellar, to retreat to for shelter." A few days later Richards was alarmed to find several shell fragments in his yard, and

Here is a picture of a bombproof dug into the ground.

added the entry, "I had our pit dug three feet deeper this week and put a barricade in front of boxes filled with dirt."[18]

A few fortunate families that lived near the railroad tracks were able to hollow out caves from the side of the embankments. However, the area around the railroads was fraught with danger and proved to be a prime target for Sherman's artillery.

A young girl named Lucy Caldwell wrote in her diary that she used the pit in her neighbor's yard, which was dug six feet in the ground and covered with timber and earth. "Within was laid a carpet and a few chairs," she recalled, "thither we would go, when the shelling began."

Historian Wallace P. Reed wrote about an unusual story that came out of the bombardment. "One hot July night," he wrote, "the members of a little family in the southern part of the city sat in their piazza trying in vain to obtain a breath of cool air. Occasionally a few shells ascended with a whish into the mid-heavens, and burst with a deafening explosion. The watchers were not afraid of these missiles, as they could see their approach a long way off. Suddenly there was a thunderclap in the next yard. Several panels of the fence were knocked down, and a few stray fragments of shell knocked off two or three of the banisters of the piazza. In less than ten seconds the family had found its way into the reliable bombproof.

'Pshaw! I am not going to stay down here this hot night," said the only man in the party. "I'll go up to my room and finish reading the 'Life of Napoleon,' and if there is any real danger I will come down to you.' There were tears in protest, but the Colonel, as he was called, was stubborn. So, he went upstairs in the wing of the building nearest to the bombproof and seated himself by window, where he had the advantage of a light, and could also look out upon the city. The shelling was terrific, but the inmates of the dugout, every time they took a peep could see the Colonel turning over the pages of his Napoleon, apparently forgetful of the stirring occurrences around him. Had a volcano broken loose? The ground trembled under the shock of the explosion, and after the lurid glare had died away, the dense fumes of sulfur filled the air, and made the atmosphere so thick that nothing could be seen. Before the terrified people in the bombproof had pulled themselves together, something very much like a singed cat, only bigger, rolled down into their midst, and then sat up with a sneeze. It was the Colonel! There were frantic inquiries, and a close inspection of the victim, but it was soon discovered that he had escaped without any more serious damage than a few bruises, and the blackening of his face with gunpowder. 'How did it happen?' asked everybody in a chorus. 'Don't ask me,' replied the Colonel irritably. 'You know as well as I do. It must've been a twenty-four pounder. I know I can't hear, and I could hardly see, and I'm all choked up with sulfur and rubbish.' Just then his wife, who had looked out gave a cry, 'Where is the left wing of the house?' she asked. 'Don't know. Don't ask me. I couldn't bring it with me, you know. It was all I could do to get here myself.'

When morning dawned the extent of the wreck could be seen at a glance. The shell had completely demolished the wing in which the Colonel had been sitting in an upper room, and his escape appeared to be almost miraculous. After that the Colonel stuck closely to his family in the bombproof, and yet during all those long weeks of the siege that followed, the house was never struck again."[19]

Wallace P. Reed described Tuesday the ninth as, "that red day in August, when all the fires of hell, and all the thunders of the universe seemed to be blazing and roaring over Atlanta." Looking up, Reed saw that a "great volume of sulfurous smoke rolled over the town, trailing down to the ground, and through this stifling gloom the sun glared down like a great red eye peering through a bronze colored sky."[20] A doctor reported that his hospital performed 107 amputations during the siege of Atlanta. His hospital was one of seven that served the city.

Sam Watkins of the 1st Tennessee visited an army hospital and came away depressed. "Great God! I get sick when I think of the agony, and suffering, and sickening stench and odor of dead and dying; of wounds and sloughing sore, caused by the deadly gangrene; of the groaning and wailing. I cannot describe it. I remember, I went in the rear of the building, and there I saw a pile of arms and legs, rotting and decomposing; and although I saw thousands of horrifying scenes during the war . . . I remember with more horror that pile of legs and arms that had been cut off our soldiers."[21]

A pile of amputated legs and feet litter the hospital floor after a Civil War battle.

It is my contention that Sherman deliberately fired his cannon into civilian areas of Atlanta. If he did not intend to do so, then why did he send to Chattanooga for long-range artillery pieces? Sherman's army of 65,000 men already possessed hundreds of rifled cannons with a range of three miles. Only 200 to 300 yards separated the Confederate trenches from the Union works. That's less than a quarter mile from the enemy defenses. So why did Sherman feel it was necessary to have long-range guns? I believe it was his intention all along not to make an infantry assault on Atlanta. In fact, he admitted this to General Halleck on August 7th when he wrote, "I am too impatient for a siege." It would appear Sherman thought that he could bombard the city into an early surrender.

To demonstrate the needlessness of shelling Atlanta consider these facts. Sherman did not resort to frontal attacks on Confederate fortifications to follow up his bombardment. This showed no real expectation of capturing the city. It only proved to kill and terrify the civilian population and destroy their property. What proved effective is when the Union forces extended their lines around two-thirds of the city and slowly cut the railroad lines. When they cut the Macon & Western Railroad to the south, they severed General Hood's last supply line, leaving him little choice but to evacuate his army. It was this strategy that captured the city, not the bombardment.

If there is any doubt in your mind about Sherman's intentions about destroying Atlanta, remember his words to General Oliver Howard the day after the heaviest bombardment of that city. Sherman said, "Let us destroy Atlanta and make it a desolation."[22] That statement makes it clear what Sherman intended.

> *The Daily Constitutionalist, Augusta, Georgia, August 28, 1864, reported:*
>
> *The shelling still goes on. "The murder of the innocents"— bids fair to be one of the most poignant tragedies of modern times— night and day it is unabated, and one continuous explosion of forty-pound spherical case balls.*
>
> *Can you imagine anything more brutal than the bombardment of the city, crowded with poor people, who are unable to get away, and are forced by their poverty to remain and to suffer? Bear in mind that this bombardment is not pretended even by the enemy to bear upon the military situation one bullet's weight. There are no stores to be destroyed; the soldiers are all in the trenches, and the thousands of shells thrown into harmless dwellings cannot possibly affect the reduction of the city. The motive is one of petty spite, the spite of cowards, who dare not attack our lines and wreak their disappointment upon women and children. But they add insult to injury, when with the cant of*

the devil upon their lips, they deny that their shots are directed towards the town.

Day before yesterday, a party of ladies, who obtained passes, crossed the lines and approached the Yankee pickets. They were halted, detained all day, and sent back. In the course of a conversation with one of the Federal artillerists, one of the ladies said she was afraid of the shells, and hence desired to get out of Atlanta." "You need not alarm yourself, for none of them are aimed at the city." The lady gave him an indignant look to show him that she knew he was a liar, as well as an assassin, and replied: "Then you must be a very poor set of marksmen, for every one of your shots fall in the heart of the town, killing women and children every day."

Historian Wallace P. Reed gave specific locations of where Union shells exploded in his book *History of Atlanta, Georgia*. I obtained an 1864 street map of Atlanta and plotted the locations he provided using a red pen. In 1864 the city was only 2 miles in diameter. All the shells impacted a mile square area in the center of the town. The lady that was mentioned in the above paragraph spoke the truth when she said, "every one of your shots fall in the heart of the town, killing women and children every day."

Atlanta's First Union Station in ruins.

When General Hood protested the shelling of Atlanta, Sherman accused him of having his defenses too close to the city so that any over shots that missed their mark went into the town. As I said before, 100% of the shells exploded in the heart of the city. This was no accident as Sherman claimed. This was a deliberate act by a man who did not care what happened to the people of Atlanta.

Even General Hood addressed Sherman's lie by saying, *"I feel no other emotion than pain in reading that portion of your letter which attempts to justify your shelling of Atlanta*

15

without notice under pretense that I defended Atlanta upon a line so close to town that every cannon shot, and many musket balls from your line of investment, that overshot their mark went into the habitations of women and children. There are 100,000 witnesses that you fired into the habitations of women and children for weeks, firing far above and miles beyond my line of defense. I have too good an opinion, founded both upon observation and experience, of the skills of your artillerists to credit the insinuation that they for several weeks unintentionally fired too high for my modest field works, and slaughtered women and children by accident and want of skill.[23]

The damage from the bombardment was obvious to the Federals. Union soldier Alpheus Bloomfield observed, "scarcely a night passes but the town is set on fire."

The Union artillerists would use the church spires of the beleaguered city to guide their shells. Sergeant James Nourse noted that Union gunners would fire towards buildings from which dense black smoke already poured to harass Confederate firefighters.

Indeed, a correspondent for the Daily Constitutionalist, Augusta, Georgia, wrote:

> *"Trying to burn Atlanta—Vandalism ran mad—Sherman the Viper—A frightful scene, etc.*
> *Atlanta, August 20, 1864*
>
> *The Vandals in front of us having failed to take the city by fair means, and in open combat are resorting to the last expedient of a baffled, unprincipled and disconsolate bully—that of its destruction by fire. Within the last four and twenty hours as many as nine buildings have touched the ground, and are now visible only in smoldering walls and charred ruins. During these conflagrations the Yankee batteries played vigorously upon the fire battalion. They obtained the range by the clouds of smoke and flame and had nothing more noble to do than to drop their shells and among the humane non-combatants at their work of charity, and the frightened and houseless women and children fleeing from the wrath of the two fierce and consuming enemies.*
>
> *Last night a shell, a forty-two pounder, struck the Presbyterian*

Church. It passed through the pulpit and floor into the basement, or Sunday school room, where a number of citizens had sought refuge: here it exploded. The scene which followed was frightful. Several were hurt and one poor fellow had his arms shot off.

General Sherman Marches on Jonesboro

Since General Sherman was unwilling to launch frontal assaults against prepared defenses he continued to bombard Atlanta even though he knew that this by itself wasn't enough to make the city surrender. Assessing the situation after a month of fruitless maneuvers and constant shelling, Sherman decided that the only way to capture the city was to sever its last remaining supply line to the south. On August 25th six divisions totaling 60,000 Federal soldiers left their positions around the city and marched west, then turned south to cut the Macon & Western Railroad. Only Henry Slocum's XX corps remained north of Atlanta with orders to guard the Federal Army's supply line's railroad bridge over the Chattahoochee River.

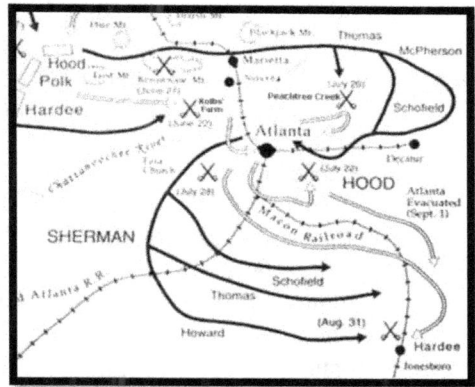

General Sherman sends 60,000 men to Jonesboro

General Hood was perplexed to discover the Union army had abandoned their trenches. He knew Sherman to be a tenacious adversary and didn't think it likely he would pull up stakes and suddenly cancel his plans to capture Atlanta. Hood suspected the Union army was up to something, but he wasn't sure what? While Hood was wondering where Sherman went, the people of Atlanta were celebrating their good fortune. They believed the Yankee army was starving and in full retreat. For the first time in five weeks the Atlantans could leave their homes and visit friends or go anywhere in the city without having to worry about a Union bombardment. On Sunday, August 28th, thousands of people gathered in their damaged churches to thank God for the end of the shelling.

Two days later Hood learned that a portion of Sherman's army was south of him and tearing up the tracks of the Atlanta & West Point Railroad near the town of Rough and Ready. The next day it was reported that the bulk of Sherman's army had reached the Flint River west of Jonesboro and were in a strong position to attack the Macon and Western Railroad. This was Atlanta's last supply line and if it were cut the city was lost. Hood immediately ordered Lieutenant General William Hardee's and Major General Stephen D. Lee's corps south to Jonesboro to attack the Union troops and protect the railroad. By

17

nightfall of the 30th over 23,000 Confederate troops were moving into position to the west of Jonesboro.

The Battle of Jonesboro: The First Day

Fighting broke out on the afternoon of the 31st when Major General Hardee ordered an attack against Union General John Logan's forces. At the same time, Confederate Major General Patrick Cleburne led his corps in an all-out assault against the right of the Union forces. Confederate troops initially met with success and broke through the outer Union line, and captured several artillery pieces. While Cleburne was engaged, General Hardee's and Lee's corps marched to attack the Union left. However, when Lee heard Hardee's men firing at some Federal pickets he mistakenly believed the main assault was underway and prematurely advance his corps to strike Howard's army. The Union soldiers had a solid defense and poured a devastating fire into the Lee's Confederates and quickly repulsed them. To the south Confederate General Patrick Cleburne's division advanced into a gully and his lines became broken. To make matters worse, the Confederate attack came upon a small body of Federal cavalry under General Judson Kilpatrick which broke up their lines further. Hardee sent word to Lee that he was to renew his assault. Lee responded that this was impossible due to the "timidity" of his troops. Hardee then ordered all Confederate troops to break off attacks and withdraw. The poorly coordinated attacks against entrenched Union positions resulted in 1,725 Confederate casualties while the Union lost only 179 men.

That evening General Hood summoned Generals Hardee and Lee to Atlanta for a conference. General Hardee appraised Hood to the deteriorating situation at Jonesboro and said the Macon and Western Railroad was in danger of being captured. He also advised General Hood that if this happened he should abandon Atlanta. Hardee pointed out that now was the perfect time to do so with the bulk of Sherman's army down at Jonesboro. Hood agreed and instructed Lee to return his corps to the city to cover the army's retreat from Atlanta. The news took Hardee by surprise. This order would leave only his small exhausted, command of 12,000 soldiers to man the over-extended Confederate line. When Hardee returned to Jonesboro his men moved in the works Lee had left when he marched to Atlanta.

The Battle of Jonesboro: The Second Day

Sherman ordered Generals George Thomas and John Schofield to advance their armies to the Macon and Western Railroad at a point several miles north of Jonesboro. Then they were to proceed south along the tracks and come in behind the Confederate lines and seize the town. Federal General Jefferson C. Davis' 14th Corps arrived first and assaulted the northern portion of the Confederate line just to the north of Jonesboro. At the same time, General Oliver Howard's troops engaged Hardee's front west of town to prevent any reinforcements from being sent to counter the attack of the 14th corps.

The fighting was vicious and for a time the Federals were held in check. But ultimately, a breakthrough could not be helped. Nor could it be plugged once the lines were breached. Seeing no other option Hardee's Corps made an orderly retreat to Lovejoy Station.

Over the course of the two-day battle at Jonesboro Confederate General William Hardee lost well over 2,700 men while the Federals lost over 1,300 soldiers. With the city captured the Federal army was free to destroy the railroad tracks and train depot and any rolling stock that was at the station. Now the final link of the Confederacy's lifeline to Atlanta was severed.

THE BATTLE OF JONESBORO GEORGIA, SEPT 1st 1864.

General Sherman had executed a very successful strategy in capturing Jonesboro and cutting the last railroad connection to Atlanta, but he committed a serious blunder when he failed to capture Hood's army. It was entirely possible that the Confederates in Atlanta could have been destroyed if Sherman had the foresight to rush two of his six corps back to the city to block any escape routes. Instead Sherman's troops were focused on crushing General Hardee near Lovejoy Station.

Hood Abandons Atlanta

Early in the morning of September 1st General Hood learned of the Confederate defeat at Jonesboro and the Union army seizing the Macon and Western Railroad. This meant the city of Atlanta was doomed because his army was cut off from any resupply. If he stayed and fought it out with Sherman, he would soon run out of food and ammunition and be forced to surrender to the Union Army. This was unacceptable to Hood, so he instructed his staff to begin preparations for the army's evacuation of the city. Orders went out to begin destroying Confederate manufacturing areas the morning of September 1st with the movement of troops to begin that afternoon.

Citizens had seen the Confederate Army leave Atlanta several days ago in pursuit of Sherman and knew there was to be a great battle. Distant sounds of gunfire confirmed this. Concern became alarm when Confederate deserters filtered through Atlanta, spreading rumors of their army's defeat. Hoping that this wasn't true residents began milling around in the streets trying to learn what was happening.

General Sherman had executed a very successful strategy in capturing Jonesboro and cutting the last railroad connection to Atlanta, but he committed a serious blunder when he failed to capture Hood's army. It was entirely possible that the Confederates in Atlanta could have been destroyed if Sherman had the foresight to rush two of his six corps back to the city to block any escape routes. Instead Sherman's troops were focused on crushing General Hardee near Lovejoy Station.

Commissary stores which could be not be removed needed to be distributed to the citizens, so the Yankees could not capture them. One of the first things Hood did was to issue extra rations to his soldiers and then throw open the commissary's warehouses to the peo-

19

ple of the city. When Hood did this it confirmed all the rumors that the citizens had heard about General Hood deserting Atlanta. Major Charles Hubner recalled "The warehouse was filled with foodstuffs of all kinds, and for several hours a large crowd of women, children and men, were kept busy rolling away barrels of syrup, sugar, etc. Upon their shoulders they carried hams, side-meat and sacks of provisions, all of which had been indiscriminately distributed to the eager, hungry populace; the sight was ludicrous as well as pathetic."[24]

Not all the plans for the removal of Confederate supplies went smoothly. General Hood ordered his ordinance train, which contained his reserve ammunition, to go south but unfortunately this was not done before Sherman seized the railroad. Therefore, Hood had no choice but to destroy eighty-one cars of munitions, supplies and equipment plus five locomotives. Also destroyed were the Western & Atlantic's depot and railroad house, the cannon foundry, the Confederate arsenal, the Confederate rolling mill and the Atlantic machine company.

That afternoon large bodies of Confederate soldiers were withdrawn from the city's defenses and began to file out of town followed by numerous supply wagons pulling light artillery pieces. The citizens of the city watched the soldiers leave with disbelief and sorrow and wondered what would be their fate when the enemy was in control. An *Augusta Sentinel* correspondent wrote of the scene, "The troops filed through the streets with a steady tread, it is true, but nevertheless with sorrow depicted on their weather-beaten countenances."

Major-General Sherman's March to the Sea

Brutal, scorched-earth tactics used by General Sheridan in the Shenandoah Valley demonstrated to Major-General William T. Sherman that a similar strategy could be employed in Georgia. The goal of his campaign was to break the will of the Southern people and hurt the Confederate army in the process. Sherman also wanted to show the Southern people that their army was unable to protect them.

He theorized that the rebel army would lose many of its men to desertion if they felt the need to rush home to Georgia and South Carolina to defend their families and property. The idea that the Southern people deserved their fate was of crucial importance to Sherman. The notion that there were no noncombatants in the South, that every man, woman, and child contributed to the Confederate cause made it easier to justify attacks on civilians. He wrote to Halleck: "We are not only fighting hostile armies, but a hostile people, and we must make old and young, rich and poor, feel the hard hand of war, as well as the organized armies."[25] It was for this reason that he felt justified in destroying private property.

Major-General Sherman marched his 60,000-man army through Georgia and the Carolina's where he destroyed southern warehouses, factories, trains, railroads, crops and burned many of the civilian homes in his path. Sherman's foraging parties went into the surrounding countryside to gather food and equipment to sustain his army. At first these foraging parties, known as bummers, did their job remarkably well. However, many of these men took Sherman's order to "forage liberally" to an extreme and became a reckless, paramilitary extension of the army. Drunk with their newly acquired power over the surrounding civilian population some of these bummers resorted to breaking the law. Numerous Southerners reported incidents of rape, murder, valuables such as silver and gold were stolen, confiscation of food, horses, mules, wag-

Sherman's bummers loot a Southern plantation. Photo courtesy of *Recollections of a Bummer*.

ons, along with household items such as tables, chairs etc. Many times, what couldn't be carried off was simply destroyed to rob the owner of its use. A few of these bummers threatened civilians with physical harm in an effort to get them to reveal the hiding places of their valuables. General Sherman largely turned a blind eye to this behavior because he wanted these stories to filter back to the men in the Confederate Army so they would cause widespread desertion.

There are numerous stories of Southern women who begged and pleaded with Union soldiers for mercy because they were leaving their families with practically nothing to eat. Such a woman was Mrs. Alfred Proctor Aldrich. Although her story is rather lengthy, I have included a section of her journal because it illustrates both the good and evil side of human nature. It is important to note that while many terrible things did occur, there were a few decent men that came forward to lend a hand when it was needed. Unfortunately, this was not always the case. Most civilians were given only a brief warning before their homes were looted and burnt to the ground.

Mrs. Alfred Proctor Aldrich was filled with dread at the approach of Sherman's army. "The Oaks" plantation in South Carolina was practically deserted because her husband and son were in the Confederate army. Fearing for the safety of her three daughters, she had sent them to stay with relatives in Columbia. The only people with her now were several trusted Negro servants to help her manage the large house. Mrs. Aldrich had heard numerous stories coming out of Georgia about how hordes of barbarians from the Union army had committed unspeakable atrocities before burning Atlanta and thousands of homes across the state. Now they had crossed over into South Carolina and she could see a foreboding cloud of smoke as the invading army drew near. Mrs. Aldrich bowed her head and said a silent prayer for her delivery while the booming of artillery could be heard as the enemy clashed with General Joseph Wheeler's Confederate cavalry.

Early in the morning on February 5, 1865 Mrs. Aldrich saw the vanguard of Union General Judson Kilpatrick's cavalry come down the long avenue of oaks to her house.

One of Sherman's Bummers leaves a Southern house with a hog, lamb and a full basket of loot while he is being chased by the lady of the house. Photo courtesy of *Recollections of a Bummer*.

"The first soldiers who rushed into the house seemed only intent on searching for food," Mrs. Aldrich recalled. "Soon, however, as they were satisfied, their tramp through the house began. They were pouring in at every door, and without asking to have bureaus in wardrobes open, broke with their bayonets every lock, tearing out the contents, in hunting for gold, silver and jewels."

"Unfortunately, a few bottles of whiskey had been overlooked in the wine closet when the milk was removed. This prize they were not long in finding, which seemed to infuriate and arouse all their evil passions, so the work of destruction began in earnest. Tables were knocked over, lamps with their contents thrown over the carpets, furniture of all sorts broken, a guitar and violin smashed."

"The infantry soon appeared and were ten days and nights passing through. When one swarm departed, another more hungry for spoil would file in. And so we live for days and nights, with guns and bayonets flashing in our faces, and the course language of ruffians sounding in our ears."

"One day a rough looking soldier appeared carrying a rope in his hand. I learned afterward he had three times hung up one of our servants. Who had been reported as having aided me in hiding my silver. Each of the three times this man suspended poor Frank in the air he would let him down, trying to make him confess. Not knowing anything, of course he could not give the coveted information. Frank's neck remains twisted to this day. With this rope shaken in my face, the monster said, 'Madam, if you do not tell me in five minutes where your silver is buried I will set fire to your home.'"

"You dare not burn my house for General Sherman has forbidden it."

"Just then I was greatly surprised to hear a voice at my back say: 'Let the lady alone; you have no right to insult her after taking everything you could find. As to her silver, I can tell you it is not here, it has been sent to Camden for bank safety.'"

"I turned and looked at the pleasant, humane looking face of this soldier in wonder and gratitude for his timely interference."

"This good man stood nobly by us in several trying scenes after, and repeatedly expressed his (disapproval) of war and his sorrow for what he saw going on around him." Unfortunately, this gentleman had to move on.

Over the next several days roving bands of infantry set fire nine times to Mrs. Aldrich's house and stables, but her faithful servants were able to alert their mistress and put them out.

One day a woman friend had followed some soldiers upstairs and discovered another fire had been set in her bedroom. "(Mrs. E.) was none too soon, for, as she reached the landing, she heard a match scratched and great laughter. Running into a chamber beyond, she found a part of the 'Boys'—this seemed to be a pet name for privates by their officers—surrounding the bed, on which they had piled up books and papers, and applied the match. She sprang forward and scattered the combustibles on the floor, exclaiming, 'My God, do you intend to burn us up?'"

Sherman's bummers were told by their commanding General to "Foraging Liberally". Here two Union soldiers are chasing a farmer's pigs.

"This greatly amused them, one fellow saying, 'No, we are only making a fire to warm by.'"

When Mrs. Aldrich informed Colonel Morton C. Hunter about his men's actions he replied with a sardonic smile, "Madam, I have very little control over the boys," he replied. "You must remember we are in South Carolina now, we entered this state with gloves off!"

"He approached nearer to me and said, 'Madam, this is war—the war which you women helped to bring on yourselves.'"

"Yes," I said, "but we did not expect to deal with barbarians—rather with men who claim to be chivalrous and honorable and who have wives and children of your own."

"You women can soon stop this thing," he rejoined, "by bringing your husbands and sons out of the Army to protect you."

"When I told him we could not bring them from their post of duty if we would, and we would not if we could, he laughed a laugh that rang in my ears long after, and said, 'Madam the end will soon come when we have finished our work in this State.'"

"As (the infantry) struck their tents and moved off, the corn-house I had tried so hard to save was discovered in flames. I always believed Colonel Hunter gave the order."

The corn house Mrs. Aldrich referred to was used to store provisions for her home. It was utterly destroyed and now she had no food.[26]

If the reader desires to learn more about these courageous women, there is an excellent book titled *When Sherman Came: Southern Women and the Great March* by Katharine M. Jones. This story and many more are in this book. This particular story was selected to show there were some decent men among the soldiers with Sherman. Unfortunately, many women had no one come forward to help them. They lost everything, including their belief that the Northern army had compassion for civilians.

As you can see this strategy had shifted to something author Mark Grimsley calls "the hard hand of war". He explains this theory in his book of the same name. Grimsley writes, "Grant's 'postwar narrative' suggests his operations during the spring and summer of 1863 saw the application of recognizably hard measures. Indeed, they inaugurated the new strategy." Grimsley goes on to write, "Nevertheless, the year 1863 marked a significant watershed, because during that year one can see the emergence of large-scale destruction carried out, in fairly routine fashion by large bodies of (Northern) troops."[27]

Was Sherman Responsible for Crimes Committed by His Soldiers?

In retrospect, one must wonder how much blame Major-General William T. Sherman should be held accountable for in the crimes committed against civilians of the South. These crimes include the wanton destruction of private property, murder, plundering personal items that have no military significance, rape of defenseless women and robbery by the threat of extreme violence. Some claim that Sherman wasn't aware of what was happening, so he should not be held responsible for the conduct of his men. Fortunately, these questions can be answered by several sources.

Major General William T. Sherman

All of Sherman's reports have been recorded in the set of 128 books entitled *War of the Rebellion Official Records of the Union and Confederate Armies*. The "Articles of War 1806" governed the army's conduct when the Civil War began. The code states, "*Any officer or soldier who shall quit his post or colors to plunder and pillage shall suffer death or other such punishment as shall be ordered by a sentence of general court-martial.*" This code remained in effect until April 1863, when the Lieber Code took over. This is a set of rules President Lincoln asked Dr. Francis Lieber to put together redefining the Union army's conduct during times of war.[28] Another source is General-in-Chief of the Union army Henry Halleck's book called *International Law or Rules Regulating the Intercourse of*

States in Peace and War. As the title suggests this gave a set of rules for the army to follow during times of war.

The most damning evidence comes from Sherman himself. It is abundantly clear from his reports that Sherman not only knew criminal activity was going on, but he held the generals and colonels of his division accountable for the men's conduct. The Lieber Code was so important that it was issued as General Order No. 100, and distributed to every regiment in the Union army. Here is what Section II, Article 44 of this code states:

"All wanton violence committed against persons in the invaded country, all destruction of property not commanded by the authorized officer, all robbery, all pillage or sacking, even after taking a place by main force, all rape, wounding, maiming, or killing of such inhabitants, are prohibited under the penalty of death, or such other severe punishment as may seem adequate for the gravity of the offense.

A soldier, officer, or private, in the act of committing such violence, and disobeying a superior ordering him to abstain from it, may be lawfully killed on the spot by such superior."[29]

It is shown by Major-General Sherman's reports that he was aware this was happening within his command. Here are several of his reports from 1862:

In July of 1862 Sherman and his army were in Tennessee and he issued Order No. 49, from Moscow, July 7, 1862.

"Stealing, robbery, and pillage has become so common in this army that is a disgrace to any civilized people." "This demoralizing and disgraceful practice of pillage must cease, else the county will rise on us and justly shoot us down like dogs and wild beasts. By order of Major General W. T. Sherman.[30]

On December 6, 1862 General Sherman issued General Order No. 2, from College Hill, Mississippi.

"The indiscriminate and extensive plundering by our men calls for a summary and speedy change. Our mission is to maintain, not to violate, all laws, human and divine."

"Each brigadier will hold each colonel or commander of the regiment responsible that when any of his men leave their ranks and pillage not only shall the stolen articles be turned into the brigade quartermasters or commissary, but the sol-

Secretary of War Edwin M. Stanton

diers be punished by fine or otherwise by sentence of a field officer. By order of Major General W. T. Sherman."[31]

Once again General Sherman had to issue an order regarding his unruly men in February 1864.

General Order No. 5:

"Information having been received at these headquarters that men of this command have been guilty of pillaging from private houses articles of no value to the soldiers, but

important to every household, such as clothing of women and children, a species of plunder unknown to civilized warfare, it is hereby ordered that hereafter during the March no soldier shall enter a house occupied by a family unless under direction of a commissioned officer; and further, that nothing is to be taken from private houses by officers or men, except provisions in such articles as are necessary for the subsistence of the Army. By order of Major General W. T. Sherman."[32]

Then in mid-1864 Sherman's behavior took a sharp turn toward violence against civilians as evidenced by this letter to Secretary of War Edwin M. Stanton.

Headquarters Military Division of the Mississippi,
In the Field, Big Shanty, Georgia, June 21, 1864

Hon. Edwin M. Stanton,
Secretary of War, Washington, D. C.:
"But one thing is certain, there is a class of people, men, women, and children, who must be killed or banished before you can hope for peace in order."[33]

Here was Stanton's surprising answer to Sherman's statement on July 1, 1864:
Major-General Sherman,
Headquarters, via Chattanooga:
"Your letter of 21 June has just reached me and meets my approval."[34]

Major-General Oliver O. Howard reported plundering homes in Sherman's command.

Was Secretary of War Stanton approving of killing Southern civilians? If he wasn't, then how do we account for the following report from Sherman? Does this sound like a man that should be honored by President Lincoln and given "the thanks of the nation"?

HDQRS. MILITARY DIVISION OF THE MISSISSIPPI,
In the Field, Rome, Ga., October 29, 1864.

Brigadier-General WATKINS, *Calhoun, Ga.:*

Cannot you send over about Fairmount and Adairsville, burn ten or twelve houses of known secessionists, kill a few at random, and let them know that it will be repeated every time a train is fired on from Resaca to Kingston?

W. T. SHERMAN,
Major-General, Commanding[35]

The next report came from a letter written on October 16, 1864. This letter did not come from Sherman but from Major General Oliver O. Howard and reports on plundering of homes near Villanow, Georgia.

"Today soldiers of our Army entered houses and opened trunks, drawers, and boxes, utterly destroying everything they could lay their hands on. They took from women and children the last morsel of food. In some cases, these things were done under the eyes of commissioned officers and in a manner as if it were a frolic. Such practices are simply dishonorable; they sullied the purity of the noble cause for which you fight. I appeal to the good sense of this army to put a stop to actions which are either thoughtless or criminal, and must lower us to the estimation of all honorable men and have a tendency to undermine our government. Pillaging is a crime prohibited by every law."[36]

General-In-Chief of the Union Army Henry Halleck

As we can see, nothing has changed regarding the soldiers' behavior, just in who was reporting it. This time it was up to one of Sherman's generals to report his command's misconduct.

However, when Sherman began his infamous march to the sea from Atlanta in September 1864 he stopped issuing orders regarding the soldier's criminal behavior. This doesn't make sense because this was the most destructive part of the campaign. I am sure that Sherman received tens of thousands of complaints from civilians, as well as his own military officers, concerning the soldier's behavior. So why was he all of a sudden silent about the men's behavior?

The answer may lie in the well-known fact that Lincoln was worried about being reelected in November. All the negative reports that Sherman was filing with the War Department made it appear to the northern voters that the Union Army was full of barbarians bent on wanton destruction and plundering defenseless women and children of the South. Is it possible President Lincoln told Sherman to "Knock it off, I'm trying to get reelected!" We can only wonder.

Politically the March dealt a devastating blow to the Confederate war machine, virtually securing Lincoln's reelection. Sherman played a major part in this victory by keeping a low profile concerning his army's unruly behavior. The problem is that most historians today perpetuate this politically correct myth by saying there was little or no criminal activity during Sherman's March to the Sea. Unfortunately, the public has heard this version so often it is now accepted as fact.

Sherman received a letter from General-in-Chief of the Union Army Henry Halleck on December 18, 1864. As you will recall Halleck was the general who wrote the book *International Law* that deals with the conduct of the Army in times of war. In this letter he wrote, "Should you capture Charleston, I hope that by some accident the place may be destroyed, and if a little salt should be sewn upon its site it may prevent the growth of future crops of nullification and secession."[37]

Major-General Sherman replied: I will bear in mind your hint as to Charleston, and don't think salt will be necessary. When I move the 15th Corps will be on the right of the Right Wing, and their position will bring them, naturally, into Charleston first; and if you have watched the history of that Corps you will have remarked that they generally do their work up pretty well. The truth is the whole army is burning with an insatiable desire to wreak vengeance upon South Carolina. I almost tremble at her fate, but feel that she deserves all that seems in store for her."[38]

It is disgraceful that a man who was the head of the Union Army, and wrote the book on how it should conduct itself, would suggest such a thing. But then these reports are hidden away in the official records and not generally accessible to the public unless they know where to look.

Sherman biographer Lee Kennett has been very lenient with this handling of Sherman in his book *Marching through Georgia*. However, even he had to admit the criminality of Sherman's behavior when he wrote:

"Had the Confederates somehow won, had their victory put them in position to bring their chief opponents before some sort of tribunal, they would've found themselves justified in stringing up President Lincoln and the entire Union high command for violation of the laws of war, specifically for waging war against noncombatant."[39]

Chapter 2

Hard-War is Applied to the Prison System

Captured Confederate soldiers were the first to experience "Hard War" in May of 1863 when the prisoner exchanges were halted. Secretary of War Edwin M. Stanton had always contended that general exchanges of prisoners who were healthy enough to return to their regiments should not be allowed. Now he was able to make it a reality. This is not to say all prisoner exchanges were halted. If a sick prisoner wanted to be exchanged, he needed to be examined by a surgeon to guarantee he was unfit to return to duty. If the prisoner did so he would be permitted to be released in a special exchange. An exception to this rule was made at Vicksburg, Mississippi. Over 30,000 Confederates had been captured July 4, 1863 and then paroled four days later. These men were paroled because an additional 5,400 prisoners had been captured at Gettysburg and Northern prisons did not have sufficient space to incarcerate such a large number of men. The government also thought caring for so many men would place a heavy financial burden on the North.

Confederate soldier drinking water. Photograph courtesy Pamplin Historical Park, Virginia.

At this point in the war many government and military officials felt retaliation was called for because of rumored abuse of Northern soldiers in Southern prisons.[1] With prisoners no longer being exchanged Secretary of War Edwin M. Stanton was free to advance his policy of retaliation against a large number of Confederate prisoners. In the next year and a half many unreasonable restrictions were placed on items that were essential to the men's survival. Among the things reduced were rations, clothing, safe drinking water, shelter, hospital care and medicine. At best it can be said that these restrictions were placed on the prisoners to hobble the Confederate army by only releasing weakened soldiers who were unfit for military duty. At worst it can be argued that halting the prisoner exchange and introducing severe reductions of food, medicine and clothing were deliberately designed to create a death camp like atmosphere.

Ration reduction was the biggest factor effecting prisoner's health. Prisoner rations were reduced on multiple occasions at the suggestion of Colonel William Hoffman, the Commissary General of Prisoners. The rations, which were scanty to begin with, were systematically reduced to half the normal ration. Although prisoners have been known to exaggerate their hardships, it is difficult to not believe the numerous prisoner's journals and diaries that consistently complain about the meals containing only a third of a ration. Without sufficient food the men's bodies no longer had the strength required to fight disease.[2]

Another problem created by halting the prisoner exchange was the overcrowding of the prisons which in turn placed great stress on their water supply. Typically, a prison had only so much freshwater available for a specific number of people. In the case of Elmira Prison camp, New York, the prisoner's supply of water became quickly polluted and spread deadly disease. Unfortunately, the scientific study of germs did not exist during the Civil War. If thirsty men could see water, they will drink it. If prisoners became sick from drinking water from a certain source, then the others knew to avoid it. This method worked fine for water that is heavily contaminated and the effects are observed right away. However, germs can be insidious creatures that do not necessarily make a person ill right away. It may be weeks or sometimes months for germs from polluted water to make their presence known. A prisoner in reasonable health is usually able to withstand and shake off an illness. He may only get some diarrhea as a result. Nevertheless, even this if continued long enough can become deadly. Now add to that equation the fact

Title page of The Medical and Surgical History of the War of the Rebellion, Part III, Volume I.

that the same man's quality of health is lowered by an insufficient diet. The bout with chronic diarrhea now robs him of any nutrients provided by his already scanty rations. Introduce a waterborne illness and the way is now open for a more lethal disease to be introduced to his already weakened system. String a few hundred of these sick men together and you have an epidemic in the making.

Overcrowding of the prison camps was a very serious problem for several reasons. Once a disease is introduced to a densely populated prison environment it can spread like wildfire. The first sign of an epidemic is when an overcrowded hospital no longer has enough beds for sick prisoners. This problem is greatly magnified because these men are then forced to remain in their barracks where they could possibly infect other prisoners.

Other problems with overcrowding of the prison include blankets, clothing, shelter and medicine. Every month the prison commandants would submit a report or requisition for what supplies were needed the following month for the prison. With more men coming in every month and none being exchanged these requisition numbers were always far behind the actual numbers. Therefore, there was never enough clothing, shelter and medicine to go around. Add to this the fact that Secretary of War Stanton and Colonel William Hoffman did their best to deprive prisoners of the supplies they needed by issuing orders that further reduced the prisoner rations.

There has been a school of thought that believes Elmira prison camp was built as a retaliatory prison because of the alleged abuses suffered by Northern prisoners of war. These claims have always been denied by the Federal government. However, there is now growing evidence to support this accusation of retaliation. The evidence I speak of was discovered while I was studying *The Medical and Surgical History of the War of the Rebellion,*

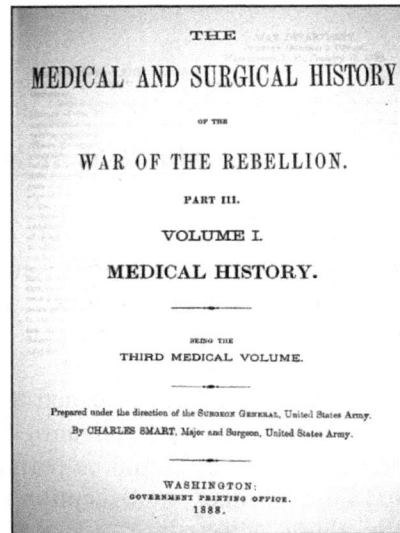

(1861-65). This is a series of medical books that were assembled by Joseph K. Barnes, Surgeon General of the United States Army. There is a table in Volume I, part 3 that contains troubling statistics regarding the death by disease at Elmira prison camp. Table XVIII lists data regarding eleven different types of disease from the nine largest prison camps in the North.[3] I wanted to find out what type of medical care the prisoners were receiving. I collected statistics from eight of those prisons, leaving out the figures for Elmira. For each prison I recorded the number of cases for a specific disease and divided that figure by the number of deaths for that same illness. This was done for each disease on the table. I compared the results to the data from Elmira. After evaluating the figures, I found the prison camp at Elmira had the worst death record for every disease on that table. Six of the eleven diseases had such an alarming difference from the other Northern prisons that I was com-

pelled to write about them. For instance, a prisoner suffering from bronchitis at Elmira was 6.4 times more likely to die from that disease than men at other Northern prisons. The grouping of "other diseases" indicated the men at Elmira were dying five times more often as at other prisons. This medical volume does not specify what these diseases were. I then checked the statistics for diarrhea and dysentery and found the men at Elmira prison camp were over four times more likely to die than at any other Northern prison. This in itself is troubling, but there is more. The list of lethal diseases goes on. "Malarial fevers" found the prisoners at Elmira four times more likely to die. The diseases of scurvy and rheumatism found the men at Elmira dying three times more often than those as in other prisons. The gap is so great in all six of these diseases that the abnormalities appear to be no random occurrence. It is becoming increasingly difficult to believe these events were merely a result of the

Elmira's Chief Surgeon Major Eugene F. Sanger

incompetence of Elmira's medical staff. If anyone bears responsibility for the conduct at Elmira's prison camp hospital it was the Chief Surgeon, Major Eugene F. Sanger. If the reader wishes to examine this table, I have included a copy on pages 130-132.

Evidence has come to light that casts Major Sanger in an incriminating position for possible criminal activity. In the hopes of obtaining a transfer from his duties at Elmira, Major Sanger sent out letters requesting a position in another part of the country. One of those letters was sent to Brigadier General John L. Hodson in which Sanger inquired about a recruiting position in Augusta, Maine. In his letter Sanger not only explained the duties of his current job as chief surgeon at the prison, but also bragged about the number of prisoner deaths under his care. This is what he wrote, "I now have charge of 10,000 Rebels a very worthy occupation for a patriot. . . . . . but I think I have done my duty having relieved 386 of them of all earthly sorrow in one month." Did Sanger indicate that he had deliberately contributed to the deaths of hundreds of patients in his care? Sanger's last sentence suggests that this was a willful act.[4]

31

Former Elmira prisoner Anthony M. Keiley worked for Major Sanger as a hospital clerk and had the opportunity to see many things regarding the hospital patients in the course of his duties. Keiley claimed that Sanger refused to sign any report that listed a prisoner's cause of death as being related to malaria. This would also include intermittent and remittent fever. The reason according to Keiley was that "in the medical department in a Yankee prison-camp . . . (there are) opportunities of plunder . . . . Vast quantities of quinine were prescribed that were never taken, the price (eight dollars an ounce) tempting the cupidity of the physicians beyond all resistance." Keiley suggested that Major Sanger was selling the medicine and attributing the resulting death to another disease. Elmira had over four times as many deaths for diarrhea as other Northern prisons. This is an unbelievably high number. Were some of these deaths caused by other diseases because there was no medicine left to treat the patients? According to Keiley's statement they were.[5]

Battlefield Prisoner Exchanges

When the war began there was an orderly system of prisoner exchange that allowed the soldiers to go home after a brief period of captivity usually lasting 30 days or less. Many times commanding generals exchanged prisoners on the battlefield using only a gentleman's agreement. President Abraham Lincoln did not condone these exchanges because to

Early in the war prisoners were exchanged on the battlefield using only a gentleman's agreement. This photograph shows a prisoner exchange at Camp Fisk near Vicksburg, Mississippi.

do so he would have to recognize the Confederate government as a legitimate, sovereign power. Lincoln was not willing to do this since he believed the Southern states were merely in rebellion. Therefore, no general exchanges could be permitted. There was another, perhaps more important reason for this. Lincoln did not want to appear to recognize the Confederacy because he did not want to show the European nations that the President of the United States considered the South a separate nation. Lincoln felt this might make it easier for England and France to recognize the Confederacy and perhaps lend the South aid militarily and financially. If this happened they could become allies with the fledgling Confederacy and benefit by receiving goods in repayment for their aid. England highly prized Southern cotton and was trying to get all they could to keep their clothing mills from shutting down because of the war overseas.

This threat was a very real possibility that Lincoln had to consider. Therefore, battlefield exchanges, which worked quite well until now, ceased to exist over the simple principle of whether the North should recognize the Confederacy.

The Dix–Hill Prison Cartel

Mounting pressure from newspapers and politicians forced Congress to act. As support for establishing a prisoner exchange grew in the North petitions were being circulated demanding an organized system of exchanges. Mounting pressure from politicians and newspapers forced Congress to act. On December 9, 1861, Congress passed a joint-resolution that read, "*Resolved, by the Senate and House of Representatives of the United States of America in Congress assembled, that the President of the United States be requested to inaugurate systematic measures for the exchange of prisoners in the present rebellion.*"[6]

With an official request from Congress President Lincoln had no choice but to renew the prisoner exchange. On July 8, 1862 Secretary of War Stanton appointed Union Major-General John A. Dix to negotiate a prisoner exchange agreement. Confederate Major-General D. H. Hill was named to represent the Confederate authorities. After much debate the Dix-Hill Cartel was created and signed by both generals at Haxall's Landing on the James River, Va, on July 22, 1862.

Several important points of the new exchange policy were that prisoners should be exchanged within ten days of capture, but paroled prisoners could not rejoin the military until their enemy counterpart had reached his own

Union General John A. Dix and Confederate General Hill created the Dix-Hill Cartel.

lines. This could be a period of several months. Paroled prisoners would be kept in special camps by their respective army while they waited for their exchange to be completed. During this time, they were not to be used for combat. The Cartel also established a scale of equivalents to manage the exchange of military officers and enlisted men. For example, one general equals forty-six privates, one colonel equals fifteen privates, one major equals eight privates, an army or naval captain would exchange for fifteen privates or common seamen, while personnel of equal ranks would transfer man for man. In addition, the agreement permitted each side to exchange non-combatants such as citizens accused of disloyalty.

Several incidents occurred that placed great stress on the Dix-Hill Exchange Cartel and contributed to its eventual breakdown. An April 1862 incident occurred in New Orleans where Admiral David D. Farragut had a chamber pot's contents was poured on his head by a woman in a second story window. Outraged, General Benjamin F. Butler issued his infamous General Order 28 which declared any woman who insulted an officer or soldier of the United States should be treated as a prostitute. When Confederate President Jefferson Davis learned of this he declared General Benjamin F. Butler was a common outlaw no Federal officers would be exchanged.[7]

Another incident occurred in July 1862 when Union Major General John Pope and officers of his command were charged by Confederate President Jefferson Davis with seiz-

ing Southern citizens and taking them past the Northern picket lines. The people were then released and warned not to return or they would be considered Southern spies and shot.[8] Union Major General David Hunter had also been declared a criminal for arming slaves and trying to start a servile war. After the Battle of Fort Pulaski, Georgia, Hunter began enlisting ex-slaves as soldiers in the occupied districts of South Carolina and formed the 1st South Carolina Regiment of African Descent. Then Hunter issued General Order No. 11 which stated that the Negroes in Georgia, Florida and South Carolina were free. General Hunter took the liberty of doing this without permission of the Federal government. This order incensed Border State slave holders which in turn upset President Lincoln. Lincoln was trying his best to keep the Border States calm so they would not secede from the Union. The President was so concerned about this that he issued a proclamation on May 19, 1862. "I, Abraham Lincoln, President of the United States, proclaim and declare

Union General David Hunter was declared a criminal by the Confederacy for arming South Carolina slaves.

that the government of the United States had no knowledge, information, or belief of an intention on the part of General Hunter to issue such a proclamation. Neither General Hunter nor any other commander or person has been authorized by the government of the United States to make a proclamation declaring the slaves of any state free, and that the supposed proclamation is altogether void."[9]

Union Brigadier General August Steinwehr was also accused of arresting peaceful citizens and holding them hostage. These hostages were threatened to be killed if the Union army was attacked by Southern bushwhackers.[10]

All ready fragile because of distrust and hostility on both sides the Dix-Hill prisoner exchange cartel finally broke down in May of 1863 when Confederate President Jefferson Davis suspended the parole of Union officers following the execution of William B. Mumford. Mumford was one of a group of men who hauled down the United States flag from the U. S. Mint at New Orleans, then tore it to pieces. Mumford was the only one caught so Union General Benjamin F. Butler ordered that he was to be hanged for his crime. On the evening before her husband was to be executed, Mrs. Mumford and her small children went to see General Butler. "Mrs. Mumford wept bitterly, as did the children, who fell about my knees," Butler remembered. The Union General remained stoic, despite her tearful pleas, and refused to pardon Mumford, saying, "Let him in the few hours he has to live look to God for his pardon." When Confederate President Jefferson Davis learned of this he declared no Federal officers would be exchanged until General Benjamin F. Butler was executed for his crimes. [11]

In early 1863 Secretary of War Edwin M. Stanton directed General Henry Halleck to drastically reduce the number of exchanges for enlisted men. On May 20th Stanton ordered Colonel William Hoffman, the Commissary General of Prisoners, to halt the prisoner exchanges. Stanton added that Hoffman was not to exchange Confederate prisoners even though they had previously expressed a desire to take the Oath of Allegiance to the Union unless the exchange was authorized by his office.[12]

Historians differ on the motivation behind Stanton's order. The most popular theory suggests the Federal government halted the prisoner exchanges because the Confederate authorities refused to exchange black soldiers. It is true the South would not exchange the black troops who had been captured. The Confederates maintained that these Negro soldiers were escaped slaves and were therefore recaptured property. Judge Robert Ould, the Confederate Commissioner of Exchange, said these soldiers would be returned to where they had been captured so they could be dealt with according to the laws of that state. He also added the South was willing to make an exception and exchange free blacks.[13] However, the Confederates refused to exchange white officers who had been captured in command of black troops. The South claimed these men were guilty of inciting servile insurrection and would either be put to death or otherwise punished at the discretion of the courts. Despite all the threats to the contrary, no white officer was ever executed for commanding a Negro regiment.[14]

Judge Robert Ould, Confederate Commissioner of Exchange

Although the Second Confiscation and Militia Act of July 17, 1862, allowed military service for persons of African descent to join the Union army, the President did not authorize the use of black soldiers in combat until the Emancipation Proclamation was officially issued on January 1, 1863. Introducing black soldiers to the Northern army did not go as smoothly as Lincoln had hoped. Officers were reluctant to use Negro troops in combat because they thought their fighting ability was inferior to white soldiers. In other instances, the colored troops were kept away from the front lines because it was thought that the Confederate soldiers would fight harder when they saw armed blacks facing them.[15]

Secretary of War Stanton said he had halted the prisoner exchange because of the Confederacy's refusal to exchange Negro prisoners. It appears the crux of the issue of whether the exchanges were stopped because the Confederacy refused to exchange black prisoners depends on how many Negro soldiers had become prisoners during the six-month period between January 1st and Secretary of War Stanton's May 20th order to halt the exchanges. Certainly, there weren't many because it had been only five months since Lincoln had allowed Negro soldiers to fight in combat. The only battle that occurred during this period where there was a sizable force of black troops on the front lines was at the battles of Port Hudson, Louisiana, and Milliken's Bend, Mississippi. At the May 26th battle of Port Hudson the 1st and 3rd Louisiana Native Guards, which were both black regiments, suffered nearly two-hundred casualties, but no soldiers were captured. The battle of Milliken's Bend occurred on the Mississippi River and involved several regiments of the Louisiana Native Guards and the white soldiers of the 23rd Iowa. The Confederate forces under General McCulloch fought a vicious, sometimes hand-to-hand fight with the entrenched Federals. McCulloch's Texas brigade inflicted 452 casualties; among these were 226 captured Union soldiers. The *Official Records* do not state if the captured troops were black or white. The famed 54th Massachusetts did not assault Battery Wagner in South Carolina until July 18,

1863. However, neither battle would have influenced Secretary of War Stanton decision because they occurred a month after the prisoner exchange had already been halted.[16]

It makes no sense for Secretary of War Stanton to halt the prisoner exchange, which would release tens of thousands suffering Union soldiers from a possible death sentence, because of the Confederates refusal to exchange a small undetermined number of captured Negro soldiers. It is far more likely that Stanton wanted to end the prisoner exchange because to do so would be a severe blow to the Confederacy. All Stanton needed to do was to find a reason for ending the exchange that the public would accept and he found it with the Confederates refusal to exchange black soldiers.

Secretary of War Edwin M. Stanton and Lieutenant General Ulysses S. Grant agreed that the burden of having to care for thousands of Union prisoners would take resources away from the Confederacy and drain its strength. It was also felt that exchanged Confederate prisoners would be healthy enough to go right back into the army while the North would only receive sick and broken men in return. From a military standpoint this move made perfect sense. From a humanitarian point of view, it was extremely cold-blooded because it failed to consider the swiftly deteriorating health of both Northern and Southern prisoners alike. Not to mention the irreparable damage done by alienating their long-suffering families of these men.

Lieutenant General Ulysses S. Grant was for halting the prisoner exchange.

The Confederacy immediately tried to resume the prisoner exchanges. There were several motives for this. One reason was because it was the humane thing to do. Another was the additional manpower it would make available to fill the depleted Confederate ranks. However, an equally important reason was that the South could ill afford to keep thousand of Union prisoners. Ever since the beginning of the war, the North had blockaded the Southern ports, capturing or destroying any ship headed for the South with food, medicines, clothing and munitions or weapons of war. After several years of an effective Union blockade food and medicine had become precious commodities in the South. In essence the South was starving and had no medicine available to treat its citizens let alone Union prisoners of war. To halt the prisoner exchanges was the worst thing the North could have done for the safety of their soldiers who had been captured. In reality the Northern authorities were abandoning their soldiers in their darkest hour; something they promised to never do.

According to the *Official Records of the Union and Confederate Armies* the first formal mention of captured black soldiers is when Colonel William H. Ludlow, the Union agent for exchange, says in a June 14th letter to Confederate Judge Robert Ould, "I now give you formal notice that the United States Government will throw its protection around all its officers and men without regard to color, and will promptly retaliate for all cases violating the cartel, or the laws." The Federal Government's claim that the exchanges were halted because of the Confederates refusal to exchange black prisoners of war does not hold up if you examine the dates involved. The fact remains that Secretary of War Stanton stopped the Prisoner Exchange Cartel May 20th, twenty-five days before the Confederates received notice about this violation. So, what was the real reason for Secretary Stanton ending the prisoner exchanges?[17]

It appears Major General Ulysses S. Grant may have provided the reason why the prisoner exchange was halted in a letter he had written to General Benjamin F. Butler. He suspected the Confederate government was violating the exchange cartel's rules by allowing paroled prisoners to re-join the military before they were formally exchanged. Grant wrote: "It is hard on our men held in Southern prisons not to exchange them, but it is humanity to those left in the ranks to fight our battles. Every man we hold, when re-leased on parole or otherwise, becomes an active soldier against us at once either directly or indirectly. If we com-mence a system of exchange which liberates all prisoners taken, we will have to fight on until the whole South is ex-terminated." Then Grant wrote these hauntingly, prophetic words. "If we hold those caught they amount to no more than dead men."[18] Surely, he did not mean that literally, but thousands of men in both armies would ultimately die because the prisoner exchange had ended. Unfortunately,

Colonel Melvin Grigsby, For-mer Andersonville prisoner

Grant did not realize this was a double-edged sword that cut both ways. Halting the pris-oner exchange would keep thousands of Federal prisoners in Southern prisons where they would ultimately die. Because of this decision Civil War prisons evolved from temporary detention facilities to long-term concentration camps and a few would become the closest thing to death camps the North had ever seen.

Secretary of War Edwin M. Stanton felt that ending the prisoner exchange would weak-en the Southern army and put an end to the war. For the next twenty-two months, from May 1863 until nearly the end of the war, general exchanges became nonexistent. Special exchanges for sick and wounded prisoners still occurred from time to time, but always at the urging of the South.

Many Union prisoners felt they were merely pawns in achieving President Lincoln's lofty goals of freeing the Negro. Former Andersonville prisoner Melvin Grigsby wrote, "If there had been any considerable number of Negro soldiers in the prisons suffering with the others, then there would have been a vital principle of justice as well as honor at stake, and the white prisoners themselves would've been the last man in the world to have sacrificed that principle in order to secure their own liberty and lives. There was not a Negro soldier in Andersonville or any other prison for any considerable time. When they were captured they were either sent back to their old masters to be put to work on rebel fortifications, and they were not starved and did not suffer. Their condition as prisoners was little worse than it had been before the war. They were property in the eyes of the Confederates, and as such were taken care of. Their condition as prisoners was little worse than it had been before the war."[19]

Former Andersonville prisoner James Madison agreed with Grigsby when he wrote, "The Andersonville delegation returning from Washington said there was not one word about the exchange of the Negro soldiers being in the way of our release. It was not then thought of. I know that for the past forty-two years that matter has never been published in the North as a reason why we were not exchanged." Madison goes on to say "the Washington authorities had concluded to stop the exchange before there were any Negro prisoners. This was the Stanton policy, and if this atrocious and inhuman doctrine is anyway meritorious, the 'War Secretary' is entitled to the credit."[20]

Chapter 3

Elmira Prisoner of War Camp

A new problem arose with the end of the prisoner exchange. If the North continued to capture prisoners and could not release any, where would the new prisoners be kept? A suitable camp was located just a few miles north of the Pennsylvania border in western New York State. In 1861 four large training camps were built to answer President Lincoln's call for 75,000 volunteers to help put down the Southern rebellion. These were officially designated as the Arnot Barracks, Post Barracks, Camp Rathbun and Camp Robinson.

Arnot barracks was located about one mile north of Elmira, New York. It was constructed on a 300 by 300-yard square plot with ten barracks designed to house 100 men each. Two hundred feet to the rear of the barracks were the officer's quarters. Across from this was a large building with six rooms for the field and staff officers. To the west stood a guard house and a mess hall with a kitchen capable of feeding 1,000 men. The camp was supplied with water from a stream of fresh water and also by two wells with good, limestone water.[1]

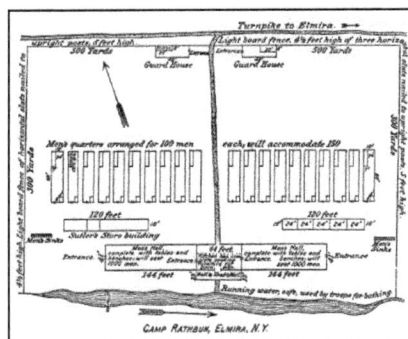

Camp Rathbun would be renamed Elmira prison of war camp in 1864.

The next training facility was the Post Barracks. This was located about one mile west of Elmira on a plot of land not easily drained and considerably lower than the surrounding country. The 400 by 200 yards area contained twenty barracks designed to house 100 men each. To the southeast stood the officer's quarters composed of six rooms. In front of the enlisted men's barracks were two guard houses, and a mess-hall and a kitchen under one roof. The water from the wells and from the junction of canal south of it was unfit for use and water needed to be brought in to supply the garrison.[2]

Camp Rathbun, which later became Elmira prisoner of war camp, was built along Water Street about a mile west of downtown Elmira. The 300 by 500-yard plot of land slopes toward Foster's Pond on the south side. The camp was as high as the surrounding country on firm, gravelly soil which did not become soft even during violent storms. Twenty barracks, 88 by 18 feet, were constructed under the specifications by Jervis Langdon, and had two rows of wooden bunks running down the sides. Each building was designed for 100 men and contains a small room for noncommissioned officers. To the rear of the enlisted men's barracks were the officer's quarters and sutler store. Behind these buildings were two mess-halls and a kitchen under one roof. The two 144 by 41-foot mess-halls occupied the two ends of the building and the kitchen the middle portion. The camp was provided with limestone water from two wells.[3]

Camp Robinson was a 400 by 360-yard area a mile and a half southwest of downtown Elmira. This camp supported 2,000 troops in twenty barracks and had two wells with abundant, pure water. To the left and rear of men's quarters was a building of 100 by 20 feet with six rooms which composed the officer's quarters. In the rear of this building were two guard houses, and two mess-halls with a kitchen under one roof. The two 144 by 41-foot mess-halls occupied the two ends of the building and the kitchen the middle portion.[4]

In the spring of 1864 Colonel William Hoffman, the Commissary General of Prisoners, was troubled by the quickly growing prison population. Union prisons were filled to overflowing and opening new prison camps needed to be considered. Most of the crowding was due to Secretary of War Stanton ending the prisoner exchange. Added to this mix was the information that General Grant had begun his all-out offensive against Robert E. Lee's army and the bloody fighting in Virginia had already captured tens of thousands of Confederate soldiers. Most of these men were sent to the already crowded Point Lookout prison camp in Maryland.

On May 14th Hoffman received a telegram from General E. D. Townsend saying, "Sir: I am informed that there are quite a number of barracks at Elmira, N. Y., which are not occupied, and are fit to hold Rebel prisoners. Quite a large number of those lately captured could be accommodated at this place."[5]

Commissary General of Prisoners Colonel William Hoffman

General Townsend had aroused Hoffman's interest because the camp near Elmira possessed everything a prison would need. It had excellent railroad connections to transfer large numbers of prisoners, a thriving lumber business to supply wood for extra barracks and fuel for the fires that were necessary to fight the harsh northern winters. It was also located in a fertile valley that produced ample fruits and vegetables and had abundant fresh water from the Chemung River. The addition of fruits and vegetables into a prisoner's diet was vital for the prevention of scurvy. Camp Rathbun already possessed twenty barracks, a large mess-hall, and with some construction could be converted into an excellent prison camp at a minimal cost. This was important to Hoffman who throughout his military career demonstrated an aptitude for thrift. Another factor to be considered was the fact that the camp was close to the seat of war in Virginia and prisoners could be transported easily.

Five days later, Colonel Hoffman sent a letter to Colonel Seth Eastman, Camp Rathbun's commanding officer, giving him instructions to "set apart the barracks on the Chemung River at Elmira as a depot for prisoners" and as many as 10,000 prisoners who would shortly be transferred there from other Northern compounds. Hoffman further ordered Eastman to construct a twelve-foot-high fence, framed on the outside with a sentries' walk four feet below the top, and built at a safe distance from the barracks in order "that prisoners may not approach it unseen."[6]

Colonel Eastman replied to Hoffman's order on May 23rd and said the camp's barracks could comfortably house 3,000 men without crowding, but he added that it could also accommodate 4,000 prisoners. Eastman further stated that there was enough room where tents could be pitched to quarter 1,000 more. He stated that the mess hall was sufficiently large enough to accommodate 1,500 men and the kitchen could cook 5,000 meals daily. There was an excellent bakery that could make 6,000 ration rations daily. Eastman cautiously pointed out that since there was no hospital, hospital tents would need to be erected.[7]

We know now that most of the deaths at Elmira prison camp were caused by overcrowding. So why was Colonel Hoffman so insistent about Elmira prison camp holding 10,000 prisoners even after Eastman told him Camp Rathbun's barracks could only accommodate 4,000 prisoners with crowding and another 1,000 could be housed in tents?[8] If Hoffman had any doubt about this figure he need only remember what East-

Lt. Colonel Seth Eastman was Elmira prison camp's first commandant.

man told him that the mess hall was large enough to seat 1,200 to 1,500.[9] Yet on June 22nd Hoffman stubbornly told Eastman, "In establishing the fence it is advisable to enclose ground enough to accommodate in barracks and tents 10,000 prisoners."[10] So why was he refusing to believe this man who had an intimate knowledge of the camp? If we examine the official records I believe can find the answer. On May 19th Hoffman wrote to Secretary of War Stanton and said, "I respectfully suggest that one set of the barracks at Elmira may be appropriated to this purpose. I am informed there are barracks available which have, by crowding, received 12,000 volunteers. By fencing them in at a cost of about $2,000 they may be relied up on to receive 8,000 or possibly 10,000 prisoners."[11] So, as early as May 19th Hoffman told Stanton, his superior, that Elmira could receive 10,000 prisoners. Hoffman then in turn related this information to Colonel Eastman. When Eastman protested by saying the camp could only quarter 4,000 prisoners and another 1,000 and tents, Hoffman wouldn't listen. As far as Hoffman was concerned he was Eastman's superior; the prison commandant had his orders and according to military protocol it was his job was to make it happen!

Camp Rathbun officially became Elmira Prisoner of War Camp in June of 1864. The thirty-two-acre site lay along the banks of the Chemung River. A one-acre lagoon, called Foster's Pond, stood within the walls of the stockade. Prison buildings were located on the high northern bank of the lagoon. The lower southern level, known to flood easily, later became a hospital area for thousands of smallpox and diarrhea victims. The entire prison was surrounded by a twelve-foot-high fence which contained a wooden walkway for the guards. This walkway was eight feet off the ground with forty-seven sentry boxes set at intervals where the guards could retreat in case of inclement weather. The sentry boxes were four feet in length, open at the sides and had a diamond-shaped window so nearly the entire prison yard could be seen.

On June 30, 1864, Colonel Eastman sent a telegram to General Lorenzo Thomas that Elmira was ready to receive prisoners. A more unhealthy site could not have been selected.

A one-acre body of water, a stagnant backwash from the Chemung River, stood within the stockade and would be the cause of several epidemics because prisoners used the pond as a convenient latrine and garbage dump. The first person to call attention to this was the prison's commandant, Colonel Seth Eastman, who reported to Hoffman, "Colonel: I have the honor to report to you that the pond inside of the prisoners' camp at Barracks, No. 3, (Elmira prison) has become very offensive, and may occasion sickness unless the evil is remedied very shortly."[12]

This was later verified by Chief Surgeon Eugene Sanger who wrote, "(Foster's Pond's) trouble does not seem to arise altogether from the decayed matter which has been thrown in, but from the daily accumulation. The drainage of the camp is into this pond or pool of standing water, and one large sink (outdoor latrine) used by the prisoners stands directly over the pond which receives its fecal matter hourly. Seven thousand men will pass 2,600 gallons of urine daily, which is highly loaded with nitrogenous material. A portion is absorbed by the earth, still a large amount decomposes on the top of the earth or runs into the pond to purify."[13]

Foster's Pond today. *Photo courtesy of Tom Fagart*

Sanger later amended his initial assessment of Foster's Pond. In a November 1, 1864 letter to Surgeon General of the U. S. Army, General Joseph K. Barnes, Sanger reported, "I have the honor to forward the monthly report of sick and wounded at prisoners' hospital, Elmira, N. Y., for the month of October. The ratio of disease and deaths has been fearfully and unprecedentedly large and requires an explanation from me to free the medical department from censure. . . . (Foster's) pond received the contents of the sinks and garbage of the camp until it became so offensive that vaults were dug on the banks of the pond for sinks and the whole left a festering mass of corruption, impregnating the entire atmosphere of the camp with its pestilential odors, night and day. . . .The pond remains green with putrescence, filling the air with its messengers of disease and death, the vaults give out their sickly odors, and the hospitals are crowded with victims for the grave."[14]

On July 1, 1864 Federal authorities announced that newly constructed Elmira prison camp was ready to receive thousands of captured Confederate soldiers from overcrowded Northern prisons.[15] It is difficult to understand how the prison was allowed to open when it did not have a hospital or medical staff available. Such things were essential to any civil war prison. In the meantime, an assistant surgeon from the U. S. army hospital in town visited the prison each day.

Surgeon C. T. Alexander, Medical Inspector for the U. S. Army, conducted an inspection of Elmira prison camp on the 11th of July. His report to Colonel William Hoffman pointed out several potentially hazardous conditions that needed immediate attention. Alexander reported the sinks, or outdoor latrines, were constructed on a slough. The Merriam-Webster dictionary defines slough as: "a place of deep mud or mire". To correct this situation Surgeon Alexander recommended either bringing water from the city of Elmira and construct new sinks with suitable drainage, or cause the Chemung River to increase the water flow to Foster's Pond so it would create a running stream through the camp. Alexander described Foster's pond as "a stagnant body of water which may soon become offensive and a source of disease."

Inspector Alexander also pointed out there was no "proper hospital organization". He said that "a surgeon from the hospital for troops in Elmira visits the prison camp daily. One of these men was an assistant surgeon who was a former medical cadet and was not a suitable person to organize or control a hospital." Alexander stated in his report, "Your attention is called to the immediate necessity of a competent surgeon to take charge." He found that the sick men did not have adequate shelter, their diets were not suitable, and some prisoners did not have bedsacks or blankets. In closing his report, Alexander summed up the condition of the sick prisoners as "bad".[16]

On July 27th the *Elmira Daily Advertiser* announced construction of a hospital for the camp using prison labor. Unfortunately, only four of the proposed seven hospital wards were completed by September 1st. It would be another month until the hospital would be fully operational. On August 6th, a full month after the prison opened its gates, Chief Surgeon Major Eugene Sanger reported for duty at Elmira. Why it took so long to get competent a doctor was never explained. Critics who consider Elmira to be a camp for retaliation say that the endless army red tape in selecting doctors can be traced to Secretary of War Stanton. Bureaucratic delays were a favorite tactic used successfully by Stanton in the months to come when he did not want anything to aid the prisoners. Although this does sound like something Stanton might dream up the author has no evidence to support such a claim. However, it was because of Stanton's order that the prison was allowed to open. The fact that Elmira prison camp did not have a hospital or medical staff should have been brought to his attention. This shows probable retaliation through careless regard for the prisoner's safety.

Maryland's Point Lookout prison camp sent the bulk of captured Confederate soldiers to the new prison camp at Elmira, New York. By June of 1864 Point Lookout's prison population had swelled to 15,500 men due to the North halting the prisoner exchange. From July through August Point Lookout sent 9,619 prisoners to the camp at Elmira— approximately three fourths of the final total of 12,123 imprisoned.[17] Because the prison camp at Point Lookout sent so many prisoners to Elmira it is important to understand what dramatic events were happening at the time that led to the North building a new prison camp. Too many prisoners were a dangerous situation since the limited well water at Point

Point Lookout prisoner-of-war camp transferred over nine thousand prisoners to Elmira prison camp between July and September, 1864.

Lookout was unable to support so many people. Barrels of freshwater had to be brought in by ship at least once a week to meet the ever-increasing demand. Also increasing the demand was the fact that Hammond General Military Hospital was located outside the prison gates. What made this a dangerous situation was the hospital's water consumption would increase dramatically after a large battle. The late spring and early summer of 1864 saw some of the most severe fighting of the entire Civil War and this had a tremendous impact on the prisoner transfer to Elmira.

Lieutenant-General Ulysses S. Grant commanded the Union armies in the Western Theater and had led them to victory in the battle of Shiloh. The following year he again had been successful with the defeat and surrender of Confederate Lieutenant-General Joe Johnston's army in Vicksburg. These victories earned Grant a reputation as an aggressive commander who refused to give up.

Despite the Northern win at Gettysburg the year before President Lincoln had serious doubts about being reelected in 1864. What he needed more than anything was a decisive victory over the Confederacy to guarantee that he would stay in office. Grant seemed the best bet to win the victory Lincoln needed so he moved his winning general east to take on the seemly invincible Robert E. Lee. He promoted Grant to general-in-chief of all Union armies, and asked him to direct the actions of

Major General Ulysses S. Grant was brought to east to battle the legendary General Robert E. Lee

the Army of the Potomac. Major-General George G. Meade was to remain in control, but he would be Grant's second in command. Grant's predecessors had always targeted the Confederate capital of Richmond and had failed. The new commander's objective was not the capture of Richmond, but the destruction of Lee's army. Grant ordered General Meade, "Wherever Lee goes, there you will go also." Although he hoped for a quick, decisive battle, Grant was prepared to fight a bloody war of attrition. Both Union and Confederate casualties could be high, but the Union had greater resources to replace lost soldiers and equipment.

The initial confrontation between Grant and Lee had all the drama of a heavyweight prizefight. On May 4th, 1864, the Army of the Potomac, 124,000 men strong, crossed the Rapidan River and converged on the Wilderness area of Virginia. General Lee had 65,000 men to oppose this newest invasion by the Federal army. The confrontation seemed to be a battle for dominance as both army's maneuvered to gain an advantage. General Lee knew this was to be a contest of will between the two commanding generals and refused to give Grant an opening. He skillfully countered every move the Union general made, never giving him a tactical advantage. The reason why Lee finally offered battle in the Wilderness was because his army was vastly outnumbered, and his artillery was inferior to those of Grant's. Fighting in the tangled woods would eliminate Grant's advantage in artillery, and the close quarters combat could give Lee's outnumbered force better odds. Lee knew that if he did not strike now, he would lose any advantage he had. Therefore, General Lee ordered his army to intercept the advancing Federals in the Wilderness.

A series of four costly battles between the Union Army of the Potomac and Confederate Army of Northern Virginia were fought between May 5 and June 15th. The two armies clashed at the Wilderness, Spotsylvania Court House, North Anna and concluded with the

devastating losses at Cold Harbor. All the battles were inconclusive except for Cold Harbor.
Grant quietly pulled his army out of their
trenches and conceded the battlefield to General Lee. Grant would never admit to being
defeated by Lee at Cold Harbor, but a look at
the statistics from the battle tells a different story. Grant suffered 12,738 casualties while Lee
lost less than half as many men with 5,287.

Throughout this campaign Grant remained
confident that his superior number of soldiers
and weapons were wearing Lee's Confederate's
down. This was true, but Lee gave more severe
punishment than he received. Unfortunately,

Cold Harbor burial party several years after the battle.

Lee could not replace his losses as easily as Grant could. The Army of the Potomac suffered 53,414 casualties while Lee's Confederate army lost 32,000. If Grant kept losing
men at this alarming rate he would have no army in four months.[18] Many of the Union's
38,339 wounded soldiers were destined to be sent to the hospital at Point Lookout. This
would dramatically increase water consumption at an already overburdened hospital and
made it essential to decrease the prison population at Point Lookout. Luckily Elmira prisoner of war camp had opened in July and received over 9,600 of Point Lookout's prisoners.

General Grant knew President Lincoln, and ultimately the public, would have a hard
time accepting this large a loss. As casualty reports became known in the North, heavy
criticism fell on Grant, who was criticize as "the Butcher" by the Northern press after taking horrendous losses since crossing the Rapidan.

On June 30th Colonel Hoffman sent a letter to Colonel Alonzo G. Draper, commanding Point Lookout prison camp, informing him to start 2,000 of his prisoners for the new
prison camp at Elmira, New York. The men were to be divided into groups of 400, with
100 guards assigned to each party.[19] Draper was relieved to hear that some of the men at his
prison camp were being sent elsewhere, but was also concerned that Hoffman didn't intend
to send a larger group.

Moving Confederate prisoners from Point Lookout, Maryland, to Elmira was an arduous three-and-a-half-day journey which involved transporting the men by steamer up the
Atlantic Coast, to Jersey City, New Jersey. There they boarded the Erie Railroad prison
train for an all-day all-night 273-mile trip from northern New Jersey through Pennsylvania
along the upper Delaware and Susquehanna rivers, then into New York where they continued on to the Elmira Railroad station. What made this process so difficult and time con-
suming was that each mode of transportation that was used made it necessary to conduct a
roll call to see if everyone was present or accounted for. If a prisoner remained hidden
aboard, the guards needed to search for the man until he was found. The prisoner-of-war
trains made frequent stops to load fire wood and take on water but were also delayed by
switching tracks to let higher priority trains through.

Prisoner Walter D. Addison remembered being loaded aboard a steamship at Point
Lookout. "(We) were crowded upon this old tub between decks with only the hatches open,

and there (the prisoners) remained crowded together like sheep for many days. The site of these holds was sickening in the extreme and the condition and the sufferings of the prisoners therein was indeed horrible."[20]

Anthony Keiley wrote, "The man who first invented going to sea was an infidel and a fool. Nature has implanted in every human stomach and instinctive and vigorous protest against this practice. We were packed like sheep on a cattle-train, in the hold of a villainous tub, in the middle of July, with no ventilation except what was afforded by two narrow hatchways."[21]

U. S. PACIFIC MAIL SHIP CALIFORNIA.

Prisoner transport USS California

Most of the men were already sick when they left the prison and the steamship's lack of ventilation and the constant motion of the ocean waves made them more ill. There was no room for them to sit down, so they continued to stand or collapsed and vomited on the floor. With the foul, stale air below decks when someone threw up it wasn't long before other prisoners became ill also. The prisoners were overjoyed when the ship docked at Jersey City so they could be on dry land once again.

Six o'clock on the morning of July 6, 1864, a locomotive bearing two red prison flags chugged into the Elmira railroad station amid clouds of hissing steam and the clangor of the locomotive's bell. This was the first of many trains to carry prisoners-of-war from Point Lookout prison camp. Three hundred ninety-nine prisoners hopped out of the boxcars under the watchful gaze of the guards. They were quickly formed into ranks and a sergeant stepped forward to take roll call. It was then determined that one of the original 400 captured Confederates managed to escape en route. A search was immediately conducted but nothing of the prisoner was found.

Hundreds of Elmira citizens gathered near the railroad station in anticipation of seeing the notorious Confederate soldiers who had given their army so much trouble. Imagine their surprise when they saw four columns of weary, dirty soldiers wearing tattered gray and butternut, marching down the street instead of the formidable army they expected. A sobering thought occurred to the crowd as they watched this ragamuffin body of men march by. If these men represented the often-victorious Confederate army; what does that say about their solder's ability to win the war.

South Carolina's Sergeant Berry Benson recollected his introduction to Elmira citizens, "As we marched through the streets of Elmira, two by two, ragged dirty faces pinched with hunger, the people came out on the sidewalks to see Lee's soldiers going to prison. Had I seen any of the men, I know I would've hated them, but I had only eyes for the pretty girls."[22]

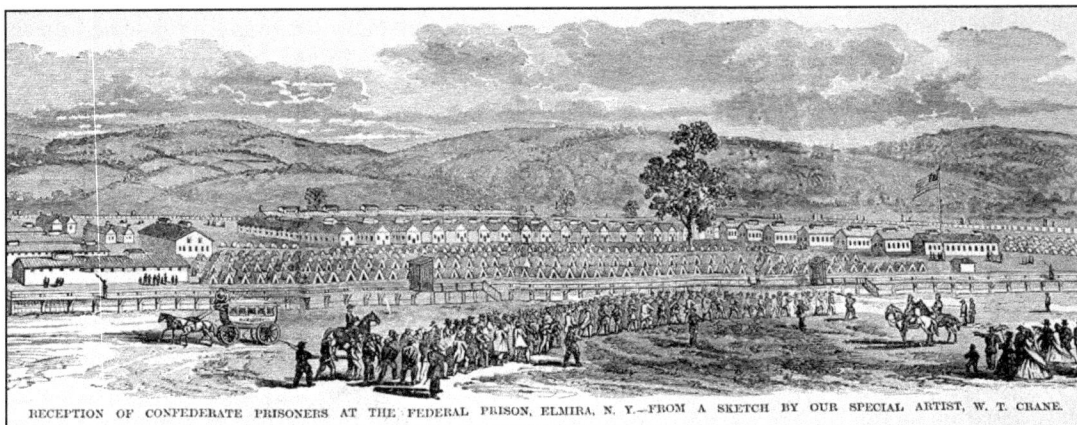

RECEPTION OF CONFEDERATE PRISONERS AT THE FEDERAL PRISON, ELMIRA, N. Y.—FROM A SKETCH BY OUR SPECIAL ARTIST, W. T. CRANE.

Prisoners marching from the train station to Elmira prison camp. Drawing is from *Frank Leslie's Illustrated Newspaper*, October 8, 1864.

In describing the prisoner's march to the stockade reporter Charles Fairman for the Elmira Daily Advisor noted:

The 'rebs,' who arrived yesterday, wore all sorts of nondescript uniforms; besides the regular dark, dirty gray. Some had nothing on but drawers and shirts. . . . They were a fine body of men physically, taller than average, for the most part, made up of two classes, the old and the young, the middle-age having a small representation. They did not exhibit a high degree of intelligence, but looked to be men that would go where they are told, let what might happen: although lean and lanky, yet evidently possessing the vigor and litheness to go through thick and thin. Of course, they were black, sunburnt and dirty;[23]

The prisoners were marched to Water Street, then turned west and went about a mile farther until they entered the tall, stockade gates. Once inside the prison the gates swung shut and the men were again formed into ranks. After roll call was taken the prisoners were separated into companies of one hundred men and assigned to a barracks. An officer was given charge of each company and an enlisted man was made the Orderly Sergeant. A Ward Sergeant was selected from the group of prisoners. His task was to supervise the company, assign men to police the barracks and grounds. He was also responsible to form the men into two columns and march them to the mess hall twice a day.

The Shohola Train Wreck

One of the most tragic chapters in Elmira's history was set into motion on the evening of July 12th as 833 prisoners, 125 guards and 3 officers of the 11th and 20th Veterans Reserve Corps prepared to leave Point Lookout prison camp. The men boarded the transport steamer *Crescent* and reached New York harbor by 3 PM the following day. Early the next morning they climbed into cars of the Erie Railway in Jersey City. Whenever prisoners switched modes of transportation a head count was conducted to see if everyone was present or accounted for. At this point it was discovered that three men were missing and likely remained hidden aboard the steamer. A search was immediately conducted of the ship and the men were found an hour later. However, during this delay a drawbridge was allowed to open and then took two hours to close. The delays set the train's departure behind almost four hours. To make up the time lost, Engineer William Ingram increased the steam locomotive's speed from 15 to 20 miles an hour.

The prisoner-of-war train which wrecked near Shohola was pulled by a wood burning steam locomotive like the one in the photograph.

The prisoner-of-war train containing three boxcars and twelve coaches proceeded through the Upper Delaware Valley and crossed the Delaware River into a mountainous area of Pennsylvania. The landscape was composed of steep ledges and woods of the Poconos as the passengers gazed from their windows at the twisting river below. Trying to keep on schedule the engineer Ingram pushed the locomotive's speed to 25 miles an hour until they reached the town of Shohola, Pennsylvania. Here the dual track merged into a single track to pass a particularly steep mountainous area. At 2:35 PM the stationmaster at Shohola signaled the train that all was clear to the end of the single-track section at Lackawaxen Junction. Douglas Kent, the telegraph operator at the next station, had been drinking heavily the night before and was sleepy. He had not heard the Shohola operator's message telling him that the prisoner-of-war train was given sole procession of the rails and the order not to let any eastbound trains through. Thinking the lone track was not in use, Kent gave the all clear signal to a heavily laden coal train of fifty cars not realizing that he had set the two trains on a deadly collision course.

By mid-afternoon on July 15th the Elmira bound train was chugging around a tricky curved section of track that reduced visibility to fifty feet. Suddenly a locomotive loomed ahead blowing an urgent warning with its whistle as it bore down on the other train. Ingram frantically reversed his engine while the engineer of the other train leaped out of the oncoming locomotive. The combined speed of both trains was 50 miles an hour. In an instant there was a tremendous boom, twisting and tearing of metal, screeching and breaking of wood as the cars collapsed into one another. Upon impact, the troop train's wood tender jolted forward and buckled upright, throwing its load of firewood into the engine cab killing fireman Tuttle instantly. In a minute all was silent except for the rushing sound of escaping steam and the heartrending cries and groans of injured and dying passengers.

The fronts of the two locomotives were raised in the air, appearing like two great beasts trying to crawl onto the top of the other. The wooden coaches either telescoped into one another, split open, or overturned in a sea of crushed wood, glass and large iron train wheels. One of the cars closest to the engine was reduced from its former length of 40 feet and compressed into barely 6 feet. The soldiers and many of the prisoners near the front of the train suf-

Removing the dead and injured from the Shohola train wreck was an all day and night job.

fered the worst. The first boxcar contained 38 prisoners and only one survivor. Hideously mangled bodies, some missing arms, legs and heads, were strewn about the wreckage. Ingram was pinned against the split boiler plate and the wreckage of the cab amid a cloud of scalding steam. He was barely conscious and warned the rescuers to stay back from the boiler because it was ready to explode. His voice became fainter as he was roasted alive.

Two miles away the village of Shohola heard the terrible collision and dozens of people rushed down the lone track to find the source. As the searchers neared the wreck, bodies and parts of bodies appeared on or alongside the track. Some corpses were so severely disfigured that they were unrecognizable. Captain Morris H. Church of the 11th Regiment Veteran Reserve Corps quickly organized a ring of guards around the site to prevent any prisoners from escaping. Rescuers, soldiers and prisoners helped remove the dead and injured from the wreckage until well into the night. A relief train from the nearby town of Port Jervis brought doctors and railway employees to help with the injured. Over several hundred injured Union soldiers and Confederate prisoners were being treated at the scene and in the town of Shohola. Within days three more guards and eight more prisoners would die. Captain Church would later put in his report that the dead "were so disfigured that it was impossible to recognize them, and five escaping whose names are unknown, I am unable to give a correct list of killed."[24] At least 51 Confederate prisoners, 17 Union guards and 3 railroad employees were killed in the wreck.

Railroad employees and prisoners dug a seventy-six-foot-long trench between the railroad track and the Delaware River to bury the bodies. Men were identified if possible and put into hastily made coffins. Most of the prisoners were buried four to a coffin on one side of the trench and seventeen Union guards were placed in separate coffins on the other. The bodies rested there until 1911 when they were exhumed and reinterred at Woodlawn Cemetery in Elmira, NY.

Elmira's Saturday morning newspaper alerted the city's population to the deadly prison train wreck near Shohola, Pennsylvania. The July 16, 1864 *Elmira Daily Advertiser* reported that a 50-car coal train had collided with a train bearing a large number of prisoners and guards destined for the prison camp outside the city. The paper went on to report that 48 prisoners and 17 guards were killed, and 100 prisoners and 18 guards were injured and required immediate medical attention.[25]

When the officers at the prison camp heard the news they sprang into action, busily making arrangements to handle the arrival of the injured. Surgeon William C. Wey enlisted all the help he could get, but the scarcity of lint and bandages crippled them in their work. The supply on hand was adequate for normal conditions, but would not be enough for a large emergency such as this. Since almost all of Elmira's doctors were at the front assisting in the war effort, Surgeon Wey was aided by nurses and medical students.

The suddenness of the tragedy and the scarcity of medical staff and supplies made it impossible to properly care for such a great number of victims. Surgeon Wey did not have time to submit an official requisition to satisfy this need; instead he notified all the cities pastors to appeal to the ladies at the Sunday service for lint and bandages. The same request was also published in the Monday morning newspaper. Not only did the ladies of Elmira respond to this tremendous crisis, but donations from adjoining cities came in as well. The Ladies Hospital Aid Association responded with dressings that they had earmarked for the soldiers at the front and instead diverted these to the prison camp.

The Shohola monument at Elmira's national Cemetery marks graves of Confederate prisoners of war who were killed in a train accident on July 15, 1864, near Shohola, Pennsylvania.

On July 22nd Captain M. H. Church of the 11th Veteran Reserve Corps was sent to Shohola with a train of twenty cars to assist the transfer of the injured to Elmira. When he returned to the city Saturday evening the train was met at the station by Colonel Seth Eastman and Surgeon Wey with a dozen hay-lined wagons to carry the injured men as comfortable as possible to the prison camp. One of the barracks had been emptied so the injured could all be placed together under the care of Surgeon Wey and the nurses. The doctor and his staff worked tirelessly from 9:30 Saturday evening until daylight the next morning cleaning and dressing wounds. Despite Wey's best efforts six more men eventually succumbed to their injuries.[26]

Several days after the train wreck one newspaper reporter described the macabre scene "the fearful groans and heart rending cries of the injured and expiring will never be forgotten. Some of the corpses were shockingly mutilated, heads completely crushed, bodies transfixed, impaled on timbers or iron rods, or smashed between the colliding beams, while one man was discovered dead, sitting on the top of the upturned tender, in grotesque and ghastly mockery of the scene around him."[27]

A week later a jury convened in Lackawaxen to investigate the cause of the Shohola train wreck and to determine a verdict in the case. Engineer Hoitt and his conductor, John Martin, from the coal train both testified that telegraph operator Douglas Kent had made a fatal mistake by telling them the track was clear that morning. When the coal train left the Hawley Branch and went on the Erie Railroad's main line, conductor Martin testified that he descended from his post in the caboose and entered Lackawaxen Station asking if the track was clear to Shohola. His question was answered by telegraph operator Kent, indicating that the track was clear for him to proceed. Engineer Hoitt then sent G. M. Boyden, the brake man, ahead to open the main switch so the train could go on to Shohola.

During the investigation it was discovered Douglas Kent had gone to a dance the evening before at nearby town of Hawley and had consumed a fair amount of alcohol. Even though the jury had a sufficient amount of evidence against Kent, they determined the accident was unavoidable. The public outcry was so great at the finding that another investigation was ordered. Although the second jury found Kent guilty, nothing could be done since he had disappeared the day after the wreck along with the incriminating evidence of his station log.

Elmira's Observatories

Making a profit on someone else's misfortune seemed to be the motivation behind a man building an observation tower across the street from Elmira Prisoner of War Camp. Near the end of July Mr. Nichols purchased the northeast corner next to the prison and built a two-story observation platform. Then he erected a sign reading, "an observation tower from which to view the prisoners—admission 15¢, refreshments served below." The *New York Evening Post* of August 17, 1864, stated that "a man of genius" "who sought his opportunity and was equal to the occasion, suddenly appeared at the camp, and apparently determined that the rebels should make his fortune."[28]

The *Elmira Daily Advertiser* reported that it was "often crowded with sightseers and must prove a paying institution." Most people had never seen

The three-story Mears brothers' observatory can be seen to the right of this photograph. Northern entrepreneurs built these towers to profit from the prisoners' misery. *Photograph courtesy of the Chemung County Historical Society.*

the enemy before and flocked to the observatory to get a glimpse of the rebel prisoners. The first level was advantageous because it had a roof over it to shelter the crowd from inclement weather, but the upper level offered a superior view. One business partner said the tower paid for itself in two weeks. *The Rochester Daily Union* reported that the proprietor of the observatory "intends to keep in this tower a powerful glass, by the aid of which visitors can see the vermin which are said to be so plenty upon the bodies of the prisoners."[29] Body lice called "graybacks" infested every part of Elmira and made their homes in the men's clothing. James Huffman remembered, "Some fellows did not wash their clothes nor themselves and you could see the graybacks crawling over their clothes on the outside."[30]

This observatory was so successful that several weeks later another tower was built down the street from the original. W. and W. Mears made their observatory twenty feet higher and charged their customers five cents less. This new tower boasted three decks instead of two and promised "a fine view of the rebel prisoners."[31] Wooden stands sprang up where hungry visitors could buy ginger cakes, crackers and peanuts or refresh themselves with a cool lemonade, beer or liquor. A writer would recall three decades later, "(These establishments) took on the look of a long row of rude wooden booths like those at a fair, or more like those that spring

One of the photographs taken from the Mears observatory of Elmira prisoner of war camp was sold as a postcard.

up in a night along a street that is the route to the grounds where a circus tent is to be spread."[32]

After observing the prisoners one man claimed they, "have a rough appearance, wearing as they do, clothing of as many hues as the rainbow but none so brilliant. The men are generally of good size, and what would be called fair specimens of the race, if they were not Rebels."[33]

A Tennessee sergeant, George W. D. Porter, recalled how "hundreds would crowd daily to get a view of the prisoners—many to gloat, perhaps, on their sufferings; some to gaze in wonder and awe upon the ragged, bob-tailed crew who had on many fields conquered their best armies; and some, no doubt, to sigh for an exchange of these men for fathers, sons, and brothers who were suffering kindred miseries at Libby, Salisbury and Andersonville."[34] James Huffman remembered there was "a constant stream of people winding their way to the top of these observatories to get a glimpse of the Rebs, as they supposed us to be like some kind of curious, monkey-shaped animals."[35]

The diary of Ausburn Towner was discovered thirty years after the war and described his visit to one of the observatories:

"It was like looking down into an immense bee-hive. There was a constant motion on all sides, but without noise or confusion that could be heard. Groups were standing here and there, formed one minute, broken up the next; some men had built a fire underneath a tree and were baking corn-meal cakes; someone was coming or going every instant to or from every building whose entrance was in sight, and many were seated in the shadow of the trees whittling or fashioning some object, the character of which the distance forbade making out. In the space between the buildings and the fence nearest sat a small circle of men, with one on his feet who seemed to be speaking and making the most violent gestures. When he finished he seated himself in his place in the ring and another rose to go through similar exercises in his turn. A few feet from these men were five men playing cards. In the corner close at hand was a large tent that had a lonesome look. Into it, during the half hour of our visit, came two men five times, bearing each time on a stretcher the dead body of a man covered over with a piece of canvas." Towner did confess that he and his friends all "speedily grew melancholy over the spectacle and cut our visit to the top of the tower very short."[36]

Both observatories and the refreshment stands did a thriving business through September. The *Elmira Daily Gazette* proudly proclaimed: "Upper Observatory (the original observation tower) should be visited by all strangers and citizens. The pictures taken from there will always be remembered with delightful interest. Photograph views of the rebel camp, and surroundings . . . have been taken and can be obtained by the public in a few days."[37]

On September 19th the lucrative observatory business came to an end. The Elmira officials were concerned that the towers could be used for communication between rebel spies on the outside and the prisoners. It was also possible, they theorized, that the towers might be used to organize an escape. The commissary general of prisoners ordered Captain John Elwell, Elmira's assistant quartermaster, to seize the ground occupied by the two observatories. The Confederates were relieved that these observatories were no longer in use. "I am surprised that Barnum has not taken the prisoners off the hands of Abe, divided them into companies, and carried them in caravans through the country," wrote prisoner Anthony M. Keiley after the war had ended.[38]

Resolution 97

Senator Benjamin F. Wade wrote Joint Resolution 97 and read it on the floor of the Senate. The resolution later became known as the Retaliation Bill.

Federal Master Sergeant Washington S. Toland of the 83rd New York wrote a letter to the editor of the *New York Times* about having been abused as a prisoner in both Confederate Belle Isle and Libby prisons in Richmond, Virginia. The newspaper printed his story in April, 1864, under the title of *Prison Life at Richmond— Its Cruelties.* Toland described these cruelties as lack of adequate food, clothing and shelter.[39] Lonnie Speer's book, *Portals Of Hell: Military Prisons of the Civil War* has a handy prison reference guide which lists different statistics of the various camps. In his book he lists Libby prison as having only twenty deaths at the end of the war and Belle Isle, 300 deaths. To put this into perspective, Belle Isle had roughly the same number of prisoners as Elmira had but only one-tenth as many deaths.[40] These facts largely discredit Toland's allegations in his letter. On the flip side of that same issue, the comparison speaks volumes about Elmira prison camp's notorious death record.

Secretary of War Edwin Stanton became enraged after reading a copy of Master Sergeant Toland's letter. Apparently Colonel William Hoffman, the Commissary General of Prisoners, had read Toland's letter also and wrote Stanton saying, "I respectfully suggest, as a means of compelling the rebels to adopt a less barbarous policy toward the prisoners in their hands, that the rebel officers at Johnson's Island be allowed only half rations; that their clothing be reduced to what is only sufficient to cover their nakedness, and that they be denied the privilege of purchasing the articles allowed to other prisoners."[41]

On May 3rd Colonel Hoffman filed a report of his observation of Union prisoners who had been returned from the prison at Richmond, Virginia. According to Hoffman the returning prisoners were so mentally and physically deteriorated that it proved Union prisoners of war were being deliberately starved to death. Again, Hoffman proposed that retaliatory measures be put in place.

Secretary of War Stanton had always suspected that Union prisoners were receiving poor treatment from the Confederates. Now, with the aid of Colonel Hoffman and the *New York Times*, he urged a retaliation bill. On May 5th Stanton wrote President Lincoln, telling him of the abuses suffered by Union prisoners of war. The Secretary of War then proposed that "precisely the same rations and treatment be henceforth practiced to the whole number of rebel officers remaining in our hands that are practiced against either soldiers or officers in our service held by the rebels."[42]

On May 4th Stanton wrote Ohio Senator Benjamin Wade, "The enormity of the crime committed by the rebels towards our prisoners for the last several months is not known or realized by our own people, and cannot but fill with horror the civilized world when the facts are revealed. There appears to have been a deliberate system of savage and barbarous treatment and starvation."[43] Then Stanton urged Wade to introduce legislation asking the President to adopt a policy of retaliation toward the Confederate prisoners.

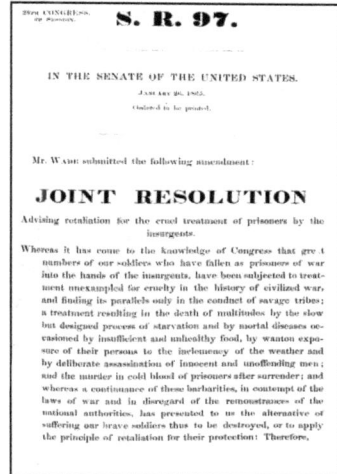

Joint Resolution 97 written by Senator Benjamin Wade.

Senator Wade then wrote *Resolution 97* and read it on the floor of the Senate on January 26, 1865. This joint resolution called on President Lincoln to declare retaliation on Confederate prisoners in Union hands for the abuses suffered by Union prisoners. The bill would have the full effect of a law if passed by both houses of Congress and signed by the chief executive. Congress passed it, but to his credit President Lincoln did not sign it. The first part of the resolution is included here to show the mindset of the Northern politicians at the time. The idea of "Hard-War", which began in the Shenandoah Valley, had broadened its scope to include the Northern prison system.

Joint resolution 97:

S.R. 97
Mr. Wade submitted the following amendment.
JOINT RESOLUTION
Advising retaliation for the cruel treatment of prisoners by the insurgents.

"Whereas it has come to the knowledge of Congress that great numbers of our soldiers who have fallen as prisoners of war into the hands of the insurgents, have been subjected to treatment unexampled for cruelty in the

history of civilized war, and finding its parallels only in the conduct of savage tribes; a treatment resulting in the death of multitudes by the slow but designed process of starvation and by mortal diseases occasioned by insufficient and unhealthy food, by wanton exposure of their persons to the inclemency of the weather and by deliberate assassination of innocent and unoffending men; and the murder in cold blood of prisoners after surrender; and whereas a continuance of these barbarities, in contempt of the laws of war and in disregard of the remonstrance's of the national authorities, has presented to us the alternative of suffering our brave soldiers thus to be destroyed, or to apply the principle of retaliation for their protection: Therefore, resolved by the Senate and House of Representatives of the United States of America in Congress assembled, That in the judgment of Congress, it has become justifiable and necessary that the President should, in order to prevent the continuance and recurrence of such barbarities, and to insure the observance by the insurgents of the laws of civilized war, resort at once to measures of retaliation." Senate Resolution 97, Library of Congress, web page:[44]

Clearly there was a recommended form of retaliation in place when Elmira Prisoner of War camp started accepting Confederate prisoners. Articles favoring retaliation frequently appeared in the Northern newspapers that autumn. The *New York Times* spoke of how the inhumane treatment of Union prisoners of war had "stained and sullied the vesture of Southern chivalry. No such disgrace, thank God, touches the North! Everything that our own soldiers are allowed by law is cheerfully given to our prisoners. Such clothing, such food as the poor Southron never enjoyed at home, is heaped before him when in our hands. . . . None suffer from want." The *Times* then proclaimed: "We believe that the most active measures should be undertaken to insure corresponding treatment of our own brave soldiers. We urge that rebel prisoners should no longer live in luxury while ours are dying of starvation and neglect."[45]

President Lincoln had a special understanding with Secretary of War Stanton.

Lincoln's Relationship with Secretary of War Stanton

Ever the politician, President Abraham Lincoln did not want anything to reflect badly on his administration. Secretary of War Edwin M. Stanton, who was already known to possess a vindictive attitude toward the South, proved to be the perfect hatchet man for the president. In his book, *The Lincoln Nobody Knows*, Historian Richard N. Current wrote that the president had an arrangement with Secretary Stanton: "Such apparently was the division of labor between Lincoln and Stanton, between lenity and the law. If a life was spared, Lincoln could get the credit. If not, Stanton would take the blame." Lincoln himself admitted, "I want to oblige everybody whenever I can and Stanton and I have an understanding that if I send an order to him which cannot be consistently granted, he is to refuse it."[46]

Historian Michael Horigan wrote, "The stark reality is this: Stanton and Hoffman wished to put forward a policy of retaliation; there is no documented objection to this idea from President Abraham Lincoln. Therefore, in the matter of retaliation, the virtually unbridled use of power on the part of the Secretary of War would have no trouble quashing any opposition to his orders that demanded a reduction in rations."[47]

Stanton had the perfect ally in Colonel William Hoffman. When the war began, Hoffman who was a junior officer in San Antonio, Texas, was captured and spent over a year in a Confederate prison. At this early date in the war prisons were tolerable for a Union officer. Still, Hoffman had an ax-to-grind with the Confederacy. Upon his release he returned to Washington and assumed a desk job. On June 17, 1862, Hoffman was appointed to head the newly created Office of Commissary General of Prisoners. Hoffman was made directly responsible to the Secretary of War so when he

Secretary of War Edwin M. Stanton was President Lincoln's hatchet man and the prisoner's worst nightmare.

took the position, he had access to the top of the military and political structure. Secretary of War Stanton was delighted because here was a man he could count on to deal harshly with Confederate prisoners.

In the rare instance where Colonel Hoffman demonstrated that he possessed a heart, Secretary of War Stanton quickly overturned any sympathetic ideas he had. Hoffman had gone to Louisville and saw thousands of Confederate prisoners lacking shoes. These men were going north to Camp Douglas in Chicago in late December and would soon face the harsh Northern winter. Hoffman telegraphed the Secretary of War and asked for permission to issue shoes to them. An angry Stanton fired back:

Defense Department, City of Washington, December 22, 1864

Brig.-General Hoffman, Louisville:
The Secretary of War desires to know whether the prisoners whom you suggest should be supplied with shoes out of the U. S. Stores are any part of that rebel Army recently engaged in killing Union troops at Nashville. If they are a part of that rebel force the Secretary does not see any occasion for such sympathetic tenderness as to give them supplies provided for our own troops.

By order of the Sec. of War:
James C. Hardy,

Inspector-General[48]

Hoffman, who was greatly stressed by Stanton's response and wanted to calm him, quickly wired:

Louisville, December 22, 1864,

Col. J. C. Hardy, Inspector-General:
Your telegram of this date is just received. The prisoners referred to in my telegram of this morning are of those captured in Nashville. It has been the practice heretofore to issue to prisoners of war such clothing as was now absolutely necessary. My suggestion to issue shoes was based on this practice. My impression is that the order for the issue of clothing has not yet been countermanded. If it has, I have not received the order.

Respectfully,
W. Hoffman,
Commissary-General of Prisoners
West of the Mississippi[49]

Tom Fagart kneels behind his great, great grandfather Pvt. Franklin Cauble's headstone. Cauble was captured at Cold Harbor and sent to Point Lookout, then transferred to Elmira July 12th. He died October 28, 1864, one day before he was to be exchanged. *Photo courtesy of Tom Fagart.*

Receiving nothing but absolute silence from Stanton, Hoffman wired back the following reply assuring the Secretary that no clothing would be issued:

Louisville, December 23, 1864, 10:50 AM

Col. J. C. Hardy, Inspector-General:
I leave for Nashville at seven this morning; will arrive there this evening. I should have said in my telegram last night that no clothing would be issued to the prisoners of war.
W. Hoffman,
Commissary-General of Prisoners West of the Mississippi[50]

It seems ludicrous for such a high ranking officer, like the Commissary General of Prisoners, to have to ask the Secretary of War for his approval to issue something so basic as articles of clothing to destitute Confederate prisoners. Yet this was the way Stanton wanted things. He desired to control everything regarding the prisoners and administer his own brand of justice. If Hoffman did not play along, then Stanton would replace him with someone who would.

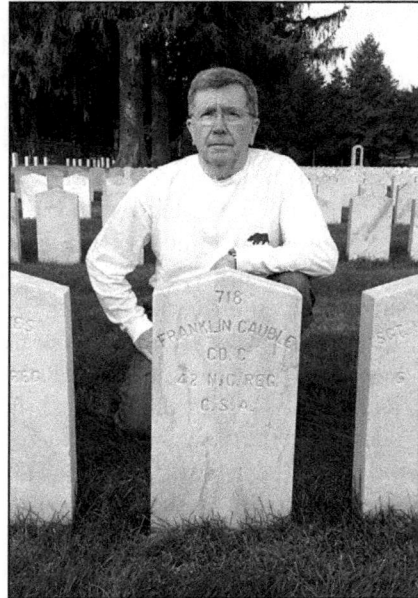

Ration Reduction

Colonel William Hoffman, who was known for being tightfisted, found a way to save the United States government thousands of dollars. His plan not only saved money, but also supported his idea of retaliation. Hoffman theorized since the prisoners were sedentary and not actively fighting or marching in the field that they could get along with less food. The rations saved could then be sold back to the commissary and the money would be put in a Prison Fund. This was like a slush fund that could be used to cover the cost of making improvements to the prison and the prisoner diet. Secretary of War Edwin Stanton liked the idea and authorized Hoffman to implement the reduction of rations on April 20, 1862.[51]

This order made no sense. If Hoffman's only motive was to save the government money wouldn't it make sense to let the prisoners have more food, so they don't become sick and fill the hospital? Sick prisoners require a doctor's care, medicine and a special diet. All of this would drive up the cost of prisoner care. If Hoffman's sole reason for the reduction of food was to save the government money, then he was doing a poor job. It is

Ration reduction at Union prison camps caused many prisoners to waste away and eventually become victims of disease and death.

far more likely Hoffman's only motive was to seek retaliation. However, Secretary of War Stanton's absolute control of the Northern prison system should not be underestimated. Stanton's vindictive nature toward Confederate prisoners was well known by his officers. Colonel William Hoffman frequently communicated with the Secretary and should be considered within Stanton's sphere of influence.

With the winter season coming Colonel Hoffman made sure the prisoners were not too comfortable by issuing the following order on November 12, 1863:

"You will issue no clothing of any kind except in cases of utmost necessity. So long as a prisoner has clothing upon him, however much torn, you must issue nothing to him, nor must you allow him to receive clothing from any but members of his immediate family, and only when they are in absolute want."[52]

Still not satisfied with the prisoners food, Colonel Hoffman advised his prison commandants on November 9, 1863, "I do not think it well to permit (the prisoners) to receive boxes of eatables from friends," "and I suggest you have them informed that such articles will not hereafter be delivered."[53] Why did Hoffman object to the prisoners having extra food? The only answer that seems to fit is that this would be interfering with the reduced rations he prescribed. Hoffman had explained earlier how reducing the prisoner's rations would be saving the government money, but now he was turning away free food being mailed to the prisoners. This fact is very telling as

Due to overcrowding of Elmira prison camp 5,000 Confederate prisoners lived in tents from the summer of 1864 until late December when new barracks were completed. *Photograph courtesy of the Chemung County Historical Society.*

it exposed his true motivation was vengeance against the Confederate prisoners entrusted to his care. Secretary of War Stanton's lack of response to this order may have been an indication that Hoffman had the Secretary's tacit approval in reducing the prisoner's food once more.

The next year Colonel Hoffman noticed that the prisoners were not adversely affected by the reduction of rations and thought their food could be decrease further. He notified the Secretary of War that the prisoner's food could once again be reduced without adversely affecting the men's health. Stanton happily agreed and ordered a 20 percent reduction in rations effective June 1, 1864.[54] It must be remembered that this order was in addition to the initial reduction of rations. A conservative estimate would place the total reduction of rations at least one-third of a full ration or possibly more.

"These orders put the prisoners on half rations," complained prisoner James F. Crocker about the ration reduction. "The result of these orders was that the prisoners were kept in a state of hunger—I will say in a state of sharp hunger—all the time."[55]

Constant hunger can influence a prisoner's everyday life through long-term depression. All prisoners have depression to a degree, but as the conditions become worse the greater the effect they will have. Prisoner exchanges had been halted so there was little hope that anyone would be allowed to leave prison anytime soon. Seeing so many of their friends die from disease, prisoners began to wonder with mounting concern if they would survive long enough to go home. Studies have been done and show there is a strong link between depression and illness.[56] If a prisoner has no hope of freedom, it is likely his resistance will go down and he is liable to catch one of the deadly diseases he had been so worried about. Many prisoners at Elmira never got the chance to go home and their remains can be found at Woodlawn Cemetery.

Former Elmira prisoner John R. King remembered how the men died at prison. "The poor fellows died rapidly, despondent, homesick, hungry and wretched. I have stood day after day watching the wagons carry the dead outside to be buried and each day for several weeks 16 dead men were taken through the gate."[57]

Former prisoner George M. Neese recalled the dark cloud of gloom which had settled over him in prison. "The true aspects, experiences, and characteristics of prison life in general can never be described, even by the most impressive writer, so that he who has never experienced its realities cannot form the faintest conception of the melancholy gloom that settles down like eternal night on the spirit of the man and crushes hope to the dark recesses of its lowest stage, so that life itself becomes a burden that may be dragged, but too wearisome to bear. No painter's palette ever held the color black enough to truthfully delineate the shadows that constantly hang around a prisoner of war in these United States."[58]

Some prisoners resorted to disgusting behavior even by lax prison standards because of the food reduction order. Prisoner Erastus Palmer remembered seeing a comrade returning from the hospital and stopped to chat. During the conversation, he noticed that the man picked up a discarded mush poultice and began scraping off the side used for treating lesions. Palmer watched him carefully remove the sickening gunk from the dirty poultice while nonchalantly mentioning that he was preparing to eat it, to which Palmer wrote, "I did not stay to see him do it."[59]

This is Private William E. Crawford's drinking cup made from a steer's horn. Crawford made this cup at Elmira when the prison ran out of tableware. Crawford was in Company G, 25th South Carolina when he was captured at Fort Fisher on January 15, 1865. Private Crawford died of pneumonia and is buried at Woodlawn Cemetery near Elmira, New York. *Photograph courtesy of Mike McCarley*

Under these new orders the Elmira prisoners were limited to two meals a day and ate in shifts that ran from 6 to 9 AM and from 3 to 6 PM. With well drilled efficiency only the army could instill, the Confederate Ward Sergeants gathered the men together in the barracks to go to the mess hall for breakfast. Every morning the men fall in between 6 and 9 AM while he called the roll. If any man was sick and unable to go, it was the Ward Sergeant's duty to bring these men their meals. The ration was four ounces of bread and a thin piece of salt pork. Dinner had the same amount of bread, but the meat was replaced by a soup or broth so clear you could see the bottom of the cup.

Starvation, manifested in stages, would become visibly evident inside the prison camp. Weight loss, headache, fatigue, irritability, insomnia, and depression were the prevailing signs that became apparent to anyone who had access to the stockade. "I have seen groups of battle-worn, home-sick Confederates," Union Lieutenant Frank Wilkeson, an officer in charge of a guard detail inside Elmira prison camp, would recollect nearly a quarter-century later, "their thin blankets drawn tightly around their shoulders, stand in the lee of a barracks for an hour without speaking to one another. They stood motionless and gazed into one another's eyes. There was no need to talk, as all topics of conversation had long since been exhausted."[60]

In the beginning, when the number of men was fewer, the prisoners sat on benches and had eating utensils consisting of a tin plate, fork and spoon. As Elmira prison camp became more crowded the benches were removed to make room for more tables. With the seats gone the 41 x 396 x 8 foot dining hall could accommodate more men. When the eating utensils ran out many men brought their own tableware to eat with. Former prisoner Anthony M. Keiley lamented, "gone were the tin plates; gone the knives and forks; gone the seats at all the tables; gone the encouragement to cry out for more (food)."[61]

Former prisoner John A. Wyeth provided an example of this when he wrote, "I know from personal observation that many of my comrades died from starvation. Day after day it was easy to observe the progress of emaciation until they became so weak that when attacked with an illness which a well-nourished man would easily have resisted and recovered from, they rapidly succumbed."[62]

As the harsh winter winds of December tightened its icy grip on Elmira's prisoners the men started to show signs of malnutrition and starvation. Prisoner James Huffman recalled that many inmates "moped about, pining away for want of sufficient food to eat, losing their humanity, eating almost anything a brute would eat—as rats, gangrene poultices and the like." Huffman remembered the prisoners at Elmira "were known by their pallid color and lifeless movements. Most of them died there, not from disease but pining away for lack of more food, some even sending word to their friends at home that they were being starved to death. These poor men grew so lean that they seemed to have no flesh at all, before their spirits left their bodies."[63]

Elmira's prisoners line up for morning roll call. Men were required to stand in line regardless if the weather was bad or they were sick. *Photograph courtesy of the Chemung County Historical Society.*

An outbreak of scurvy became so acute in August and September that it soon reached epidemic proportions and prompted Post Surgeon Eugene Sanger to ask Colonel Hoffman to increase the supply of vegetables. Colonel Hoffman, who had previously forbidden the sutler from selling fruit and vegetables, complied with the request and permitted him to resume selling these items to the prisoners. Still the question remains why Surgeon Sanger, who knew that the lack vitamin D would cause disease, did not say anything until there was a serious outbreak of scurvy? It appears that this disease was a real threat since Elmira's records indicate that over forty prisoners died from the disease.

The disease caused assorted spots and irritations on the body, but John R. King noted that it also "attacked the mouth and gums, becoming so spongy and sore that portions could be removed with the fingers."[64] In addition to losing their teeth, victims frequently saw their hair fall out and felt their stomachs cramp, leaving some men too weak to walk.

If this were not bad enough, the beef rations were reduced on October 3rd by Special Order No. 336 issued by post commandant Colonel Benjamin Tracy. The order reads, "Whereas the fresh beef now being furnished at this post is in the opinion of the Colonel commanding unfit for issue, and inferior in quality to that required by contract. Therefore: Colonel S. Moore and Major Henry V. Colt are hereby designated to hold a survey upon said beef and to reject such parts or the whole of the said beef as to them appears to be unfit for issue, or of a quality inferior to that contracted for."[65]

The daily meat inspection frequently resulted in large amounts of beef being rejected. The supposedly inferior beef was then sold to local meat markets while the prisoners simply had to do without meat.

In 1878 the flawed nature of Special Order 336 was revealed by Brigadier General Alexander S. Diven when he wrote a letter which stated that he accompanied Colonel Tracy to the slaughter yard where the beef was inspected. He recalled Tracy rejected "beef, which, though it was such as I would often be glad to have for myself and my command."[66] General Diven's observation that he would have been glad to receive the unwanted beef brings into question the reason Colonel Tracy had for rejecting it. It appears he could have been seeking his own brand of revenge against the Confederates or perhaps more accurately his superiors' demand for retaliation. No doubt the starving prisoners would have loved to have had some of the beef rejected by the uncaring Colonel Benjamin Tracy.

"The meat ration," prisoner Anthony M. Keiley wrote, "was invariably scanty; and I learned, on inquiry, that the fresh beef sent to the prison usually fell short from 1000 to 1200 pounds in each consignment." Keiley added that "when this happened, many had to lose a large portion of their allowance; and sometimes it happened that the same man got bones only for several successive days. The (things) resorted to by the men to supply the want for animal food was disgusting. Many found an acceptable substitute in rats, which the place abounded."[67] Keiley bitterly added that "in a nation, whose boast is that the people of the United States do not feel the war, and supplies of all sorts are wonderfully abundant, it is simply infamous to starve the sick as they did there [Elmira]."[68]

If the meat was substandard, as Colonel Tracy claimed, why was it good enough to be sold to Elmira's citizens? Many historians agree that Secretary Stanton's approval of this controversial order was intended to force a bread-and-water diet on the prisoners without actually going on record as ordering it. It can be argued that a systematic reduction of rations was intentionally ordered to lower the prisoner's resistance to more deadly diseases. If one considers Elmira's 25% death rate, which was more than twice as high as the rate for the other Northern prisons, the numbers seem to support such a claim.

Confederate prisoners sold rats at five cents apiece. This became a thriving business in the camp. *Photograph courtesy of the Chemung County Historical Society.*

The New Prison Meat: Rats

Thousands of rats migrated into the prison camp attracted by the foul stench from tons of garbage rotting outside the cookhouses. These rodents grew to alarming size and hid under buildings and burrowed in deep holes alongside the pond. Encouraged by the gathering darkness of evening, the rats became bold and would venture out to make forages on the trash heaps.

Former prisoner Berry Benson recalled, "Another item of fare which was not on the list furnished by the government was—rats! The prison swarmed with them—big rusty fellows which lived about the 'cook house' as the kitchen was always called, and also under the house used as quarters. The floors of these houses were close to the ground, and the sides came down all the way. The rats burrowed holes underneath to go in and out, sometimes as large as a man's leg."[69]

One evening a prisoner was arrested for prowling around the camp during the night. The next morning, he was taken to headquarters and questioned by Major Colt, who asked, "What were you doing?" The prisoner answered, "Huntin', sir." Colt wondered what type of animal would be in his prison camp at night and asked, "What are you hunting?" The man replied, "Rats!". Toward dusk, prisoners armed with rocks and clubs waited for the rats to gather. One prisoner remarked, "[when a rat was seen] such a hurrah and such a chase and such a volley of stones! You would have thought it was our Battalion of Sharpshooters in charge."[70]

After the rats were killed and cleaned they were either grilled or fried. Marcus Toney remembered men catching and then eating the rats. "I am glad that I did not have to go on this diet; but I have tasted a piece of rat, and it is much like squirrel."[71] Everything on a rat was used. No part of the rodent was wasted. After a prisoner got every bit of nourishment from the animal possible, he would sew several hides together to make gloves for the winter months.[72]

Walter D. Addison wrote, "Rats, dogs, cats nor any other animals wouldn't long exist amongst that hungry throng of prisoners. Catching rats and selling them for food became quite a business, and they pursued the avocation with quite a profit, the demand being steady."[73]

Former prisoner James B. Stamp remembered that in December 1864 the "insufficiency of food increased, and in many instances, prisoners were reduced to absolute suffering. All the rats that could be captured were eaten, and on one occasion a small dog that had followed a wood hauler into camp was caught and prepared for food."[74]

Killed and dressed rats were an important commodity in the prison camp and sold anywhere from four to twenty-five cents apiece. Former Elmira prisoner of war R. B. Ewan recalled, "Our mart of trade was about in the center of the ground, and at 10 o'clock every day dressed rats on boards and tin plates, and sick prisoners' rations were offered for five cents and sometimes more."[75]

Tobacco and Hardtack Were Used as Money

Since money was not allowed at Elmira the prisoners needed some form of exchange for goods. Tobacco proved to be the ideal substitute since it could easily be divided and was readily available. One pound of tobacco was worth about a dollar. The pound was usually divided into twenty squares or quids. These were often referred to as chews. The value of each quid was five cents. This system of trade made it possible to have a thriving marketplace.

Former prisoner Berry Benson wrote, "Tobacco I found to be the medium of trade, the currency, and the chew was the unit thereof. But tobacco and hardtack had the same value. One cracker equals one chew. A user of tobacco, feeling that he must have a chew, saves a cracker from his dinner (ill can he spare it!), walks up to an exchange table, deposits his cracker and takes up a chew, saying never a word, the relative value is so well-established."[76]

Prisoner carved hickory pipe bowl. Prisoners created things to sell at the Market Place inside of the prison. *Photograph courtesy of the Chemung County Historical Society.*

Private James Elliott noticed that, "Tobacco was the most common medium of exchange. Pieces of tobacco cut up into chews, the larger cuts passing for five or ten chews."[77]

Apparently, nothing was wasted in prison. Not even tobacco after it had been chewed. Former prisoner Thad Walker recalled, "Tobacco was a very scarce and valuable article at Elmira, and happy was the individual fortunate enough to secure any. I have often seen men following a lucky chewer and waiting for him to finish his chew and beg it for himself. The poor fellows would daily hunt for discarded chews and consider themselves lucky if they found one."[78]

Former prisoner George M. Neese remembers, "I have seen men walking along the streets gathering up chewed cud's of tobacco for smoking purposes. They picked the little ground-up quids to pieces and spread them in the sunshine until dried, then smoked the debris."[79]

Trades Flourished at Elmira

Like all forms of society, people with money fare better than those without. So, it was the same with the prisoners of Elmira. A few prisoners were fortunate enough to have friends and relatives send them money to make life easier in prison. Yet ninety percent of the men either did not receive any money or very little and had to rely on what the United States government furnished them. Sadly, this was never enough. Many prisoners' immune systems were weakened by a lack of food and disease was the inevitable result.

Prisoners sought to supplement their inadequate diet and clothing through profitable activities. Men with some education or skill were able to increase their chances of survival by making goods to sell to other prisoners. Others practiced a trade or learned a new one. The benefits of having a trade were many. First, it kept the inmate occupied and made the time go by faster. Second, he earned a wage which allowed him to purchase items that would make life in prison more comfortable. Food and clothing were the most sought after things because it was nearly impossible to live on what the government issued the prisoners.

Prisoner carved bone necklace. *Photograph courtesy of the Chemung County Historical Society.*

All that was needed for creative prisoners to setup shop was to hang the appropriate sign outside his tent, and display his wares on a cracker-box table. These items could range from artwork, coffee, fans, rats, rings, watch fobs, and many others. Some men performed a service such as barbers, tailors, shoemakers and laundry men. There was practically no end to the possibilities if a prisoner had the desire to succeed and set his mind to it. Private David Holt remembers many men sold a service to other prisoners. "In our tent we had a barber. Every man who had a trade or profession was trying to follow his calling. As I had neither, I followed my nose and roamed around like a roaring lion."[80]

Men gathered together at the prison market place, buying and selling various goods they had made. A fiddler entertained the men by playing an instrument he designed from a cracker box and string. Prisoners traded cups of coffee, slices of bread, and meat rations for tobacco. Many used old wooden crates as makeshift stands, so they could display their wares. In his book Berry Benson wrote about the trades that flourished at Elmira. "It was a curious sight to see, different trades being plied, such as cobbling, perhaps some kind of small carpenters work."[81] It should be explained here that the extra meat rations sold generally came from prisoners who were in the hospital and either had no appetite or passed away. Other times the extra rations had been stolen or flanked by other prisoners. One example was 11th Mississippi infantryman James M. Gilmore who worked as a waiter in the mess hall. Gilmore admitted stealing twenty-five to thirty rations during his daily shift. "After eating all I wanted, I sold the remainder. We aggregated the amount to be something like 10,000 (rations), so you can see we cared little about how the government issued rations."[82] Unfortunately, activity like this did not come without a price as other prisoners were deprived of a meal.

John R. King wrote, "The prisoners passed the time making trinkets. Capt. Munger and Capt. Peck, secured the material and after the articles were completed they sold them in the city for the best price possible, always remitting the money. In passing through the prison one would see a boisterous lot playing cards or some other game, numbers making rings out of Gutta-percha buttons and riveting sets on to them of real silver which the captains

Prisoner carved bone thimble. *Photograph courtesy of the Chemung County Historical Society.*

had purchased, others were making pretty trinkets out of bone, such as tooth picks and seals for watch chains, with birds, squirrels and other figures designed on them. Some made watch chains out of horsehair with single links, with two links interlocked and others with three links interlocked making a round chain. This was done with horsehairs and two common needles. Others in our pen made fans out of white pine wood, the board was cut in the shape of a paddle with a fancy handle, then the part which formed the paddle was notched and cut into thin slices with a very sharp knife. The wood was softened with warm water and then the slices bended like a fan. Different colored ribbons were worked through the notches and the ends tied in a bow around the handle. They were very pretty, but frail. One man made a small parasol on the same plan."[83]

Prison Letters and Packages

One of the most enjoyable pastimes for prisoners was reading letters from loved ones. These letters from home were extremely important for the men's morale and they provided a brief respite from the woes of prison life. When a prisoner was writing a letter to his family it could only be a single page and not mention anything critical of the camp or their treatment. The envelope remained unsealed, so it could be examined by a censor. If a letter contained anything forbidden, it was not mailed.

Packages were especially looked forward to. Many times, the prisoners would receive money or clothing which was intercepted by the prison censors. When mail for a prisoner was received the sensor would open it and see if it contained anything that was

Prisoners letters sent from Elmira had to be left open, so censors could inspect the letter for anything forbidden. This letter passed inspection and bears an "Examined, Elmira, N. Y." stamp from the censor.

contraband. All Federal uniform clothing, boots, or equipment of any kind for military service, weapons of all kinds and intoxicating liquors, were among the contraband articles. All money prisoners received was taken by the Provost Marshall, and he gave the prisoner a receipt for it. These funds were recorded in a ledger by the camp sutler and the prisoners were given credit for any purchases made at the sutler's store. When prisoners were paroled their money was returned to them.

Former prisoner Anthony M. Keiley recalled there were ways to send a letter longer than one page. "One had to acquire a telegraphic habit of writing, or be content to say very little. Some geniuses were in the habit of writing their letters in the usual long length, then sending them by detail (separate envelopes). Others cultivated a microscopic penmanship."[84]

Somehow Elmira prisoner John Brusnan got a letter past the military censors to his sister in Maryland.

> *"I will give you some idea of my situation,"* Brusnan wrote. *"I would have never written to you for money, but I am almost starved to death. I only get two meals a day, breakfast and supper. For breakfast I get one-third a pound of bread and a small piece of meat; for supper the same quantity of bread and not any meat, but a small plate of warm water called soup. When I came here this prison contained 10,000 prisoners, and they have all died except for about 5,000. They are now dying at the rate of twenty-five a day."*[85]

On January 10, 1865, Lieutenant P. E. O'Conner sent a copy of Brusnan's letter to his sister to the War Department where it caused quite a stir. O'Conner pointed out that the letter had somehow gotten past the censors at Elmira.[82] Colonel Benjamin F. Tracy, Elmira prison camp's commandant, was informed of this letter and asked for his comment. Tracy examined the letter and wrote back, "it is almost unnecessary for me to say that the statements made by the prisoner Brusnan are out-rageously false. The daily rations for each prisoner is uniformly as follows: For break-fast, 8 ounces bread, 8 ounces meat; for sup-per, 8 ounces bread, 1 pint and a half soup of excellent quality, made from the meat, pota-toes, onions, and beans." Tracy also stated, "as regards to letters prisoners of war secret out of camp, I have the honor to state that about January 1st we discovered that letters were mailed which did not pass through the

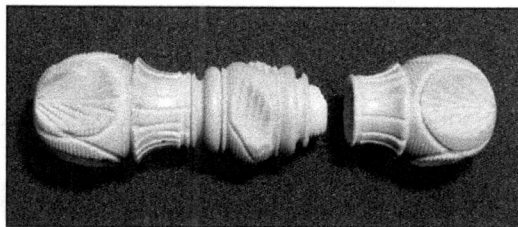

This carved beef bone needle case was made by prisoners. *Photograph courtesy of the Chemung County Historical Society.*

hands of the examiner. We have intercepted some hundreds of such letters and discovered the parties engaged in this business. One commissioned officer, one acting assistant sur-geon, and two enlisted men have been arrested and charges preferred against them. We have adopted such measures for the future for the detection of parties attempting to secret letters out of camp and it will be very difficult, if not impossible, for them to escape dis-covery."[86]

Tracy's letter is very enlightening, but what Union Lieutenant Frank Wilkerson says about the prisoner rations can shed more light on the meals. It is important to note that Wilkerson was a guard at Elmira and had no ax to grind regarding the prisoners. In a book he had written after the war, he said, "The prisoners, it was alleged, were allowed the same rations, excepting coffee and sugar, that their guards received. They did not get it. I repeat-edly saw the Confederate prisoners draw their provisions, and they never got more than two/thirds of a ration."[87]

So, who do you believe? Apparently, the full ration Colonel Benjamin Tracy spoke of was only on paper. It has already been shown that because of the two ration reductions the full ration had shrunk by at least 25%. By the time the prisoner's food was issued by the commissary, the ration was pilfered by men in the handling and preparation of the prison-er's food. So, on one end of the spectrum, you have Colonel Tracy saying the prisoners were issued a full (reduced) ration. On the other end of the spectrum, there are hundreds of prisoners who say they received 4 ounces of meat and an inch-thick slice of bread. In the middle is Lieutenant Wilkeson who says he never saw the prisoner receive more than two/thirds of a (reduced) ration. Historians have always cautioned readers not to believe everything a prisoner says because his words may be influenced by his hatred for his cap-tors or a bitter memory of his time while he was in prison. While I can't discount so many accounts from prisoners, I also can't believe Colonel Tracy saying that the prisoners re-ceived a full (reduced) ration. I believe the truth lies somewhere between, probably closer to Lieutenant Wilkeson's 2/3's ration. Wilkeson's testimony has several things going for it. The first thing is the time element. Due to the reductions and availability of certain foods, rations would vary in size and content. The time he had written about was the winter of 1864-65. Brusnan's letter was written on December 30, 1864. This would be about the same time that Lieutenant Wilkeson made his observation of the 2/3's ration being issued to the prisoners. Another thing his account has going for it is that he was merely reporting what he saw day after day. As stated before, he was not being partial to either side. If Colonel Tracy said a full ration was 8 ounces of bread and 8 ounces of meat, two/thirds of the same ration would be 5.3 ounces. This amount seems far more likely to be fairly close to the actual amount the prisoners received.

Since Lieutenant Wilkeson did not comment on the soup it is difficult to determine if it was of excellent quality as Colonel Tracy said it was. I will note that virtually all of the prisoners complained about the soup not having any meat in it and three or four beans.

Prisoner Marcus B. Toney had charge of the Ward—a duty that required his calling the roll once a day, and submitting a report of the sick men who went to the hospital. "In the cookhouse," Toney stated in the Civil War memoir, "were a large number of iron kettles or cauldrons in which the meat and beans were boiled. I suppose these cauldrons would hold 50 gallons. The salt pork was shipped in barrels and rolled up to the cauldrons, and with a pitchfork tossed in, then the beans—I have heard the boys say four beans to a gallon of water. Now when this is boiled down it gets very salty, and after three weeks of a diet of this kind the prisoner will commence to get sick." [88]

A straw watch chain made by prisoners and sold at the prison market. *Photograph courtesy of the Chemung County Historical Society.*

Under Colonel Hoffman the prison fund was growing by leaps and bounds. Not only did the fund save money by selling rations back to the commissary, but it also collected money belonging to deceased prisoners and a 3 ½ cent sales tax on any money made by the sutler. The money from this fund could be used to purchase materials for the prison camps that were not provided by the War Department. Although Elmira existed only a year, the prison camp fund amounted to $239,857. Fifty-eight thousand dollars remained unspent at the end of the war and was returned to the Federal Government. The prisoners of Elmira could have certainly used this money to stave off death by buying extra food and clothing. If Northern officials were doing all they could to prevent prison deaths, why wasn't this money used to help these prisoners? To carry this idea a step further, $1,845,126 remained in the collective Prison Fund from all the Northern prisons at the end of the war.[89] Why on earth was this money unspent? Who knows how many prisoner's lives could have been spared by releasing the money in the prison fund. It was after all, their money not the governments. The main reason this money was not spent to aid the prisoners is because Colonel Hoffman tightly held the purse strings. Was Hoffman's motivation to show the government what an excellent job he was doing by returning a large portion of the money, or was his cost-cutting measures really designed to further his retaliation against the Confederates?

In a November 14, 1864, report Medical Inspector Surgeon William Sloan said when he asked the quartermaster about the lack of insulation for the prisoner's barracks at Elmira he was told, "I was informed that everything being referred to the Commissary-General of Prisoners, (Colonel William Hoffman) the requisition of lining (insulation) the buildings to make them comfortable for the winter was disapproved and the stopping of cracks and open places ordered." Was this another case of Hoffman's being frugal or was it really retaliation in disguise by stopping up the cracks? Inspector Sloan goes on to say this was imperative because the barracks were "hastily erected of green lumber, which is cracking, splitting, and warping in every direction. An inside lining would prevent the access of cold winds, snow, and rain." Sloan pointed out that the barracks at Elmira needed this insulation as it was currently being ravaged by pneumonia and scurvy.[90]

During the late summer days of 1864, 5,000 Confederate prisoners were housed in tents. Some men slept in tents through late December until the last of the winter barracks were completed. *Photograph courtesy of the Chemung County Historical Society.*

71

Chapter 4

Disease at Elmira Prison Camp

One of the leading causes of disease was the water supply. Foster's pond was a stagnant backwash of the Chemung River running through most of the camp. Prisoners were using this water for bathing and also as a latrine. On November 1, 1864, Surgeon Eugene Sanger wrote a lengthy report critical of Elmira's sanitary conditions to Surgeon General Joseph K. Barnes. Sanger wanted to absolve his department of any wrongdoing in regard to the overwhelming sickness and death among the prisoners. Sanger also noted there were serious delays in getting the medical supplies he needed and in building better hospital facilities. "Foster's Pond," he wrote, "remains green with putrescence, filling the air with its messengers of disease and death, the vaults give out their sickly odors, and the hospitals are crowded with victims for the grave." He estimated that "Seven thousand men will pass 2,600 gallons of urine daily. A portion of this is absorbed by the earth or runs into the pond to purify." Sanger concluded with, "Unless the laws of hygiene are carefully studied and observed in crowded camps, disease is the inevitable consequence."[1]

Elmira's Chief Surgeon Eugene Sanger called attention to the hazards of Foster's Pond. *Photograph courtesy of the Chemung County Historical Society.*

In August, Sanger requested that a drainage system be built to flush the pond and remedy the problem. Surgeon Sanger was not alone in sounding the alarm about the dangers of Foster's pond. At least four other officers, including Colonel Eastman, Colonel Tracy, Lt. Colonel Alexander and Captain Munger, wrote more than a dozen letters to the Commissary General of Prisoners recommending a drainage system for Foster's Pond. These letters were largely ignored.

On October 23rd, 101 days after this unhealthy condition was brought to his attention, Colonel Hoffman finally gave his approval to build a drainage trench to the Chemung River, specifying that the money would come from the prison fund and the labor was to be performed by the prisoners. The trench was to be dug six feet deep and a two-inch wooden pipe would carry water from the river. Earlier Colonel Tracy had estimated it would only take two weeks to complete the mile-long drainage project, but now there were delays because the ground was frozen. Twelve hundred sixty-three prisoners died of disease before work on the drainage system was completed in early January. Secretary Stanton and Colo-

nel Hoffman had once again succeeded in bringing their policy of retaliation to fruition through the use of delaying tactics. Historian Michael Horigan wrote:

> The failure of the Commissary General [Colonel Hoffman] to launch a work project in good weather of late summer is puzzling. It now appeared, in the eyes of some, that a tactic of deliberate delay was beginning to come into being. That tactic would become part of the Elmira Prison Camp's legacy.[2]

Federal Lieutenant Frank Wilkeson wrote a book about his experiences during the Civil War. During this time his unit happened to be assigned to help guard the prison camp at Elmira. One of his duties was to take a detail of Confederate prisoners outside the prison walls to dig the six-foot-deep trench for the drainage system. Wilkeson testimony is extremely important not only because he was a Federal officer, but his statement was unsolicited. No one asked him to comment about the Elmira prisoners. He did so voluntarily. Wilkeson wrote, "They (the prisoners) were eager to work, to earn money to buy tobacco. On pleasant days a few hundred of them were employed outside the stockade in digging ditches and trenches. For this work they were paid about twenty-five cents per day, which sum they promptly invested in tobacco. And they worked faithfully and honestly, and earned their scanty pay. Thinly clad, with blankets wound around them instead of overcoats, poorly fed, hopeless, these unfortunate soldiers swung heavy picks, and bent low over

Captain Frank Wilkeson, 4th US Artillery, guarded prisoners digging a ditch in the frozen ground from Foster's Pond.

their shovels, as the cold wind swept through their emaciated frames as through a sieve. It was pitiful to see the poverty-stricken Confederates breaking the hard, frost-bound earth."[3]

Another factor affecting the water quality was the number of people in the camp. Camp Chemung was built to house 2,000 men. When it was converted into Elmira Prison Camp over a thousand tents were added, increasing the capacity of the camp to 4,000 men. Until the new barracks were completed the following January, 5,190 men camped outdoors in tents while 3,873 were housed in barracks. The camp designed to accommodate 4,000 men now had over 9,000 going into the harsh northern winter.

The severe winter weather of 1864-65 became a major story in Elmira's newspapers. The *Advertiser* noted January 16th "as being one of the wildest and most blustery days of the season. We were favored with blustery, blinding snow squalls which seem to have swept generally through this part of the state."[4] On February 11th the *Advertiser* reported that snow in the wooded areas near the town was two and a half feet in depth. Prisoner John N. Opie recalled in a memoir the cold winter mornings and said, "Imagine if you can, with the weather ten or fifteen degrees below zero, one hundred men trying to keep warm by one stove. Each morning the men crawled out of their bunks, shivering and half frozen, when a scuffle and frequently a fight, for a place by the fire occurred. God help the sick or the weak, as they were literally left out in the cold."[5] John R. King wrote, "The man who looked after the fires made only two fires in 24 hours. The first fire was made at 8:00 in the morning, the other at 8 p.m. Near noon and midnight we were comfortable, but during the twelve hours between fires when the temperature of the stoves lowered we often suffered with the cold."[6]

Prisoner James Huffman remembered the "weather being so extremely cold that some of the men froze their feet while standing on the snow and ice at (morning) roll call."[7] John R. King wrote, "While in the house I wrapped my feet in old rags which kept them warm, but in the late winter we were compelled to stand in the snow every morning for roll call, consequently my feet and shins were badly frozen. Many besides myself had frozen feet."[8] Nine Fort Fisher prisoners died from disease that was attributed to gangrene. Gangrene is characterized by decay of body tissue where the flesh turns black and dies due to severe trauma or frostbite. These deaths occurred in February and March which suggests these men died as a result of frostbite.

Captain Bennett F. Munger inspected Elmira on August 17, 1864, and reported that, "two hundred twenty-six prisoners were sick in hospital and a large number in quarters." He noted that a number of prisoners in their barracks were unable to attend sick call, and in some cases had not been visited by a surgeon in four days. "Some are destitute of blankets and proper underclothes, and all without hospital rations; clothing of prisoners deficient, especially in blankets and shirts. The stench arising from the stagnant water in the pond is still very offensive."[9] Prisoner Anthony M. Keeley recorded in his diary August 28, "The regulations of the pen are growing more strict. No food is permitted to be sold to us by the sutler." On September 11th Keeley made another entry in this diary, "The restricting of the prisoners to a uniform diet of bread and meat, and denying them the privilege of purchasing other food, are showing their affects in an epidemic of scurvy."[10]

Lt. Colonel Eastman sent a letter to the War Department asking what he should do with packages of clothing sent by prisoner's relatives. The government's lack of action appalled clothing giant Noah, Walker & Co. *Photograph courtesy of Minnesota Historical Society.*

In late September, Captain Munger conducted another inspection of Elmira and noted the weather was unseasonably cold. "There is still great destitution and those in tents especially suffer." The report told of a lack of stoves in the hospitals and barracks, and overcrowded hospital conditions that deprived about a hundred sick prisoners of war of a hospital bed. Captain Munger wrote, "During the past week there have been 112 deaths, reaching one day 29. There seems little doubt numbers have died both in quarters and hospital for want of proper food."[11]

John R. King wrote, "The poor fellows died rapidly, despondent, homesick, hungry and wretched, I have stood day after day watching the wagons carry the dead outside to be buried and each day for several weeks 16 men were taken through the gate."[12]

The Elmira prisoners also became sick due to the lack of adequate clothing. Between August 22nd and February 1st of the following year four attempts were made by different individuals to provide the prisoners with winter necessities. All four were thwarted by Secretary Stanton and General Henry W. Wessells. Wessells became the perfect ally of Stanton because he had been a prisoner of the Confederacy and readily accepted the idea of retaliation. Circular No. 4 dictated that clothing might be furnished to "destitute" prisoners of war by their relatives. "The outer garments must be gray, and only one suit and change of underwear would be allowed."[13]

Sergeant George W. D. Porter recalled, "A great number of the men were in rags, and but a small quantity of clothing was issued by the United States Government. Of that received from home and friends the amount was restricted, and only obtainable on a permit approved by headquarters. When the mercury got down to 35 degrees below zero in the winter of 1864-65, I saw numbers of my comrades with frost-bitten hands, feet, ears and faces."[14]

Noah Walker & Co., a Baltimore clothing retailer, notified Colonel Eastman that it had a number of clothing packages ordered by relatives of prisoners that were to be delivered to Elmira. The company explained the War Department restricted all deliveries

Confederate jacket

of clothing to prison camps and asked Eastman if he would accept the packages for Elmira.

Colonel Eastman sent a letter to the War Department asking what he should do. No record was ever found regarding the War Department's reply. What they said can only be surmised by Eastman's refusal to allow the shipment of clothing from the Baltimore firm.

In another attempt to send clothing to Elmira, The Baltimore Relief Organization in early September sent John J. Van Allen to Elmira to see about providing a shipment of clothing for the prisoners. Colonel Eastman received Van Allen with courtesy and informed him that the prisoners of war at Elmira "were destitute of clothing and blankets; that one-half of them did not have a single blanket; that most of them had been captured during the hot summer months with nothing other than thin cotton clothes, which in most instances were in tatters."[15]

The War Department refused to allow Van Allen to enter the prison camp. He contacted the Secretary of War in hopes of being allowed to help the prisoners. Stanton's response, Van Allen claimed, would only allow gray color clothing to be brought to the prison. Van-Allen was told he could not distribute the clothing or moneys himself, but would have to leave it with prison officials. Van-Allen was convinced that the Confederate prisoners would never see any of the clothing or money that he had brought. "I was actually forced to give the matter up in despair," a disappointed John Van Allen wrote, "The brutal Stanton was inexorable to all my entreaties, and turned a deaf ear to the tale of their sufferings."[16]

In April of 1876 *The Southern Historical Society Papers* reported that the Honorable A. J. Beresford Hope wrote Secretary Stanton for permission to raise money in England to alleviate the status of prisoners in Northern prisons. Stanton said, "Almighty God! No! The government of the United States is rich enough to provide for its prisoners and needs no foreign help."[17]

Colonel Tracy submitted Elmira's December clothing requisition for 1,000 jackets, 2,500 shirts, 3,000 pairs of trousers, 8,000 drawers, 7,000 pairs of socks and 1,500 caps.

Tracy was informed by General Wessells that "a large amount of cotton has been shipped for New York . . . the proceeds to be applied for the purchase of clothing . . . for the comfort of rebel prisoners of war. In view of this fact it is desirable that no more clothing shall be provided by the Government than is absolutely demanded by the ordinary dictates of humanity." (The cotton shipment will be discussed on page 82) Wessells then closed his letter with the instruction, "You will please report your views on this subject."[18]

Colonel Tracy waited all month for the clothing he ordered in December, but no shipment ever came. Finally, Tracy wrote General Wessell's on January 5th and informed him he was still waiting for his December allotment of clothing to be delivered. Colonel Tracy asked, "that these amounts . . . be furnished immediately for issue to prisoners, unless the department is advised that supplies will be speedily forwarded by the rebel authorities."[19]

Wessells responded to Colonel Tracy on January 19th and told him that his clothing requisitions for Elmira were not sent because Tracy had failed to report his views of the government's plan as ordered. This bureaucratic red tape was all part of Secretary Stanton's delaying tactics to exact punishment against the Rebels. If he could holdup the clothing shipment long enough, it would virtually have the same effect as refusing to fill it.

In September 1864, with the end of the war in sight and apparently in favor of the North, the War Department reinstituted the prisoner exchange. Commissary General of Prisoners, William Hoffman, telegraphed Colonel Tracy, "By authority of the Secretary of War all invalid prisoners in your charge who will not be fit for service within sixty days will in a few days be sent South for exchange." This order refused to release men "who are too feeble to endure the journey." Those to be exchanged were to be accompanied by at least one medical officer and several able Confederates who had served in the camp hospital as attendants and nurses. Elmira's medical staff was to select only those prisoners who were healthy enough to survive the journey. Colonel Tracy hoped the prison hospital would be improved by eliminating over twelve hundred invalids.[20]

Surgeon Josiah Simpson told Colonel Hoffman that many prisoners were unable to bear the journey south.

On the morning of October 11th, the 1,264 prisoners to be exchanged made the two-mile trip from the prison camp to the town's railroad depot. Nearly 300 men, who were unable to walk, rode in wagons to the depot and then were loaded onto boxcars. They were described by Anthony Keiley, an assistant nurse, as "hospital patients on crutches, borne in the arms of friends, creeping some of them, on hands and knees, pale, gaunt, emaciated; some with the seal of death stamped on their wasted cheeks and shriveled limbs. They were a ghastly tide, with skeleton bodies and lusterless eyes, and brains bereft of but one thought, and hearts purged of all feelings but one—the thought of freedom, the love of home."[21]

The prisoners were loaded onto three trains of boxcars for the 260-mile trip to Baltimore. During the forty-hour trip death claimed five of the Confederates and another prisoner died shortly after he arrived at his destination. Medical officials in Baltimore were dismayed to learn no doctors had accompanied the men.

Surgeon Josiah Simpson, medical director of the Middle Department, VIII Army Corps, angrily reported to Colonel Hoffman that many of the prisoners arriving from Elmira were gravely ill. "I made a personal inspection of the men," Simpson stated, "and found a number unable to bear the journey. Many should never have been permitted to leave Elmira."[22]

Surgeon Artemus Chapel boarded the steamer at Baltimore to examine the Elmira prisoners going to Point Lookout. He reported to Surgeon Simpson that someone "is greatly censurable for sending such cases away from camp even for exchange."[23] Surgeon C.F. Campbell told Simpson that sixty of the men were suffering from extended illnesses and too debilitated to make the trip. "Such men," Campbell wrote, "should not have been sent from Elmira. If they were inspected before leaving the place in accordance with orders it was most carelessly done, reflecting severely on the medical officers engaged in that duty and is disgraceful to all concerned. The effect produced on the public by such marked displays of inefficiency or neglect of duty cannot fail to be most injurious to our cause both at home and abroad."[24]

Surgeon Simpson sent a letter to Colonel Hoffman regarding the Elmira exchange. An angry Simpson suggested there was "criminal neglect and inhumanity on the part of the medical officers in making the selection of men to be transferred."[25] Colonel Hoffman forwarded all the reports regarding the October prisoner exchange to Secretary of War Stanton. Stanton remained silent about the matter and never took any disciplinary action.

A woman from Baltimore witnessed the dramatic scene at Elmira's train station involving the transfer of prisoners and wrote a letter to the *Daily National Intelligencer* in Washington, D. C.. Mrs. Mary W. Rhodes described seeing the emaciated prisoners, and wrote, "I saw the condition of the fifteen hundred who were taken away for exchange, many of them in a dying condition." Then Mrs. Rhodes complained on the corruption that allowed this to happen, and she appealed to her country men to correct this terrible wrong. "It is useless to appeal to the Secretary of War. It rests with the men of the North to remove this foul stain from our country. I cannot, will not, believe that my countrymen of the North will permit this state of things to continue.... Those fifteen hundred [sic] pale faces are before me as I saw them pass me at the depot.... I would plead for all the prisons, though I have only seen the horrors of Elmira."[26]

Superintendent of Nurses Dorothea Dix was called in to examine Elmira prisoner of war camp.

Because of Mrs. Rhodes' letter *The Daily National Intelligencer* contacted the Sanitary Commission about investigating the conditions at Elmira prison camp. The Commission wanted to have a highly respected figure conduct the inspection, so they asked Miss Dorothea Dix. During the war Dorothea Dix served as the civilian superintendent of Women Nurses for the Union. When Miss Dix requested to inspect Elmira prison camp she was initially refused by

Major General Ethan A. Hitchcock who was the commissioner for the exchange of prisoners. However, Hitchcock did change his mind two days later. It's possible Hitchcock was influenced to change his mind by his superiors, or perhaps it was due to the *Elmira Daily Advertiser's* November 19th article. The newspaper noted that her, "visit is at the instance of the government, which avails itself of her life-long experience in connection with the amelioration of the condition of the criminal as well as the sick and wounded."[27]

Miss Dorothea Dix's visit to Elmira prison camp took place November 20th and 21st of 1864. Everything was carefully orchestrated to only show her what Colonel Benjamin Tracy intended her to see. Her whirlwind two-day inspection began when she was greeted by a distinguished group of Elmira's leading citizens. During her tour of the prison camp Miss Dix was escorted by Colonel Tracy and his staff who made sure she only saw what they wanted her to see. The prison grounds and barracks were carefully policed and spotless for her visit. The mess halls and hospitals were scrubbed, sanitized and anything objectionable removed for her visit. If

Exchanged prisoners being given rations aboard ship.

this was truly to be an impartial inspection her visit needed to be a complete surprise, so no one could have time to prepare the camp for her inspection. She also needed to have unlimited access to go wherever she wished. But this never happened.

When Miss Dix completed her inspection, she filed a favorable report with the War Department on November 25th. In it she claimed to have "visited the prisons [sic] and hospitals at Elmira, in both which the rebels are receiving all necessary care, and provision fully adequate to all necessities; health, good; sick-call, moderate; serious illness, but few serious cases; mortality, low; prisoners, about 8,000; probably 7,400 fully able for field service."[28]

Let's consider what was said in Miss Dix's report. I will quote her exact words. Were the prisoners receiving "all necessary care"? When one considers Elmira's death toll for November listed 207 prisoners, and twelve men died in the two days Miss Dix was there, you have to wonder which prison camp she was inspecting. Certainly, it wasn't Elmira where several hundred men died from disease during the month of her visit.[29]

Miss Dix also reports that medical supplies were "fully adequate". This was the same month that Elmira's Chief Surgeon Eugene Sanger filed a report to General J. K. Barnes, the Surgeon General for the U. S. Army for the Department of the East, saying he was prevented from obtaining medical supplies and it made it virtually impossible for him to properly manage Elmira's hospital.[30]

Miss Dix also said, "health, good". Let's look at the figures as reported to the United States War Department. Elmira prison camp had 666 sick men in the hospital in November and 207 of these men were destined for Woodlawn Cemetery. Does this sound like good health to you? It doesn't to me, either.[31]

Miss Dix goes on to say, "sick-call moderate; serious illness, but few serious cases; mortality, low." All one has do is look at Elmira's atrocious November figures to realize how false her report was! And yet her inspection is supplied by numerous historians as evidence that conditions weren't so bad at Elmira prison camp.

When the exchanged prisoners from Elmira sailed to Savannah, Georgia, they were met at the dock by Richard H. Dibrell, a member of the "ambulance committee". Dibrell testified to the Committee to Investigate the Conditions and Treatment of Prisoners of War in March, 1865. "I have never seen a set of men in worse condition. They were so enfeebled and emaciated that we lifted them like little children. Many of them were like living skeletons. Indeed, there was one poor boy about 17 years old, who presented the most distressing and deplorable appearance I ever saw. He was nothing but skin and bone, besides this, he was literally eaten up by vermin. He died in the hospital in a few days. . . The mortality on the passage from Maryland was very great as well as that on the passage from the prisons to the port from which they started. I cannot state the exact number, but I think I heard that 3,500 were started, and we only received about 3,027"[32]

W.W. Gramling wrote this in his diary entry for Feb 28, 1865. "Another load of 500 signed the paroles today. Don't know when they will get off. Have a load of sick made up also. Hope I will get out soon. Trust to Providence. Just whoever has money to buy his way out can go."[33]

On one occasion an examining surgeon approached a rebel prisoner who claimed to have a painful gunshot wound that would prevent him from carrying a musket for at least sixty days. This was the time agreed upon where an invalid prisoner could not return to the Confederate army. The man carefully rolled up his sleeve so only the doctor could see his arm. Instead of a wound the doctor found a five-dollar bill. Apparently, this was sufficient incentive for the medic to tell the parole clerk that the prisoner had a "gunshot wound in the left arm."[34]

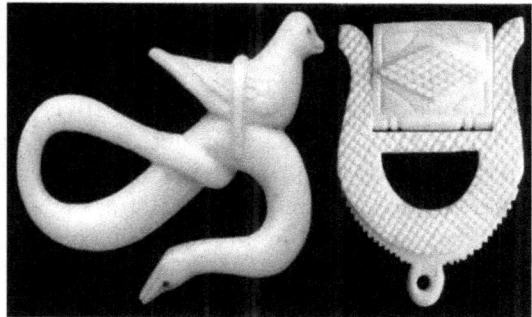

Two trinkets made by George W. Davis at Elmira Prison. Both the bird and snake and the watch fob were carved from beef bone. *Photograph courtesy of the North Carolina Museum of History.*

Another reason for exchanging gravely ill men seems more likely. The officers at Elmira were trying to prove to their superiors, and to the public, that conditions were healthful and not any worse than other Union Prisoner of War Camps. What better way to instantly improve the health of their camp than to get rid of hundreds of terminally-ill prisoners? Is it possible the officers at Elmira deliberately planned to exchange terminally ill prisoners before they died inside the camp? If they could to do so, those deaths would not go on Elmira's permanent record and the public would never know that they had occurred.

Anyone in a position of authority at a prisoner of war camp with a high death rate should not be surprised to find himself the target of intense scrutiny and criticism. The spotlight was especially harsh for Chief Surgeon Eugene Sanger because the prisoner's health was his responsibility. If prisoner reports are to be believed, the good doctor was not as benevolent as he appeared. Prisoner Anthony Keiley was one of the most severe critics of the medical department. Keiley was given the job of clerk in the prison's medical department because he had once been a newspaper editor in Petersburg, Virginia. One of his jobs was keeping a record of the deaths in the hospital wards each morning. After a particularly disturbing day he wrote about high number of prison deaths: "As I went over to the first hospital this morning early, there were eighteen dead bodies lying naked on the bare earth. Eleven more were added to the list by half-past eight o'clock!"[35] In October Keiley wrote, "The deaths yesterday were twenty-nine. Air pure, location healthy, no epidemic. The men are being deliberately murdered by the surgeon, especially by either the ignorance or malice of the chief."[36] Another prisoner, James Huffman, allegedly heard a doctor say, "He (Sanger) killed more Rebs than any soldier on the front."[37]

In his book *In Vinculis* Anthony Keiley wrote, "Sanger is simply a brute, as we learned the whole truth about him from his own people. If he had not avoided court martial by resigning his position, it is likely that even a military commission would have found it impossible to screen his brutality to the sick."[38] Historian Clay Holmes wrote that many prominent citizens who personally knew the Chief Surgeon, believed "something was wrong with Dr. Sanger." Many believed that he "took a very considerable amount of the medicine which the Government furnished for the sick prisoners."[39] Further accusations came from within the hospital. Medical steward W.P. Whitesides commented that there were "plenty of stimulants, but a good deal of it drank by the doctor."[40]

In Sanger's defense it must be noted that between August 13th and October 17th he wrote nine detailed reports that told of unhealthy conditions in the prison camp. Historian Michael Horigan wrote, "No other officer, in the duration of the camp, did so much in such a short period of time. Undoubtedly, the single greatest irony of the Elmira Prison Camp is this: the officer who most vociferously called attention to the unsanitary conditions and other major shortcomings of Barracks No. 3 (Elmira Prison Camp) became the nearest thing to a scapegoat in this very sad story."[41]

On December 23, 1864 Sanger got his wish and was replaced by Major Anthony E. Stocker as Chief Surgeon at Elmira Prison Camp. It should be noted that the two most deadly months, February and March, 1865, occurred at the prison after Sanger had left. However, it must also be remembered that this high death toll may have been a result of insufficient clothing during the unusually harsh winter.

Because of retaliatory articles in Northern newspapers a great number of people felt the South was guilty of brutal behavior in its treatment of Union prisoners of war. The South was hard-pressed to provide food and medicine for their own people, let alone prisoners of war. The devastating impact of three years of war had seriously depleted the region's agricultural production. General Sherman's "March to the Sea" and up through the Carolinas devastated cropland which until that time had produced substantial amounts of food. Sherman's powerful 62,000-man army carried out a scorched earth policy and destroyed all crops and centers of transportation. This seriously impaired any attempt to properly feed Union prisoners of war at places such as Andersonville.

Most people in the North were unaware that their own government was partly responsible for the mistreatment of Union prisoners. The Northern blockade of Southern ports slowed to a trickle the foods and medicine that might have helped Union prisoners. Every time the prisoner of war exchanges were halted it was done by the North. The Confederacy wanted to relieve itself of the burden of caring for thousands of Union prisoners and tried repeatedly to re-establish the exchange but all too often their appeals fell on deaf ears.

A Guard walks his post as he keeps an eye on the barracks at Elmira Prisoner of War camp.
Photograph courtesy of the North Carolina Museum of History.

Several years after the war Federal Major-General Benjamin Butler wrote about the starving Confederate soldiers and reasoned they could only give a small amount of food and clothing to prisoners.

> While I do not mean to apologize for the manner in which our prisoners were treated, I feel bound to say that from careful examinations of the subject I do not believe that either the people or the higher authorities of the Confederacy were in so great degree responsible as they have been accused. In the matter of starvation, the fact is incontestable that a soldier of our army would have quite easily starved on the rations which in the latter days of the war were served out to the Confederate soldiers before Petersburg. I examined the haversacks of many Confederate soldiers captured on picket during the summer of 1864 and found therein, as their rations for three days, scarcely more than a pint of kernels of corn, none broken but only parched to blacken by the fire, a long piece of meat, most frequently bacon, some three inches long by an inch and a half wide and less than a half an inch thick. Now, no Northern soldier could have lived three days upon that, and the lank, emaciated condition of the (Confederate) prisoner fully testified to the meagerness of his means of sustenance.
>
> With regard to clothing, it was simply impossible for the Confederates at that time to have any sufficient clothing upon the bodies of their soldiers, and many passed the winters barefoot. Necessity, therefore, would seem to have compelled the condition of food and clothing given by them to the

81

Federal prisoners, for it was not possible for authorities to supply it without taking the clothing from their soldiers in the field.[42]

Elmira, with its 24.4 percent death rate, was without a doubt the worst camp in the North. Its comparison to Andersonville in southwestern Georgia cannot be avoided. During the war some 45,000 Union prisoners of war were incarcerated at that prison camp. Today there are 12,914 Federal graves in its National Cemetery, making Andersonville's death rate of 28.7 percent the highest of any Civil War prison.

The unusually high death rates of Andersonville and Elmira are comparable, but this is where the similarity ends. Elmira had so much more than Andersonville. Elmira had excellent railroad connections which made it possible to ship in any supplies that the prison camp needed, plus an unlimited supply of fresh water from the Chemung River and plenty of timber for the construction of barracks. Elmira was also located in a valley that was known for growing an abundance of fruits and vegetables. Local newspapers in the summer of 1864 boasted of bumper crops of apples, pears, peaches and a variety of vegetables. There were also herds of cattle and sheep to supply healthful meat for the prisoners. It is difficult to understand why Elmira Prison Camp should be in need of anything in this land of plenty. Many of the deaths at Elmira could have been prevented by sufficient food, clean water, clothing and proper quarters, but officials in Washington chose to ignore the reports about the unsanitary conditions of the camp.

In a letter to President Lincoln, Secretary of War Stanton admits to retaliation and threatens strict measures if Union prisoners do not receive better treatment.

War Department, Washington City, December 5, 1863

Mr. President: The rebel prisoners of war in our possession have heretofore been treated with the utmost humanity and tenderness consistent with security. They have had good quarters, full rations, clothing when needed, and the same hospital treatment received by our own soldiers. Indulgence of friendly visits and supplies was formerly permitted, but they have been cut off since the barbarity practiced against our prisoners became known to the Government. If it should become necessary for the protection of our men, strict retaliation will be resorted to.

Respectfully submitted,
        Edwin M. Stanton
                Secretary of War[43]

Secretary of War Edwin M. Stanton had written President Lincoln urging "strict retaliation" against Confederate prisoners.

Did Secretary of War Stanton ever implement the "strict retaliation" he referred to? The record seems to indicate he may have. Certainly, the situation of the Northern prisoners did not improve. It probably got worse. The war had another year and a half to go and the South had yet to experience Sherman's devastating March to the Sea and up through the Carolinas. This invasion burned buildings and crops, butchered livestock and tore up the railroad tracks. All of these things were needed to feed and clothe the Federal prisoners.

After reviewing all the evidence presented it is difficult not to arrive at the conclusion that there was some form of retaliation taking place. Admittedly, there is no hard proof such as documents that distinctly outline a plan of retaliation. However, we can put the pieces together to form a picture. The picture that takes shape is not very pretty because it clearly shows man's inhumanity toward man. Worse still, it reflects man's vindictiveness against helpless prisoners of war.

These examples suggest that during the last year of the Civil War certain officials of the United States War Department sought retaliation in the form of delaying or rejecting reasonable requests from prison personnel. These orders emanated from one man, Secretary of War Edwin M. Stanton, and were passed down to like-minded officers, ie, General Henry W. Wessells, Colonel William Hoffman, General Ethan A. Hitchcock and others. Soldiers at Elmira enforced these mandates and turned Elmira into a death camp. In his own way, Stanton succeeded in creating his own Andersonville in the North.

Northern Prisons Become Overcrowded

When Camp Rathbun was constructed in 1861 to train Union troops and could only accommodate 1,500 troops. Rathbun was closed in 1863. In early 1864 the Northern command began searching for an available space to build another prison, so it could handle the thousands of Confederate prisoners from General Ulysses S. Grant's spring time offensive against Lee's Army of Northern Virginia. This campaign produced 20,000 more Confederate prisoners that were sent to the

Every morning a death wagon would make rounds of the camp and pick up the dead bodies from the night before. *Photograph courtesy of the Chemung County Historical Society.*

prison at Point Lookout, Maryland. Point Lookout became so overcrowded that it caused Colonel William Hoffman to send a letter to Secretary of War Edwin M. Stanton, recommending that the Maryland prison send some of its prisoners to a new prison camp to relieve the overcrowded conditions.[44]

Camp Rathbun in New York had been closed the previous year and was examined for the possibility of a new prison. Officials liked what they saw when they toured the facility. Located in the east, the existing camp was near railroads to haul the prisoners and the fertile valley could produce plenty of farm fruits and vegetables, and it had abundant freshwater from the Chemung River. The area was wooded to provide lumber to build twenty new barracks and dozens of other buildings, mess halls and thousands of feet of twelve-foot-high fence. It was estimated the new prison camp could accommodate two thousand prisoners and another thousand could be housed in tents. When Elmira opened its gates in July, ten more barracks were hastily erected. As it was discovered later, the new lumber was not seasoned properly and was not ready to use yet. In November medical inspector William Sloan explained to his superiors at the Medical Department that the winters were cold and harsh at Elmira and the lumber for the barracks was cracking and splitting. Sloan described that this left gaps between the joints where bitter winter winds could penetrate the buildings promoting deadly diseases like pneumonia.

The prison at Point Lookout, Maryland, sent over 8,500 prisoners to Elmira between July and September, 1864. The overcrowding began almost as soon as Elmira Prisoner of War Camp opened its gates. The prison officers did their best in trying to keep Elmira prison camp clean, but sickness still plagued the camp because it was grossly overcrowded. Every prisoner who came to Elmira was immediately vaccinated. If someone was suspected of having smallpox, the prisoner was put in the Contagious Diseases hospital until he either died or became well.[45]

Woodlawn Cemetery with the original wooden headboards. These headboards became weathered and cracked and were replaced with granite stones by the United States Government in 1907. Unfortunately, the grave numbers were changed from the original numbers listed in the soldier's records. *Photograph courtesy of the Chemung County Historical Society.*

Introduction of Smallpox at Elmira Prison Camp

The first incidents of variola, or more commonly known as smallpox, occurred at Elmira Prison camp when infected prisoners from Fort Morgan, Alabama, were captured on the Gulf Coast. These prisoners were held in New Orleans, Louisiana, then sent to Ship Island, near Gulfport, Mississippi, sent briefly to Fort Columbus in New York Harbor and finally transferred to Elmira Prison Camp.

A few of the prisoners from Fort Morgan, Alabama, developed symptoms of smallpox in October. By December 12th two of these men became the first smallpox related deaths at the prison. These were Privates Alcide Carmonche, Company K, 2nd Louisiana Cavalry and Oscar Davidson, Company G, 37th Texas Cavalry. Both men were captured near Morganza, Louisiana, and sent to a temporary prison in New Orleans, then on October 4th they were transferred to Ship Island, Mississippi. The men were again transferred November 16th to Fort Columbus, New York Harbor, and then to Elmira Prison Camp. It is important to track where the men had been to see if we can determine the source of the dreaded disease. They probably weren't exposed to the virus in Morganza since the two were captured a month apart. The first incidence of them travelling together is when they were sent to Ship Island, Mississippi, on the same boat. From then on the men traveled along with the other prisoners. It is not known if the men shared the same tent once they reached Elmira. When these prisoners developed symptoms of the disease in October the prison did not have a hospital that could handle cases of smallpox.

On December 23rd Major Anthony E. Stocker replaced Eugene Sanger as chief surgeon and immediately had his hands full with an out of control smallpox epidemic. On Christmas morning Captain William Jordon reported that the virus had been transmitted to sixty-three more men and two more deaths had occurred that week.[46] With the epidemic increasing Colonel Benjamin Tracy was advised on January 5th by General Wilson T. Hartz that if the disease spreads further he should isolate the carriers by building a hospital some distance away from the prison population.[47] A mere three days later there was more bad news when an inspecting officer reported that there were now 126 cases along with 10 deaths.

Shortly after this Tracy ordered a "Smallpox Hospital" be erected in a remote corner of the prison on a strip of land that existed between the Chemung River and Foster's Pond. This hospital, if it could be called that, consisted of several rows of A-frame tents which house three patients and a wood burning stove. Another inspection January 24th reported a total of 397 smallpox cases proving that the disease was on the rise.[48]

Despite several attempts to halt the spread of smallpox everything proved futile except for the moderating spring temperatures of 1865. Smallpox during the Civil War was considered a seasonal disease. Doctors noticed that during the warm months of the year the rate of smallpox cases was considerably below average and during cold months increased to well above normal. The season for this disease typically lasts from October through April with its peak being in March.[49]

One of the precautions taken to halt the spread of smallpox was when a patient recovered from a case of the disease he was required to take a bath and put on new clothes. In the meantime, his old clothes and blankets were burned to destroy the smallpox virus. Surgeon Stocker and his staff busily administered 5,600 vaccinations in January, but they had some terrible side effects. Many of the prisoners developed an ulcer on their arm and a few even had to undergo amputation which sometimes resulted in death.

Former prisoner Walter D. Addison wrote about the horrors of 19th century vaccinations. "The courageous manner in which men were vaccinated excelled anything I have ever witnessed even surpassing the acts of savages. The modus operandi was to assemble the men in long lines with coats off and arms bared; then the butchering began by illiterate and irresponsible men. They would take hold of a thick piece of flesh, dip a lancet into the diluted virus, and then thrust it entirely through the pinched up flesh. The spurious virus soon produced such fearfully disastrous results that it became necessary to construct gangrene hospitals, from which arose a dreadful stench. Scores died from the effects; others losing arms. I have seen the sickening effects of their villainous vaccinations. There are many who can verify the above."[50]

Medical Director Charles S. Tripler presented an interesting report on the large number of prisoners who had developed bad ulcers from smallpox vaccinations. The Medical Department suspected that the vaccine purveyors had provided tainted serum. The ulcers on the patient's arm were described as occurring on the third day with a cyst which filled with pus. This speedily became an irritable sore, from 1 to 4 inches in length, and finally degenerated into an ulcer that was extremely slow to heal. At the time of his report Surgeon Tripler cited 1,580 cases of ulcers. Of these 668 had healed while 912 remained obstinately open.

Tripler noticed that the same vaccine was used on Federal troops as the prisoners and they suffered very little occurrence of ulcers from the vaccinations. Tripler said that the only difference between these men was their diet. He therefore concluded, "The prison diet in this department (prison system) is sufficient in quantity, but it lacks those component parts which are essential to health. Aside from soft bread the only vegetable issued is 30 pounds of potatoes to 100 men per day. This is not sufficient to ward off scurvy, and as long as it is continued a mortality not credible to our government may be expected among our prisoners of war."[51] According to prisoner Marcus Toney the medical staff largely ignored the men in the smallpox hospital. On January 25th Toney was experiencing "a severe chill, with pains in my spine and back of head." He also said his bunkmate's were worried because he had been delirious for two days. Being the Ward Sergeant Toney goes on to say, "When I came to I was out calling the roll of the ward. I noticed that my hands were badly pimpled, but as we did not have a mirror I could not see my face. Before I finished the roll call along came Doctor Burchard, one of the prison surgeons. The doctor looked at me and said: 'Toney, you have the smallpox.'"

Toney then went to the smallpox hospital where he spent a total of four days. He goes on to say, "It was way below zero, and the hospital was across a little lake inside the prison walls, and the patients were in A tent, tents shaped as the letter A, and having a capacity of three patients each. I walked across the lake on the ice and commenced my search at the head of the row of tents, trying to find some bedfellows that had a light attack as myself. Nearly all the tents were filled with patients who had the confluent type, but finally I found a tent with two patients—one very bad and the other lighter—and I crawled in.

We did not see a doctor while there, but once a day a waiter brought us some tea and bread. As the hospital was some distance from the cookhouse and the weather was below zero, the tea was cold when it reached us. My bedfellows could not eat or drink anything, and I had all the rations, yet I could not get enough. The second night one of our bedfellows died, and all the vermin came to us, and we had plenty of company. The vermin will leave a body as soon as it gets cold. We had about eight blankets, but could not keep warm; and to make the situation worse, the men who died were dragged out and left in front of the tents, and in whatever position a man was when death overtook him in that position he froze. Some with arms and legs extended presented a horrible sight."[52]

If Tony's account is to be believed, where were the doctors? Apparently, the smallpox victims were ignored by the medical staff and left to fend for themselves.

Here's an intriguing fact that I think you should be aware of. *The Medical and Surgical History of the War of the Rebellion, (1861-65),* volume I, part III, presented an interesting fact when it reported "No case of smallpox or varioloid was reported among the 49,394 men of the Confederate Army of the Potomac during the nine months, July, 1861-March, 1862, while 380 cases occurred during this period in the United States Army. Smallpox may, therefore, be considered as having invaded the South during the progress of the war."

As you recall Elmira received over 9,000 prisoners from Point Lookout from July through August 1864. It has been confirmed that Point Lookout prison had 466 cases and 212 deaths from smallpox that began as early as November 1863.[53] Isn't it conceivable that the virus had already been at Elmira when the Fort Morgan prisoners arrived? Since small-pox has a two to three-week incubation period this would place full-blown smallpox at Elmira prison camp in September. It had been reported that the first cases of variola appeared in October. This is not to say the disease was carried to Elmira in this way, but this information is given as an alternative scenario that could have taken place.

The Fort Fisher Prisoners

One of the most tragic events in the history of Elmira was set in motion when 1,128 Confederate prisoners arrived in late January from Fort Fisher, North Carolina. These men had endured great suffering during two battles barely three weeks apart. These Confederate soldiers withstood a tremendous bombardment by the largest federal fleet to sail until D-Day in World War II. This fleet contained 58 Warships mounting 644 cannons, unleashing more than 30,000 shot and shell in three days. These guns ranged in size from 6" Dahlgren's and Brookes rifles to monstrous 15" smooth bore Dahlgrens cannon on five ironclad-monitors.[54]

Harper's Weekly **drawing of Federal Infantry assaulting Fort Fisher, North Carolina.**

The Fort's Confederate defenders were under constant bombardment for several days and nights and were unable to come out from their bombproofs to retrieve or bury their dead. The men were suffering from untreated wounds; they were cold and hungry because the January night time temperature had dipped into the 40's and 50's and they hadn't been able to make a fire or have a meal for the last two days. At the height of the bombardment Fort Fisher's commanding officer, Colonel William Lamb, estimated 130 shot and shells exploded inside the Fort per minute. Admiral David D. Porter of the Federal fleet agreed with Lamb's figure and reported, "The fort is nearly demolished, and as soon as troops come we can take possession. We have set them on fire, blown some of them up, and all that is wanted now is the troops to land to go into them."[55]

The third and final day of the bombardment the Union army and Navy launched an 8,000-man, two-pronged assault at the east and west end of the fort simultaneously. The Confederate defenders beat back the assault on the fort's northeast corner with great slaughter, but the Union army desperately struggled to gain entrance through the fort's west gate. Men of the 117th New York penetrated the swamp near the river and flanked the Confederates at the gate, forcing an entrance into the fort. With hundreds of federal troops rushing into the fort the Confederate defenders fought a losing struggle against an overwhelming attack. There was little room for the opponents to maneuver on the fort's parapets because of the growing number of dead and wounded that littered the gun chambers. Men fired their muskets point-blank into the enemy, then plunged into brutal hand-to-hand combat—grappling with each other and killing the enemy with clubbed muskets, knives or any way they could.

One of Fort Fisher's gun batteries lies in ruins following the battle.

The wild melee for the fort would go on for seven hours in the gun chambers, the parade ground and among the rubble of burned barracks. Twice the Confederate defenders succeeded in pushing the enemy back, but their attacks would ultimately grind to a halt with severe losses as a fresh wave of Union troops would arrive on the field. These precious soldiers could not be replaced. Finally, the overwhelming number of Union soldiers pushed them back, capturing more of the fort.

At 10 PM, with the darkness of evening all around them and their ammunition nearly exhausted, the embattled Confederate soldiers were ultimately pushed to the last corner of the fort and forced to surrender. Thus, ended one of the great defensive battles for a Confederate fort in the annuals of the Civil War. The fall of Fort Fisher ultimately led to the surrender of the Wilmington, North Carolina, the last open seaport to the Confederacy. General Robert E. Lee had warned that Wilmington was so important that it must be "defended at all hazards," because if Fort Fisher fell he could not maintain his army (and that meant losing the war).

The reason I am mentioning the Fort Fisher prisoners here is to dispute something that was written in *The Medical and Surgical History of the War of the Rebellion, (1861-65)*. The statement I am referring to was made by an inspector who was trying to explain the large loss of life at Elmira Prison Camp. This inspector wrote, "This is due to the broken-down condition of the prisoners on their arrival."[56] Let's examine the statement he made. In the instance of the Fort Fisher prisoners I am sure that these men were not "broken-down." I speak from authority because I have written a book titled *Fort Fisher to Elmira*. This book not only describes the battle, but the prisoner's experience at Elmira Prison Camp. During my research for this book, I had examined the Fort Fisher soldiers under the discerning eye of a writer. The soldiers at Fort Fisher, North Carolina, were garrison troops. Yes, they received the standard Confederate rations like everybody else. However, the fort was surrounded on three sides by water. Two of these bodies of water were the Atlantic Ocean and the third was the Cape Fear River. This being the case, the soldiers at the fort were able to supplement their diet with fresh fish

A few of the graves in front of Fort Fisher's sally-port.

and oysters. Colonel Lamb regularly detailed men who had had previously worked as fishermen to go out in boats and catch fish for the garrison. The fort also had its own vegetable garden tended by the soldiers. As a result, these men were extremely well fed for Confederate troops. As for being rundown, these men slept in wooden barracks every night. They were not marching hundreds of miles in a campaign and eating meager rations. These soldiers were in the best of health up until the moment they became prisoners.

Now let's examine how these men fared at Elmira and Point Lookout Prison Camps. During January 1,128 Fort Fisher prisoners entered the prison at Elmira and 643 prisoners entered Point Lookout, Maryland. Forty-seven percent of the soldiers who went to Elmira died from disease within five months of captivity. Of the 643 soldiers who went to Point Lookout only nine percent died.[57] Both groups of men had the same diet and experience before being captured. What made this huge difference? Obviously, it was the men's prison environment and diet. A clear majority of the men who died at Elmira succumbed to chronic diarrhea. This was due to overcrowding of the prison which led to water pollution. The second deadliest disease for the Fort Fisher soldiers was pneumonia. These men went north to prison the last week in January. This is the coldest month of the year in upstate New York. "The condition of the patients is pitiable," a federal inspector wrote. "The diseases are nearly all of the typhoid type, and much of the sickness is justly attributable to crowd-poisoning. In addition to this the clothing during the winter was insufficient." The inspector goes on to say, "The Fort Fisher prisoners, especially, arrived in cold weather very much depressed, poorly clad, and great numbers were soon taken sick with pneumonia and diarrhea, rapidly assuming a typhoid character."[58]

It is a known fact that the Union prison system reduced rations several times during the course of the war. When the Fort Fisher prisoners arrived in January, 1865, the men were eating approximately one half the original ration and their meager diet often lacked vegetables. It is known that chronic diarrhea depletes the men's bodies of vital nutrients and electrolytes needed to maintain a normal heartbeat and blood pressure. Unfortunately, this severe diet did nothing to relieve their suffering and in actuality made it worse. Is it any wonder why the prisoners died at such a terrific rate?

On February 20th and again on March 3rd the Fort Fisher prisoners at Elmira participated in an exchange. The men were examined by a medical officer to insure they were

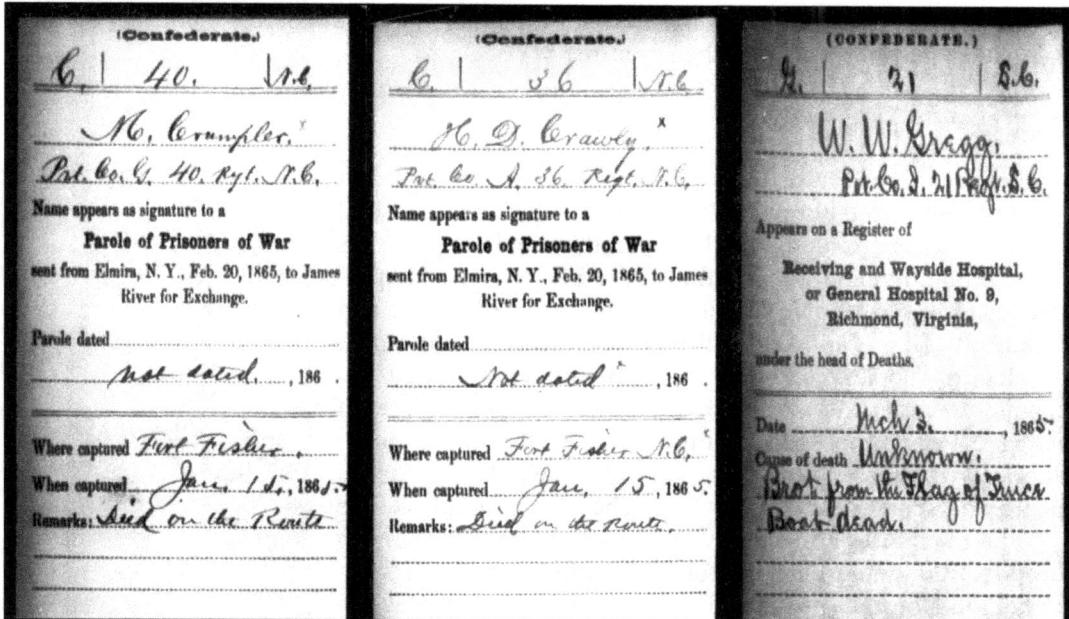

These soldier's records were found at the National Archives. All three men "died on the route" to be exchanged in February, 1865. The author had found sixty-five Confederate soldiers from Fort Fisher who were exchanged and then died of disease before they ever made it home. Were these soldiers released even though the Union medical officers knew the men were terminally ill? *Photograph courtesy of National Archives.*

invalids who were healthy enough to survive the trip. Of the 259 men exchanged 65 did not live long enough to return to their homes. There are several possible reasons why these gravely ill men were allowed to leave the prison camp. The first explanation suggests that the prisoners might have paid the medical officer to release them regardless of their condition. Since money was not allowed in prison, it would be difficult for a prisoner to have enough money to bribe anyone. If the man was fairly healthy and industrious, it was possible for him to earn some money by selling items that he had made. However, any sales inside the prison were paid for in chewing tobacco. If a man wanted hard cash, he needed to sell his trinkets outside the walls of the prison. Many of the Union soldiers were willing to sell the prisoner's wares for a percentage of the money made. In this way it would be possible for a prisoner to earn enough to bribe his way into an early exchange. However, there was still a catch he had to overcome. Any money an inmate earned while working at the prison would have been collected by the prison treasurer and entered into a ledger. Credit was then issued to the prisoner, so he could purchase items from the sutler's store. It is unclear how inmates could obtain money to buy their freedom. Below are several examples of prisoners bribing officials. On one occasion an examining surgeon approached a rebel prisoner who claimed to have a painful gunshot wound that would prevent him from carrying a musket for at least sixty days. This was the time allotted where an invalid prisoner could not return to the Confederate army. The man carefully rolled up his sleeve so only the doctor could see his arm. Instead of a wound the doctor found a five-dollar bill.

Apparently, this was sufficient incentive for the medic to tell the parole clerk that the prisoner had a "gunshot wound in the left arm."[59]

Judge Robert Ould, the Confederate agent for prisoner exchange, wrote a letter on October 30th to Lieutenant General Ulysses S. Grant. Ould pointed out that thousands of prisoners of war would be held through the winter of 1864-65. He proposed a plan to ease the suffering of both the Confederate and Union prisoners. Ould said if the Federal Army would send a shipment of supplies to Union prisoners in the South the Confederate government would forward these supplies free of charge. He also proposed that if the North would send a ship to Mobile, Alabama, 1,000 bales of cotton would be loaded aboard and sent to New York City. The cotton could then be sold and the money collected would be used to purchase much needed clothing and blankets for the Confederate soldiers being held in Northern prisons. General Grant thought this was a wonderful idea since it would help both Union and Confederate prisoners and perhaps save the government money. Grant agreed so quickly that he could send his reply to Judge Ould with the same messenger who brought it.[60]

Judge Robert Ould proposed sending 1,000 bales of Southern cotton to New York to be used to purchase clothing for the Confederate prisoners.

Shortly after Grant and Ould reached an agreement on the delivery of the Union supplies and sale of the Southern cotton, Secretary of War Edwin M. Stanton set into motion a series of delays. Stanton objected to Ould's selection of Confederate Major General Isaac R. Trimble as the officer to handle matters concerning the sale of Southern cotton in New York City. After three weeks of debate, Stanton finally approved of Confederate prisoner Brigadier General William N. R. Beall and said that he would be paroled from Fort Warren so he could manage the transaction of the Southern cotton.[61]

Secretary of War Stanton was not alone in seeking retaliation against the Confederate prisoners. General Henry W. Wessells, who at that time was Commissary General of Prisoners, Major General Ethan A. Hitchcock, Colonel William Hoffman and a handful of other ranking Union officers joined the Secretary of War and instigated delays to hamper Confederate efforts to relieve the suffering of Southern prisoners of war.

It must be remembered that the goal of the Confederacy was to purchase winter clothing for the prisoners, so time was critical. Since this deal was not agreed upon until November any delay would set this arrangement back and make it more difficult to get the clothing to the people who needed it. Perhaps Stanton thought there was no harm in delaying the supplies to the Northern prisoners because they were in the warmer climate of the South, but the captive Confederates would soon be in the freezing winter in the north and could suffer illness and possibly death without the necessary clothing. Nine hundred Elmira prisoners spent Christmas day in ice encrusted, snowbound tents until the new barracks were finished in early January 1865. Secretary Stanton's plan was to create needless delays

92

so the extra clothing for the Confederate prisoners would have a minimal impact and may even miss the winter altogether.

Ever since the "Ould-Grant agreement" had been finalized a thousand bales of Southern cotton sat on the wharf in Mobile, Alabama, for over than a month waiting for a Federal ship to take it north. Somehow Secretary Stanton managed to delay the departure of the USS *Atlanta* by six weeks before allowing her to pick up the Southern cotton and take it to New York so it could be sold.

Finally, on December 16th the USS *Atlanta*, sailed into the harbor at Mobile, Alabama, under a flag of truce. However, the endless series of delays which plagued this undertaking did not end here.[62] The USS *Atlanta* only had storage capacity for 830 cotton bales. After the cotton was loaded aboard it was discovered the ship was too heavy to navigate some underwater obstructions in the harbor. It would take three weeks to find a ship light enough to safely navigate the obstacles.[63] As soon as the Confederate steamer *Waverly* was found another delay occurred when the northern stevedores refused to load the cotton onto the lighter ship and transfer it to the Union vessel once she had cleared the underwater obstructions.[64] Ultimately, it would take another week to locate thirty men to move the cotton bales.

A thousand bales of cotton sat on a New Orleans wharf for thirteen weeks waiting for a Union ship to transport it to New York, so it could buy clothing for the Confederate prisoners.

After a month and a half of delays the USS *Atlanta* cleared Mobile Harbor on January 21st and did not arrive at the New York waterfront until the 24th. This was a full thirteen weeks after the Ould-Grant Agreement had been made. Unfortunately, the price of cotton had dropped 50% from the time that the proposal had been made in October to the time it had been sold. This alone would determine that only half the winter clothing the Confederates had intended to purchase could be bought.

The remaining 170 cotton bales were eventually shipped to New York harbor in April aboard another Union vessel. Why it took another three months to transport the remaining cotton has never been adequately explained. It is likely that Secretary Stanton had something to do with this since only a portion of the clothing and blankets destined for Northern prison camps could be purchased.[65] The cotton, sitting on the Mobile wharf since November, had deteriorated over the six months was because it had been exposed to the elements and rough handling by stevedores as they loaded the bales on board several ships. These bales were in such bad condition that they had to be repacked and re-bailed before they could be offered for sale. As it was, the cotton did not fetch the $.82 per pound that the original 830 bales did. Instead they sold April 18th for the paltry price of $.29 per pound.[66]

The cotton was not sold until February and partial shipments of clothing were made to the eight largest Northern prisons. Elmira received her first shipment containing 984 blankets and 2,000 socks on February 6th. The next shipment came on February 9th and included 150 coats and jackets and 150 pairs of trousers. This is a far cry from Colonel Tracy's December clothing requisition for 1,000 jackets, 2,500 shirts, 3,000 pairs of trousers, 8,000 drawers, 7,000 pairs of socks and 1,500 caps. Tracy did not order any blankets at all! The remaining shipments came February 17th and 27th, but they still fell substantially short of what Colonel Tracy had ordered. Unfortunately, the shipments of clothing never came close to what Elmira prison camp wanted. Tracy still needed 750 pairs of trousers, 1,000 shirts, 4,500 pairs of socks and 1,500 caps from his original order! Consider this, during the three months since the December clothing requisition was submitted 1,577 additional prisoners were sent to Elmira. There was also three months of wear and tear for the clothing and blankets the prisoners already possessed. Among this group were 1,131 prisoners from Fort Fisher, North Carolina. Many of these prisoners had no winter coats or blankets because they were stored in the barracks during

Sergeant Thaddeus C. Davis, 3rd Company G, 40th North Carolina

the fight. Unfortunately, their barracks had burned down during the Union attack and when the prisoners had gone north they were not given any clothing to replace what they had lost.[67] Since Colonel Tracy had not received any clothing for two months he had nothing to give these new men. On March 3rd an inspector wrote after examining the shipment of clothing, "The clothing sent here by Confederates . . . [is] not in quantities sufficient to supply all that are in need."[68]

Fort Fisher prisoner Sergeant Thaddeus C. Davis recalled what happened when they arrived at the train station in New York. "We arrived (at Elmira) about eight o'clock in the evening, in four feet of snow, and many prisoners had neither blankets nor coats. We were kept standing in ranks in the street for half an hour before starting for the prison."[69] The soldiers then trudged two miles through ice and snow to the prison camp. With the creature comforts we have today, it's difficult to imagine what it was like for over a thousand newly arrived prisoners who lacked winter clothing or even blankets in Elmira's freezing weather. No wonder inspecting officer Lieutenant James Reid reported February 12th, "General health of prisoners—very bad; increase of sickness principally caused by the arrival of the Fort Fisher prisoners, of whom more than half are sick."[70] Unfortunately, hundreds of those men would die in the next several months.

While all this was going on another drama was unfolding that concerned the December clothing requisition for Elmira's prisoners. These two stories were inextricably interwoven since they both involve the Confederate cotton shipment and the shortage of prisoner's winter clothing. Again, the heavy-hand of Secretary Stanton, aided by his close ally General Henry Wessells, tipped the scales in favor of retaliation after the cotton arrived in New York City.

On December 1st Colonel Tracy submitted Elmira's clothing requisition for that month. General Wessells did not send him any clothing, but instead sent a confusing telegram on December 12th. Wessells message acknowledged that he had received Tracy's December requisition for prisoner's clothing. He also explained the agreement between the United States and Confederate authorities where they would supply extra clothing and blankets for the prisoners in the North. The next part of Wessels' telegram is rather confusing. "In view of this fact it is desirable that no more clothing shall be provided by the government than is absolutely demanded by the ordinary dictates of humanity. You will please report your views on this subject. Very respectfully, your obedient servant, H. W. Wessells, Brig. Gen. of Volunteers and Commissary General of Prisoners."[71]

What did Wessells mean by "it is desirable that no more clothing shall be provided by the government than is absolutely demanded by the ordinary dictates of humanity." Wessells January 31, 1865, telegram sent to General H. E. Paine removes any doubt what he meant. In essence he was saying the clothing, which should've been sent regardless, would not be sent unless the cotton shipment arrived. Did Wessells really believe the cotton shipment would relieve the government from having to supply the Confederate prisoners with winter clothing? If he did, the cotton the Confederacy sent north did not buy the prisoners one single stitch of extra winter clothing. Judge Ould's proposal made it clear that these supplies were to be "ancillary", or in addition to, the prisoners normal winter supply requisition. Aside from being the moral thing to do supplying clothing to prisoners is something the Union and Confederate governments were required to do according to the Lieber Code of 1863.[72]

General Henry W. Wessels believed the Confederate cotton shipped to the North released the Union from having to supply clothing for the prisoners.

The second part of Wessells' telegram asked Tracy's views about the previous statement. Colonel Tracy was not aware his December clothing requisition was dependent on his answering this question. By inserting this seemingly insignificant question, on which hung whether or not the prisoner's clothing shipment would be sent, shows how General Wessells was colluding with Secretary Stanton by seeking to delay sending the winter clothing going to Elmira prison camp.[73] First he demonstrated this by not sending the required clothing and supplies for December, then he reaffirmed his stance by inserting a question on which hung whether or not the prisoner's clothing shipment would be made.

Colonel Tracy waited all month for the clothing he ordered but no December shipment ever came. Finally, Tracy wrote General Wessell's on January 5th and informed him that he had received a partial shipment but was still waiting for the rest of his December allotment of clothing to be delivered. Colonel Tracy asked, "that these amounts . . . be furnished immediately for issue to prisoners, unless the department is advised that supplies will be speedily forwarded by the rebel authorities."[74]

Wessell's responded to Colonel Tracy's letter on January 19th and said, "The (December) requisitions were held awaiting your reply to the letter of the 12th ultimo from this office, which explain the necessity of strict economy in the issue of clothing to rebel prisoners at the present time, and requested that you would report your views on the necessity of such issue at Elmira, N. Y. No reply to this letter has been received, and the requisitions are still in this office." Then Wessells stated, "The clothing received by you was sent to Elmira by mistake and was no part of that required for by you it was reported as issued before the error was discovered."

This bureaucratic red tape was all part of Secretary Stanton's delaying tactics to exact punishment against the Confederate prisoners. If he could holdup the clothing shipment long enough, it would virtually have the same effect as refusing to fill it.

After receiving no reply from Colonel Tracy about the government not furnishing any more clothing because of the impending shipment of Southern cotton, General Wessells should have reminded him after two weeks by telling him he would not receive the clothing requisition until Tracy sent the reply that he asked for. Since Wessells did not say anything, Tracy waited five weeks for his December clothing to arrive for the prisoners at Elmira. When he did not receive it, he telegraphed General Wessells who then informed him the clothing was being withheld because he failed to respond to his first telegram. The fact that Colonel Tracy waited five weeks before asking about the December requisition is incredible! It was not as bad as what General Wessells had done intentionally, but this shows a serious dereliction of duty on Colonel Tracy's part. According to Captain Benjamin Munger's December 4th inspection of Elmira prison camp he reported, "Clothing—insufficient for this climate." Munger goes on to say, "One thousand six hundred and sixty-six (prisoners) are entirely destitute of blankets, or have blankets nearly worthless."[75] Why on earth did Colonel Tracy wait over a month to ask where his December shipment of clothing was?

Elmira commandant Colonel Benjamin Tracy failed to answer a simple question from Wessells and was denied any winter clothing for the prisoners at Elmira.

It was not until February 7th that a partial shipment of three boxes of clothing finally arrived at Elmira for distribution among the prisoners. More boxes arrived in the following weeks, but these never contained anything close to what Tracy had ordered.[76] The question remains, how many prisoners died as a result of the lack of clothing and blankets during the harsh winter season?

The Ould-Grant Agreement stipulated that three Confederate officers on parole would distribute the clothing to the prisoners. Since Elmira had no officers who were prisoners, Lieutenant Colonel H. J. Price, Major John P. Thompson and Major Daniel S. Printup arrived at Elmira February 7th from Camp Johnson's Island, Ohio, for the purpose handing-out the supplies received from General Beall to the prisoners. The Confederate emissaries stayed at the Brainard House under guard. No clothing shipments from General Beall had arrived yet, so they decided to go to the prison camp to make their presence known and make a preliminary assessment of what supplies were needed in the prison. When they tried to gain entrance Colonel Tracy refused to let them in the stockade. Confederate Major Daniel Printup complained in a February 13th telegram to General Beall that he and the other officers were not allowed freedom of action to do what was required of them. "It is very necessary that we should visit the express office, railroad depot, and especially headquarters of the post." Printup went on to say, "We feel confident that Colonel Tracy, commanding post, will approve any extension or further privilege in our paroles asked."[77]

Was this delay intentional? Probably not. But it is characteristic of all the little delays that plagued this undertaking. Perhaps problems should have been expected when this sort of task got so large that it involved too many people. Inevitably not everyone will be in the know and familiar with what is going on. Still, one wonders why someone as important as the commandant of Elmira prison camp was not notified that these Confederate officers were arriving and needed to have access to the prison, so they could distribute clothing.

On February 15th the Confederate emissaries were allowed to move from the Brainard House Hotel to the officer's barracks at Elmira prison camp. Even then Colonel Tracy did not allow them to move about freely inside the prison camp. They were required to have a pass to move from the officer's barracks to designated areas only. The Confederate officer who was selected to distribute the clothing to the prisoners was Major Printup. The first shipment of clothing and blankets from General Beall were distributed among smallpox victims. Then the prisoners who needed clothing and blankets were given

Confederate General William Beall distributed clothing to the prisoners.

preference. The names and rank of the men who received clothing were written in a ledger, so no one would receive more than his fair share.

While the Confederate officers were determining the needs of the men and receiving boxes of supplies from General Beall, Major Printup learned that Elmira prison authorities had given local clothing merchant J. Gladke the impression that if he designed and manufactured Confederate clothing that he would be granted permission to sell these items to the prisoners. Gladke had already produced a large quantity of items when he found out that he would not be able to sell them at Elmira prison camp. Sensing that he might be able to obtain a good deal, Major Printup contacted Gladke and was told the Elmira clothier wanted to sell $5,000 worth of clothing to the Rebels. Printup explained to General Beall that the local clothing merchant was willing to produce more clothing and that he had examined samples and found it to be "of good quality & seems to us fully within the prices asked."[78]

Major Printup's discovery of local clothing merchant J. Gladke with a large quantity of Confederate uniforms and blankets readily available seems to shed light on another aspect of the Union Army's clandestine plan to deliberately deprive Confederate prisoners of war of winter clothing. The fact that the clothing necessary could have been purchased with the money in the Prison Fund was well known to Union officers both at the Commissary Gen-

97

eral of Prisoners office, and at Elmira, but they declined to pursue it. In February 1865, there was $127,000 available in the fund for just such emergencies. Why wasn't this used?

It seems obvious why General Wessels or Colonel Hoffman did not want to use the funds available, but what about Colonel Tracy? In the past Tracy seemed to be genuinely concerned about the lack of clothing for the prisoners. Then why didn't he suggest the possibility of using the prison funds to purchase the necessary supplies? There is no evidence that Tracy made any attempt to approach the subject with either of the Commissary General of Prisoners. Even if he had, Colonel Hoffman would hardly have allowed this to happen. If past behavior is any guideline, Colonel Hoffman stubbornly clung to his miserly ways as demonstrated in this November 15, 1863 letter to the prison camp commander at Camp Morton: "So long as a prisoner has clothing upon him, however much torn, you must issue nothing to him, nor must you allow him to receive clothing from any but members of his immediate family, and only when they're an absolute want."[79]

Elmira Prison Camp Flood

A sea of tents housing 5,000 Elmira prisoners dominates this photo, but illustrates the contention of the author that the hills surrounding the camp were practically barren of trees. This was a result of building the prison and providing firewood for the camp's stoves. *Photograph courtesy of the Chemung County Historical Society.*

The extreme weather for the years 1864-65 made headlines in the newspapers of New York State. The area suffered under a severe summertime drought that wilted fruits and vegetables and also affected the cattle that were sold to Elmira prison camp. Scurvy patients at the prison hospital suffered the most because the dry weather also made it difficult to obtain fresh onions, potatoes, etc. Farmers did not have enough grass to fatten their cattle and found it necessary to sell their stock before they became too weakened and died from lack of food. Elmira farmer Roswell R. Moss said, "In the summer of 1864 there was a severe drought; hay and grain crops were almost nothing, and pastures dried up. Because there was no feed, father sold a number of young cattle that otherwise he would have kept for a year or two longer."[80]

Captain Benjamin Munger's inspection report of December 4, 1864, confirmed this by saying, "The beef is very lean. Cows milked through the summer and too poor for a respectable farmer to winter are slaughtered and the beef issued to the prisoners."[81]

Colonel Tracy issued controversial order No. 336 on October 3rd because he thought that the government was being cheated because the prison's shipments of beef were consistently underweight. This order declared the prison camp's beef would be inspected by Colonel S. Moore and Major Henry Colt and if it did not meet the government contract specifications it would be rejected as being inferior.[82] The consequence of this order was that the prisoners did not receive any meat for three or four days. String enough of these rejected shipments of beef together and the prisoners would be forced to subsist on a bread and water diet. Certainly, this matter could have been resolved without making the prisoners suffer unnecessarily. Any amount of beef in a prisoner's diet would have been preferable to having none.

The next big weather event happened October 10th when an Arctic blast of cold air brought four inches of snow to the Chemung Valley. Heavy snow fell throughout the winter and temperatures plunged to 18 degrees below zero. It was so cold that from January 1st through the first week of March that the thermometer seldom got far above zero.[83]

Frigid winter winds gave way to warmer temperatures on the 14th of March, melting the two-and-a-half-foot blanket of snow in New York. Freshets of water ran down the hills around Elmira and drained into the Chemung River, turning the normally slow body of water into a raging torrent that threatened to overflow its banks. Normally this was not a problem because these hills were heavily forested, and the dense canopy of trees held in the cooler temperatures, which kept the snow from melting too quickly. The water that gathered would be held in place and consumed by the rich vegetation. On arriving at Elmira prisoner Anthony M. Keiley wrote, "The whole site is a basin surrounded by hills which rise several hundred

Major Henry Colt inspected beef to be sent to Elmira prison and rejected many shipments for being of inferior quality. *Photograph courtesy of the Chemung County Historical Society.*

feet, and are covered richly and thickly with the luxurious foliage of the hemlock, ash, poplar, and pine." However, this was not a typical winter because these hills were largely denuded of trees to provide lumber to build the prison camp. What trees had not been cut down during the summer months were harvested that autumn to provide fuel for the stoves of Elmira prison camp to combat the frigid winter weather. Thus there were no trees to keep the snow from melting and very little vegetation to provide a barrier against the water draining down from the hills.[84] Many consider this terrible flood to be an act of nature, but man helped it to become the epic disaster that it was by removing the only natural obstacle to flowing water there was.

On the morning of March 15th the river reached flood stage and began to overflow its banks; the muddy water continued to get higher, reaching the edge of the stockade. Being worried about the rising water, Colonel Tracy held an emergency meeting with the other prison officers at 9 PM that evening. The smallpox hospital was located on lower ground close to the river, so it was decided to evacuate the 300 sick prisoners to land farthest away from the rising water. A dozen men under Major Norton were assigned to build several large rafts from two-inch planks to ferry the sick men from the hospital. The construction of the flat boats was finished by morning and the process of rescuing the prisoners got underway.[85]

Hand drawn map of Elmira prisoner of war camp by inmate David J. Coffman. *Photograph courtesy of the Chemung County Historical Society*.

It was soon discovered that the large, unwieldy rafts became unmanageable in the strong current. The men secured two ropes and tied one to the front and the other to the rear of the rafts. Teams of prisoners worked in relays allowing the raft to drift toward the hospital, where it was loaded with prisoners, and then pulled it back again. It was reported the men became so exhausted from their labors that as soon they accomplished their task each one was given a cup of whiskey.[86]

A few hours after the smallpox hospital was evacuated, the water continued to rise until it reached every building in the prison. Former prisoner John A. King remembered, "We were surrounded by a wilderness of water. A great part of the prison wall was gone, and we could see about half of the cookhouse extending above the water."[87] The water not only covered the prison camp, but had crossed Water Street, flooding the camp of the 19th Veteran Reserve Corps.[88]

The prison barracks were built on stilts several feet off the ground to discourage the prisoners from digging tunnels to escape. Now the water had submerged the stilts, entered the barracks and covered the lower bunks, forcing the men to climb up to the second or third tier of bunks. The near freezing water crested at four feet above the barrack floor. The men remained in the upper bunks for two days and were visited by soldiers in rowboats several times a day to bring them something to eat. King remarked, "Men came into our wards through doors in rowboats, passing near where we were roosting. They gave us something to eat. My, but it tasted good!"[89]

The flood's high-water mark was reached when it overflowed the river's 20 foot slope, engulfing the prison camp and invading the appropriately named Water Street. The morning of the 17th the muddy waters began to recede, revealing what damage had been done to the prison camp. Twenty-seven-hundred feet of the stockade's fence had been washed away requiring the guards to stand watch until it could be repaired. Several of the older barracks were so badly damaged by the flood that they were no longer safe to occupy and needed to be destroyed. Other buildings had stairs ripped off, boards loosened or swept away completely. All the buildings were coated with several inches of foul smelling mud and dead fish and eels were scattered everywhere.

The Elmira Daily Advertiser urged its readers to use caution when looking for firewood and items from the flood ravaged pris-

Camp Douglas barracks on stilts were similar to the ones built at Elmira. Barracks on stilts allowed guards to observe any escape tunnels being dug and greatly helped to eliminate them.

on. Some of the objects had been contaminated by the smallpox virus which remained viable for up to eighteen months. "Several tents and the flooring of the board barracks occupied last winter, for the rebels having small pox, passed down the river yesterday, and everybody therefore along the river looking after flood wood and refuse should handle these articles gingerly."[90]

There is some confusion as to the loss of life due to the flood. In his March 21, 1865, report to General William Hoffman, Colonel Tracy says his command responded to the flood and "accomplished (their task) with great promptness; with no escape of prisoners, and, what is still more remarkable with but slightly increased loss of life."[91] Tracy statement concerning loss of life is rather vague because it never gave exact numbers. You would think that four days after the tragedy that Tracy would've conducted a roll call to see who was still among the prisoners. When Prisoner John R. King waded out to the pump near the dead house to get some water, he made a gruesome discovery. "On the way to the pump I noticed several old blankets near my feet. Looking closer I discovered a number of dead men concealed under them. The high water had prevented the people from taking them to the graveyard."[92] It is assumed these men were washed out from the dead house, but they could have also been victims of the flood. Prisoner James Huffman recalled, "The sick were taken out in boats and a great many died before they returned."[93] However, Lieutenant James R. Reid conducted an inspection of the prison camp and noted that the flood caused but "slight increase of mortality among patients."[94] One prison guard is reported to have said "affects of the flood were plainly visible upon the health of the men for some time"[95] Certainly moving so many deathly ill prisoners had a consequence. We know from the Official Records that the March death total was the highest month in Elmira's history with 491 deaths.[96] However, we will never know how many of these deaths were caused by the flood.

Escapes from Elmira Prison Camp

All soldiers know that one of their first duties as prisoners of war is to try and escape.[97] Since this knowledge is so well known it is remarkable that only seventeen men managed to breakout of Elmira prisoner of war camp during the twelve months of its existence. The lack of successful escapes wasn't for a lack of trying. Many captive soldiers attempted this feat, but few succeeded. The reason for this can be attributed to several factors. The first of these is that these men were on half rations and many of them were too sick or in the hospital to try and escape. These prisoners needed to conserve their energy just to survive the harsh day-to-day existence that prison life entails. They could not dig hundred-foot escape tunnels because they did not possess the physical stamina for such a demanding task. Another reason for the lack of escape attempts was the fact that five months out of the year, Elmira prison camp has the coldest weather of all northern prisons and digging in the frozen ground was impossible. An added component was the vigilance of the guards. Elmira had a famous spy by the name of Sergeant Melvin M. Conklin whose chief employment was that of secret police or detective. However, Conklin was aided by a network of spies known as Confederate "oath takers" who in hopes of being released early reported their fellow

Union spy Lieutenant Melvin Conklin *Photograph courtesy of the Chemung County Historical Society*.

prisoners for digging tunnels. Conklin went about the camp in all sorts of disguise, often pretending to be a Confederate prisoner to find out any plans to escape. This man was so successful at ferreting out tunnels that he discovered every single one except for the big one on October 7th which allowed ten prisoners to escape.

After the war Conklin was interviewed by author Clay Homes in 1912 when he was writing his famous book titled, *The Elmira Prison Camp*. "The first tunnel I found was started under Hospital No. 1," Conklin recalled. "The men worked nights. In the daytime they covered up the hole with boards and put sod on top. I found it and reported it. My orders were to let the men dig." Conklin checked the hole every day and dropped into the tunnel to see how it was progressing.[98] When it was near completion extra guards were assigned to watch the area where it was expected to come out. "The night they chose for escape happened to be a bright moonlit night. When they broke through and the first "Johnnie" stuck his head up he discovered, much to his surprise, that he was right in the midst of the guard camp, with a dozen guards looking right at him." The prisoner disappeared down the hole, but before he could get back to the entrance with his companions, Conklin and the guards were waiting for them.[99]

Sergeant Conklin remembered that some of the prisoners were quite ingenious in their tunnels. He recalled that, "The occupants of one tent built the chimney at the rear of the tent, and tunneled down from inside the chimney. This one was directed northward and would have come out very near where Ed Warner's grocery now stands near Hoffman Creek. There were two started in the tents on the flat near the fence, next to the river, and two started in the barracks next to the east fence, about halfway between Water Street and the pond. There were twenty-eight in all. Most of the tunneling was on the east side of the camp, and someone was digging nearly all the time during the fall of 1864. All being discovered, they finally became discouraged and none were attempted after November."[100]

The first escape occurred shortly after Elmira prison camp opened its gates. The initial group of prisoners to arrive at Elmira on July 6th tested their new home the next day by planning an escape. Privates Charles D. Slack and Edwin James of Company G, 7th Louisiana Infantry, escaped on the night of July 8th by successfully scaling a fence. Slack was recaptured in Newport, PA, and taken back to the stockade in chains. James eluded his pursuers and made his way back to Dixie.[101]

The next prison break was October 7th and involved ten men tunneling out of the prison. This escape is perhaps the single most remarkable story of Elmira prison camp. Fortunately, six of the men who participated in the escape left written accounts of their harrowing exploits. Sergeant Berry Benson of the 1st South Carolina infantry and Private John Fox Maull of the Jeff Davis Artillery, have written accounts so fascinating that they seem to take the reader along with them as they dig the tunnel. Their efforts become so real that you practically cringe when the men are nearly discovered, and you want to cheer when they reach the fence and finally make their escape to freedom![102]

Elmira prisoner Washington Traweek worked tirelessly on the escape tunnel. *Photograph courtesy of the Chemung County Historical Society.*

Their story begins when Private John F. Maull is transferred to Elmira from Point Lookout on August 15, 1864. As luck would have it Maull was assigned to occupy an A-frame tent near the prison's fence. He quickly explained his plan to escape to his tent mates, but only J. P. Putegnat liked his idea and thought it had a chance to succeed. Since the rest of his tent mates were not on board with his plan, the two men needed to move to a vacant tent. However, they had to get the Ward Sergeant to agree to remove them both from the tent, so they pretended to have a fight with the others and then moved angrily out. At this time Private Washington B. Traweek of South Carolina joined the two men. Traweek was a valuable addition since he was a daring man who never seemed to tire no matter how much work he did. With their hands on a bible the men took a solemn oath pledging their "sacred honor that if betrayed we would follow the betrayer and knife him, that if caught at work by any of the prisoners, the discoverer must join us or die."[103]

On August 24th the men stole a spade from a contractor that was constructing trenches for the prison camp's streets and began digging their tunnel at nine o'clock that evening. "We were all young and ambitious," Maull would write later, "and we thought we could dig our way out in four or five days, but soon discovered it was no easy task."[104] They dug a round hole three feet in diameter, carefully removed the sod, and dug down until the hole would hide the digger's head when sitting down. Another man laid planks across the hole

and sat on the wood until the dirt needed to be taken from the digger below. A candle was used to illuminate the tunnel where the men were working. They discovered the shovel made too much noise when it scraped against rocks, so the prisoners chose to dig with a knife. This pocket knife was later exchanged for a stronger 12-inch knife made from a file. The next problem was how to hide the dirt. This was solved when J. P. Putegnat donated his extra shirt to make bags to haul away the dirt.

While the others were in the tunnel, a man wearing a special jacket and cape carried the bags of dirt outside. His coat had a slit on either side where two or three-pint sized bags could be hidden in the pockets. The bags were then emptied of their contents in the street. Imagine the men's horror the next morning when it was discovered the fresh dirt was a different color than that in the street! Fortunately, no one noticed and future bags were emptied in Foster's pond.[105]

One day as Traweek was emptying rocks from his pocket, a fellow prisoner came up to him and said, "You'd better take care of yourself."

Surprised, Traweek asked him what he meant.

"I saw you put the stones in the water." Sergeant Berry Benson replied.

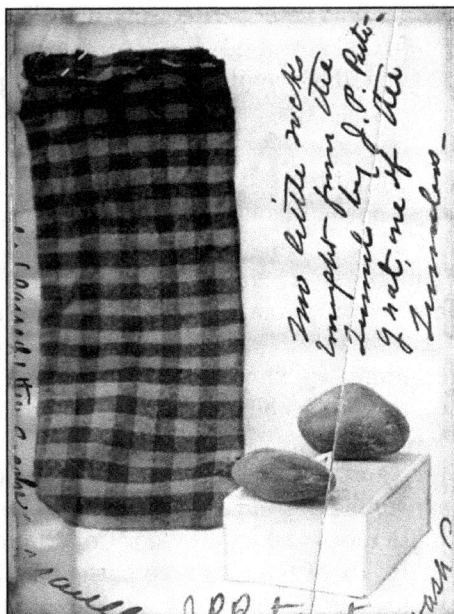

Elmira prisoner Putegnat made some bags to carry dirt from an extra shirt. *Photograph courtesy of the Chemung County Historical Society.*

Traweek shrugged his shoulders and told him, "Well, there's no harm in that, is there?"

Benson shook his head, and said, "No, if you were not digging a tunnel. No man would take such pains if you were not digging a tunnel. Here, I'll stand between you and the crowd. Empty your pockets."

Without another word, he got rid of all of his stones; then rising Traweek said, "Walk with me a little way."[106]

Traweek finally admitted, "We're all bound by an oath not to tell it nor hint of it to the dearest friend, but you've found it out without my telling it, and now, if you want to join us, I've no doubt the boys will all be willing enough to take you in."[107] The man, Sergeant Berry Benson of the first Regiment South Carolina infantry, said that he would. Benson proved to be one of the best men in the group. He was ready to work at all times and had excellent ideas to improve the men's efforts in digging the tunnel. "One of his first suggestions was there was too much crawling to get out a little dirt, which could be saved by getting a box with a cord in each end, so it could be pulled into the digger, and pulled back when full. We got the box, attached two long cords to it, and put it to use. It was a great success, saving much time and crawling back-and-forth."[108]

Berry Benson recalled that he had a unique way to get rid of stones. "A favorite place to deposit stones was in rat holes. I would sit by a rat hole and drop the stones in until I could see the top of his stones, then move to another hole. The next day it could be filled again, for during the night the rats would move all the stones away in order to get in and out of their holes."[109]

One would think the best time to dig would be at night, but this was not the case. Actually, the best time was between dusk and eight o'clock. This was when men were walking about and activity was at its peak. A silence would settle over the prison after lights out and any little sound could be easily detected. Another good time to dig was during the day because everybody was up and creating noise that would drown out any sounds coming from the tunnel. To keep their clothing from getting covered with fresh dirt and attracting attention, the men turned their clothes inside out and worked in them that way. When a man was finished for the day, he reversed the process and exposed the clean side.[110]

Sergeant Berry Benson *Photograph courtesy of the Chemung County Historical Society.*

In his book, Sergeant Berry Benson eloquently described what it was like working in the tunnel. "After the blankets and dried grass were removed and the planks taken up, you got into the vertical section of the shaft. Then on hands and knees you crawled into the tunnel and lay flat. Beyond the first body length, the tunnel decreased in size until it was only large enough to admit the body, and in some places it was a squeeze at that. Thus, only the toes and the points of the elbows were used in propelling yourself forward. Having got to the end of the tunnel, your body blocking the way behind and leaving the least bit of air in front to breathe, you began to dig with a butcher knife. In less than a minute you were panting like a dog for air. A minute was enough to give you the most violent, racking headache, and you knew perfectly well in entering the tunnel that you had this to expect."[111]

The longer the tunnel became the more difficult it was to breath because of the lack of proper ventilation. The digger then crawled forward and resumed digging, meanwhile fighting against suffocation. After an hour of this, the man, his hand sore from scrapping with the knife and his head groggy from breathing "poisoned air", would call over his shoulder, "Back out!" The two men would crawl backward until they reached the entrance, stood and exited the shaft, gasping for air. After the exhausted men left the hole, a fresh team dropped down the shaft and crawled out of sight.[112]

About this time John F. Maull got sick from lack of air in the tunnel which became so fouled every day that a candle would not burn. "It was torture to all, and used me up completely, so that I could do no work inside. The dust created in digging, and the lack of air so affected my lungs, but I was useless for inside work, and I suggested taking in two fresh men from our artillery company, George Jackson, and William Templin, both good and tried men. They accepted and took the oath. From this time, I did little but carry away dirt and rocks."[113]

The men had been excavating the tunnel for nearly a month now and found the work was much harder than anticipated. So much so, they decided to take on another member. J. P. Putegnat suggested S. Cecrops Malone, one of his friends from the 9th Alabama. Everyone agreed so he took the oath and was added to the group.

One day a surprise inspection was announced. The men were terrified because they had two men in the tunnel digging at that moment. They quickly placed the planks in the hole, back filled it with dirt, placed sod on top along with a layer of dried grass, and finally covered it with a blanket that would serve as a bed. Agonizing minutes turned into hours as the men waited for the guards to search their tent. While standing at attention in front of their tent, Maull and Putegnat would glance nervously behind them, praying the two men in the tunnel would remain quiet and not try to come out of the hole. Finally, a guard entered their tent and began moving things around and stamping on the ground to see if there was a weakness in the sod

Cecrops Malone helped dig the escape tunnel.

that might reveal a hidden tunnel. Finding nothing, the guard left and continued on to the next tent. A shaken Maull remembered, "We were badly frightened by this sudden (inspection) and decided it would be safer if we had our Orderly Sergeant on our side to keep us posted. He was a good man, from South Carolina named Brawley. He did us good service by keeping us advised about everything, but he did no work on the tunnel on account of a sore arm, through a bad vaccination."[114]

As work on the tunnel progressed the men grew weary from the demanding excavation and the progress slowed. It was then decided that the men doing the hardest work needed more food. The problem was solved by taking in J. P. Scruggs, who was a "sick sergeant". Scruggs routinely ordered and delivered food to the men of his company who were too ill to walk to the mess hall. He would go to kitchen and claimed he was getting food for sick prisoners in their tents. "He brought us two water buckets full of soup and plenty of fresh bread every day, which gave us renewed strength and put us in fine shape for hard work."[115]

The length of the tunnel was measured with a string and compared with the estimated distance of sixty-eight feet to the camp's northern fence. It was found that the tunnel should be within three feet of the fence. But the men who worked at the end of the tunnel could hear the footsteps of the guards making their rounds just inside the fence. The guards did not appear to pass overhead but some distance away. To find where the end of the tunnel was, Benson suggested that someone should stand where he thinks the end of the tunnel is and make some noise. This way the man in the tunnel could tell if he was left or right of where the noise was. It was decided to get a piece of tin and strike it with a rock on the pretext of making a spoon. Prisoners were hammering on pieces of tin all the time trying to make trinkets and fashioning tableware for the mess-hall, so it was thought this would not arouse the guard's suspicions.[116]

Major Colt arrested Washington Traweek for digging a tunnel. *Photograph courtesy of the Chemung County Historical Society*.

Four men went outside and walked over to where they thought the tunnel should end. They took turns banging on the piece of tin, using a stone as a hammer. Pretty soon word came to them from the man in the tunnel that they were to move six feet to the right. He'd move to the spot indicated and start banging on the tin again. After several more adjustments, the man banging on the spoon stood over the end of the tunnel. Word came to him that he was to halt right there and mark that location with a several stones.[117]

To the men's surprise the tunnel veered to the right about fifteen feet from where it should have been. At first the men were perplexed by this, but then Benson suggested that since the men were all right-handed, this could've caused the tunnel to shift its course to the right. From then on the men had a rifle ramrod in the excavation and every so often they would poke it through the ceiling. Other men would be watching for it. When they saw the ramrod poke up through the grass they would hurry over and step on it, marking that spot with a distinctive stone. The word was then passed to the man in the tunnel if he needed to go right or left to go in the direction of the fence.

Benson suggested they enlarge the ramrod hole to let more air into the tunnel. This was done, and it was widened to a width of three fingers. An enlarged chamber was also dug out where a man could sit up and catch his breath before continuing. This part of the tunnel was called the ventilator and was very important because the longer the tunnel became the more difficult it was to breathe.[118]

One day an order came from Major Colt for Traweek to report to headquarters. Supposing that he had gotten a letter containing money or a box from home, he went to retrieve it. When Traweek didn't return to the tent the other men became worried. Finally, the Orderly Sergeant went to inquire. He came back with the news that Traweek was not only in the guard house, but locked up in a cell under close confinement! The rest of the men were sure their plot had been discovered and that they would all be arrested and thrown in jail. They figured that Traweek was a good man and had given his solemn oath not to tell on the others, but who knew what cruel ways the Yankees would use to make him talk. Meanwhile Traweek wondered who had betrayed him. It was then he remembered talking with some friends and unwisely bragging about his part in digging tunnels. A prisoner, who volunteered to take the Oath of Allegiance to the Union, overheard his remarks and reported him.

"Well, lad," Major Colt said, "you are a tunneller I suppose." Traweek replied that he did not know what the major meant that he was a tunneller. Major Colt told him that he had ways to make him talk. The major then asked Traweek again who his partners were.

109

"When I answered that I did not know, he ordered me placed in a straight jacket. I was bound down and the pressure applied. For possibly a minute the breath was squeezed nearly out of my body, and the agony was fierce. I was released in a few minutes and again asked to tell names. "I said, "Major Colt, you are a coward and no soldier, and I will see you in hell before I will tell you a thing."[119]

About that time an officer standing near the room walked forward and said to Major Colt, "You let this boy come with me and I am sure he will tell me everything he knows." The officer, Captain Bennett Munger, questioned Traweek about the tunnel. As they spoke, Traweek learned that Munger taught Sunday school at the same church that he went to. This made for a pleasant conversation until the cap-

Drawing of prisoners heating water for coffee.

tain asked Traweek to tell him about the tunnel and who his friends were. Traweek finally persuaded Bennett that he did not know the names of the others because it was dark, and he couldn't see anyone distinctly. The only name that he was aware of was a man named Jim. This of course was a figment of Traweek's imagination as he would never reveal anything about the others.[120]

Captain Munger went back to Major Colt with the story, and Traweek was ordered to be held in close confinement in the guard-house. During the Civil War "close confinement" is described as being in solitary confinement on bread and water.

Three weeks after his arrest Major Colt sent word that he would release Traweek if he would give his honor not to try to escape from prison again. Traweek sent back word and thanked him, but he could not in justice to himself make such a promise, for if an opportunity to escape should present itself, he would feel bound to take advantage of it. To this the Major replied, "Oh, very well! There is no other tunnel going on that I'm aware of, and it's hardly probable that you'll break down the fence."[121]

The longer the tunnel became the more men were required; one man was needed to dig, one man rested in the ventilator catching his breath, one in the shaft and one to stand at the door and keep anybody from coming into the tent. At least one other man was required to dispose of bags of dirt and stones.

Two days before the escape the prisoners knew they were near the fence because they could hear the guards walking their post. The men worked steadily and planned their escape for 10 o'clock on the night of the sixth.

On the day of their escape, the men gathered everything they would need to take with them. For Benson this was two pocket knives, half a mess kit to cook in, a few matches, a pencil map that he had drawn of the area, a pocket compass, and a strong cord to serve as a bridle on the chance he could steal a horse.

It was soon discovered that a little more work in the tunnel needed to be done than expected. By 10 o'clock the men had still not reached the fence. In the tunnel Benson was hastily digging with his knife and the box with the dirt slid back and forth. It was decided to leave the dirt in the tent that night because it didn't need to be hidden anymore. Benson

could stand the suffocation no longer, making it necessary for both him and Traweek to back out of the tunnel and change places.

The next section I am quoting directly from Benson's book because I want to convey the unbelievable tension that he experienced. "In the tent I was eagerly listening to the faint sounds from the tunnel, low whispers, a grasp on a fellow's arm to any sound from without. In all hearts were hope, fear, and anxiety, as long as the box slid back-and-forth and the knife pegged away."

"Fighting suffocation all the while, I became wretchedly sick, with a violent headache and nausea, and so did Traweek. Once as I crawled back to the ventilator, the roof of the tunnel broke in, quantities of dirt and stone falling on my legs. I called quietly to the shaft-man, who came and removed the dirt. This consumed so much time. It was now past midnight."[122]

"Once as I occupied the ventilator, I worked my hand up and widened the hole a little, to admit more air. This could do no harm now, it being the last night. Traweek called, 'Benson, let's change; I can't stand it any longer.'"

"This time, instead of inching slowly backward the length of the tunnel, I squeezed my back against one side of the ventilator, saying, 'Traweek, see if we can't pass one another here.' Down he came slowly, first his feet in my face, then further and further, while I jammed myself against the side of the tunnel. Now we were face-to-face. I tried to move forward, but could not. He tried to move down, and he could not. We couldn't move either way—we were wedged! We had begun to think we had made an end of it, when a desperate effort set us free, and I went to digging, he to the ventilator."

"And now as I plied my knife, my head seemed on the point of bursting. My mouth wide open, tongue protruding, panting like a dog, I felt the lack of breath not in my lungs only, in my whole body. With every beat of my heart, great throbs of pain coursed through me. Having stood it as long as I could, I was relieved by Traweek, we passing one another more easily at the ventilator this time."

"During his turn at digging, Traweek called softly, "Benson, I've struck a fence post!"

"Good!' I whispered back, for this meant that our digging was near an end. Taking my turn, I worked to the right around the post, until I knew the end of the tunnel was outside the fence. Feeling that I was dying for air, I reached out my hand and worked it through the pebbly soil, which came raining down in my face—my eyes shut, for of what use are eyes in the tunnel? I felt cold air on my fingers, and withdrew my arm, the cold stream following. I lay on my back, enjoying that feast of air, that luxury of breath. Then I crawled back and sent Traweek up to get his share of it."

"Pretty soon we had hollowed out all but a thin shell on top, and our last work was to dig a hole under that for the dirt to drop into when the break was made. Then Traweek and I went out and announced the tunnel was ready, and the boys began gathering up what they needed to take with them."[123]

It was agreed that everyone should leave in the order that they had joined the group. The men could not go all at once because of the lack of air in the tunnel, so it was decided that they would go in groups of two. The first couple of men, Washington B. Traweek and James W. Crawford, eagerly climbed into the hole and disappeared down the shaft. The others were required to wait for ten minutes to allow the first group time to exit the tunnel. Next John F. Maull and J. P. Scruggs lowered themselves into the tunnel. Ten minutes later they were followed by S. Cecrops Malone and J. P. Putegnat. Webster was too sick to leave with the others, Sergeant Brawley, with his bad arm from his vaccination, thought he stood a good chance of exchange so he decided to stay.[124]

While all of this was going on Benson, still groggy and light headed from lack of air, could no longer stand on his feet and lowered himself to the ground. "I lay down, to get some ease for my head, which almost crazed me. Directly I fell into sort of a doze, only half conscious of what was going on in the tent. I was suffering such pain in my head that I didn't care whether I went or stayed."

Waking up a few minutes later Benson found all the others had gone before him except for Glenn Shelton and his partner. Shelton was convinced he could still hear the others in the tunnel and they had not left yet. Benson told him that was impossible, and he would prove it by going first and calling back to him that the way was clear. Shelton agreed and Benson crawled into the tunnel. After several minutes Benson found he was all alone in the tunnel and called back to Shelton and his partner that the way was clear for them to escape.[125]

Benson raised his head through the tunnel's opening and looked around. Across the street were three sentinels with rifles sitting around a fire. He crawled out and went along close to the fence. From the platform above Benson could hear the sentinels tramping above his head and got down on his hands and knees so he could move more quickly. As he neared the street, Benson rose to his feet and walked away rapidly, "I felt every moment that I would hear a shot and feel a bullet pierce my back. But there was no shot and no challenge."

Reaching the other side of the street, Benson walked down the pavement and then jumped into a yard and ran behind the house where a dog barked and growled at him. He quickly jumped the back fence and fled towards the mountains.[126]

Nine of the ten men made their way back South.

The October tunnel escape is perhaps the single most remarkable story of Elmira prison camp. The men's escape from prison is even more miraculous when it is considered that ten prisoners needed to work in absolute secrecy for seven weeks in an overcrowded environment. Not only that, but they had to overcome terrific obstacles in digging the tunnel such as cave-ins, lack of air and choking dust. Each time the men encountered a seemingly insurmountable problem they did not give up, but worked to solve it and continue toward their ultimate goal of freedom!

One of the more humorous escapes occurred in November, 1864, and involved a prisoner named Jimmie Jones. Jones earned the nickname buttons because he wore so many shiny brass buttons on his bluecoat that he appeared to glow in the dark. Jones convinced the prison doctors that he was infected with smallpox and was immediately transferred to the hospital for that disease far away from the other prisoner's barracks. This was also near the dead house where his friend and fellow prisoner F. S. Wade worked. Jones snuck unobserved to the dead house, wrapped himself in a blanket and climbed into one of the coffins. His friend later discovered him, and Jones revealed his plan along with a bribe. Buttons handed him a small package of flour and told him, "Sprinkle my face and hands with flour, then fasten the coffin lid slightly down, and when the dead wagon comes around, be sure to put my coffin on top of the other dead."

Sometime later the dead wagon came by for another load of bodies to take to the cemetery. Wade carefully loaded it as instructed and sent the wagon on its way. Jones waited inside the casket, listening until the creaking wagon was far enough from the prison before attempting to surprise the driver. Wanting to play the part of a dead body coming to life, Jones began knocking on the coffin lid. When this failed to draw the driver attention, he opened the lid and sat up, calling in a scary voice, "Come to judgment." The startled Negro driver turned around and saw the ghostly white, cadaver sitting up in his casket. This was more than the wide-eyed black man could take. He threw down the reins and leapt from the moving wagon, yelling, "Ghosties! Ghosties!" With shaking arms raised to the heavens, he ran to the safety of the nearest woods.[127]

John W. Jones

One of the men who profited from Elmira's war-time economic boom was the sextant of Woodlawn Cemetery. John W. Jones had been a slave in Leesburg, Virginia, and escaped along the Underground Railroad to Elmira, New York. Some might think that Jones was born under a lucky star, but it appears he made his own good fortune. Immediately after his arrival, this industrious man not only found himself a job, but enrolled in a school where he received an education. This helped him advance in his current position to that of sextant at Woodlawn Cemetery. The only part luck played in his story is the timing of Elmira prison opening its gates in June of 1864.

At the end of that month Commissary General of Prisoners Colonel William Hoffman approved spending $300 from the Prisoner Fund to purchase a half acre of land to bury deceased Confederate prisoners. Hoffman also authorize the purchase of a wagon to help the sextant transport the bodies for burial. Prison carpenters fashioned the pine coffins to have straight sides so six caskets could be loaded on the wagon at one time. Every morning the wagon would pick up the dead bodies from the prison

Former slave and Woodlawn Cemetery Sextant John W. Jones. *Photograph courtesy of the Chemung County Historical Society.*

morgue and deliver them to the cemetery. The government paid Jones $2.50 per burial for his services instead of the accepted rate of $40 per month. This proved to be greatly in his favor.

To help Jones, twenty-eight Confederate prisoners were employed by the government to dig graves for the deceased. Jones services included directing where the graves were to be dug, collecting pertinent information such as—name, state, regiment and date of death and transcribing this information inside the coffin's lid. He also wrote this information on a piece of paper, placed it in a bottle and tucked it under the arm of the deceased to be buried

with him. Jones job wasn't through after the burial, however. He needed to make sure the headboards were straightly aligned, contained the correct information and were on the proper graves. This attention to detail caused former prisoner Marcus Toney to comment sarcastically, "(This) admirable system took care of the dead better than that bestowed on the living."[128]

The Confederate prisoners began to die so rapidly that Colonel Hoffman leased another 1/2 acre of land on January 1, 1865. Several years after the war had ended sextant Jones would comment, "The first day that I was called in my capacity of sextant to bury a prisoner who had died, I thought nothing of it. . . . Directly there were more dead. One day I had seven to bury. After that they began to die very fast." The most burials performed by Jones was forty-three in one day. The highest month occurred in March of 1865 where 495 men died from disease in prison.

During the year Elmira prison camp remained open, thirty-six trenches were dug containing 2,973 Confederate soldiers who had died at the prison in Elmira. At $2.50 per burial this amounted to $7,432.50 for Jones making him the wealthiest black man in the state.[129]

A TYPICAL CONFEDERATE SOLDIER.

Chapter 5

President Lincoln's Refusal to See Union Prisoners

In early August 1864, Union prisoners at Andersonville, Georgia, had become so alarmed at the increasing number of deaths of their fellow inmates that they held a conference to see if they could help reestablish the prisoner exchange. The men signed a petition and planned to give it to President Lincoln, asking him not to abandon them and to reinstate the prisoner exchange. They wanted to let him know that 38,000 Union prisoners at Andersonville were sick and dying at an alarming rate. The Union prisoners approached the prison commandant, Colonel Henry Wirz, and asked if they might present this petition to President Lincoln. The Confederacy had tried everything to get the prisoner exchange reestablished so when Jefferson Davis learned of their efforts he agreed to help. He gave a delegation of four Union sergeants a temporary pardon to go and see President Lincoln with the stipulation that when negotiations were over these men would return to prison. The Union sergeants all agreed.

Lincoln not only did not meet these men, it seems he was nowhere to be found. What business did the President have that was so important that he could not listen to these men who risked their lives to preserve the Union? If Lincoln was truly unaware of the horrors the prisoners faced he would have gladly seen these men, so they could discuss their situation and try to improve it. However, the President chose not to see them. Why would he do such a cruel thing? Could it be that Lincoln already knew what the prisoners were going to tell him, and he had no suitable reply to give them? One thing regarding the prisoners is certain though, the President would never allow the government's policy of halting the prisoner exchanges to be jeopardized by a few Union prisoners. Lincoln's decision is difficult to understand in light of the fact that the North was winning the war when the Andersonville prisoners came to see him in August of 1864.

Lincoln told Secretary of War Edwin M. Stanton to meet with the prisoners August 23rd. Stanton informed them there was nothing that he could do for them because the Union would be exchanging healthy prisoners, who would return to the Confederate ranks, while they would get sick, broken men in return.

Disheartened, Sergeant Edward Wellington Boate said after the affair, "It distresses me to state that the representatives of 38,000 Union prisoners were treated with silent contempt, the President declining to see them or have any communication with them!

"A policy like this is the quintessence of inhumanity, a disgrace to the administration which carried it out, and a blot upon the country. You rulers who make the charge that the rebels intentionally killed off our men, when I can honestly swear they were doing everything in their power to sustain us, do not lay this unflattering unction to your souls. You abandon your brave men in the hour of their cruelest need. They fought for the Union, and you reached no hand out to save the old faithful, loyal, and devoted servants of the country. You may try to shift the blame from your own shoulders, but posterity will saddle the responsibility were it justly belongs."[1]

Former Andersonville prisoner John W. Urban wrote, "Men who had cheerfully faced death on many battlefields, lay down and died brokenhearted as the terrible suspicion forced itself and their minds that the government they love so well, and fought so hard to save, was indifferent to their sad fate."[2]

Before the prisoner delegation left the north, they contacted the *New York Times* and the *New York Evening Post* and told them what had happened. The *New York Evening Post* printed the entire petition the prisoners had brought for Lincoln in its August 23rd issue.

The Confederacy was still eager to continue the prisoner exchanges. The most important reason why they wanted the exchanges to be resumed was for the sake of humanity. Prisoners were needlessly suffering because the Lincoln administration had declared all medicines contraband of war. This occurred when the Northern blockade was initiated in 1861. As a result of this, the Confederacy had no morphine, opium, calomel or quinine to treat Northern prisoners.

When the North refused again to exchange prisoners in the summer of 1864 the Confederate Commissioner of Exchange, Judge Robert Ould, contacted Northern authorities and offered to pay gold, cotton or tobacco for medicine to be used exclusively for Union prisoners. Ould never received a reply to his offer. Ould thought perhaps Union officials did not trust the Confederate government to do this, so he told them they could send their own surgeons with medicine to treat Federal prisoners. Again, the North ignored Ould's proposal.[3]

Confederate Commissioner of Exchange Judge Robert Ould

Another reason the Confederacy wanted the exchange to continue was because they did not have the food and supplies needed to provide for the men they had captured. Sending Union prisoners North would relieve the Confederacy from the burden of having to provide for these men. This was substantial because there was not enough food to give the Confederate soldiers in the field let alone Federal prisoners.

During the summer of 1864, Judge Robert Ould wrote to Union General John E. Mulford, the Assistant Agent of Exchange, and offered to send 13,000 sick and wounded Federal prisoners to Savannah, Georgia, without requiring the North to exchange any Southern prisoners. Ould urged Mulford to respond quickly because of the terrible mortality at Andersonville prison. For some unknown reason the Federal authorities did not respond to this offer until November. Even though Judge Ould did not request any prisoners in return, he was glad to see 3,208 Confederate prisoners step off the flag-of-truce boat at Savannah. Unfortunately, the Confederate prisoners were so ill that 292 of them died during the two-day voyage.[4] How could such a terrible thing happen? Union prison commandants had been told by Colonel Hoffman to medically inspect the men to be exchanged so they would be healthy enough to survive the trip.[5]

When reading the following article, the reader must remember it was written at a time when the news media was extremely biased against anything Confederate, especially something pertaining to the Confederate prison system's handling of captured Union soldiers. It also must be kept in mind that it was the North that halted the prisoner exchange, implemented the blockade which treated food and medicine as contraband of war. Northern soldiers had been burning Southern crops in the field that could have feed these prisoners.

New York Times

August 24, 1864

Union Prisoners at Andersonville

A delegation, consisting of four Union prisoners just released from Andersonville, Ga., will have an early interview with the President, for the purpose of presenting the case of the thirty-five thousand Union soldiers now penned up at that place as prisoners of war. The statement which these men are prepared to lay before the President is horrifying to a degree far beyond what the experience of this war has brought hitherto. In an inclosed field of thirty acres of ground, exposed to the heat of an all but tropical sun, fed upon a daily ration for each man of three-quarters of a pound of dirty corn bread and two ounces of rancid swine flesh, and supplied with water from a stagnant ditch, which forms the receptacle of the excrement of the camp, are thirty-five thousand of our bravest soldiers -- the men who were the foremost in the hard-fought field, and the most daring in the final grapple and crisis of battle. There they swelter and rot, or go raving mad, or find an end to it by crossing the "dead line," where the friendly rifle of the sentinel brings them final release without the aid of cartel or Commissioner. A seething, reeking pen, surcharged with horrors unimaginable. Pestilence in every form of deadly fever, scurvy and nameless disease raging with undisputed sway; and death making its daily harvest of half a hundred.

Such is military prison life in rebeldom. And yet we hesitate to make a general exchange, until we shall see whether the rebels shall gain a few hundred more able-bodied men than ourselves by the transaction. Able bodied men forsooth! How many score of our brave fellows will there remain in this soldier's pound before another moon has passed, either to return to the field or to bear witness to the atrocities of Southern despotism or repeat the story of their wrong? Raise an army strong enough to affect their release, says the chief scribe of the stoics, who is quite as eager to join such an army as to exchange places with a Union soldier at Andersonville.

The duty of the military authorities is surely clear. Exchange the white prisoners man for man at least; if no better can be done for the negro troops now, their time will come again, unless the South is to have a monopoly of the capture of prisoners. It is doubtless true that the maddening tortures and exposures our men have to endure form parts of the rebel scheme to compel us to make an exchange. What if it is so? They will have the odds in their favor in any case, in all that is most savage in this war. But let our authorities see to the release of our brave and patriotic soldiers.[6]

117

Did President Lincoln Have Knowledge of Prisoner Abuse?

President Abraham Lincoln was the consummate politician. After his first tumultuous year in office Lincoln learned how to avoid controversy and remain unscathed. Sometimes the job of president means making unpopular decisions. Since Lincoln did not want to tarnish his image, he needed someone with authority to carry out his more controversial policies. The man for the job was Secretary of War Edwin M. Stanton. In November 1861 Stanton, who was then Attorney General, urged Secretary of War Cameron to issue a report arguing that slaves should be armed to fight against the Confederacy. Therefore, it was no surprise to learn about Stanton's negative attitude regarding the South, so his retaliatory orders, such as reducing rations for the Confederate prisoners did not shock anyone. Stanton became the perfect scapegoat for Lincoln. It must be remembered that all the orders Stanton issued had the approval of President Lincoln. Therefore, it can be assumed Lincoln gave tacit permission for these orders to be carried out. If they proved unpopular, Stanton knew how to take the blame, so nothing would touch the President.

President Lincoln received many requests from prisoner's families who described the horrendous conditions in the prisons. It is known Lincoln read at least some of these letters because he did grant a few paroles. To believe he knew nothing of the prisoner's situation would be naive. This knowledge coupled with Lincoln's refusal to see the prisoner delegation from Andersonville in August of 1864 raises suspicions that the President not only knew about the brutal conditions that prisoners lived under, but tends to make him appear insensitive to their desperate situation. These men were living under dreadful conditions that saw 29% of their fellow prisoners die from disease. The prisoner exchange

This note from President Lincoln asks for the release of Union 1st Lt. Edward P. Brooks.

had been halted during the summer of 1863 by the vindictive Secretary of War Stanton and it only needed President Lincoln to step in to reestablish the prisoner exchange, but he refused to do so. It is for these reasons that I believe President Lincoln had full knowledge of prison brutality, but did nothing to alleviate it.

118

Chapter 6

Who Is Responsible?

So, who is to blame for the corrupt prison system which eventually gave birth to Elmira prisoner of war camp? There is a lot of blame to go around, but I would like to single out one person who started the ball rolling and kept it going throughout the war. Let's begin at the top with President Abraham Lincoln. Since the President is the Commander in Chief of the United States the ultimate responsibility rests with him. As you will recall it was Lincoln who put an end to battlefield exchanges even though those exchanges satisfied everyone involved. His decision imprisoned Confederate soldiers in small, hastily built stockades for an indefinite period of time. Northern prisons eventually became grossly overcrowded, a condition that soon led to water pollution, disease and death. The truth of that became apparent when numerous prison records were examined. It was easy to see that the longer a soldier was in prison the more chance he had to develop a disease and possibly die. Another fact that does not bode well for President Lincoln is that he ignored requests by the public to begin a prisoner exchange, so these men could come home. It finally took an act of Congress to formally ask the President to "inaugurate systematic measures for the exchange of prisoners in the present rebellion."[1]

To his credit Lincoln did established the Dix-Hill Cartel, but it lasted less than a year before it was temporarily suspended by Secretary of War Edwin M. Stanton. What prompted Stanton to suspend the exchange? We have always been told this was done because of the South's refusal to exchange captured Negro soldiers. It is true the South would not exchange the black troops who had been captured. The Confederates maintained that these Negro soldiers were escaped slaves and were therefore recaptured property. However, less than two hundred black troops had been captured at this point. Not many when you consider that tens of thousands of white soldiers were also prisoners and would suffer disease and possibly death if they were left in prison. It is an established fact that the Northern government had always wanted to stop the prisoner exchange because they did not want to release Confederate soldiers so they could rejoin the army.[2] Did the North use the Confederate's refusal to exchange Negro soldiers as a red herring to confuse the issue, so the public would not object to halting the exchanges? It is very likely that President Lincoln knew the Confederacy would not exchange captured Negro troops and the South's refusal would be viewed as a legitimate reason for ending the prisoner exchange. So, we are back to the question, "Why did Secretary of War Stanton suspend the prisoner exchange?" Stanton answered this question in a letter dated November 22, 1865. The Secretary wrote "he (President Lincoln) gave instructions to suspend the prisoner exchanges." So, it was Lincoln, not Stanton, who had clung stubbornly to his original idea about ending the prisoner exchange.[3]

It was finally up to Lieutenant General Ulysses S. Grant to permanently end the prisoner exchange in April 1864. When General Grant wrote Benjamin F. Butler about his decision he did not try to be devious about his reason for halting the exchange, but told the truth as he saw it. "It is hard on our men held in Southern prisons not to exchange them, but it is humanity to those left in the ranks to fight our battles. Every man we hold, when released on parole or otherwise, becomes an active soldier against us at once either directly or indirectly. If we commence a system of exchange which liberates all prisoners taken, we will have to fight on until the whole South is exterminated."[4]

The South made several attempts to reinstate the general exchange, but it was never agreed upon by Northern authorities. Only a few "special exchanges" were allowed for sick prisoners who would not fit for combat within sixty days. Many of these men died before they could reach home because they had remained in prison too long.

The final nail in the proverbial coffin was provided by Lincoln who in August of 1864 refused to see a delegation of captured Union soldiers from Andersonville prison camp in Georgia. These men had brought with them a petition containing thousands of signatures of fellow prisoners who were asking President Lincoln to reinstate the prisoner exchange. The reason for this request was that thousands of men at Andersonville had already died and more would die if nothing was done. These prisoners had every hope that the President would keep his promise to do everything in his power to bring them home soon. Instead they were met by Secretary of War Stanton, Lincoln's hatchet man, who relayed a message from the president that the prisoner exchange could not be reinstated because this would release thousands of Confederate soldiers.[5] These Union prisoners recalled seeing Northern newspapers from time to time in prison and reading articles that mentioned with pride that the Confederacy was losing the war on every front and the bitter conflict tearing the nation in two would be over in less than a year. After reading how well the war was going for the North, Lincoln's words of "No prisoner exchange was possible" rang especially hollow. These men sadly returned to Andersonville with the heartbreaking news that Lincoln wouldn't even meet with them, abandoning them to suffer their fate alone.[6]

However, most of the guilt for inflicting death and disease on Confederate prisoners of war rests with Secretary of War Edwin M. Stanton. Stanton has done more than any other person to make the lives of Confederate prisoners of war miserable. It would appear decisions regarding their fate was a high priority on his agenda. Whenever he was asked by the Commissary General of Prisoners William Hoffman to approve something that might improve the health of the prisoners, he would delay the proceedings through red tape or by some other devious means. This way Secretary Stanton could accomplish his goal of depriving the prisoners while at the same time avoid having to go on record as refusing a legitimate request.

When Colonel Hoffman suggested cutting the prisoner's rations to save money, Secretary of War Stanton went him one better by trimming his proposal even more. A circular for a 20% reduction of rations for prisoners went into effect June 1, 1864. Hoffman also issued an order that prohibited the prisoners from receiving food packages in the mail from friends and family. Apparently, this was not enough for the Commissary General of prisoners, he issued another order that halted all food sales from the sutler.

Secretary Stanton also refused to build wooden barracks at Camp Douglas, Chicago, Illinois, and Point Lookout, Maryland. In both cases these structures were suggested by the prison commandants because of the approach of winter. These requests then were forwarded to the Secretary of War by Colonel Hoffman. The Commissary General received this curt reply back from Stanton's adjutant saying, "The Secretary of War is not disposed at this time, in view of the treatment our prisoners of war are receiving at the hands of the enemy, to erect fine establishments for their prisoners in our hands."[7] Stanton's reply was so bold it even admitted to retaliation against Confederate prisoners.[8] Stanton declared that the prisoners at Point Lookout would be housed in tents that were rejected by the US Army as being too old and leaky. None of these tents would be equipped with stoves to keep the men warm during the winter.

Secretary Stanton also refused a request by Colonel Hoffman to issue shoes to barefoot Confederate prisoners who were going north to Chicago in winter. When Secretary Stanton heard the request, he became angry and refused to do so because these prisoners had killed Union troops in battle. Stanton's response doesn't make sense since every soldier, North and South, must kill the enemy. That was his job!

Commissary General of Prisoners William Hoffman could also be accused of being the worst enemy of Confederate prisoners. After all it was Hoffman who suggested cutting back on prisoner rations on May 19th.[9] Having researched Hoffman extensively for this book I can say that all his life Hoffman had been guided by a desire to save money. He also wanted to win the approval of Secretary of War Edwin Stanton. He knew of Stanton's desire to retaliate against Confederate prisoners of war and, so he sided with the volatile Secretary.

Something that is a little harder to explain away than his penchant for thrift is the four-month delay in digging a trench to drain Foster's Pond. Hoffman was appraised of the situation in July by Chief Surgeon Eugene Sanger and prison Commandant Colonel Seth Eastman.[10] Hoffman had even asked Eastman for a cost estimate and how long it would take to construct the drainage ditch. His answer from Eastman was "There would be no cost to the military at all." The labor would be provided by the prisoners and any cost for the wood would be paid for by the Prison Fund. Eastman estimated the project would only take two weeks to dig the six-foot-deep drainage ditch a half-mile to the Chemung River. Hoffman finally gave his approval in late October to dig the drainage system, but the severe weather of November and December prevented a timely completion of the project.[11] Now the ground became frozen under a foot of snow and needed to be broken up with a pick. Quicksand was encountered in several places and not only delayed the project, but raised the cost $2,000. Thus, the two-week project during the summer was now extended to a two month job in winter. How many men died at Elmira prison camp while they were waiting for the six-month drainage ditch to be completed? This appears like another case of delaying tactics where Hoffman or Stanton were hoping to inflict as much damage as possible to the Confederate prisoners.

Secretary of War Stanton also failed to issue orders to build winter barracks for over 5,000 prisoners until October 3rd. Like the drainage ditch, this construction would cost the government very little. All costs for the project were to be paid from the Prison Fund and the labor provided by the prisoners.[12] There was absolutely no reason to delay building winter barracks for prisoners still living in tents. It would've been advantageous to begin construction of the barracks during the summer for several reasons. Obviously, the weather was pleasant, and the work days were longer because of the extra sunlight available. Also by starting the construction in the summer the barracks would've been completed in a timely fashion, probably by early fall. Beginning the project during summer would also be beneficial because the workers would not be exposed to cold temperatures and heavy snow.

This way they could get more work done. Another factor for starting the barracks during the summer concerned the men available for the workforce. During the summer there was no major project going on. However, in November there were 200 men employed in digging the half-mile drainage ditch from Foster's Pond to the Chemung River. Since the barracks were also constructed in November, these men would not have been available.

During the 1864 cotton exchange Secretary of War Stanton also figures prominently as the major source of irritation for Confederate prisoners. Stanton managed to delay the exchange of Southern cotton for clothing for destitute Confederate prisoners of war for five months. This is something which should not have taken more than a month. However, because of Stanton and his accomplice General Henry Wessels efforts, the government did not provide the usual clothing allotment for the prisoners as intended. Instead it had the opposite effect! Now the government, represented by General Wessels, felt they did not have to supply any more clothing for prisoners. Now the prisoners got less clothing and this shipment was delayed for four months. Unfortunately, the months when this occurred were December, January, February and March, were the coldest months of the year.

So who was the main source of abuse for Confederate prisoners? If Lincoln had not halted the exchange, Stanton could not have done his dirty work. Conversely, if the exchange was allowed to continue, there would be no prisoners to abuse.

Colonel Hoffman is not a significant factor in this equation since anything he did was more or less influenced by the Secretary of War. The same goes for General Henry Wessels.

I believe President Lincoln's halting of the exchange setup the Confederate prisoners to be abused by Stanton. Remember earlier when I had said that the President was the ultimate politician, and that he did not want anything to soil his image as a great president. Lincoln needed someone who was close to him to carry out the unpleasant tasks of his office while he kept his hands and reputation clean. Stanton fit the bill perfectly as Lincoln's secretary of war. He was a great organizer, and more importantly he was pro-retaliation and possessed a vindictive personality. Remember when Lincoln refused to see the Union delegation from Andersonville? He sent Stanton do his dirty work for him. Stanton also said Lincoln had instructed him to end the prisoner exchange in 1863. Because of these reasons, I have to think that Lincoln bears the greatest responsibility for being the worst enemy of the Confederate prisoners.

Chapter 7

Deadly Civil War Diseases

All prison officials were either consciously or unconsciously guilty of promoting disease; whether this was due to overcrowding, which led to water pollution or merely ignoring sick prisoners until they were too ill to save. Either way, they shared responsibility for the alarming number of deadly diseases in their prison.

The deadliest diseases that preyed upon the Elmira prisoners listed according to severity were: chronic or acute diarrhea, pneumonia, typhoid fever, smallpox, erysipelas, scurvy and chronic dysentery.[1]

Let's follow the health of a typical prisoner who is sent to Elmira. When men are captured and go north to prison they are extremely depressed, and uncertain of their future. One of the first influences on their health occurs when they drink a cup of water. In the case of Elmira, the water in Foster's Pond became extremely polluted because the prison camp held more than twice as many prisoners as it was designed to hold. The prisoners usually develop acute diarrhea because the water contains harmful bacteria. Eighty percent of the men who came to Elmira experienced acute diarrhea in the first few weeks of entering the prison camp. If his initial bout of acute diarrhea goes on for over a week the prisoner can develop chronic diarrhea. A symptom of chronic diarrhea is that it causes frequent, loose or liquid stools. Numerous bowel movements can deprive the human body of water, electrolytes and nutrients through a rapid passage of the stool through the intestine. Electrolytes are vital minerals that regulate many important body functions such as maintaining a normal heartbeat, nerve functions and blood pressure. Once a man's body is depleted of these nutrients his chronic diarrhea then provides a clear path for the introduction of more harmful diseases.

The majority of the prisoners who died at Elmira prison camp had more than one disease which brought about their demise. Surgeons typically only list the main cause of death in their reports, not what other factors contributed to it.

After the war former prisoner William R. Greer wrote about the medical situation in Elmira, "In spite of all hygienic precautions, including an enforced vaccination, illness and mortality steadily increased. Pneumonia, typhoid, and smallpox simply raged even in the wards. The hospitals, being inadequate to meet the situation, the daily death rate of smallpox alone was registered as forty cases. Finally, I became ill, partly from exposure to the intense cold and from insufficient and improper food. I lay in my bunk without medical attention and was gradually sinking from sheer weakness and exhaustion."[2]

Former prisoner Walter D. Addison wrote about the horrors of 19th century vaccinations in *The Southern Historical Collection of the North Carolina* at Chapel Hill. "The courageous manner in which men were vaccinated excelled anything I have ever witnessed

123

even surpassing the acts of savages. The modus operandi was to assemble the men in long lines with coats off and arms bared; then the butchering began by illiterate and irresponsible men. They would take hold of a thick piece of flesh, dip a lancet into the diluted virus, and then thrust it entirely through the pinched up flesh. The spurious virus soon produced such fearfully disastrous results that it became necessary to construct gangrene hospitals, from which arose a dreadful stench. Scores died from the effects; others losing arms. I have seen the sickening effects of their villainous vaccinations. There are many who can verify the above."[3]

Diarrhea

Chronic diarrhea was the leading cause of death at all military prisons during the Civil War. Diarrhea is a bacterial disease with severe abdominal discomfort, cramping and causes frequent, violent defecation which produces a liquid stool. The stools often contain mucus and may be blood streaked. The chronic diarrhea patient is likely to be anemic and suffering from malnutrition. One of the harmful effects of diarrhea is severe depletion of body fluids leading to an electrolyte imbalance. Electrolytes are essential minerals in your body that are necessary for nerve and muscle function and other critical processes. Potassium supply is especially depleted by diarrhea. Ignorant of germs, men in prison shared eating utensils which helped this disease to spread. Diarrhea and dysentery claimed 1,394 lives making it number one on the list of Elmira's most deadly diseases.[4]

Reverend I. W. K. Handy, of the Presbyterian Church of Virginia, remembers what a difficult time men who suffered with chronic diarrhea had. "Sick men, perfectly emaciated from diarrhea, have been obliged to stagger through their quarters to the outhouse on the bank of the river, with filth streaming upon their legs; and then, unable to help themselves, they have fallen upon the pathway, and have been found dead in the morning. Barefooted, bareheaded and ragged men, tottering with disease, have been left to suffer long for the necessary clothing or medicines, which might have been abundantly supplied."[5]

"I was in the hospital myself a month with (diarrhea). Weakness and starvation had caused me to lose my sight, consequently often times when wandering some distance from our ward spots appeared before my eyes that I was dependent upon some kind comrade to lead me home. The blindness left me as I grew stronger. Others suffered the same way. Many times a poor fellow staggered along until his old shaky legs fail to support him, and then he staggered until he was on his feet again with a ghastly smile trying to bear it bravely. It was touching to see the poor, ragged gaunt, half famished, much abused, noble fellows trying to be cheerful through it all."[6]

Former prisoner Anthony M. Keiley wrote that diarrhea was so common that the disease affected everyone. "Visited all my comrades today, and, with one exception, found them all suffering like myself from exhausting diarrhea, induced by the poisonous water."[7]

Dysentery

Many prisoners died of chronic dysentery, but not at the alarming rate of diarrhea. Dysentery is a bacterial infection whose symptoms are intestinal inflammation especially that of the colon, abdominal pain and cramping, a high fever, chills, and frequent foul-smelling stools often containing blood and mucus. Quite often there is straining to evacuate the bowels and the stools are accompanied by a fluid discharge. Although commonly confused with diarrhea, this disease is caused by a different type of bacteria. Dysentery was spread by malnourished prisoners who shared eating utensils and water.[8]

Erysipelas

Erysipelas is a bacterial infection in the upper layer of the skin that normally only affects the legs or the face. It is a highly contagious disease that can cause death if left untreated. Also known as St. Anthony's fire, erysipelas is a disease which produces a fever, reddened, bumpy texture to the skin plus a fiery red rash with raised edges that can easily be distinguished from the skin around it. More severe infections can result in vesicles or pox-like marks on the infected areas. The symptoms include stinging and itching lesions, inflammation of the skin, vomiting, fever, headache and sore throat and sometimes complete prostration can occur. Erysipelas infections can enter the skin through minor trauma, such as a bruise, ulcer, burn, wound, or incision.

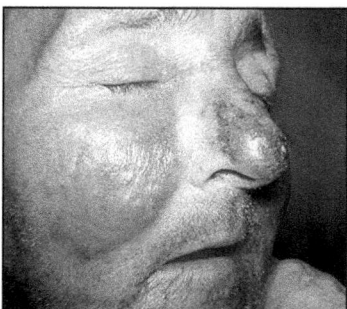

Facial Erysipelas on cheeks and nose.

Records show Elmira prison camp had 52 cases of erysipelas in which 10 patients died. Elmira patients with this disease died almost 20% of the time while the average for other Northern prisons was only 10%.[9]

Intermittent Fever

Intermittent fever has recurring elevated temperatures separated by intervals during which the temperature is normal at least once during a 24-hour period. A variation of intermittent fever is alternate day fever, which can occur in patients with malaria.

Typical symptoms include a high fever of 105°, headache, tiredness, fatigue and chills. In acute cases these symptoms become chronic, intensify and result in death.[10]

Measles

Measles is a highly contagious, viral disease that produces a distinctive, three to five-day rash, 103° to 104° fever and swollen lymph nodes. It usually begins as flat red spots that appear on the face at the hairline and spreads downward to the neck, trunk, arms, legs, and feet. Small raised bumps may also appear on top of the flat red spots. The spots may become joined together as they spread from the head to the rest of the body. Often considered to be an early childhood disease it usually infected the younger soldiers and could possibly be deadly. This disease is caused by the rubella virus and is transmitted through contact with blood, urine, stools or infected persons. Records show Elmira prison camp had 130 cases of measles in which 15 patients died.[11]

Pneumonia

Pneumonia is a severe bacterial infection of the lungs which often impairs gas exchange. This disease is characterized by a persistent cough, sharp chest pain, shortness of breath, blood-streaked or brownish sputum and a high fever. Pulse and respiration increase to almost twice their normal rates. Pneumonia frequently killed one out of four victims. Often this illness got worse because of the poor prison diet. Due to the water pollution at the prison camp, pneumonia has become closely linked to chronic diarrhea which robbed the victim of further nutrition. Records show Elmira prison camp had 1,882 cases of pneumonia in which 773 patients died. With 773 deaths pneumonia is second on the list of Elmira's deadly diseases.[12]

"The Medical and Surgical History of the War of the Rebellion" has this to say about pneumonia contributing to other diseases. "Many diseases were of more frequent occurrence than pneumonia, but only diarrhea and dysentery and the continued fevers furnished a larger death list. It has been shown, however, in discussing the points of interest connected with these grave camp diseases, that pneumonia was present and caused or hastened the fatal issue in 21.6% of the deaths from diarrhea and dysentery and in 68.3% of those attributed to the continued fevers; the mortality from measles also resulted largely from inflammatory processes in the lungs. In fact, the importance of pneumonia as a destroyer of life in our camps and hospitals can hardly be overestimated."

Civil War soldiers were under tremendous stress when they got captured and went North to prison because they were constantly worried about what would become of them and their families. The men heard many horror stories from other soldiers who had been in prison and it was understandable the new men were frightened. A prisoner's ability to fight disease was weakened by stress, worry, a poor diet, inadequate water, clothing and shelter. Given all these sources for disease it was now possible for a simple cold to develop into pneumonia.

126

Remittent Fever

Elevated body temperature showing fluctuation each day, but never falling to nomal.[13]

Scurvy

Hundreds of years ago sailors at sea were commonly affected by a disease that attacked the gums and teeth. Doctors quickly diagnosed the problem as a lack of fresh fruit and vegetables containing vitamin C. By the time of the American Civil War scurvy was a well-known disease which could be easily prevented with a proper diet. There was absolutely no reason for the appearance of this disease in civil war prisons. The existence of scurvy was due to a callous disregard by prison officials for a prisoner's nutritional needs. There were 356 cases of Scurvy at Elmira which claimed 20 lives.[14]

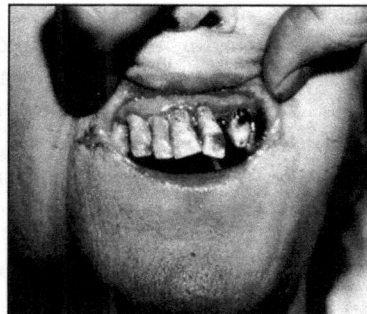

Scurvy victim suffering from bleeding, receding gums and loose teeth.

A person suffering from scurvy has a serious lack of vitamin C in his system which is essential for the production of collagen, a substance that binds teeth and bones. Symptoms include weakness, swollen and bleeding gums, loose teeth, poor wound healing, black and blue spots on the skin and depression.[15]

All prison officials were either consciously or unconsciously guilty of promoting disease; whether this was due to overcrowding, which led to water pollution, or merely ignoring sick prisoners until they were too ill to save. Either way, they shared responsibility for diseases in their prison. Scurvy, however, is unlike other diseases since it can be traced directly to prisoner's diet. Colonel William Hoffman, the Commissary General of Prisoners, insisted on controlling every aspect of a prisoner's life; whether it was shelter, clothing or diet. This being the case, the men's food was his responsibility. Hoffman could not plead ignorance of scurvy because he had been warned many times by prison commandants and surgeons about the presence of the disease.

Trying to combat scurvy the Federals added vinegar to the prisoner's diet. Since vinegar was made from fermented apple juice the liquid contained some vitamin C.

Former prisoner Luther Hopkins remembers the vinegar on his meals. "The dinners consisted of a tin cup of soup (generally bean or other vegetable), a small piece of meat on a tin plate, on which a little vinegar was poured to prevent scurvy."[16]

Another prisoner, Private Malachi Bowden remembers the Yankee antidote for scurvy. "They (prison officials) did allow us to draw a copious supply of vinegar. I ate this with my diet, and drank it with water, hoping that it might help to keep down the disease."[17]

Smallpox

An overcrowded prison environment where the men have a poor diet and live in filthy conditions can be a breeding ground for deadly diseases such as smallpox. This highly contagious disease became so severe at Elmira that 31% of the individuals who were infected did not survive.

This disease begins with a headache, fever and chills and may include pains in the back and the head. Within a two-week period, pimples breakout all over the body and develop into pus filled blisters. Scratching the irritating sores causes them to break open and form scabs which can permanently scar the body. One benefit of surviving a case of smallpox is the individual generally becomes immune.

Since the smallpox virus can live on clothing and blankets for up to 18 months, it can spread with a vengeance inside the prison.[18] If an individual survives he is ordered to take a bath and put on a new set of clothes. His old clothing and blankets are then burned to destroy any trace of the smallpox virus. The most effective way to combat smallpox is through vaccinating the entire prison population. However, 28% of prison vaccinations resulted in painful ulcers on the arm where the virus was administered. Sometimes these sores deteriorated further causing amputation or death.

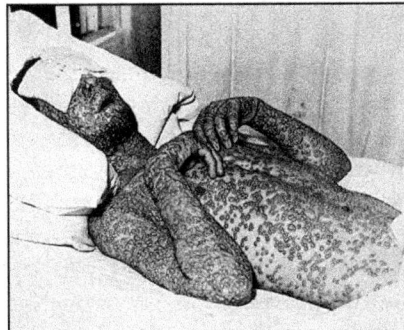

Smallpox victim

Ninety-eight percent of the smallpox cases occurred from October to the end of March 1865. During this period 1,186 cases of smallpox claimed 363 lives at the prison making it the third most deadly disease at Elmira prison camp. A few of Elmira's death certificates during this five-month period failed to list what type of disease caused the prisoner's deaths. It is probable that some of these deaths were caused by smallpox.[19]

Typhoid Fever

Typhoid fever is a bacterial disease, often recorded by the Civil War surgeons as remittent fever. Its symptoms includes abdominal tenderness headache, sweating, cough, high fever of 104°, bloody stool, confusion delirium and severe fatigue or weakness. Typhoid fever bacteria are deposited in water or food by a human carrier and then spread to other people in the area. Victims can develop a fever that may reach 105° and have a severe headache while lying exhausted with half-closed eyes in what's known as the typhoid state. Periods of chills and sweating may occur with a loss of appetite. Victims often become carriers and pass the bacteria to others through their urine and feces. Where sanitation is poor the organisms may enter the water supply.[21]

In the twelve months Elmira was in operation there were 235 cases of typhoid fever which claimed 140 lives. This means an astounding 60% of the prisoners who were unfortunate enough to have developed this disease died from it.[22]

128

Twelve percent of typhoid fever victims die from the disease. Typhoid fever is listed as a "Continued Fever" in the table on page 113.

Photograph by Mathew Brady taken of a Civil War hospital ward.

The Medical and Surgical History of the War of the Rebellion Table

Part III, Volume I, Table XVIII, page 46, part 1 of 3

	Camp Douglas, IL, Feb 1862 to June, 1865		Alton, Illinois, Sept. 1862 to June 1865		Rock Island, Illinois, Feb. 1864, to June 1865	
Number of Months Recorded	41		34		17	
Mean Strength	5,361		1,008		6,030	
All Diseases and Injuries	Cases	Deaths	Cases	Deaths	Cases	Deaths
	70,088	4,009	29,095	1,475	13,678	1,604
Wounds, Injuries and Unspecified Diseases	1279	80	329	20	225	15
Specified Diseases	68,809	3,929	28,766	1,455	13,453	1,589
Continued Fevers	1,116	351	190	70	52	54
Malarial Fevers	10,151	233	7,206	177	2,384	52
Eruptive Fevers	4,671	823	2,632	537	1,797	436
Diarrhea And Dysentery	13,455	698	5,580	229	3,874	363
Anemia	585	4	465	27	47	8
Consumption	259	113	47	27	26	76*
Rheumatism	3,212	37	518	7	700	1
Scurvy	3,745	39	390	6	439	14
Bronchitis	1,628	27	400	4	391	25
Pneumonia And Pleurisy	4,655	1,296	1,134	276	1,464	397
Other Diseases	25,332	308	10,204	95	2,279	163
Total Specified Diseases	68,809	3,929	28,766	1,455	13,453	1,589

Nineteenth century medical officers divided fevers into three separate categories. Typhoid and typhus fevers constituted two of the Continued Fevers on the table above. The category Eruptive Fevers encompassed erysipelas, measles and smallpox. The category Malarial Fevers was made up of intermittent and remittent fevers.

* Rock Island post mortem evidence was taken as cause of death while no corresponding change was made in the diagnosis of the case.

The Medical and Surgical History of the War of the Rebellion Table

Part III, Volume I, Table XVIII, page 46, part 2 of 3

	Camp Morton, Ind., June 1863 to June 1865		Johnson's Island, Ohio, June 1863 to June 1865		Camp Chase, Ohio, Feb. 1864 to June 1865	
Number of months Recorded	25		25		17	
Mean Strength	2,865		2,114		3,570	
All Diseases and Injuries	Cases	Deaths	Cases	Deaths	Cases	Deaths
	9,122	1,187	3,697	161	24,687	1,771
Wounds, Injuries and Unspecified Diseases	259	12	126	5	741	32
Specified Diseases	8,863	1,175	3,571	156	23,946	1,739
Continued Fevers	55	42	93	26	115	53
Malarial Fevers	1,954	119	417	10	4,258	34
Eruptive Fevers	548	85	160	17	1,865	362
Diarrhea And Dysentery	2,241	315	1,855	46	4063	226
Anemia	68	4	35	1	402	24
Consumption	34	26	14	7	24	12
Rheumatism	190	5	106	1	988	0
Scurvy	778	6	58	0	828	5
Bronchitis	178	1	57	1	240	1
Pneumonia And Pleurisy	1,351	495	99	25	1,681	954
Other Diseases	1,466	77	677	22	9,482	68
Total Specified Diseases	8,863	1,175	3,571	156	23,946	1,739

The Medical and Surgical History of the War of the Rebellion Table

Part III, Volume I, Table XVIII, page 46, part 3 of 3

	Elmira, New York, July 1864 to June 1865		Fort Delaware, Delaware, August 1863 to June 1865		Point Lookout, Maryland, Sept. 1863 to June 1865	
Number of Months Recorded	12		23		22	
Mean Strength	6,591		6,406		9,610	
All Diseases and Injuries	Cases	Deaths	Cases	Deaths	Cases	Deaths
	10,455	2,931	44,388	2,218	44,934	3,704
Wounds, Injuries and Unspecified Diseases	277	4	817	19	1,399	65
Specified Diseases	10,178	2,927	43,571	2,199	43,535	3,639
Continued Fevers	239	140	432	156	267	217
Malarial Fevers	628	65	4,725	175	6,864	161
Eruptive Fevers	1,368	388	2,593	472	1,033	333
Diarrhea And Dysentery	4,379	1,394	9,659	644	20,474	2,050
Anemia	202	17	792	38	613	33
Consumption	23	13	32	11	76	46
Rheumatism	360	9	1,494	19	772	16
Scurvy	356	20	6,351	94	3,312	167
Bronchitis	116	19	965	34	513	21
Pneumonia And Pleurisy	1,882	773	1,128	401	925	425
Other Diseases	625	89	15,400	155	8,686	170
Total Specified Diseases	10,178	2,927	43,571	2,199	43,535	3,639

Chapter 8

Prisoner's Statements

Private Walter D. Addison

Breathed's battery of Jeb Stewart's Horse artillery

Recollections of a Confederate Soldier of the Prison-Pens
of Point Lookout, Md., and Elmira, New York

This article is from the Southern Historical Collection of the University of North Carolina Library, Chapel Hill.

So many exaggerated accounts of the treatment of Union soldiers in Southern prisons have been published from time to time creating as they have done such a wide spread prejudices throughout the country and which of course have been accepted all over the North as truth, the wonder is that such silence should be kept by Southerners as to the treatment of Confederate prisoners within Northern prison pens.

The writer having more than six months experience at Point Lookout, Maryland; and Elmira, New York, recalls that which he has witnessed himself, and desires to state truthfully herein, it being ever green in his memory.

I was a private in Company A, Breathed's battery of Stewart's Horse artillery commanded at the time by Captain Preston P. Johnson of Baltimore, Md., and now a resident of Kentucky. Major James Breathed of Hagerstown, Md., in command of the Battalion.

I was a captive in the summer of 1864 at the time of the Wilderness Campaign, and was sent to Point Lookout and there confined a few weeks, and when there was confined about sixteen thousand Southern prisoners many having been there as long as two years owing to the refusal on the part of the North, to exchange prisoners. During my entire confinement at Point Lookout we were under guard of Negro soldiers whose conduct and treatment of the prisoners was infamously cruel and in many instances they conducted themselves in a savage manner. I have witnessed them fire their muskets indiscriminately into crowded masses of prisoners, shooting two or three men at a single shot, and such outrages were tolerated by their white officers, and they never were punished nor their cases investigated. This repeatedly happened at Point Lookout, and I never heard that one was even reprimanded.

There was at one time an apprehended raid of Mosby's cavalry upon Point Lookout for the purpose of releasing the prisoners confined there. Stringent orders were given to the guard to fire upon any prisoners who were seen out of their quarters after eight o'clock at night. Many prisoners were unaware of the orders, and incautiously ventured out for the performance of nature calls, when they were ruthlessly shot down. Several cases of the kind occurred. All these outrages were perpetrated by Negroes as there were none others on guard.

133

Water for the use of the prison was collected in barrels distributed about the prison grounds, and the vessel for drinking purposes was conspicuously absent in many places, when the prisoners would drink from the barrel. The audacious Negro was always at hand, and seemed to delight in immersing the head of the drinker, and then gloat over the fun. All this was allowed, and there was no redress. Repeated remonstrances were made to the authorities, but were unnoticed, and such outrages continued to be of daily occurrence.

The Rev. Mr. Eddy, an English gentleman residing in Texas at the breaking of the war, and who espoused our cause, and gallantly fought in the ranks was a prisoner at Point Lookout, and attempted to expose to the outside world the outrageous shooting of our prisoners by the Negro guard was detected in his good work. He remained at Point Lookout after my transfer to Elmira. I next saw him in the guard house at Elmira, after suffering as he did cruelties which befitted a savage than the so called Samaritan of the Federal army. Mr. Eddy was for weeks confined at Elmira when all sorts of indignities were imposed upon him and when I was undergoing similar punishment for writing an article upon the treatment of the prisoners and which was intercepted in the Elmira PO. The Post Office was cautiously watched and it was almost impossible for a letter to pass such watching eyes as were employed, and the dread of having letters which could contain anything pertaining to the inside workings of the stockade. In any other prisoners served their sentence in the guard house for the same offense, and some marched at the command of the Negro guard with a barrel shirt.

From Point Lookout, and various other Northern prisons there were about Ten thousand prisoners transferred to Elmira, NEW YORK in the summer of 1864, the writer being amongst the number. The first installment from Point Lookout was dispatched by sea via New York City in the month of July upon a miserable old Government transport only fitted to carry cattle. About twelve hundred men were crowded upon this old tub between decks with only the hatches open, and there they remained crowded together like sheep for many days, only allowing one or two at a time on the main deck for a few minutes, when they were ordered into their horrible quarters below. The sight of these holds was sickening in the extreme, and the condition and sufferings of the prisoners therein confined was indeed horrible, and a large number of the men being already sick when placed on board their wretched condition upon the voyage can be imagined better than described. After reaching the harbor of New York we were released from the ship until the following day, and upon clearing the vessel the sight presented can never be forgotten. Think of their journey by sea, several hundred miles, crowded together as we were, with so many sick in the sweltering heat of July. It was on a par with the condition of the Yankee slave ships with a cargo of human souls purchased with a cargo of Boston rum. Our rations consisted of fat pork and a loaf of bread.

No beds nor straw to lie upon, only a blanket spread beneath us on the filth covered hard boards only comparable with hog or cattle pen. Never upon the whole voyage was there any attempt made to sweep or clean the floors. There was scarcely an inch of space where there could be a step between the crowded mass of human freight. The insufficient ventilation of the ships holds rendered the stench and the foul air unbearable, and many deaths were the result. The writer owes the preservation of his own life to the kindness of one of the prisoners (now residing in San Francisco) who was fortunate enough to enjoy a little more freedom than the rest, and who managed to smuggle me a small lump of ice, and a swallow of tea when I was lying jammed in amongst the rest of the hold and sick almost to death. Some were already dead when the ship reached New York, and I feel certain that many died afterward from the affects of that horrible voyage. The continuation of the trip afterward to Elmira was attended with less suffering.

When showing the prisoners on the ship at Point Lookout they were supplied with their rations for the voyage, consisting of a piece of very fat mess pork and a loaf of bread, and it can be imagined what was the condition of things between decks when rolling on the billows of the deep, and hardly one escaped the effects of his first experience at sea. It reminded me of only one other scene I witnessed when passengers upon a ship at sea, which was converging at market nearly two thousand huge densely crowded together upon deck, the animals having been fed upon raw potatoes just before starting. The sea affects them as it does a human being. Those swine were accommodated better than we, they being upon the upper decks in the fresh air, whilst we were between decks almost poisoned by the foul air, which was intensely polluted by human excrement.

The return trip to Richmond from Elmira was no more comfortable than the one described. We were marched from the prison to the depot in Elmira through about two feet of snow—the weather intensely cold—in February 1865. Upon reaching the depot wet and cold we were crowded into cattle cars wherein was a little dirty straw scattered over the floor, and not a particle of fire. Thus we were transferred to Baltimore in nearly forty-eight hours, including two whole nights. At Baltimore we were marched a long distance through a blinding sleet and snow storm to the steamboat upon the wharf from noon till night, when we were placed upon a dilapidated government cattle transport and landed at City Point below Richmond. A violent storm of wind, sleet, and snow raged the entire night of our passage down the bay, and unprotected as we were upon the hurricane deck with only a blanket the night was a hard one. Many of the sick of which there were a large numbers were placed below decks in the stalls formerly for cattle, and but slightly protected from the weather, and but little more comfortable than there on the hurricane deck. There can be no doubt that it was the grossest indifference on the part of the Government in thus permitting sick prisoners to be conveyed in such an inhuman and cruel manner. I do not believe that in any instance during the war when Northern prisoners suffered as much, if as, it was for lack of provisions and the refusal on the part of the North to exchange prisoners, it seeming their intention to let the latter die rather than refrain from their endeavor to eat out the substance of the South.

The conduct of many of the physicians in charge of the hospitals herein named deserves especial notice, and the strongest condemnation. If they had been dumb brutes, instead of human beings as they were supposed to be, they could not have exhibited greater brutality. I was ward master in one of the hospital barracks at Elmira which contained from eighty-five to ninety patients crowded, as they sometimes were to or three in a bunk. The physician, a doctor Van Ness made his visits once and sometimes twice every twenty-four hours. For the many different diseases incidental to such places, nearly every patient received opium pills. That being the favorite prescription no matter what the nature of the disease. On one occasion, three persons so being treated were visible shaking, the surgeon-in-chief, a Dr. Sanger, was called in. He directed Dr. Van Ness to write four or five drops of Fowler's solution of arsenic. He wrote forty-five and the patients in a very short time breathed their last breath. No investigation ensued. No reprimand. Dr. Van Ness continued in his position.

Hundreds of our prisoners died. I can truthfully say not twenty percent of those in the hospital left it alive. This is no exaggeration of what I believe was a terrible crime growing out of, to put it mildly, the deplorable ignorance of the medical men in charge, if not willful murder.

They had our poor helpless soldiers at their mercy. Often have I heard them, when gathered together in the dispensary discussing their experiences of the day, exult over the numbers of the Rebs they had put through, i.e. killed' and expressing their desire to, in this way, get rid of the whole number of the Confederates there, thus avoiding an exchange. All in authority at Elmira seemed to be of this opinion. Who that was confined at Andersonville can recall a single instance where there was a greater outrage than at Elmira, where thousands of prisoners were confined in small tents until early winter in such a dreadfully severe climate as that of northern New York where is situated Elmira. I have known persons to be frost bitten, and when some of them provided for themselves little mud chimneys to their tents, gathering chips and other small fuel, the Yankee officers would send a guard to ruthlessly destroy them and Major Beall, who was then in command, would go to the rounds himself, in the middle of the night and deprive them of the extra blankets which were their own personal property, leaving the soldier to freeze to death. No coffee, no tea, no vegetables but a few beans to make tasteless watery soup consisting of the liquid in which the pork had been boiled. After many months the old soldier barracks—barns were used as hospitals. Hundreds were wedged in, and crowded together like packed sardines. Two and frequently three in a bunk. They had no opportunity to cleanse themselves of vermin there first found, therefore who can wonder at the fearful numbers of deaths, arising from ignorant medical supervision, and total lack of proper ventilation. Of the false statements of the humanity then boasted by the Yankee, the bored will get a truthful statement. Humanity equal to that shown at the time they burned, so termed witches. The Northern people, not descended from Yankees, will when the whole truth is known, believe the palm of humanity be-longed to the South, and will see through the intentional falsehoods of a prejudiced press.

There is no doubt in my mind as to the intention of our enemies to rid themselves of as many of our prisoners as was possible, no matter what the means to which they resorted. Witness in various instances when contagious diseases were introduced into crowded prisons. I recollect, in one instance at Elmira hundreds of deaths were the result of small-pox introduced by patients from Blackwell's Island, New York. Up to that time not a case of the disease had been known there. In a few days it manifested itself in one of the new importations. Instead of being isolated, he was placed immediately adjoining one of the wards used as a hospital, and there remained for days. Other cases rapidly developed, and soon broke out in a virulent form. Tents were them placed inside the stockade where hundreds were confined, and immediately upon their convalescence were again distributed amongst the well prisoners, even occupying the same beds, thus spreading the disease to an appalling degree. No comfortable buildings were provided for the wretched victims, even when the temperature fell twenty degrees below zero. Very few small-pox patients survived. When discharging small-pox cases they were led to a pump, and there stripped and washed in the coldest weather, and then assigned new quarters for a brief time, when they were returned to the hospital to meet their deaths. Their sufferings were laughed at. Considering their ill usage, premeditated torture, insufficient food, and the prevailing lack of any show of humanity it seems a miracle that one again reached his home. I repeatedly heard it said by Federal officers that the mortality at Elmira far exceeded that at Andersonville. I will say in justice to two officers, Captains Whiton and Munger, that they did what they could to alleviate the sufferings of the prisoners, but were almost powerless to render the aid they deserved.

The outrageous manner in which men were vaccinated excelled anything I have ever witnessed even surpassing the acts of savages. The modus operandi was to assemble the man first in long lines with coats off and arms bared; then the butchering began by illiterate and irresponsible men. They would take hold of a thick piece of flesh, dip a lancet into the diluted virus, and then thrust it entirely through the pinched up flesh. The spurious virus soon produced such fearfully disastrous results that it became necessary to construct gangrene hospitals, from which arose a dreadful stench. Scores died from the effects; others losing arms. I have there seen the sickening effects of their villainous vaccination. There are many who can verify the above.

A most horrible instrument of torture used at Elmira was called a sweat box. For trivial offenses our men were therein confined for hours, in the scorching suns of July and August, without food and water, and removed in many cases only when the victim was more dead than alive. I vividly recollect when one man dropped with rigid limbs swollen and almost paralyzed, and died in a few days from the effects. This instrument of torture consisted of a narrow upright box, about seven feet high, and wide enough to fit an ordinary sized man. It stood in a perpendicular position with its victim without ventilation, and the poor victim and left to sweat to death.

Another instrument of torture used at Elmira was the dreaded barrel shirt. What was known by that name was a very heavy barrel with one head out, and the other containing a hole large enough to admit the head of a man through it. All offenders, twice a day, for two hours, had to wear it. They were drawn up to form a circle, the barrel adjusted over the head the inside of the barrel resting upon the shoulders and the parade commenced. This death dealing instrument would have been a burning shame amongst savages.

This afforded the Negro guard amusement every day, and also seemed to gratify their beastly officers. Upon the back of every barrel, on a board twenty-four by six inches, was written in large letters the supposed offense, such as, "Liar;" "Liar No. 2;" Liar No. 3;" "Dogeater;" "Dogeater No 1;" and so on. Multitudinous outrages no less revolting were of continued occurrence under the eyes of men high in rank under the Government.

As an explanation of the term "dog-eater" mentioned above I will state on one occasion an officer came into the stockade accompanied by his favorite dog. No sooner was the dog discovered by several hungry prisoners than he was seized and converted into food. A search of the camp soon revealed the dog quartered and dressed and hid away in the rafters. The parties to the wrong were quickly discovered, and were for a long time clothed in barrel shirts.

Rats, dogs, cats nor any other animal would long exist amongst that hungry throng of prisoners. Catching rats and selling them for food became quite a business, and the pursued the avocation with quite a profit, the demand being steady. Would men eat dogs and rats unless suffering from extreme hunger? Many died from insufficient and improper food. I have seen men, almost starved fish scraps from barrels containing hospital refuse and devouring it ravenously, although be so doing were poisoning themselves with the putrid filth they were swallowing. Can it be imagined that human beings imagined that human beings—officers could witness such sights and then return to their sumptuous meals without a thought of the terrible suffering of their starving Confederates.

The customary prison diet consisted of three or four crackers and a small slice of fat pork in the morning. In the afternoon a half pint of water in which the pork was boiled, and a piece of bread—nothing else. There were entirely insufficient to properly preserve health. The diet in the hospital was better, and answered fairly well. No vegetables, tea nor coffee were ever seen. It was repeatedly said, in my presence, that the reason we were denied vegetables, was in retaliation for the refusal of tobacco to their prisoners in the South. On many occasions vegetables sent by friends outside were denied to the prisoners. This occurred oftener at Point Lookout than at Elmira. At the later prison clothes sent to me they refused to deliver, also boots and shoes. In case they did deliver a coat it was not until the tail had been cut off and the tops of boots were similarly curtailed. At Elmira I was one day notified that there was a box at headquarters for me. Upon reporting there for it was opened in my presence by the order of Major Colt who was in command. The articles of clothing therein were of a valuable character. They were refused me. After pleading some time for the new coat, Major Colt consented to having it exchanged in town for another, he said of more suitable color, and detailed. Sent Major Rudd to attend to it. The overcoat was a very handsome and costly one; in re-turn, after charging me five (5) dollars for his trouble he delivered to me a miserable shoddy one almost worthless.

I could relate dozens of other outrages equally disgraceful, but enough is said to illustrate what was the condition of thousands of our Confederates confined in the Northern prison-pens. I hope that many of those who had similar experiences will, some day, make known to the world, the disgraceful scenes they there witnesses.
Walter D. Addison, San Francisco, Sept. 30, 1889

Private Albert Marion Baldwin

Company K., 40th North Carolina heavy artillery

Text copied from *Wilmington Morning Star News*, 12/4/1927

Dr. Albert Marion Baldwin, Confederate veteran, was born in Columbus County, February 9, 1845. He enlisted from Wilmington, Company K., 40th North Carolina heavy artillery, at the age of 18. "I was sent to Fort Fisher where I served one year and was then sent to Bald Head Island, where ten companies were stationed. Here I witnessed the first bombardment of Fort Fisher. I remained one year at Bald Head and was sent back with four other companies to the second bombardment. The coast from Carolina Beach was lined with gunboats about 50. The ironclads came near in shore. We could make no impression on them with our small guns. In front of Fort Fisher there was a channel called the New Channel. It has since filled in by building the wall from the lower end of Fort Fisher to Zeke's Island. This channel was valuable to the blockade runners. I saw the wreck Modern Greece. She was attacked by the Yankees and ran in near shore and was wrecked. She can still be seen off the seas beach at low tide—24 sister blockade runners shared her fate along our coast.

The fort faced the ocean a mile. About every 200 yards a 64-pound gun was mounted and manned by eight to ten men. The largest gun we had was the Armstrong gun. We only had it at the last. I was instructed to stand on tiptoe when the gun went off; I did, and was alright. The bombardment was too terrible to describe. It was a rain of fire, shot and shell over us three days and two nights. Our barracks were all burned. The bombproofs saved some of us, when we could crawl in at night. When the firing ceased and we were captured, we were exhausted, but the Yankees marched us up the beach a mile. Here we camped, with a strong guard around us. They were kind. A soldier gave me something to eat from his haversack. We had no time to eat during the bombardment. We spent two nights on the beach. I had two blankets and the sand was soft. We were marched back and through the fort and put on two transports where the prisoners were taken through the New Channel into the ocean. There were 800 prisoners on the transport I was on.

Our captors were kind and kept the companies together. We put to sea, steaming due north. We entered the Delaware River, cutting through the ice. It was about the 20th of January, and the ice being so heavy our transport was ordered back and we put into New York harbor where we awaited orders from Washington, which was to proceed to Elmira. Our friends on the other transports were taken to Point Lookout. We were to have been sent to Fort Delaware, but our transport could not get through the ice we encountered. From New York we went by train to Elmira. Everything was covered in snow. Crowds came to look at us but no one said anything. We got off in the snow and marched a mile and a half to prison, but it seemed like 10 to me, leaving our southern climate, where I had been put to sleep with the rustling of the palm trees and the warm ocean winds from the Gulf Stream, it was a bitter exchange for this ice and snow—but so I entered my prison January 31, 1865. The officers and guards had icicles hanging from their moustaches.

139

They paid no attention to it, but it was new to me, being from the South, where gentlemen wore no such ornaments.

My bed was a board—we slept in tiers of three along the wall, two to each tier. I occupied a center with a friend, James Lesesne, a member of my company and a comrade at Fort Fisher. I had held on to my two army blankets, and he had two, so we encountered the zero weather. We had two meals a day. We were marched by barracks, 100 to be fed at a time. We ate with our fingers, no plate, knife, fork or spoon. A thin slice of bread—with a thinner slice of meat—pork or corned beef—on it served as a plate. This was breakfast. The next meal and the last of the day was a cup of bean soup and a slice of bread, I was always glad to get the end slice, because it was a little thicker. I was so hungry I felt worse after eating than before. It was just a teaser what they gave me. One day James Lesesne received five dollars from a friend in Vermont, and then we felt as if we had come into a fortune, and so we had. We used it little by little, never more than 75 cents at the time for something to eat, cheese and crackers, which were bought from the sutler, the prison merchant. When money came it was posted on the bulletin board, and what glad news it was; some friend would tell us if we did not see it. I was so thin and weak and hungry that I felt like I was starving to death, and I was. I knew with the fall of Fort Fisher the South could not hold out much longer, and now the question was, would I hold out.

When a prisoner broke a rule he was marched around, up and down through the barracks with a barrel shirt on. The barrel shirt was a barrel with the heads knocked out and a place for the prisoner to put his arms through. The weather was getting better, snow and ice were melting and I could walk outside some days.

The news came, "Lee had surrendered!" Mr. C.C. Covington's uncle was the means of my get-ting released as soon as I did; he sent my name to Washington. At last the day came when we were ordered to the dining room under strong guard and on the way Lesesne saw on the bulletin board another five was waiting for him. We were so happy release was near. Lesesne was eager to hurry on, but I knew what the money had done for us and would do now, so I had consent to try and get it. I asked permission to see the treasurer, and a guard was given me, and I got the money and again laid in a supply of cheese and crackers. We had to take the oath, then we were marched through a large gate and on to the station.

I was in prison in Elmira four and a half months. I was released June 13, 1865. When I entered I was weighed and measured and a description taken of me. I was six feet and two inches tall and light in weight, 120 pounds, and far less now. From Elmira we went to Baltimore and took a boat to Old Point, changed to a smaller boat and went up the James River to Richmond, from there to Danville, in boxcars to Greensboro, Raleigh, Goldsboro and Wilmington, where I boarded the steamer A.P. Hurt, to Fayetteville, which was my home. My parents were not living, but my sister was there to welcome me—she did not recognize me when I appeared—I was so emaciated and had grown a long black beard. I spent my 20th birthday in prison."

Sergeant Berry Benson,
1st South Carolina Infantry

Text has been reprinted from "Berry Benson's Civil War Book", pages 126-150;

"We were put on board a train of freight cars, with a guard in each car—maybe two—and guards on top of the cars. I had made up my mind to seize the first chance I had to jump from the cars, but decided to wait for the night decreasing the chance not only of being shot by the guards but also of recapture.

"In Baltimore, we were marched through the city. I remember very well passing by the Cathedral, along Cathedral Street. While waiting in the depot, the citizens crowded upon us very close, looking at us with great interest, and, I thought, with sympathy. Once or twice my heart was in my mouth as a chance seemed about to be offered of slipping out amongst them, but the guards always drove them back too soon. During the journey, one of Mosby's men escaped, so I heard, by cutting a hole in the side of the car. The noise of the train prevented the guard from hearing, and other prisoners stood or sat around to hide him at his work. It was intended that others should follow, but the hole was discovered just after he got out.

"When night came on, I took a place by the door, and waited, hoping the guard would drop off to sleep. Then just when I had resolved to jump anyhow, the car shot pass some large rocks many feet below in a ravine, which I would've met instant death. And so, always deterred by one thing or another, I let the whole night go by. I certainly must have been unusually devoid of courage that might, and I have always been ashamed of it.

Reaching Elmira, Sunday, July 24th, we were marched through the streets to the outer edge of the town, where stood the prison, it being a camp like Point Lookout, with the same kind of wooden fence around it. Before getting inside the prison, I marked one object which seem to promise a hope of escape. This was a large tree-I think a walnut-which grew in one corner, throwing its limbs out beyond the prison walls. Climbing it some dark night, one might go out on a limb and drop to the ground. Outside, near the entrance gate, were the guards quarters-plain pine houses.

Inside, we were drawn up and the roll called, and assigned to our quarters, Baxter, Atkinson, and I being assigned to the same long room with bunks fitted up on both sides, in two tiers. The bunks were made of on planed pine boards, and as we had no blankets, they were left bare during the day, and at night occupied simply by ourselves. Later Baxter was given a blanket and a piece of cloth by a friend, and these he shared with me.

The prison was said to be a mile in circumference. In rear of it ran to the Chemung (or Tioga) River, some 20 yards distant. Through the middle of the prison, paralleling the river, lay a pool of water, probably 3 to 6 feet deep and about 40 feet wide. We were told this was the old riverbed, its course having been changed by a freshet. One end of the pool did not quite reach the fence; the other end ran underneath it, extending into the common beyond. Here a narrow bridge crossed the pool, a sentinel standing on it to keep anyone from going to the other side of the prison, at that time unoccupied.

The occupied part of the prison was, I believe, smaller than the other, the soil being hard, mixed with stones, while the unoccupied portion was low and sandy. When we arrived I think there were no tents, all prisoners then our being lodged in the long wooden buildings. The Sergeant of our ward was one of the guards, and we never saw him accept a roll calls (reveille and tattoo).

Shortly after arrival, I came across Savage, Russell, Ferneyhough, and Johnson, whom I had left at Point Lookout. Russell had taken care of the things I had left at Point Lookout-my vest, shoes, etc.-and now he gave them to me; and he also paid a barber (a prisoner) to cut my hair, which had grown very long. Of course I had to tell them the whole story after leaving them, first making them promise not to repeat it to anyone, lest it reach the authorities, and get me into trouble here at Elmira. I shortly met up with a member of my regiment, Sergeant Hood, who had been captured just a week after I was, by the very same troops, including the corporal who had pricked me with his bayonet. The corporal had shown him the knife with "Z. Benson" cut in the handle, which I had dropped during the struggle, and told him the story of my capture and attempt to escape.

Talking with Hood as to the prospect of escape, I now came to the conclusion that our best chance was to swim across the pool in the night crawl long on our bellies to the fence and lying flat against it, dig a hole under it the chief difficulty lay in being able to reach the fence, unobserved by the Sentinel, and to remain unobserved while digging the hole. To minimize this danger, one should go first, leaving the others lying down at a distance, to be signaled by a stone thrown to them when the hole was dug. Baxter, Wood, Russell and I assembled one night to make the attempt. It being a bright, clear, starlit night we waited for a darker night, preferably a stormy one. And the very next night, big locomotive lights were put all around inside the fence, so that the prison was like a gas-lit sidewalk.

I found here in prison in old schoolmate, John Perrin, who lived in a house in the North East corner of the enclosure. With him was another Augusta boy, James Bohler. Between their house and the next one below it was a space only about 3 feet in width, making a long narrow alley way, boarded up at both ends. I saw that if one were in the narrow alley way, he could crawl under the adjoining house and start a tunnel, with little danger of being seen by anybody. So I proposed a plan to Perrin and Bohler, to which they agreed. They cut a little door in the side of their bunk, hinging it at the top with pieces of leather. To inquiring friends, they explained that this door was handy to spit out of when lying in their bunks smoking, or chewing tobacco. The first night after the door was completed, Perrin and I went out through it, and started a tunnel. We let in two or three others, to join in the attempt. After a few days, one of the newcomers took me aside saying he had something private to discuss with me. He told me that he belonged also to another gang of tunnelers, whose leaders asked me to visit them "on business." I went and was introduced to Joe Womack, a Confederate Sargent Major. He propose that we join forces and combine on one tunnel saying that both tunnels could not succeed because of the first escape, a rigid search would be made, and the other inevitably discovered. Also, by combining forces, we could shorten the time of digging.

I was quite of the opinion of my new friends and promised them a coalition of forces. As their tunnel started from under one of the hospitals on the west side of the prison, and was much closer to the fence, we agreed to continue it and abandon ours. We had worked only three nights, when strange men were seen going in and out of the adjoining hospital, and we suspected that another tunnel was being dug under the adjoining hospital. Investigation the following night disclose the tunnels were being dug from under all three hospitals. We sought out the leaders and held a council of war, at which was decided to abandon one of the three tunnels, continuing the other two. Both should be opened on the same night just as the Sentinel on the fence called 11 o'clock.

The night agreed upon came (August 28/64). Going early to the scene, I was surprised to see so many men about. There must've been scores lounging around--all talking about the tunnel and the prospect of its early completion. The chance of escape grew wonderfully small to me all at once. A few men might get out without discovery, but not the scores! Determined to be one of the early ones, I went under. The ground under the building was almost covered with men lying down! Fearing that the attention of the guards would be attracted, and the men under the house captured, I crawled out, but continued to loiter near-by, chatting with a friend I had recently made, Jack Kibler, a Virginia cavalry scout. Directly men came streaming out from under the house, making off, some of them at a run. A few words they let drop made the group scattered about retire hastily too. Finally we halted one long enough for him to say, "The Yankees have found us out and have driven stakes in the end of the tunnel."

I told Jack, "That isn't so. The Yankees wouldn't be so foolish as to stop the tunnel with stakes. They'd watch and catch the tunnelers. The leaders are just telling this tale to frighten the crowds away."

Jack agreeing with me, we crawled under the house. Two or three men were near the tunnel's mouth. When I asked whether anyone was in the tunnel, I was answered, "No." So off went my shoes, and I crawled in. Coming to the tunnels end, I found solid dirt—no stakes. I backed out of the mouth and asked for a knife to dig with. A voice asked, "Is that you, Sullivan?"

"No," I answered. "Give me a knife."

They gave me one, and I set to work, working hard for some time, the air in a tunnel growing more and more foul as I breathe it over and over, until I was nearly suffocated, and had to come out for fresh air. I went back soon, taking a lighted candle someone gave me, and some matches. Soon the candle sputtered out and the matches refused to light. I kept working as long as I could stand it. When I came out again, someone took my place. So the work went on, by reliefs.

It had now grown late, probably 2 o'clock, August 29th. Nearly everybody had gone, but I lay near the mouth of the tunnel, determined to stick it out to the end. After a while the tunneler came out and said he had opened the tunnel by a small hole, and found that it was just inside the wall. "Give me a tuft of grass to stop the hole up," he said.

The grass being given him, he crawled in to stop the hole, and came back saying, "The tuft won't hold, but I pulled the grass over it, and I don't think it will be discovered."

There was some little talk between the two men as to completing the work the next night, neither aware of my presence within three feet of them, it was so dark. Then the man in the tunnel's mouth said to the other, "We'll go out tomorrow night if this is not found out. But if it is, why I've got another tunnel under way that was just begun before this was thought of. I'll see you tomorrow."

"But," objected the other, "you don't know me by sight. We've never met except in the dark."

"Here," said the first voice, "you'll know me by this."

Nothing more was said, I crawled away, certain in my own mind that I knew exactly what was meant by, "You'll know me by this," and just what action accompanied words. Several times I had noticed a young man hanging around the hospital while the tunnel was being dug. Barefoot, dressed in a long gray jeans frock coat, sometimes reading or pretending to read, sometimes whittling, I had identified him in my mind is one of the other digging party. One thing that I noticed about him in particular was that the nail on the little finger of his left hand was an inch long. When I heard the words, "You'll know me by this," I was certain in my own mind that it was this man who put out his left hand to his companion, to feel the nail.

I crawled out and found it almost day, August 29/64. After breakfast, I went to my bunk and turned in for a good long nap, telling Baxter to be ready for a long tramp that night. But sometime during the day a friend came in and said, "Have you heard the bad news? The tunnel has been betrayed."

The commandant of Elmira Prison was Major Henry V. Colt, a brother of the Colt pistol fame. Though our tunnels were broken up with pickaxes, and what workers could be found out, lodged in the guardhouse, the commandant is reported to have said: "I must keep those fellows close, or they'll getaway yet. If we hadn't caught them, they'd be halfway to Dixie by now. Well, I feel sorry for them, they deserved to succeed." This made me feel kindly toward him, realizing that he did not punish the men from cruelty, but merely to restrain them from and repetition of the attempt. The attendance at the guardhouse honored the tunnelers with the title of the "Engineer Corps," and would not allow them to do any of the dirty work about the guardhouse, making the criminals do it all.

Now that the old tunnel was broken up, I felt anxious to gain admittance into the one I had heard mentioned before, and so began to look for my barefoot friend in the long coat and with the Chinese fingernail. But amidst several thousand people you can't find the man you want whenever you want him, and so my search for some time went unrewarded.

Meanwhile daily life at Elmira followed a routine regular as clockwork. Roll call came first, then breakfast at eight. The menu to, followed a regular routine—so many days we had pork, so many days beef, so many days being soup for dinner, so many days vegetable soup. The vegetable soup was made of a compound of several kinds of vegetables dried and pressed together in cakes resembling a plug of tobacco, not much liked by our men, the bean soup being much more popular. The "early settlers" reported that they had been serve coffee at breakfast until July 4th it was abruptly discontinued, no one knew why.

Since we couldn't be made to fight under the stars and stripes, we were made to eat under them, for along the joists above lay two immense flags that the boys cracked an infinite number of jokes about. The table furnishings were all of tin; the plates were shallow and didn't hold much soup. At first there were plenty of spoons, but the boys stole so many that a fellow was lucky to find a spoon alongside his plate, and many times we had to drink it from the sides of our plates. Sometimes soup would be left over in the kitchen, and then the officers would kindly announced that all who wanted extra soup might fall in line. The falling in was pretty general, it may be well believed. Once there was a line of men formed to go in, when, seeing in it a man I had something to say to, I walked up to him, not getting into the line, but simply standing alongside to speak to him, when an officer came up and ordered me off, struck me. Under this indignity, I had such feelings as never before in my life. To this day, I can hardly forgive myself for not striking back. I went straight to my quarters, trembling all over for a long time.

I have told how the men traded in crackers and tobacco at Point Lookout. At Elmira there was a regular marketplace where all the trading was done. I think it was the first day after my arrival that I was drawn thither by the sound of a fiddle, and there was a man playing away, with a crowd around him, on a fiddle which he had made of white pine (probably cracker boxes) and now offering for sale. Here, too, the currency was tobacco, the value of a "ration" being a third of a plug. Since coffee was no longer served us, certain prisoners took to vending it. Having bought coffee, one would make a big boiler full and carry it around to sell— hot coffee, so much for a cracker, a cup full for so much tobacco cut off a plug. The place where this or anything else was cooked was the edge of the pool. Clever little fireplaces or "furnaces" as the men call them, were constructed, in which all the heat was so well utilized that a whole meal might be cooked of a single shingle split up fine. Shingles and bits of pine were obtained by begging the Carpenters for waste when new buildings were going up. If not given away, it was stolen, which was just a satisfactory. To steal from prison authorities was considered a worthy exploit, but to steal from a comrade a man had to sink to the lowest depths of depravity.

When we first came, the water in the pool was clean; the men caught a good many fish there. But after a while the pool became so foul from the kitchen slops being thrown there that it began to stagnate and the authorities had some chemicals thrown in, which turned the water green and killed all the fish. Every morning the shore would be lined with the white bellies of dead fish.

I have said that the far side of the pool was low and sandy; it was also covered with grass and weeds, and the men would sometimes go there and gather "lamb's quarter" or other such wild stuff as was known to be edible, of which there were a good many kinds that were known to those skilled in such craft.

Another item of fare which was not on the list furnished by the government was—rat! The prison swarmed with them—big rusty fellows which lived about the "cook house" as the kitchen was always called, and also under the houses used as quarters. The floors of these houses were close to the ground, and the sides came down all the way. The rats burrowed holes underneath to go in and out, sometimes as large a man as a man's leg. Down on the bank of the pool they burrowed great holes extending far underground. It was a usual sight at dusk, when the rats would be scampering about, to see men down on the bank with stones watching for a rat to come out, and when he appeared, such a chase and such a volley of stones! You would've thought it was our Battalion of Sharpshooters in charge. Most of the boys followed this kind of chase for excitement. But I think there is little doubt of the truth of the stories told that some broiled and ate them.

Among the prisoners was one named Williams who had a little dog, a terrier, and the two together made an unceasing war upon the rats. The dog, of course, was worth his weight in—I can't say gold; I must say tobacco—and the spoils of the chase kept him well fed. Once Williams was arrested for prowling around camp in the middle of the night. Taken to headquarters next morning, he was asked by the Major, "What were you doing?"

"Hunting, sir."

"What were you hunting?"

"Rats."

Inquiring further, the major was told that the rats were fed to the dog, the skin sold to make gloves, and that the nightly catch usually a dozen or more. After thinking a moment, the major call the sergeant and instructed: "Sergeant, have this man detailed on special duty—to catch rats. Have double rations issued to him—one for himself and one for his dog." Turning to the prisoner, he continued, "Now Williams, report to me every morning with the rats you have caught."

After that, every morning, Williams was seen at headquarters with the string of rats in his hand—or so the story was told to me.

Our drinking water came from wells, into which the rats used to fall down and drown, the water becoming so unbearable that somebody would have to go down and clean it out; it seemed to me that we were always cleaning out the wells.

There was a strange character in a prison who went by the name of Buttons. A large man, he wore a large gray frock coat and rather long tails, which at a distance looked like a veritable coal of mail. For this coat was literally covered with brass buttons, hundreds of them, so that in the sunshine he fairly glistened. Where he got the buttons to gratify his strange taste, I never heard; and I never heard him called by any other name then "Buttons." It was generally true that whenever soldiers would hit upon a nickname which was in any way characteristic, that name would take preference over the legitimate one. Examples are: "Gator" of Co. H.; Munnerlyn was always called "Old Son"; Rothwell was called "Promptly"; Peagler, invariably addressed as Mister Peagler; and a Scotsman named Smythe, who was dubbed "City of Glasgow". In prison, where there were men from all sections, the most frequent nickname was that of one state. At Elmira I was called "South C'lina" more often than "Benson."

The prison kept growing in population until there was said to be 10,000—quite a little city in itself. Tents were set up on the far side of the pool and occupied as quarters, and free passage was allowed between the sections except at night. Amongst so many prisoners deaths were necessarily frequent, and at one time the mortality rate was pretty bad. It was reported amongst us that one of the Federal surgeons said this excessive mortality was the result of insufficient food—that we got enough to sustain life, but not enough to resist disease. Personally I never believed that a Federal surgeon said this.

One day a number of prisoners were brought in, and as usual we crowded around to see if any friends were amongst them. I noticed a prisoner standing apart, who appeared to be under special guard, and so we proved to be. He had attempted to escape on the route, and by now was to be punished by close confinement. While close confinement may have been warranted, the abuse I now saw heaped upon him by some of the officers certainly was not. He was treated as though he had done something mean in criminal. This man was a sort of lay preacher. He was called insulting names, and even told that his attempt to escape was inconsistent with his profession of religion, as though to remain a captive when caught were a sacred duty. There were a good many preachers in prison; we used to have preaching every Sunday and sometimes oftener; and there were constant prayer meetings in various parts of the camp. Once a brother of Henry Ward Beecher came to preach to us, and afterward for a long time he returned on every third Sunday.

During this time I considered various plans of escape, even trying to figure out how I might go out the covered wagon that drove out daily with the dead. Most of all, I continue to look for my fellow workmen of that eventful night in the destroyed tunnel, him of the

146

Chinese fingernail. I hunted all sorts of places, preachings and prayer meetings, the market—any place where numbers of men gathered together. I even stayed about outside the dining room stirring meal hours, inspecting the various boards as they marched in. Finally one morning early I was strolling down by the pool when my eyes fell on the familiar long frock coat, and the figure of the man I sought.

He strode deliberately and unconcerned ability down to the edge of the pool and there took a seat, I watching him. He put his hand in his coat pocket, and taking out something, dropped it gently in the water at his feet. The motion was repeated. Then again and again. But I did not need even the second movement to know exactly what he was doing. He was getting rid of stones that he had dug out of his tunnel! I felt alarmed lest amongst the men standing around, there might be someone sharp enough to define the meaning of his actions—some oath taker may be, who would betray him.

I walked down to him, when seen me approach, he stopped his work and folded his arms across his knees. I said quietly, "You'd better be careful; some fellow may see you and tell on you."

"Tell what? I'm not doing anything!"

"I saw you putting stones in the water."

"Well, there's no harm in that, is there?"

"No, if you are not digging a tunnel. No man would take such pains to dispose a few stones if you were not digging a tunnel. Here, I'll stand between you and the crowd. Empty your pockets."

Without another word, he get rid of all of his stones; then rising said, "Walk with me a little way."

When we were away from the crowd, he said, "Yes, I am digging a tunnel. There is a party of us, and were bound by oath not to even hint of it to the dearest friend. But since you found out without my telling you, I have no doubt that if you want to join us, the boys will be glad enough to take you when. We need another good hand."

I told him that was exactly what I wanted, adding that I had been with him in the other tunnel though he did not know it. He then appointed the time and place of the meeting— the third tent from the end in the second row from the wall. Arriving at the appointed time, I found in the tent a little party of 45—all strangers. Introduced by my Alabama friend, whose name was Traweek, we shook hands all around. When all had been assented to by becoming a member, a Testament was brought, and with my hand upon it, I took solemn oath not to divulge by word or sign the existence of the party or its operations. In order to avoid disputes as to precedents, it was a law of the group that the men should go out of the tunnel, upon its completion, in the order in which they had been admitted to the society. There were nine before me in the group, of which several were not present. As the 10th man, I felt my chances of escape would not be great, for I believe that not more than three or four were likely to get away without discovery. Still there was a chance, and I determined to go to work with all my energy, not neglecting meanwhile any other opportunity that might offer.

The oath being taken, a blanket was turned back from the bed, the dried grass used as a bed scraped away, two short pieces of plank taken up, and the mouth of the tunnel revealed. It was a pit about waist deep in between 2 and 2 ½ feet square. At the bottom on the side nearest the fence was the beginning of the tunnel proper. The tent from which it started was near the northeast corner of the prison, and the distance to the fence or wall was roughly estimated as between 50 and 60 feet. One line of tents being between it and the fence, we would have to pass under one tent. At the time I joined, the tunnel had attained a length of about 15 feet. Its entrance was a great improvement on that of the one I had started, for I had begun mine by slanting it down at the proper depth, and it was hard to back out of it. But as this one began with a perpendicular shaft, all one had to do was to straighten himself up when he got to the shaft.

I now set to work in good earnest. It might be supposed that night was the best time for this work, but seldom was anything done after nine at night, the dangers of detection being greater after silence had settled over the prison. Our best time was between sundown and 8 o'clock when activity was at its peak, and actually a good deal of digging went on during the day. Luckily the sergeant of our ward was a Confederate and moreover he was one of us. He would always announce to us when an inspection was to take place. But sometimes we had to wait two or three days before the officers finally came, and during that time nothing could be done, for fear of discovery.

One great trouble was disposing of the dirt and stones taken from the tunnel. Sometimes one of the men would venture on taking out a haversack full of dirt under a big coat. But the usual means was a little sacks we had made to fit into our pockets. Some of this was emptied into the sinks, some into the rat holes, while the bank of a new ditch being dug was regarded as a splendid place. Once during a rain at night we strew dirt along the street, expecting the rain to obliterate all traces. It did well enough to escape general observation, but we could detected in the morning, and were uneasy.

The stones, except for the biggest ones, where an easier matter. A few large ones we had to sneak out with after dark and drop them quietly in the pool. I'm not sure but that some of the biggest were buried in the tent. The smaller stones were easy to get rid of. I would fill my coat pockets with them take a book, which I pretended to read, sit down with my back against one of the buildings where the floor came nearly to the ground and with a twitch of my hand send a stone far back under the building. One building was a favorite of mine until finally I had thrown so many stones under that house that I could not throw another without hearing it hit some stone that had gone before. A favorite place to deposits stones was in the rat holes. I would sit by a rat hole and drop the stones in until I could see the top stones, then moved to another hole. The next day it would be filled again, for in the night the rats would move all the stones away in order to get in and out of their hole. Then when in the dusk the rats were running about, the men after them with stones, we would fill our pockets and join in the chase. There was no such lavish expenditure of ammunition amongst other hunters as with us. All our stones, moreover, were so thrown as to bounce eventually into the pool, lest their fresh, earthly look might next day excite suspicion. And we did not at all need to see a real rat. In the dusk and imaginary one might be chaste, with cries of, "Here he goes--kill him!" and a terrific bombardment of stones. Outsiders coming up to join the chase never guessed that there was no rat, but thought simply that he had got away.

That was the way the stuff was disposed of; the tunneling itself was harder. The blankets and dried grass having been removed and the planks taken up, got into the shaft. Then on hands and knees you crawled into the tunnel and lay flat. Beyond the first body length, the tunnel decreased in size until it was only large enough to admit the body, and in some places it was a squeeze at that. Thus only the toes and the points of the elbows were used propelling yourself forward. Having got to the end of the tunnel, your body blocking the way behind, and leaving the least bit of air in front to breathe, you fell to with a butcher knife, one of a supply the boys had managed to steal from the cookhouse. In less than a minute you were panting like a dog--for air. A minute was enough to give one the most violent, racking headache, and you knew perfectly well in entering the tunnel that you had this to expect.

When the digger had loosened so much of the dirt and stones as to incommode him, he laid down his knife and crawled backward, scooping the earth back with his hands and arms until he had carried it about the length of his body. Then he crawled forward and resumed his digging, by now fighting against suffocation. An assistant crawled in behind him and removed the dirt to the tunnel's mouth, scooping it along with his hands and arms as he inched himself laboriously backward. When the man at the end could stand the suffocation no longer, his head seeming about to burst with pain, his tongue thrust out, breathing fast to keep his blood supplied with the poisoned air, he called to the man behind him to "back out," and both backed to the shaft, and a fresh couple went in.

To keep our clothes from getting so covered with fresh dirt as to attract attention, those of us who managed to secure extra shirt and trousers or drawers, kept them especially for excavation. But those of us who could secure no change of clothes turned our clothes wrong side out to go into the tunnel. Traweek was the best tunneler in the party, and I was generally accounted second best, this being gauged by what we could accomplish under the suffocating conditions which we must endure. One of our best workmen, Fox Maull, had to give up work in the tunnel entirely, being seized with nausea and violent vomiting, from breathing the poison air. But he made up for it by zeal at other tasks.

Being bound by oath, I could not say a word to Baxter; but from a few things he let drop, I inferred that he attributed my prolonged absences to the right cause. Nor could I hint of it to my friends Adams and Atkinson, both of whom were most generous in sharing with me gifts they had received from some friends they had in the north. When I coveted a pocket compass on sale at the camp for 30cts, Adams bought it and presented it to me, and I could not tell him the use I hoped to make of it. He also told me the name and address of the lady in Baltimore who had befriended him, and I stored it in my mind, thinking it might be useful if I found myself a fugitive in that city.

A new friend I had made in the prison was Jack Kibler, a cavalryman from Virginia, whose hardihood, strength, and knowledge of the border country would have made him an ideal companion in an attempt to escape, and he was as bent upon escape as I was. I fell in with the plan of his for scaling the wall with the ladder, helping him to steal lumber, and make the ladder, which, in sections, he hid under his bed. Being extremely doubtful that fugitives from the tunnel could escape detection so far as the 10th man, I was ready to participate in alternate plans which might prove feasible.

But the tunnel continued undiscovered so long that we grew more and more hopeful every day, and worked harder than ever. Dirt went out by the haversackful, and stones by the score. With the prospect of early completion, I determined that for the present I would do nothing in any other direction, but bend all my efforts towards the completion of the tunnel.

The length of the tunnel was measured with a string and compared with the estimated distance from its mouth to the fence, and it was found that we ought to be within three feet of the fence. But as we worked at the end of the tunnel, the footsteps of the guards passing on the rounds just inside the fence did not appear to pass overhead but some distance away. We held a conclave and I proposed that one of us should go to the end of the tunnel and listen to blows which on some pretext should be struck on the ground. So a piece of tin was procured, and a piece cut off in her rough imitation of a spoon. About four of us took this out on the grass about where we thought the end of the tunnel should be. Sitting down, one began hammering away on the tin, using one stone is a hammer, another as an anvil, making all the noise possible, for the benefit of the listener in the tunnel. If the sentinel on the fence heard us talking about "making a spoon" and "bringing it into shape" he paid little attention, for he had seen Johnny Reb hammering out a tin spoon before.

Directly a man came from the tent and joining us quietly said, "He says you're too far to the left."

We shifted position to the right and commenced hammering again.

Presently came another man strolling from the tent, who sat down casually, took the spoon and looked at it, with the remark, "He says you're still too far to the left."

We shifted position to the right and commenced hammering again.

Watching until the two nearest sentries turned their backs, we shifted again, further to the right, and again commenced hammering. Directly we saw the man from inside the tunnel standing unconcernedly outside the tent door. Leaving our stones to mark the spot, we adjourned with our spoon, such as it was. When the tunnel are declared that the last knocking had been right over his head, we felt sure that he must be somehow mistaken. But we dared not repeat the experiment right away, lest so much activity excite suspicion.

Then he thought struck me and I said, "Let's run a little hole up through the roof from the end of the tunnel. I know where we can get a ramrod, and the small hole it will make won't be noticed."

The men agreeing, I went in search of a man I'd seen that morning with an iron ramrod. With this heated red hot, he had been hollowing out a hole in a walking stick he'd made. Guessing his purpose, I had said, "Going to send a letter home, aren't you?"

Looking up surprised he said, "No. Why do you think so?"

"You're boring that hole to put a letter in, and you'll give the stick to a friend in that batch of prisoners there making up for exchange. You don't want Major Colt reading your letter—that's all." The man still looking at me in surprise, I added, "Don't be afraid of my telling on you. I'm no oath taker."

I found my man easily, and he lent me his ramrod willingly, grateful that I had not told on me. While a man inside the tunnel worked the ramrod slowly up to the surface, several stood around talking, about where we expected it to come up. Directly one made a step forward, putting his foot on the end of the ramrod is a came through a tuft of grass very close to the stones with which we had marked the spot. We now knew exactly where we were. But what a crook in the tunnel this indicated! We were about 10 feet off from where a straight line drawn from the tunnel's mouth to the fence.

After talking it over we came to the conclusion that the curve in our tunnel was due to right handedness. To get the proper use of the right hand, the digger had to lie on his left side. The tendency was thus always to work a little to the front, and the tunnel continually

150

inclined to the right. Someone now suggested that the aperture made by the ramrod be enlarged a little, thus obtaining for the diggers a supply of fresh air, which was increasingly needed as the tunnel grew in length. So we widened the tunnel a little at this point, and dug away some of the dirt overhead, making a little chamber from which a man could sit hunched, his knees drawn up to his chin. Then we enlarge the ramrod hole to about the size of three fingers, and the "Ventilator" was made. When we worked at night the hole in the surface was left open, without fear of discovery. In the day, two or three men would set around reading, talking, or playing mumble peg, ready to cover it if need arose. When we were not at work, a stone was laid over it.

One day an order came from Major Colt for Traweek to report to headquarters. Supposing that he had got a "money letter" or a box from home, we awaited his return without alarm. We waited and waited, but he did not return. Finally the Orderly Sergeant, who as I have said, was of our party, went to inquire. He came back with the dreadful news that Traweek was not only in the guardhouse, but locked up in a cell! This had only one meaning for us—our plot was discovered, we would all be arrested and lodged in cells, escape further away than ever. As the moments slipped by, we wondered why we are not arrested.

At dinner time, the Orderly carried Traweek his dinner, and Traweek told him what it happen. Talking with some friends, Traweek had unwisely bragged about his part in digging the other tunnels, the ones from the hospital that have been destroyed. An oath taker, overhearing his remarks, had reported him. It was a great relief to know our tunnel was safe. But how about Traweek? He had been originator and moving spirit of this enterprise, and all agreed that we could not desert him. I don't know just how it was managed, but tools were secured and smuggled into him, and Traweek managed to loosen the planks across the top of his cell so that they could be removed at any time. Through the opening thus made, he could reach the loft, once through a back window he could let himself down to the ground. We would send him word when the tunnel was ready and he could escape from his cell that night and join us.

Major Colt had questioned Traweek as to his confederates in the hospital tunnel, but Traweek had declared that he didn't know a soul. He finally admitted under pressure that he did know one man named Jim but insisted that he knew neither his other name, nor his ward. The Major finally said, "Very well, I'll lock you in a cell until you find this Jim." Every now and then the Major would drop by the guardhouse, have Traweek brought out, and ask him in a joking kind of way, "Well, have you found Jim yet?" knowing full well that Jim was a Johnny Reb born of Traweek's imagination. And Traweek would laugh and answer, "No sir, Major, not yet."

Finally the Major sent Tray week word that he would release him if he would give his word of honor not to try to escape from prison again. Traweek sent back word that he thanked him but could not in justice to himself make such a promise, for if an opportunity to escape should present itself, he would feel bound to take advantage of it. To this, the Major is said to have replied, "Oh, very well! There is no other tunnel going on that I'm aware of, and it is hardly probable they'll break down the fence." (How we tunnelers chuckled over this, for that very moment our tunnel was near completion, and we had a little army prepared with a ladder ready, if not to break down the fence, in any rate to climb over it.)

After we had progressed a little way beyond the Ventilator, we experienced the same suffocation while digging as we had before. But the Ventilator caused some change and improvement in the way of working. The diggers still haul the dirt as before to the one behind him. But the dirt-remover now stayed huddled in the ventilator, getting fresh air, until signaled. He still must rake the dirt with hands and arms as far as the ventilator, but there he deposited it in a small wooden box which had two long, strong chords fastened to it, one at each end. He then gave a rap on the box as a signal, a man in the tent pulled it in, the man at the ventilator letting the cord slip through his hands. The passage of the box, however, was never made smoothly; it was always catching on some projecting rock and having to be pulled back a little way and given a fresh start.

So, besides those who kept going in and out of the tent, disposing of dirt and stones, the work took four men—one to dig, one in the ventilator, one in the shaft, and one to stand at the door and keep anybody from coming in. For any friend would just have parted the flaps of the tent and walked right in, if no one had been at the entrance to prevent. Coming to pay a visit, such as a friend would be told, "Don't go in right now; Traweek is washing all over" or "Don't go in now; Maull is dressing." Such visitors must have thought these dwellers in tents to have been a remarkably modest set of men.

It was now early in October. On Wednesday, October 5th we knew by measurement that we're close to the fence, and our ears confirmed this, for we could hear the guards tramp right over our heads as they walked their beat just inside the fence. We worked steadily on the 5th or 6th fixing the time for our escape at 10 o'clock that night of 6th. Our Orderly Sargent, who did no work inside the tunnel on account of a wounded arm, but had been invaluable in other ways, now decided not to go with us. Besides being handicapped by his wound, he had been given reason to hope for an early exchange, along with some other sick and wounded. This would've advanced me to 9th place instead of 10th. Looking north towards the mountains, we could see a broad highway winding around the fields. Some of the men said, "That leads to Canada; that's the road I'm going to take." As for me, I had no other thought nor wish than to go south and rejoin Lee's army.

On the sixth I got everything ready: 2 pocket knives; half of a kit to cook in; a few matches; I pencil map; my pocket compass; and some strong cord to serve as a bridal if I could steal a horse. We fixed a point of woods in the mountains to meet and have a last talk and final goodbye. Most of the men were going in couples. I was again going alone.

As it grew dark we prepared for action. No dirt was to be carried outside tonight; it was to be left in the tent. Traweek took first turn at the digging, I in the ventilator. Being the fastest workers, we were to do the remainder of the digging. But there was more work to be done than had been expected. At 10 o'clock we had not yet reached the fence. About that time a heavy storm passed over—just the thing for an escape! It looked as though fate had made an appointment with us and we had failed to come to time.

In the tunnel the knife plugged away steadily, the box slid back and forth with its load of dirt. Traweek would stand the suffocation as long as he could, then we must both back out all the way to the tent and change places, I going in first to take my turn. In the tent was an eager listening to the faint sounds from the tunnel, low whispers, a grasp on a fellows arm at any sound from without. In all hearts were hope, fear, and anxiety, as the box slid back and forth and a knife pegged away.

152

I became wretchedly sick, with a violent headache and nausea, and so did Traweek. Once as I crawled back to the ventilator, the roof of the tunnel broke in, quantities of dirt and stone falling on my legs. But as no rush of fresh air followed, I knew that the surface had not been broken. I called quietly to the shaftsman, who came to remove the dirt. This consumed much time. It was now past midnight.

Once as I occupied the ventilator, I worked my hand up to widen the hole a little, to admit more air. This could do no harm now, it being the last night. Traweek called, "Benson, let's change; I can't stand it any longer."

This time, instead of inching slowly backwards the length of the tunnel, I squeezed my back against one side of the ventilator, saying, "Traweek, see if we can't pass one another here." Down he came slowly, first his feet in my face, then further and further, while I jammed myself against the side of the tunnel. Now we were face-to-face. I tried to move forward, but could not. He tried to move down, and he could not. We could move neither way—we were wedged! We had begun to think we had made an end of it, when a desperate effort set us free, and I went to digging, he to the ventilator.

And now as I plied the knife, my head seemed on the point of bursting. My mouth wide open, tongue protruding, panting like a dog, I felt the lack of breath not in my lungs only, but in my whole body. With every beat of my heart, great throbs of pain coursed through me. Having stayed as long as I could, I was relieved by Traweek, we passing one another more easily at the ventilator this time.

When he next called for relief, Traweek told me that he had struck a big rock which projected downward from the roof of the tunnel. He was afraid to use force against it, as it might break the surface. I found it as he said, and very much in the way. After feeling all around it carefully, I gave a quick French and it fell, broken into, the upper part remaining in the roof. During his next turn at digging Traweek called softly, "Benson, I've struck a fence post!"

"Good!" I whispered back, for this meant that our digging was near an end. Taking my turn, I worked to the right around the post, until I knew the end of the tunnel was outside the fence. Feeling that I was dying for air, I reached up my hand and worked it through the pebbly soil, which came raining down in my face--my eyes shut, for what use are eyes in the tunnel? I felt cold air on my fingers, and withdrew my arm, the cold stream following. I lay on my back, enjoying that feast of air, that luxury of breath. Then I crawled back and sent Traweek up to get his share of it.

Pretty soon we had hollowed out all but a thin shell on top, and our last work was to dig a hole under that for the dirt to drop into when the break was made. Then Traweek and I went out and announced that the tunnel was ready, and the boys began gathering up what they needed to take with them, I slipping into my quarters to get my coat and shoes. Baxter was awake, late though it was. Because of my oath, I could only say something unimportant, and with a sad heart leave him, not even saying goodbye.

Back in the tent, the exit had not yet begun, and as the departures were to be made at considerable intervals, it would take some time. So I lay down, to get some ease for my head, which almost crazed me. Directly I fell into a sort of doze, only half conscious of what was going on in the tent. I was suffering such pain in my head that I didn't much care whether I went or stayed. In this half conscious state I heard someone say, "They are still working in the tunnel."

153

I started to my feet. It was Shelton speaking; only he, the seventh man, and his companion, the eighth, remained in the tent. He said that he had been down in the tunnel and had heard those who had gone before, down at the end working. When I protested this could not be the case, since Traweek and I had finished the tunnel, he still believed that he had heard the men inside.

I said, "Let me go in then, I'll find them out."

He agreed, saying, "If you find the way clear, call back to us."

Having crawled nearly to the ventilator, I knew that six men could not be stowed in the remainder of the tunnel, so I called back to Shelton come on. In a few minutes I was at the outer mouth of the tunnel, finding all open, above me the platform running around outside the fence. I raised my head and looked out. On the other side of the street stood three sentinels with rifles, around the fire. I crawled out and wormed my way along under the platform, close to the fence, toward the town. After a little, I got on my hands and knees and went faster, the sentinel tramping along above my head. When I had got a tree between me and the three sentinels, I rose to my feet and walked rapidly along under the platform to the corner of the prison. What I had now to do was full of risk. I had to step out from under the platform in full view of the sentinels on it. At a brisk pace, not hurrying, I stepped out across the street diagonally, not turning my head, though I felt every moment that I would hear a shot and feel a bullet pierce my back. But there was no shot and no challenge. Reaching the other side of the street, I walked quickly down the pavement about 40 yards. Then fearing I might meet some sentinel or patrol, I jumped into a front yard, and ran into the backyard and then into a vegetable garden, when a big dog made at me. I jumped the back fence into a lane, and away I fled toward the mountain.

I ran until exhausted, then stopped and looked back. There lay the prison under its bright lights, white with tents, populous with a sleeping multitude. And there were the pickets, the blind pickets, calmly walking their beats. It is to be wondered at that I should give vent to my joy in unseemly ways, jumping up and cracking my heels together, throwing my hat in the air? As I made my way to the point of woods where we had engaged to meet, it was all I could do to keep from shouting "The Bonnie Blue Flag" at the top of my voice.

Sergeant Thaddeus C. Davis

36th Regiment, 2nd Artillery Division

A Tarheel Soldier's Story

Thaddeus C. Davis enlisted as a private in the 36th Regiment, 2nd Artillery Division, North Carolina troops in Beaufort, NC. Davis was sent to Fort Fisher and was promoted to 3rd sergeant in 3rd Company G on November 14, 1862. He transferred to the 40th Regiment NC, 3rd Artillery division on November 4, 1863 and was stationed at Fort Holmes. During this period, he maintained a home at Smithville, NC. On November 22, 1864 five companies of the 40th NC were ordered to Georgia to reinforce Lt. General William J. Hardee, who was contesting Sherman's advance on Savannah. In December the 40th NC along with the 60th NC infantry served as a rear guard as Hardee's army retired through Savannah, Hardeeville, and into Charleston, SC. On December 30th, 1864, the 40th Regiment received orders to return to Wilmington, NC, and reinforce Fort Fisher. Sergeant Davis was captured at Fort Fisher on January 15th, 1865, and sent north to Elmira Prison. After the war he wrote an article about the second battle of Fort Fisher and his imprisonment in Elmira Prison Camp that was published in the *Confederate Veteran* Magazine in the February 1899 issue. Here is a reprint of that article:

Sergeant Thaddeus C. Davis, 3rd Company G, 40th North Carolina

T. C. Davis (Fortieth Regiment, North Carolina Troops), of Morehead City, N. C.:

In January, 1865, after the evacuation of Atlanta, five companies of the North Carolina Regiment of Hardee's command were ordered to reinforce the command at Fort Fisher, N. C., which, at that time, was the "key to the Confederacy."

We arrived on the 13th of January, 1865, at the beginning of the second attack on that fort, which was garrisoned with about twelve hundred soldiers. The Federals had a navy of eighty-four vessels, carrying six hundred heavy guns. After bombarding the fort for three days and nights, and disabling all of our guns except two or three, they landed about eleven thousand infantry, under the guns of their navy, and assaulted the fort. They succeeded in making lodgment in the fort about three o'clock Sunday evening, January 15, and the contest kept up until ten o'clock at night. The fort, with its garrison, was captured.

The Federal loss, as stated by Gen. Terry in his official report, was 1,445. The Confederate loss is not known, though it is estimated at 500, including Gen. W. H. C. Whiting and Col. William Lamb.

155

On January 16 we were put on board a ship and sent to Fortress Monroe, Va., from whence we were to be sent to Fort Delaware; but we got stuck in the ice at the breakwater, and the ship backed out and took us to New York City. We were sent by rail for that den of misery known as Elmira Prison, about one mile from Elmira, N. Y.

We arrived about eight o'clock in the evening, in four feet of snow, and many prisoners had neither blankets nor coats. We were kept standing in ranks in the street for half an hour before starting for the prison. We were halted in an old warehouse and robbed of all valuables by Lieut. Groves and an unknown Sergeant Major; then we were sent to the barracks-board shanties about fifty yards long, containing one stove. Our beds were planks without blankets.

There were about seven thousand prisoners confined there, and those who had preceded us were in much want. They were dirty, pale, emaciated, and scantily clothed. Our rations consisted of loaves of stale bread an inch thick, tough pieces of steak, and occasionally broth. When prisoners died, their bodies were put in a box and stacked up in a "deadhouse" as high as they could stack them before taking them out for burial.

The Federal Sergeants who had charge of the prison "wards" (as they were called) were the meanest men I ever saw-demons in human flesh. There was a young soldier about eighteen years old, without blanket or coat, who had become deaf from exposure. When he was found near the stove, he was beaten and kicked about unmercifully. Gen. Weyler's treatment of the Cuban prisoners is nothing, compared to the treatment the Confederate' soldiers received at Elmira, N. Y. After the war, we were turned out in squads of two hundred, by taking the oath. I was truly glad to get out of prison, but sorry to be deprived of my watch and ring, which were stolen by Lieut. Groves and the sergeant major. I arrived at home on June 1, 1865, and while memory lasts I shall not forget the Great War and the cruel prison.

Private Wilbur W. Gramling

Company K of the 5th Florida Infantry

The following excerpts are from a diary kept by Wilbur Wightman Gramling after he was wounded and captured as a Confederate soldier in the Wilderness campaign and while in prison in Washington and in Elmira. A copy of the Macon, Ga., *Southern Christian Advocate* in Mr. Gramling's possession carries an obituary of W.W. Gramling. The newspaper, dated Jan. 25, 1871, said W.W. Gramling was born March 30, 1843, in Spartanburg District, S.C., son of Andrew P. and Elizabeth Gramling. After being captured in the Battle of the Wilderness, he spent 15 months in a federal prison camp and while there contracted pneumonia. He died in Leon County on Dec. 3, 1870, apparently from the effects of this disease, the newspaper said.

The daily diary was kept in ink (some of the entries being badly faded). In the front of the diary is this entry, "W.W. Gramling, May 25th. 1864. Colonial Hospital, Washington, D.C." Inside the back cover are some arithmetic calculations and the entry, 'I-want-to-go-home-so—bad."

Please Note: All spelling and grammatical errors are as they were written by the author of the diary.

Friday, May 6, 1864. Went into battle 2 o'clock. Wounded in the right arm and taken prisoner. Sent to rear in great pain. Had ball out and wound dressed. About 600 prisoners with me.

Saturday, May 7, 1864. Went to Hospital 1st Div. 9th Army Corps. Wound dressed and doing well. Started to rear but cut off by Moseby. Camped on Rappadan River. Considerable uneasyness afraid Mosby will make a dash on them.

Sunday, May 8, 1864. Came back by Chancellorsville and camped near Fredericksburg. All fair weather and wound doing finely. Got on the road to Moseby again today and had to turn back. I have been wishing he would recapture me. Did retake one from my regiment.

Monday, May 9, 1864. Arrived at Fredericksburg only this morning. Established hospital in a Presbyterian Church. Nothing to eat but hard bread, coffee, beef, and tea and every two or three days 2 oz. boiled beef.

Tuesday, May 17, 1864. All quiet. Weather fair. Three butter crackers for supper. Wound still improving. A great many vague rumors among the Yankees in regard to their successes. They have had it read to them on dress parade that Richmond was theirs.

Wednesday, May 18, 1864. A great many wounded came in last night from the front. I asked Dr. to let me walk out for recreation but would not allow me even with a guard. Reports from the front say the forces attacked with bayonets. They repulsed or captured a force including our battery of artillery, their report.

Saturday, May 21, 1864. Arrived at Washington this morning at daybreak. Now in hospital on the north side of town, is called Columbian Hospital. Saw Abe Lincoln's house. Very comfortably situated. Baked bread, coffee, meat, apples, some corn meal and syrup. Another cot to lie on.

Sunday, May 22, 1864. A beautiful morning. Shower rain at noon. Health good and wound doing well. I see negroes riding out in fine carriages with their driver sometimes a negro.

Man & a white woman riding together in a carriage with a negro driver. Frequently see them walking together.

Thursday, May 26, 1864. Rainy all day. 200 more wounded came in. Papers are full of vain rumors. Lee is still retreating and nearly cut off from Richmond, Jeff Davis is captured by Grant and paroled. Don't know whether he will be summarily hanged or not. Some believe it, therefore are all very jubilant.

Tuesday, May 31, 1864. Every thing quiet today. The weather fair & pleasant. My health good, wound doing well. Some ladies in today to see Col. Manning. Brought him some grub. Still at Lincoln Hospital. Now what composes it is a building 100 feet long & 25 feet wide forming a triangle and a large number to tents. In all I suppose there is over 3000 wounded here and perhaps 200 rebs. I think this is nearly the last place in creation. It is right out in the open field. It is so very hot. I understand that 18,000 men are to leave here tomorrow for the front. Yanks still in good spirits & are looking up to Grant expecting him to crush out the rebellion this summer. If he does it by the 5th of June will be nominated as candidate for President. He won't do it.

Friday, June 24, 1864. Very fair and warm this morning. Sold $10.00 in gold for $18.00 in green-backs & bought 1 plug tobacco, 2 boxes of matches & pr suspenders this p.m. Suffering good deal with backache again. The boys all keep in pretty good spirits so far.

Wednesday, July 6, 1864. Weather fair and pleasant. No change in things generally as I know. The wounded are most all doing very well. Some cases of gangrene which I think will be fatal.

Thursday, July 7, 1864. Very fair and pretty day though quite warm. No change in things generally, good deal of excitement about Frederick and Hagerstown, Md. Our forces making pretty good head-way. Last dispatches state all the rebs have recrossed the Potomac. Men here sick.

Friday, July 8, 1864. The 8th day of July has passed & nothing has transpired worth note nor to make the day memorable. It has been a rather fair day and quite warm & sultry. The Yankees can't ascertain what force we have invading them with nor their whereabouts.

Sunday, July 10, 1864. The day has passed off very quiet. Nothing of note occurred. It is reported that our boys drove the Yankees 18 miles, killed Gen. Wallace and captured one other general—for-get his name—and are now within nine miles of Baltimore. I think Washington is threatened pretty strongly this morning.

Monday, July 11, A.M. Great deal of excitement. Won't allow any one to go out of the ward. Ward master got his repeater on caused from the invaders say they have just about got Baltimore and are coming now to take Washington. Foiled in my plan to escape. Sent part of my party off. Wrote to Irvin. P.M. Things have got a little more quiet. Reports say that they are fighting within six miles of here at Fort Manassas.

Tuesday, July 12, 1864. Fair~& pleasant this morning. Left today at noon & arrived at the old capital prison. They are very strict here. Won't let you get close to the window. Eat twice a day. Quite a dirty place, just alive with chinches one or two out at a time. Think I will get along.

Saturday, July 16, 1864. Every thing quiet today. Nothing occurred worthy note. My principal amusement is looking at the women pass. Some very pretty ones in the city of Washington. Quite a lot of cavalry are passing just now. Weather moderate.

Sunday, July 17, 1864. Today seems a great deal like Sunday & I can't help thinking of home and wishing I was at Old Pisgah. Everything remains about the same. A funeral procession passed. It was a member of the fire company. Five very pretty young ladies passed by in a carriage and one of them waved to me which is frequently the case.

Tuesday, July 19, 1864. Weather quite fair & not very warm. Our room is about 25 or 30 ft. square and has 42 men in it. Pretty well crowded about 600 or 700 prisoners. Prospects are good to be sent away soon but can't judge to what place. Rations are very short, 2 meals per day & is rumored that we will only get one hereafter.

Saturday, July 23, 1864. Left Washington 1 o'clock for Elmira. Arrival at Baltimore at 7. A great many spectators on the street. Got off the cars at Mountain House on Howard St & turned down Franklin. At Franklin house drew rations and left at 8 o'clock.

Sunday, July 24, 1864. Traveled all night and find we 170 miles from Elmira. Corn crops are very sorry. Wheat is gathered. Oats is pretty good. Traveled through the Catskill Mountains up the Susquehanna River. Crossed it 20 times. Got here 6 o'clock.

Monday, July 25, 1864. Raining all day. Very sloppy. Elmira is noted for pretty women and a good many of them. The prison is about 10 acres square with Barracks inside large enough to hold 112 men each. This is Barracks No. 3 commanded by Maj. Colt.

Wednesday July 27, 1864. It is fair & quite warm today. Though the nights are quite cool. We eat twice a day, morning at 7 o'clock & evening at 3 o'clock. Our camp or Barracks are surrounded by mountains, not very high ones though.

Friday, Aug. 5 , 1864. No news today. Everything perfectly quiet & dull as is natural in prison. Weather remains fair and quite warm. Everything seems to speak in favor of the South. The prisoners are expecting an early exchange or parole.

Thursday, Aug. 11, 1864. Everything very quiet & have rumors of exchange pretty soon but it don't amount to anything, only a falsehood. My health is still improving. Am taking salts in broken doses. My blood seems to be very thin.

Friday, Aug. 12, 1864. This is a beautiful day. The sweet little birds are chirping from branch to branch. There are a great many rumors but I don't pay any attention to these, Dear Friend, when what you do remember is the Guns.

Friday, Aug, 19, 1864. Fair and pleasant today. Suffering very much with jaw-ache. Tried to have an old root extracted & instead of getting it broke a good one off at the gums. Recd. a letter from Irvin today. He was well, also one from Washington. Have some clothes on the road.

Saturday, Aug. 20, 1864. The exchange question is still being agitated very much. Report says (said to be reliable) commencing 10th Sept. all over plus to be paroled & all to have 60 days furlough on our return. Still suffering good deal with neuralgia. Morgan of Co. D died today of Chronic diarrhea.

Friday, Aug. 26, 1864. No change in things generally. It has been a very pleasant day. Little rain this evening. Neuralgia is about well. Received the clothing today that I have been expecting from Washington. Very well pleased. No fine clothing nor provisions are allowed to be brought in—all that come are confiscated.

Saturday, Aug. 27, 1864. Wrote Miss Thomson today. Report says that Lee made a flank movement on Grant & fully demoralized his army. The news generally is very cheering. More rain this evening, I am feeling very well now.

Wednesday, Aug. 31 1864. Last night & this morning was cold, the coldest weather I ever experienced in August. It is quite pleasant this evening. August has been tolerably pleasant and pretty rainy & cloudy most all the time The news generally has been quite cheering. Most all the prisoners are looking forward for an early exchange, also are expecting peace soon. The last report (which are many in regard to exchange) is that Jeff has agreed to exchange the Negroes for the men that have enrolled their names to take the oath of allegiance to the U.S. Thomson is sick with pneumonia. Also Wilford with fever, both in the hospital. My health has been good except neuralgia. The rest of the company are well & doing as well as could be expected. So ended August.

Thursday, Sept, 1, 1864. Good deal of excitement in town last night caused by the nomination of McClellan for President. Quite a number of guns were fired. Weather remained the same as everything else does. No change in anything.

Saturday, Sept. 3, 1864. Weather still remains cool and cloudy, but no rain. Seems be more like November than September. Rumor says Atlanta has fallen with 20,000 prisoners, also that Lee has lost 15,000.

Sunday, Sept. 4, 1864. It is reported that Lee has whipped Grant again & driven him 6 miles. He calls for reinforcements, will have to retreat if not received. Papers advocate a retreat. I think more about home Sundays than any other day, not only home but old Pisgah house. Long to see the dear spot again.

Saturday, Sept. 10, 1864. Rumor says that the exchange is to take place between the 15th & 25th of this month. I can't put much faith in it though I hope it is true. Still fair & very pleasant. We have pretty strict orders. Have to be very careful what we do or how we act.

Friday, Sept. 16, 1864. This has been the most pleasant day we have had in some time. Fair & not cold. There is no news today. Wrote a letter to John T. Desellum for Blanket, draws, pants socks and money. Some rumor about the wounded & sick being sent off.

Wednesday, Sept. 21, 1864. Reported that Gen. Rhodes & Gordon are killed & 15,000 prisoners captured. Am little better today but feel quite bad yet. Men are dying up very fast, average 16 or 18 per day.

Thursday, Sept. 22, 1864. Have got about well again though my breast is very sore yet. The ex-change & parole question is being agitated again. Great many are taking the oath. Weather same. Read a letter from Irvin. Is dated the 15th.

Friday, Sept, 23, 1864. There is no news about today. Weather fair & pleasant. Am feeling some better. Wrote to Irvin today. Men are dying very fast, from 15 to 25 per day.

Saturday, Sept. 24, 1864. Surgeons have been round today examining the sick and wounded, they say to parole them. Weather very pleasant though a little cooler this evening. Health improving. I long to get back in Dixie.

Saturday, Oct. 1, 1864. No news of interest stirring today. Weather is cloudy & very cold and unpleasant. Don't expect to sleep much tonight as I only have one blanket to cover with and it is quite thin. Don't see how I am to live this winter without more cover.

Wednesday, Oct. 5, 1864. Weather remains the same. No news at all. Received a letter from & wrote to Mr. Desellum today. Taking names for clothing this evening. Health remains very good.

Friday, Oct.7, 1864. A.M. fair and pleasant. 25 army men made their escape last night by tunneling. They got 25 horses. Commenced 19th of Aug. They dug 64 ft. No news today. Report says the sick leaves in the morning. P.M. cloudy but no rain. Still hauling wood.

Tuesday, Oct. 11, 1864. Elmira Gazette states that all prisoners captured up to June are to be exchanged except those captured by Butler in front of Petersburg. The sick and wounded have got off at—last near 2000. They seemed to be very cheerful.

Thursday, Oct. 14, 1864. No news stirring today. Fair and quite cold. Received a letter from Mattie today of Sept. 17th. All well as usual. Rave not caught any of the men yet that made their escape.

Tuesday, Oct 18, 1864. Still fair & pleasant. Papers says that Sherman's army is completely annihilated. Jeff Davis speaks very cheeringly to the soldiers. I had a mess of cabbage & Irish potatoes today.

Wednesday, Oct. 19, 1864. No change in the weather & no news of any kind. The general health of the prisoners are a great deal better. Instead of 15 to 20 it is only 5 to 10 per day & it seems to be the general impression that we will winter here.

Thursday, Oct. 20, 1864. Weather somewhat unsettled but no rain. Frost every morning though the weather remains quite moderate. Prisoners are generally pretty well supplied with clothing, shoes especially.

Friday, Oct, 21, 1864. Papers state that England & France have recognized the independence of the Confederacy. Nothing else new. Weather remains the same. My health is still very good.

Sunday, Oct. 23, 1864. Cloudy but no rain today. My health has generally been good ever since I have been captured. Read my Testament almost every day. They have a Library here now & I have a book reading. The title is the Story of a Pocket Bible. Very good.

Monday, Oct. 24, 1864. More tunneling been going on but were reported by some galvanized demons. Would soon have been through. Weather cloudy but little rain. Wrote to Miss Ida Dun-canson today.

Tuesday, Oct. 25, 1864. Reported in camps that Grant has given up Petersburg and is falling back to Washington. My health remains very good. Weather very mild, fair & pleasant. The people of Elmira has kept the old cannon pretty busy today.

Monday, Oct. 31, 1864. Weather warm & wet. We have a very good market here. The principal articles of trade is apples, cooked cabbage, Tobacco, clothing, potatoes, knives &c. Officers have tried several times to break it up but have not succeeded & are not likely to. Received a letter from Mrs. Sawyer yesterday. Boxes of clothing &c, and money are being sent in daily to the men from their relatives & friends but I am somewhat among the unfortunate. The way I spend my time. 1st. Set the table & then clean up afterwards, then 2nd read & knock about until 3 O'clock & 3rd it is dinner, which I have to take an active part in, working after the rest.

Monday, Nov. 7, 1864. Weather fair & pleasant. It is very changeable, one day freezing, the next almost boiling. Comparatively no new dispatches today. Tomorrow is looked upon as the great day. General impression is that it will be a close run between Abe & Mc.

Tuesday, Nov. 8. 1864. Nothing has occurred today more than usual. Far as I know it is quite still for election day. Generally thought that it will be a close run between Abe & Mc. rather in the latter's favor.

Wednesday, Nov. 9, 1864. It is reported that Lincoln is a head as far as known. Little hopes of an exchange. Health good, weather fair & quite pleasant.

Friday, Nov. 11, 1864. Great speculation about the election. Some say that Lincoln is elected & some say Mac. Very fair but some colder though pleasant. Great many boxes packages of clothing come in daily for the rebs.

Monday, Nov. 14, 1864. Have not heard who is elected yet for president—it is a very close run. I believe it inclines to be in Lincoln's favor. Weather unsettled. Little snow & very cold. Health generally very good.

Friday, Nov. 18, 1864. Weather cloudy & warm. Fresh report about exchange. Officers are getting tighter on us every day. Keep trying to break up our market but cant quite outwit. Rebels are too smart at every point.

Saturday, Nov. 19, 1864. Unusually pleasant today & fair. seems to be no doubt but Abe is re-elected. Health improving. Everything very quiet in camp. Bought a blanket today for 75 cents.

Wednesday, Nov. 23, 1864. Weather broken & a little snow. Very cold. I am well except a severe cold. N.Y. Papers say Gen. Lee is killed. Beauregard has taken the oath & Jeff is not to be found. Wrote to Mrs. Sawyer and Mr. Wagener.

Thursday, Nov. 24, 1864. No news stirring today. Very strict with the men now. Don't allow the men to bring their rations out of the messroom. Two men were caught tunneling last night.

Friday, Nov. 25, 1864. All quiet along the line today. Fair & pretty warm. Good deal of snow on the ground. Wrote to pa today There is between 7000 & 8000 men in here and about 4000 have applied to take the oath. I am some better this evening.

Saturday, Nov. 26, 1864. Cloudy & a little snow. N.Y. Herald say that Mullord has gone to prepare terms of exchange to Jeff which not doubt he will accept, also that Lee has whipped Grant again, capturing 20,000 prisoners. It predicted that all of us will doubtless eat our Christmas dinner at home.

Thursday, Dec. 1, 1864. No news again today. Weather fair & pleasant. Health very good. Up roar in the cook house. I will try & give a minute description of our camp quarters & surroundings vicinity as well as possible.

Saturday, Dec. 3, 1864. Weather remains the same, No news. On the South Side is the old river bed holding water. Along on the north bank is the cookhouse and mess room & apothecaries &c, then a street 30 ft wide, then a row of Barracks 30 in another street same width.

Sunday, Dec. 4, 1864. Everything remains the same. Next is two more rows of barracks. Along the north side in the west half is the officers quarters, gate in the center along the west side are the Hospital Barracks & kitchen, seven in number.

Monday, Dec. 5, 1864. Everything the same. Major very strict. On the north side of the camp is part of the city, two observatories, 1 regt. in camp & mountains dotted with country farms. On the east side is the principal part of town, depot & another regiment in camp & one 4 gun battery.

Tuesday, Dec. 6, 1864. Our new Maj. is very tyrannical. Had a fight in the ward. Mountains also on the east. On the south side is battery River, broad plain & mountains, slaughter house & farm house &c.

Monday, Dec. 19, 1864. Cloudy but quite pleasant. More prisoners came in today from Washington. Good many cases small pox. Three have died. Prisoners are very sickly as a general thing. My bed fellow Cay is sick with pneumonia.

Tuesday, Dec. 20, 1864. Fair and very cold. Everything is frozen hard. No news again to-day. Am in very good health. Cay is not any better. The rebs are enjoying themselves daily skating on the pond in the south side of the camp.

Saturday, Dec. 24, 1864. Weather fair & has moderated a great deal. Jeff Davis has poisoned him-self, Bob had whipped Grant. There is 40 cases of smallpox, 4 have died. Prospects are bad for Christmas.

Sunday, Dec. 25, 1864. Fair and very pleasant. Christmas but it seems no more than any other day. ground is melting which makes it very slippery.

Monday, Dec. 26, 1864. Cloudy, warm but no rain. It is reported that Savannah has fallen with 20,000 prisoners. Quite sickly in camp again, from 15 to 25 die a day. Small pox is growing worse every day. Wrote to Mrs. Sawyer.

Thursday, Dec. 29, 1864. Heavy snow last night. Colder today & a little snow. Started to school today. Am taking French lessons. No news. My health remains good. Getting Sunday school lesson, 1st Chapter Acts of the Apostles to 16th verse. Nearly know it.

Tuesday, Jan. 3, 1865. Weather has moderated. A great deal from reports. Confirmed my vaccination has taken finely. Very sickly in camp now. Progressing pretty well in French.

Wednesday, Jan. 4, 1865. Cloudy & a little snow and very cold. Health very good. Arm is pretty soar & is still inflamed. Had quite a fight in my ward this morning between Dunn & Harper about insulting language.

Sunday, Jan. 22, 1865. Had considerable snow again last night. Not very cold. Reported that the authorities have agreed to parole all prisoners. Am not feeling very well this evening. My feet are frost bit again. Lady in camp today.

Tuesday, Jan. 24, 1865. Cloudy but not very cold. Recd. a letter from Matt yesterday. All well but for several deaths. No school today nor no news of interest. All dull.

Thursday, Jan. 26, 1865. Cloudy, no snow nor rain and not very cold. Reported that Buffalo was burnt last night. Supposed to be done by the raiders from Canada. Everything is quiet. 2000 prisoners sent from Point Lookout. Worked on bunk today. (These prisoners were from Fort Fisher. Author)

Thursday, Feb. 2, 1865. Fair and quiet pleasant and beautiful scenery. Mountains all around & perfectly white with snow. Received box & contents today from Mrs. Sawyer & a pair of girls drawers (astonishing).

Sunday, Feb 5, 1865. Very blustery and unpleasant. Thank God the exchange is about to commence at last—have been taking names today. Texas, Louisiana, Tennessee, Kentucky, Arkansas & Missouri are to go first with the sick.

Tuesday, Feb. 7, 1865. A.M. cloudy & moderate. No person allowed to go to Dixie who has applied to take the oath, I entertain very good hopes of getting back soon. Col. Moore says is a general ex-change. France seems to be meddling with affairs. P.M. snowing very fast.

Monday, Feb. 13, 1865. Weather fair and pleasant. At noon 300 sick & 200 well men leaves this evening in an hour or more. Are now calling the roll. Reported that they will continue to send fast as possible.

Thursday, Feb, 16, 1865. Reports say there is 1000 to go next load, 600 sick & 400 well also Va. and N.C. will be the last exchanged. Am anxious for my time to come. Am afraid they will only exchange three thousand & stop & leave me here.

Friday, Feb. 17, 1865. Weather very moderate & fair. I have pretty reliable information that the commanding officer has recd orders to clear the camp as quick as possible. Trust to God it is true. Great deal of sickness.

Tuesday, Feb 28, 1865. Another load of 500 signed the paroles today. Don't know when they will get off. Have a load of sick made up also. Hope I will get out soon. Trust to Providence. An unfair way of sending them off. Just whoever has money to buy his way out can go. Some sent an application to the Col. and got off in that way. Great deal of sickness in camp now and the smallpox is more fatal. Great many deaths, from 20 to 30 every day out of about 7000 man. More now than there was last summer and fall when there was some 10,000 here.

Monday, March 13, 1865. Weather quiet moderate. Reported that 13,000 of Earley's men are captured, also that 17,000 of Sherman's surprised old Jube. I don't believe either report. As the saying is those tales have not got any hair in them.

Friday, March 17, 1865. Weather remained the same. River is still rising. Is all over camp 4 or 5 ft deep, in cook house & some of the wards. Moved out all the sick and commissary stores to higher place. Commence fall in it at 6 o'clock.

Saturday, March 18. River has fallen nearly to its old water mark. Mess house 7 & cook houses 4 in deep in mud. Had a bad time cleaning them out. Some houses washed away.

Wednesday, March 22, 1865. Little sleet and rain today, reported that the load on which my name was is broken up. I think it true. They have made up another load of the first on the rolls as we came here. I am knocked out.

Monday, March 27, 1865. Very fair & pleasant. Boys are catching fish today out of the creek. Catches some quite nice perch. Tried my hand but met with no success. Nothing new. All quiet.

Tuesday, March 28, 1865. Weather remains the same. Everything quiet. Papers say Lee attacked Grant thinking his strength was weakened to reinforce Sherman & was repulsed with a loss of 5000 or 6000 men while Grant only lost 500 or 600 men.

Wednesday, March 29, 1865. Very pleasant weather. Every thing very quiet. Discharged from the mess because they were dissatisfied with me but simply good union men. Bob Lee whipped. room today, not to put in some.

Thursday, March 30, 1865. My birthday, 22 years old. A very wet morning. More of the waiters discharged. No news about when and more men will leave for Dixie. I think not before next week. Have made one more effort to get off.

Friday, March 31, 1865. Still cool & raining. No news of importance. I hope the Yankees are satisfied now they have discharged all the rebs who were waiters in the mess room and put in oath takers or good union men as they call them. The winter is about over now and it has not been so very hard. I have toughed it out very well. Can't say that I suffered any either from cold or hunger for which I am very thankful. Have been blessed so far. Tried to get off on the next load but I think my chances are very slim. Lt. Smith said the rolls were full. Wards are all consolidated into 30.

Monday, April 3, 1865. Weather same. Reports say that Richmond is evacuated & that it will be a month yet before the Baltimore road is repaired. Commenced work today.

Monday, April 4, 1865. A.M. fair and pleasant. Richmond gone up. 12,000 prisoners, 50 pieces artillery. P.M. cloudy and little rain. Nothing new.

164

Monday, April 10, 1865. Tolerably pleasant today. Reports say, it is published on bulletin board that Lee has surrendered his army also that we are to be paroled immediately.

Tuesday, April 11, 1865. No change in things generally. Still rumors & seems to be confirmation of the surrender of Lee & army. Some seem to be glad, some sorry.

Wednesday, April 12, 1865. Cloudy & rainy. Papers give a list of officers captured, Gen. Finegan one of the number. Great many are confident we will all soon be paroled.

Thursday, April 13, 1865. Seems to be settled that Gen. Lee & Army has surrendered of Grant. Some seem to rejoice while others lament the capture of so noble an army.

Friday, April 14, 1865. Great rejoicing throughout the U.S. Great exultation & blowing in the papers. fairly glowing picture. Richmond is entirely destitute of provisions. Recd. Federals with great joy.

Saturday, April 15, 1865. Excitement has only begun. Abe & Seward was murdered last night, first rumors that a Virginian, lastly S.s. clerk Rumored that all Rebel officers at Washington were killed.

Sunday, April 16, 1865. Cloudy and Quite cold. Lincoln's murderer is supposed to be one Booth. Johnson to his seat yesterday at 2 o'clock. Seward considered dangerous. The assassin not apprehended yet.

Monday, April 24, 1865. Weather fair & cold. Great excitement. Took the names of all citizen oath takers, all who willing to take the oath & those who won't take the oath. I am still a R E Reb.

Tuesday, April 25, 1865. Fair and very pleasant. Nothing new. Johnson has not surrendered yet. He & Sherman has been negotiating terms of peace. Lines extend from the Potomac to the Rio Grande. Washington authorities dissatisfied. All armies to be turned over to state authorities just as before the war.

Wednesday, April 26, 1865. Fair & pleasant. Still great excitement. Most all have applied to take the oath & I was weak enough to do so also. Sorry for it since try and & live in the hopes that it will prove for the best.

Thursday, April 27, 1865. Warm & broken. A thunder & shower reminded me of old times very much. Am feeling troubled today, afraid I have done wrong.

Friday, April 28, 1865. Weather broken. No rain & tolerably cool. Latest dispatch is that they com-mence paroling Monday, Virginians first. Don't place any confidence in the rumor. Health good, smallpox departed

Saturday, April 29, 1865. Another thunder shower. Otherwise fair and pleasant. No news today. All very quiet. Bought some leaf tobacco. These are very dull and all have on hand.

Sunday, April 30, 1865. All quiet. Reported a load leaves tomorrow for Baltimore. There has been a great deal of excitement this month, the whole confederacy has gone. Sad to think of but might be hope.

Friday, May 5, 1865. Fair & warm. No news of importance. Everything quiet. Wrote to Pa of the great improvements going on in camp, and fixing up quite a garden.

Private William R. Greer
25th South Carolina Regiment

Nineteen year-old William R. Greer enlisted in the Confederate Army on January 4, 1863 and was assigned to Hagood's Brigade, 25th South Carolina Regiment. He fought at both battles of Fort Fisher, was captured and sent to Elmira Prisoner of War Camp. This is a small portion of a larger story he had written about his experiences during the War Between the States. His story begins in the trenches of Petersburg, Va., just before the first attack on Fort Fisher. William R. Greer's story is courtesy of the Manuscript Department, William R. Perkins Library, Duke University, North Carolina.

Recollections of a Private Soldier of the
Army of the Confederate States by William R. Greer

At 3:30 A. M. December first 1864 there rang out through the bitterly cold air, it was sleeting heavily, the bugle call of "To the Colors" and our brigade started in heavy marching order, south-ward, destination not divulged. After toiling wearily through heavy mud for ten miles that night we reached Richmond early in the morning. We received no welcome there and no coffee or anything else, although we were bitterly cold and suffering greatly. We were then packed, like cattle, into box cars with no seats therein and so closely packed that we could not move, the redeeming quality of this arrangement being the warmth of such intimacy saved us from freezing to death. We traveled in this fashion all night, reaching Danville, Virginia, the next morning. Upon disembarking one comrade was discovered dead from cold and exposure, a dozen more were hustled to the hospital.

Later on we continued our journey South but with improved Transportation facilities, but owing to the condition of the roads, the rolling stock, and careless or treacherous human assistance, every-thing pertaining to the transportation department was beginning to disintegrate, we did not reach Wilmington, North Carolina, until December 25th. Rations were not, at that period, superabundant as I recollect while enroute Christmas day, I enjoyed for dinner a large uncooked sweet potato.

On reaching Wilmington we embarked for the neighborhood of Fort Fischer (sic) situated at the mouth of the Cape Fear River. Before our arrival at this destination, an expedition for the reduction of the fort, the land forces under B. F. Butler and a large naval force commanded by Admiral Porter had appeared, but although Porter inaugurated a determined attack, Butler failed in his support and the expedition sailed away December 31st. We were ordered back to Wilmington and there held in reserve.

January 13th a second attack on the fort was imminent. The expedition this time being under command of General Terry supplanting old Butler. Terry's land force of 8,000 men was auxiliary to Porter's fleet officially numbering 58 vessels of various grades.

The garrison of the fort being deemed insufficient our regiment and one other was ordered to proceed with all haste to the point of attack. This journey, my last under Confederate rule, was noteworthy as to the unwillingness or treachery of the Captains of the river steamers to risk their precious lives in close proximity to the bombardment now in progress. My recollection is that the application of a loaded weapon near the head of the recalcitrant sailors proved a persuasive argument, and on to our fatal destination we sailed.

It was a clear, cold morning, Sunday January 15th, when our forces disembarked at the extreme inner end of the landing under cover of a high battery, although we were witnesses of the progress of this continuous and terrific bombardment (up to this time there had been no demonstration from Terry), Porter evidently wished to reduce the fort first; we were soon in a position to realize the magnitude of this unceasing torrent of iron missiles which were being hurled at us. Finding a barrel of "hardtack" flavored with worms, our last ration from Dixie, and thus being prepared for the ad-venture, we were ordered to proceed singly, keeping a reasonable distance apart, into the main fort, under this enfilade of fire, and ordered to protect ourselves "as well as possible", this was somewhat possible, from gun projectiles as we hugged the intervening batteries and bomb-proofs closely on our hazardous journey to the ramparts of our 1,700 yards but mortar shells are deadly missiles which are difficult to elude. The result of this maneuver which was absolutely correct insofar as necessity demanded, was not quite successful, inas (sic) much as many men perished or were disabled, and many more in consequence partly of the disorganization of the different companies, officers and men being widely apart, and furthermore, many tired out and utterly disheartened men took shelter in the bombproofs on the route and refused to budge, so that only a portion of our force joined the organized garrison on the front who themselves had been of necessity in the bombproofs nearby.

A determined attack by sailors from the fleet who marched up the beach with drawn cutlasses was quickly defeated by our force who manned the breastworks very rapidly. The loss to the attacking party was reported very heavy. Shortly after this incident, a squad of Union soldiers appeared in the fort at the extreme left, the sallyport not only unprotected but left wide open. A larger force appearing there ensued a struggle between the contestants fighting from each bastion when it became useless to resist any further, and Fort Fischer (sic) surrendered.

It was recalled to the memory of the writer that one of the members of our command had in his rapid movement while dodging shells witnessed my complete entombment in the sand from the explosion of a nearby shell and as stated "only one foot sticking out."

As the prison camp (Elmira) was a very large enclosure we did not happen to meet, and it was thirty years after the close of the war, that after much persuasion, he was convinced that the fact of my having one foot out encouraged my extrication.

After a time squads of Federal soldiers marched through the fort gathering up the prisoners saying "fall in" and "Johnny got any tobacco?" We were marched out of the fort in a body and placed on the beach, cold, wet, and hungry, sentinels closely guarding us. The only diversion being the pyrotechnic display from the fleet celebrating the victory. One regret connected with this situation was that before I was ordered to "Fall in" I had unwisely destroyed the diary of my services in the Virginia Campaign, for this proved to have been unnecessary. The possession of this record, written under fire, would have been very valuable in assisting memory at this juncture.

The following morning there occurred a heavy explosion in the magazine of the fort in which it was reported the Confederate who fired the fuse perished as did a number unknown to us of the Union force. As I have no memory of any food being given us I presume we were still hungry, living on the memory of the last Confederate ration mentioned above.

The weather was clear but quite cold, but we were ordered to wade knee deep in the surf and were then hauled in launches, and after boarding a tug, were loaded into a "Greyhound" named General Lyon, said craft being noted as having only one live boiler, its companion having perished as a result of the high rate of speed characterizing the ship, this was confirmed by the fact of its taking ten days to speed from Cape Fear, North Carolina, to Jersey City. The memory of this sea voyage lingers like a sinister dream. I re-visualize the situation in the whole as comparable only to an enlarged box of sardines, the temperature ranging in the 90's and when it is remembered that on deck the yard arms as well as the deck were coated with ice, there could have been only one result, which was speedily achieved by the mortality list shortly after our incarceration in the prison camp, Elmira, N. Y.

Rations for the prisoners appeared to be of the least consequence to our guardians. One day we had, I distinctly recollect, four soda biscuits and some rice gruel. I desire here to emphasize the thought, that what is written about my captivity, that may appear censorious, is related and has lain in memory without sectional prejudice, the term "War" covering the situation and further, if any statement of hardship or suffering is emphasized it is with the view of picturing the horrors of war to some extent with the hope, that even this slight contribution, may assist in producing a situation as outlined by Tennyson "Till the war drums throbbed no longer and the battle flags were furl'd."

On landing at Jersey City we were at once transferred to a train of cars in waiting and then, under guard, commenced our journey to a prison camp on the outskirts of the city of Elmire (sic) in New York State. The journey was long and uncomfortable and on landing at the depot we were marched through the streets, almost waist deep in snow, and being gazed at from the dwellings as if we were wild animals. As the sinister walls of the camp, which proved to be my home for six months, or might, as it was the case of thousands whose graves lie nearby, in mute evidence of their suffering and endurance, have resulted in my relief from earthly existence, the familiar quotation from Dante which I had memorized in my early youth, "All hope abandon ye who enter here." On entering this miniature city, for such it was in a sense, having its own hospitals, guard house, post office, express office, etc. We were at once assigned to barracks, being wooden houses with triple rows of bunks on each wall and two large coal stoves in the center. Being imbued at the time with ideas pertaining to my personal welfare such as warmth and sustenance, I did not interest myself as to the extent of the grounds, number of prisoners, etc., but I did observe that this large area was surrounded by high wooden walls and that sentinels were stationed on platforms on the outside overlooking the camp, and that there existed an area, a prescribed distance from the walls, aptly termed the "Dead Line". This I believe exists in all institutions. There was as far as topography is concerned a river, the name of which is forgotten, flowing past one side of the camp but closely guarded. Still I do not imagine that at that time it was flowing very freely as the whole landscape appeared to be composed of ice and snow; the icicles from the barracks of great lengths and apparently never melting. As an instance of the severity of the climate which so hardly tested our Southern blood and was the cause of great mortality, it was officially stated that on a certain morning in February the relief guard found three sentinels dead from exposure.

On our arrival and assignment, we were ordered to partly unclothe and perform some ablution; as this was effected outside of the building it was performed with great celerity. Our hair being trim-med and very proper instructions given as to keeping away from the stoves we began to settle down and await further orders. I was informed that the number of prisoners at that time was eight thousand.

The most important regulation of the camp was the roll call, outdoors, early morning and again in the evening.

On arrival the prisoners were offered the choice of either remaining loyal to the Confederate cause, or of swearing allegiance to the United States Government, including our oath of never bearing arms during the continuance of the war. Those who availed themselves of this latter opportunity were placed as hospital stewards or assigned other light duties, and furthermore abundantly fed. All of my comrades of the W. L. I. (Washington Light Infantry) decided to remain loyal to the Southern cause. Our duties were in addition to the care and cleanliness of the wards, and our own personal portion thereof, the policing of the streets and other sanitary work. Our rations were poor both in quality and quantity and altogether insufficient for sustenance in such a rigorous climate. In spite of all hygienic precautions, including an enforced vaccination, illness and mortality steadily increased. Pneumonia, typhoid, and small pox simply raged even in the wards. The hospitals, being inadequate to meet the situation, the daily death rate of small-pox alone was registered as forty cases. Finally, I became ill, partly from exposure to the intense cold and from insufficient and improper food. I lay in my bunk without medical attention and was gradually sinking from sheer weakness and exhaustion, when a messenger sent by a friendly hand, appeared at my bedside and silently left a package containing a flask of brandy and some soda crackers. This timely and welcome sustenance restored my strength to an extent that I was again on my feet.

The following narrative may prove of momentary interest, among my messmates in the company there was a gentleman who, for a short period before the secession of South Carolina, had left his native state, Massachusetts, and had come to Charleston with the intention of residing here. In addition to having engaged in mercantile business, he at once evinced a decided interest in the building (sic) of our Y. M. C. A. His sterling qualities expressed in his various activities very soon resulted, in spite of sectional prejudices, in his acquiring a large circle of friends. This popularity became much greater on his enlisting as a private soldier in the ranks of the W. L. I. (Washington Light Infantry) giving as his reason, his belief in the justice of the Southern cause. Brave soldier as he proved to be in every engagement, he was intensely interested in religious work and whenever occasion offered would assist our chaplain in conducting prayer meetings. He was captured at Fort Fischer (sic) and as, in my case, imprisoned at Elmira. The following information was given me after the close of the war—George S. Baker, such was his name, was the son of the Rev. A. R. Baker of Medford, Massachusetts, this latter being also an author of works more particularly of Sunday School literature. Soon after reaching our prison camp my comrade became desperately ill of pneumonia. Word having been conveyed to his father of the critical situation, he hurried to Washington D. C. and after much difficulty was granted an interview with President Lincoln. After narrating the serious condition of his son he besought the president to grant a pardon and to give an order for his release which might result in saving his life. This plea was at first denied, but as the grief stricken father was on the point of leaving his presence, Mr. Lincoln, for some reason unknown, recalled him, and after some inquiry ascertained that the petitioner was the author of a publication that he (Mr. Lincoln) had used as a textbook while teaching a Sunday school class in former times in Springfield, Illinois. He now signed the order of release and pardon. The patient having, as soon as practicable, been carried to his old homestead, was carefully nursed back to health. It was, as I definitely ascertained, this good hearted messmate, who had directed the conveyance of life saving material by a trusted messenger to my bunk in the prison.

One more rather disagreeable climatic experience in prison is recollected. In the early spring as a consequence of the thaw, the adjacent river overflowing its bank invaded our territory, and for several days the water surged through out barracks to the depth of six feet necessitating an adjournment of the upper banks. After this occurrence things began to grow brighter. The war was over and the gradual release of the prisoners, beginning with the earlier ones, was in inaugurated.

As stated above the earlier prisoners were being released thereby leaving certain positions, clerical and otherwise, to be filled. My vigorous home training being properly brought up supplemented by camp discipline had inculcated a habit of order and neatness not only personally bit in my intimate surroundings. It was, therefore, from habit that my bunk when put in order for the day, was not only proper but was duly decorated with a fringed shawl. So accordingly the established order of little events and their resultant growth, it happened one day, being temporarily on the parade ground and an officer passing through our barracks stopped immediately at my bunk and after obtaining my name left instructions for an immediate appearance at headquarters. Thither I sped with some trepidation, but upon reporting to the said officer and satisfactorily answering certain queries, I was directed to report at Major Beale's tent, the Commandant of the camp, to act as clerk and perform certain duties. I found the Major quite affable and reasonable. He was the ideal expression of an elderly army officer, florid of complexion and in his genial make up gave evidence, from his ample girth, of never permitting any of the comforts of life escaping his vigilance.

After a time the Major, who off duty was really a charming genial personality began to evince a kindly interest in the Confederate boy. I was only twenty years old, and granted the privilege of going into the city during the day. Finally as time wore on and the date of my release from captivity drew near the kind hearted Major expressed a wish that I should remain with him as an adopted son. But, the home urge to a Southern boy, in whose memory of his home in Charleston, South Carolina, with its care, comfort and family affection, dwelt so vividly, and made such an appeal, that I, with grateful thanks and warm appreciation, declined this most unusual tender. I have often thought of the dear old Major who I presume has long since responded to "Taps" of the English—the "Last Post"— "Peace be to his ashes."

On a certain day in August 1865, exact date forgotten, three months after peace was declared and after the administration of the oath of allegiance and other formalities and after twenty-four hours stay in Elmira at the home of a kindly, gracious and elderly Southern gentlewoman, I embarked on a train from New York City enroute for my uncle's residence at Yonkers on the Hudson. There I was graciously received and cared for. After a time, (illegible) and elder brother, (this officer escaped capture with me, being on a furlough at the time, but returned to Virginia and remained with the remnant of the brigade until the surrender of Lee's Army), arrived at Yonkers by invitation and the information that certain business arrangements could be effected for the resumption of the disrupted mercantile business that had existed prior to the war. It can be imagined how this reaction from the hardships and miseries for so long a period was enjoyed, but after a brief period it was determined, that, as our family, then residents of Graniteville, South Carolina, were sorely in need of funds, I was entrusted with a sufficiency of "greenbacks" for first aid. So I took passage on the initial voyage of the steamer "Quaker City" from New York to Charleston. My memory is, that as the good ship entered our ever grand and beautiful harbor and neared her dock, I became deeply despondent at the spectacle of such dilapidation and ruin as our once beautiful city presented at that time. I immediately took passage on the old South Carolina Railroad, and after a varied itinerary of railroads, and crossing streams in lighters and other adventures, arrived safely at Graniteville where I was accorded a joyous welcome.

A pleasant sojourn in the country soon came to a close, as arrangements had been effected for the resumption of the book business in Charleston. The family returned to the old homestead, which fortunately had been out of range of shell fire and was in fair condition for habitation.

I, in company with my father and brothers began the arduous task of rehabilitation of the old business.

Private James Huffman
10th Virginia Infantry, C. S. A.

The following account has been reprinted from
Ups And Downs of a Confederate Soldier,
pages 95 to 107

A Prisoner at Elmira, New York

This Elmira Camp was entirely different from Point Lookout. Sod and grass covered the ground. Green trees and mountains covered the landscape. This camp contained approximately 45 acres, on the Chemung River, a tributary of the Susquehanna. This river's banks usually confine the stream in ordinary freshet's; then there is a wide bottom, then a hill, something like 18 or 20 feet high and on this were our quarters. In the river bottom were located the pest houses or hospital for smallpox and other contagious diseases. Two thirds or more of our camp was in this bottom. Our hilltop was about on a level with Elmira city. There was a pond or a lake along the foot of our hill, which was part of our boundary line. Streets and roads were graded nicely all over our camp on the hill and trees were planted along on each side. The camp was kept strictly clean which made it attractive to outsiders, but not so much to our eyes.

We were quartered at first in tents but as winter approached, they put up buildings, each about 50 feet long and 18 feet wide and containing three tiers of bunks. The floors were from 1 ½ feet to 3 feet above the ground and each had two large coal stoves, one in each end of the building.

Private James Huffman, 10th Virginia

Then there was a row of hospital wards across the end of the camp, I think 12 or 14 and number and generally full of patients. A large cookhouse stood on the brow of the hill, and about the center of camp was a carpenter shop were coffins of white pine were made for the dead. Rebel carpenters were detailed to this work. When not busy at that, they made some beautiful walnut furniture for the Yanks. They received ten cents a day and extra rations. I had a friend in the shops and got many little scraps of walnut and other kinds of nice wood which I worked with my knife into picture cases in book form. These I sold from $.75 to $1.25.

We also had a subtler's store where was sold cheese, crackers, candy, apples and almost anything more that we had money to buy. This camp, at first sight, seemed a very healthy place, but it was just the reverse proved to be a very sickly place for our men. The death rate was much higher than in the Army during active hostilities. About half of us Virginians and I think three quarters of all Southerners died here in 8 to 10 months. Out of twelve of our company, half died. In the winter, a large number of North and South Carolinians had been captured at a fort on the North Carolina coast, hale, hearty looking fellows as ever were, except that they were yellow from lying in the trenches. These men crowded us very much at first, but in two or three weeks they were nearly all gone to the hospitals, and most of them died. The well water looked pure and good but was deadly poison to our men; thousands taking chronic diarrhea and all kinds of bowel and kidney trouble, from which they died.

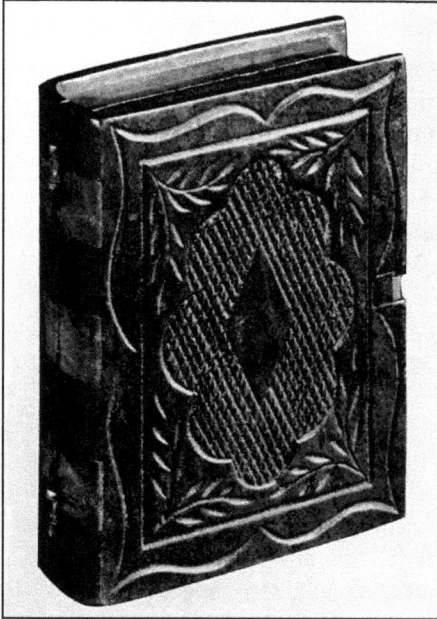

We had smallpox almost all the time. One of our company had it, got well, but afterwards died there. His brother took measles and died in two or three days. One doctor there said he killed more Rebs than any soldier at the front.

We could buy things at the sutler's, if we had the money. Well, we had some money, but we had to use strategy. If anyone had money on arrival, it was taken from him when he went in and you could get an order to the store for one or two dollars at a time. If we wanted money in our pockets, we would buy at the store and then sell to others until we had the whole amount in our pockets. If a friend send in money, it would be held at headquarters and the name placed on the bulletin board— John Smith, $10. Not over two dollars at a time on an order. You will be surprised when I tell you we did as much business in a small way as a town or city.

James Huffman carved this picture frame from wood and sold these at the Elmira market place. Many of the guards would purchase these items and resell them to the citizens.

Half or more of the well man were earning money one way or another. When first put in prison, we only stood around and looked at each other, not knowing what to do except to await the call to the mess house for the mite of food allowed each man. Fortunately, there were some mechanics and jewelers who procured some tools—I don't know how—and went to work making very pretty things and selling them for big money. We looked on with stomachs pinching until the thought came, "I wonder if I could make anything. I will try."

Here is one of the most important lessons of life. Believe you can do a thing and have patience and try it thoroughly. Have confidence and patience. "I will try," beginning to believe, puts the whole being into action and the thing is done. If at first you don't succeed, try again and put the whole mind, being and soul into your work, thinking of nothing but success.

Our noble General Jackson started in life with this motto—"I can do all things through Christ. He strengthened me." Stonewall Jackson never failed to defeat the purpose of the enemy. At Kearnstown only, was he forced from the field against great odds, but succeeded in drawing back a large column that had started to reinforce McClelland and held them there until he could get them in position to flog and defeat the last one of them. And then Jackson took his own little army and helped Lee to drive McClelland away from Richmond's door before they knew where he was. His accidental death, by his own men, was the defeat of the Confederate cause.

Have faith or confidence in yourself to do whatever you will do. It was this confidence that, forced on me under the most unfavorable circumstances, caused me to make an effort. I had never done anything but run sawmills, haul logs and farm. I had no tools, no material and was shut up in prison. How could I do anything? Hunger puts the mind to action. Mind says to nerves and muscles, "Get a move on and try."

I got a big 6-inch spike nail and drove it through a neat stick. This was my hammer. I got a file at the store. Out of two spike nails I made a neat pair of pinchers, broke the point off of needles and fasten them in a rod, bow and sweep completed a drill and a pocket knife made up the outfit with which I made nice rings that sold well and at good prices. A good workman well supplied with tools could make a nice work with ease. But one who never did anything of the kind must have a storehouse full of confidence, patience and energy to achieve success. I mention this to illustrate the energy of thousands who worked up beef bones, horsehair, little scraps of lumber, pearl, silver, gold, Gutta percha and other waste, into every conceivable fancy article of such attraction and beauty that the most fastidious appreciated. Some of us were manufacturing, some selling at wholesale, some retailing, and altogether making a perfect network of business.

Yet there were a lot of drones or lifeless, do less persons who moped about, pining away for want of sufficient food to eat, losing their humanity, eating almost anything a brute would eat—as rats, gangrene poultice and the like. These were known by their pallid color and lifeless movements. Most of them died there, not from disease but pining away for lack of more food, some even sending word to their friends at home that they were being starved to death. These poor men grew so lean that they seem to have no flesh at all, before their spirits left their bodies.

Our manufactured articles were purchased mostly by outside people. The guards who came on the inside bought largely and sold again to others outside. At first it was hard for visitors to get in and high observatories were built on the outside and the owners charged admission fees for people to go up and look at the Rebs. No doubt the reader thinks my anxiety for school waned away. The authorities here would not let us organize anything. I got a slate and an arithmetic and studied it with the assistance of some friends. I had to work to get about $.75 worth of extra grub each day. Then we had to wash and boil our clothes every week.

With all our care and caution, we could not keep rid of vermin. We called them gray backs for short. The only way we could keep them down was in this manner. My bunk mates and myself would get up in our bunk, strip off and hunt in the seams of our shirts and drawers. This we did every day to prevent nits. If all would have done as we, they would soon have exterminated the lice. Some of the fellows did not washed her clothes nor themselves and you could see the gray backs crawling all over their clothes on the outside. There were other bitter doses that I will not mention. There were all kinds of mixtures of men and morals in our ward. Some were talking, some were swearing, some singing, others playing cards, some laughing and engaged in all sorts of amusements.

I persuaded another fellow to assist me and we read a chapter and sang a hymn and had prayers at night before retiring. These services were respected and enjoyed by most of them, but not all. There was not the religious feeling that had existed at Point Lookout, but we kept this up until I was assigned to attend the hospital wards, where we read and had prayers and song service and talk to some of the patient's—poor, sick and dying people whose friends were a thousand miles away. Four of us would go together and attend three or four wards each night. Other groups would attend other wards, so all hospital wards had services each night, twelve or fourteen in all. Few of our sick ever came away. Oh, it was so horrifying to see all these poor men dying needlessly, so far from their friends! The prison wards would be crowded sometimes when a fresh lot was brought in, but they soon vanished away as snow on a warm, sunshiny day.

The Great Flood

This state of things continued until the last days of February, 1865, when there was a sudden change in the weather. From 1st December to the last of February, all the snow that fell lay on the ground and pack down to a depth of three or four feet. During this time the weather was extremely cold, some of the men froze their feet while standing on the snow and ice at roll call of the mornings. The last of February, I was elated at being on the list to be exchanged. Everything was already and we were waiting for the government train, when a warm rain set in and melted all the snow in the Pennsylvania and New York mountains. The riverbanks soon began to overflow.

Water spread over the wide bottom, sweeping away our pest hospitals and over the prison walls to the foot of our hill, but it didn't stop there. We were to have the biggest flood in the history of Elmira. It rose until our entire camp was underwater. The sick were taken out in boats and a great many died before they were returned. One of my bunk mates died. Our number had been greatly reduced by so much sickness and death and one boatload of sick had been exchanged a short time before, so that the rest of us could get in the second and third tier of bunks and keep out of the water. There we had to remain until the water receded and food was brought it on boats.

Remember that the river had banks that usually held freshets. There was about four hundred yards of bottom, then a hill on the second rise, eighteen or twenty feet high; then the barracks were one and a half to three feet off the ground and the water was from one to four feet in the buildings. Now can you picture in your mind the volume of water that flowed down this Chemung Valley? All the prison walls were swept away except the side next to Elmira, and there had been much current some of the buildings on the hill would have gone. The railroad down this river to Harrisburg was torn to pieces, and much of it carried away. This flood foiled my hopes and my exchange never came.

As soon as the water began to fall and before it left the cook houses, some of the boys waded in and got some choice hams intended for Yankee officers, but we feasted on them all the same. They tasted "moreish." On this hill, the water had not much current. Perhaps you can form some idea of the sediment or mud left all over the camp, in the buildings and under the buildings and everywhere you would turn your eyes. Still we had to live or die in it, as chance made it. Some of us lived, but we had lost much of our humanity. The death rate was about thirty-two a day for a while, even though our number was reduced to a little over half. I would like to revisit the boneyard of Elmira Confederates, where thousands of poor fellows bones were laid to rest, for there was little else than bones when life ebbed away.

Preachers came in from the outside to preach to us some with good gospel sermons. Others were possessed with devils before they came in. We gave good attention and enjoyed many good gospels, but had no time to waste on old political hypocrites and would leave.

One Sunday one of these last named, after announcing his text, said, "I want you all to understand that I am a Union man and my great grandfather was a Union man." I don't know how much farther the old political crank went grinding out his Unionisms, for the most of us were too far on the way to our quarters to hear any more.

Sometimes Sunday school papers were distributed among us. The first page was half covered with a magnificent flag of the Stars and Stripes. Then the reading went on to pictures of how the Southern planters drove the Negroes through the day with long whips like oxen and penned them in boarded lots like cattle, at night, and all kinds of other black falsehoods, on the order of the infamous, "Uncle Tom's Cabin." I believe the Northern preachers did more to bring on the great slaughter between the States than all the other combined forces. The Northern literature so pictured the Southern people, that there was almost a constant stream of people winding their way to the top of these observatories to get a glimpse of the Rebs, as they supposed us to be like some kind of curious, monkey shaped animals. After their long trips over the railroad and their observations, they saw only some poorly clad men, like others in form but far better in principle and character.

After the big flood we had to wear the time away as best we could, being forbidden to organize in any form by which we could have made better use of our time. We dragged through March and into April, when Lincoln was assassinated—on the night of April 14, 1865. All Southerners, prisoners and all, were accused of the crime and we were made to suffer for it, when outside of John Wilkes Booth and his pals, no one had any knowledge of it or anything whatever to do with it.

Booth's brother-in-law was caught and tried as a spy, convicted and sentenced to death, and Booth went to Lincoln asking for a respite for him. Lincoln told him he could not do anything and for him to go to Seward, and when Seward refused to do anything Booth determined the two should pay the penalty and he shot Lincoln, at the same time his pal cut Seward's throat as he lay in bed, but not quite deep enough to be fatal, and this is the whole story in a nutshell.

The war was over now and the Southern soldiers had returned to their homes (where they had not been destroyed) and were trying to make an honest living for themselves. But now depredations, torture, robbery, murder, carpetbagging and Negro rule, scaly-wagging jurors of the lowest grade of whites and Negroes being selected to try our leaders for treason—even putting President Davis in irons—all this the Southerners had to bear.

Under this rule much of the private property left was destroyed by the cruel, heartless, brute beasts of Federal officers who went through the country, burning and robbing cities, destroying private property, houses, barns, mills, grain and feed, shooting down livestock that they could not carry off, torturing helpless and innocent people. This brute beast carpetbagger and Negro rule wasted and destroyed what had been left. General Butler was noted for stealing spoons from the Southerners and went by the name of silver spoons Butler. The loss of property to the South cannot be estimated. About 4 million slaves were liberated without any compensation, besides public and private property destroyed amounting to billions of dollars. All railroads and other institutions were now bankrupt. Wide regions of country were laid waste. Hopes were blighted, fortunes ruined, plans frustrated and all now were subjected to Freedmen's bureau agents and the swarm of hungry carpetbaggers that came South to devour the little the war had left. This tyranny lasted some years, and had it not been for the secret organization of the Ku Klux Klan would have completely ruined the South. The prisoners were now being sent away gradually. I find the records of history state that about four more Rebels died in the Northern prisons then Yanks died in Southern prisons.

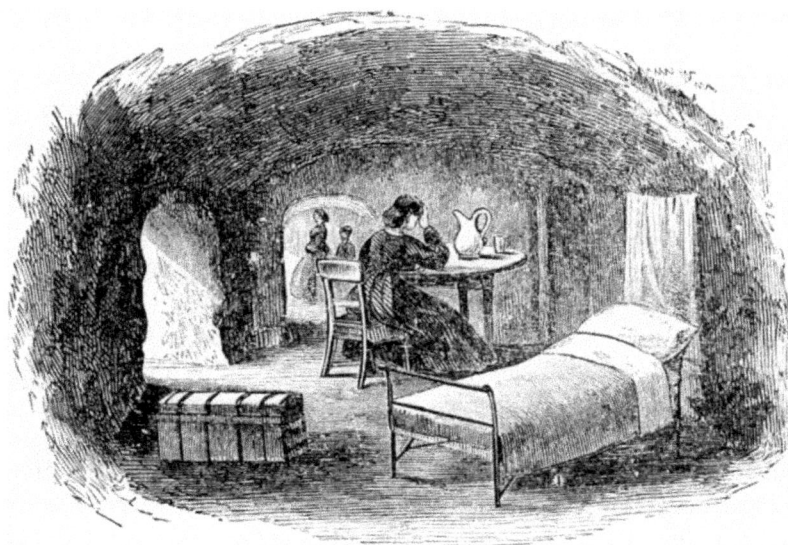

Private Anthony M. Keiley

Company E, 12th Virginia Infantry
This text is copied from Keiley's book, *In Vinculis or,*
The Prisoner of War: Being the Experience of a Rebel In Two Federal Pens

The man who first invented going to sea was an infidel and a fool, a misanthrope, and probably a marauder, a superintendent donkey and a filibuster, *hostis humani generis,* and should have been outlawed accordingly. The element is proverbially treacherous, the dangers are great, the inconveniences infinite, the results moonshine, and, to crown all, beneficent Nature has implanted in every human stomach an instinctive and vigorous protest against the practice, which ought to satisfy any reasonable being that it never was designed that a creature innocent of fins, tail, or a shell, should go out of sight of land. I admit that the whale-oil supply was for a long time an obstacle to the general acceptance of my view of the case, but the vast fields of petroleum recently discovered knock the wind out of that argument, and allow me to indulge the reasonable hope that if Pit Hole holds out, and Oil Creek does not suffer from a drought, I shall one day have the satisfaction of participating in a general auction of all marine properties, "on account of whom it may concern."

The fact is, there is nothing redeeming about the infernal sea-going system. You get up in the morning, and there is no newspaper; you stroll out to settle your bitters, and a dozen paces in any direction will introduce you to a shark; you stagger into breakfast, and the coffee slides into your beefsteak, and both into your lap; you get up, and in 10 minutes you discover, in the language of the luckless Yellow-plush, "Wot tin basins was made for;" the day passes, and there is no post office, no business, no counting room, no children run over, no street cries, no omnibus, no dogfight, no civilization: it snows, and you can't go sleighing; it is fair, and you can't take a drive; it rains, and you can't roll tenpins, or get satisfactorily drunk; pale specters with pendant jaws and watery eyes, all by a strange centrifugal force flying towards the outside of the ship, pass you at every instant; and after a day dismally dragged through in every conceivable discomfort, you turn in at night to a closet not large enough to swing a cat in, and tumble into a berth which looks so much like a coffin, that you dream, before you are well asleep, of attending your own funeral!

So your days creep along, if you have vitality enough to survive, destitute of fox-hunts or flirtations, law or literature, politics or opera, fashion plates or scandal, telegrams or taxes; and if the old scythe-bearer comes to your relief, you are sewed up in a sack with a thirty-two pound shot at your heels, and tossed to the fishes as remorselessly as the beef bones from yesterday's soup.

"Now would I give a thousand furlongs of sea for an acre of barren ground: Long heath, brown furze, anything. The wills above be done, but I would fain die a dry death."

All these objections are valid, if you are a first class passenger aboard a first-class steamer. "Phancy our feelinx," then, when you remember that we were packed like sheep on a cattle train, in the hold of a villainous tub, in the middle of July, with no ventilation, except what was afforded by two narrow hatch ways (there being no sidelights), and permission to put our heads above the deck being only accorded to two at a time, and then for five minutes, so that it required one hundred-fifty times five minutes, or over half the day, to elapse before you could get your second gasp of fresh air! And then our ship was such a crazy and unseaworthy craft, that in the event of a storm there was little prospect of our ever seeing land again.

In this delightful situation, the sun melting the pitch in the seams over our heads, and not air enough stirring to raise a ripple, we stretched ourselves on the lower deck in a desperate state of disgust, with only energy enough to pray for a short, passage or a heavy gale, blessings craved in vain. Many of us were seasick, all were hungry, and there was a unanimous devotion of all Yankeedom to the devil. During the night I stole aloft once, but was ordered down by a sentinel with the manners of a hog the accent of a New England clock-peddler.

Anything short of a wheel barrel ought to make the run from Point Lookout to New York (our destination) in thirty hours, or thirty-five at the most; took us just forty-six, although the sea was as calm as a river, nothing breaking the smoothness of its treacherous surface, except that infernal stomach pump, known as the "groundswell,"—a submarine wave which constantly beats from the shore, and was intended by beneficent Nature to prevent her children from the folly of navigation, by circling the whole ocean with this (unheeded) warning against leaving land.

Sunday, the 10th, was a brilliant day. I took my five minutes ration of the deck at sunrise this morning. How the calm, superb majesty of such a scene, the golden god scattering his largesse of rubies over the great deep, crowning each wavelet with a gem; the swelling ocean broken by no ruffling storm, but surging with long unbounded waves to the very gates of the morning; a sky warm and glorious with the purple flush and splendor of the full dawn,--how such a scene, in its beauty, grandness, immensity, tranquility, contrasts with and rebukes the petty blustering and passions and paltry ambitions of men!

From 10 AM, Saturday the 9th, until we arrived in New York Harbor, a period of over fifty hours, her only food was one ration of bread and a couple of ounces of adipose; and what with this and a slight dose of seasickness, I was consummately miserable by the time we got into "the Narrows," early Monday morning. I stole up on deck, and hunting up the officer commanding the guard, asked permission to purchase a cup of coffee from the cook, and leave also to remain on deck till I could drink it. He assented readily; and having made the contract with the presiding genius of the galley, I took my seat on a bit forward, and drank my fill of the beautiful scene around me.

As we got well up in the channel you little boat rowed off from shore to us, we stopping the while, and with about ten seconds of conversation to the captain, its tenant rode back with a fee in his pocket. He was the incumbent of the most lucrative office probably in America— the New York Health officer. The screw revolves, and again we are off.

Those who have entered New York harbor by this channel will remember the richness and luxury of the Jersey coast for thirty miles below the city. The land is high, handsomely wooded, and almost every summit is crowned with a stylish country villa— the urban residences of the princes of Wall Street and Broadway;--while in every reach of shore where a surf breaks, a handsome hotel fronts the sea, and rows of piquant little cottages dot the hill slopes to their tops. As you approach the city, these evidences of wealth and taste increase in number and in magnificence; and you are ushered into the teaming port of the American Venice through a highway of palaces, with here and there a powerful fortress interspersed, to give security to all this rural luxury and elegance.

179

I was musing on this, indulging my taste for the beautiful, but amazingly hungry and uncomfortable withal, when a Yankee corporal, a German Jew, named Bernstein, as I afterwards learned, came to where I sat, with a smoking cup of coffee in his hand, his own ration for breakfast, and with a courteous apology for having nothing better to offer, insisted on my drinking it. It was idle to tell him that I had engaged to get some from the cook, for he replied, that the cook might not have it to give me, and on my objecting that he would lose his own breakfast, he assured me that he could get another cup, and would be offended if I did not take it. So I accepted it very gratefully.

There is no likelihood that these lines will ever meet his eye, but I could wish that such might be their fate, that my friend Bernstein might see that his little act of kindness is not, and will not be forgotten. Before I had finished, he hunted up his haversack, and laid before me as many hard-tacks as I could eat, so that when, half an hour afterwards, the cook told me he had a breakfast for me, I was able to administer alimentary consolation to a couple of hungry "Rebs" below.

It was near midday when we hauled up the channel just off and below the Jersey city end of the lower ferry to New York; and there we lay till the train on the Erie Railroad, whose eastern terminus is here, was ready. I am quite familiar with New York Harbor, and many a spire of the city was easily recognized as those of my Virginia home. Everything seemed as busy, as "alive," as stirring, as in the same month, four years before, when I last saw the gay city. The war was apparently little felt here. The docks were as crowded; the same unvarying hum filled the sultry air; the ferry-boats passed with the same surcharged loads; the wharves were crowded with the same rushing hordes of porters, hackman, stevedore's, newsboys, and thieves; and I doubt not, Broadway echoed to the same endless tide of wheel and foot, and Wall Street choked its crooked throat with as excited in thronging a congregation is have ever "bulled and beared" it in the shadow of old Trinity, on any July day this quarter of the past century. In the face of all this wealth, development, material power— all these vast appliances of conquest—I felt a new pride in our beleaguered Confederacy, which has had nothing to oppose to this unexampled affluence of resource except the unconquerable gallantry of her children, and yet has fought this fight against such odds as have never yet stood in the way of freedom, with a calm confidence in the cause, a noble acceptance of sacrifice and undaunted courage, a patient hope, a chivalric devotion, that fearlessly challenge the comparisons of history.

While I am indulging in these moralizing's, a little boat is shooting out from shore, and in a moment more an officer boards us, who probably brings news that the train is now waiting, for our "tub" is now turned toward the dock. We are soon alongside, an officer stands in the hatchway to count us as we come up, lest some may conceal themselves in the ship. The count seems satisfactory (yet it was not, for two born idiots remain the board), we are marched into the depot, a few paces off, and put aboard a train of box and passenger cars, standing ready for us.

Our Advent is unexpected, or the Jerseyans are not as curious as their compatriots elsewhere, for there is but a small crowd of spectators, and these gaze on us with a stolid air, which may mean sympathy; probably, however, indifference. By 1:30 all was in readiness, the locomotive gave that preliminary shriek, which, according to the Sydney Smith, is most like the scream an attorney may be expected to give when the devil gets hold of him, and off we started for Elmira.

The Erie Railroad, as I presume everyone used to know, runs through the northern counties of New Jersey, and the southern counties of Central and Western New York. It passes through some handsome towns and cities but the country is considered far inferior to that which lines the Central road. At almost every station we make a lengthy halt, to give way to some regular train passing up or down, and, wherever we stopped, we were the subjects of very great, and, generally, respectful interest. The guards rigidly excluded the people from all intercourse with us, and forbade, under various sanguinary threats, any assistance being tendered us; still they found it impossible to guard every avenue of approach, and many a piece of tobacco, package of crackers, and the like, was handed us by the good people on the route. The gentler sex was conspicuous in these charities, and more than one surprised us by furtive exhibitions of little Confederate flags which they had concealed about their persons. At Port Jervis, there seemed to be a fair prospect of a difficulty between our guards and the citizens, many of whom persisted, despite all orders, in making such contributions to our wants as accidentally lay in their power. Of course, these agreeable incidents were occasionally diversified by the insults with some sleek noncombatant, whose valiant soul found congenial occupation and fearful threats of our indiscriminate massacre, if he could only lay hands on us. These gentry work, in the main, of that physical and sartorial type which we always associate with the ideas of extreme orthodoxy— your sanctimonious, high-seat in-the-synagogue worthies, who
"Compound for sins they are inclined to,
By damning those who have so mind to;"
and from the serene heights of their sublime self-conceit, hurl worse anathemas than that prolix profanity of Bishop Ernulphus, at the forlorn publicans below. You know the canting breed, good reader mine, wherever you see them; and at home or abroad, in pulpit or Tribune, in Church or State, they everywhere exhibit the same harmonious blending of Heap's hypocrisy with the villainy of Carker. Of these lovely lambs Butler is the God and Kalloch the prophet. He would be a most unreasonable "rub" who would look for anything but a snarl from these curs.

And thus, amid friends and foes, through gorges and around bluffs, now skimming gaily along a level metal, and anon "wiring in and wiring out, and of quote apparently in the absurd effort to avoid crossing the Susquehanna— a stream so crooked that the engineers who built the road seem to have fancied that, by following up one bank, they would, sooner or later, find themselves on the other—on we steamed till about 8 o'clock, Tuesday morning, when we pulled up in the pretty little city of Elmira, which, albeit only about 20 years old, as I hear, contains 12,000 inhabitants and is situated on the left bank of the Chemung, a tributary of the Susquehanna. Although at the door of the prison, we realized a comparative comfort by contrasting our condition with what it was aboard the "El Cid." This being the last time I shall have occasion to mention this miraculous sample of naval architecture, I hear deliberately devoted to the infernal gods, with his honest and unction is ever filled the bosom of the most patriotic Moor, and the times of the great namesake—a gentleman who must have served Moorish mothers with impracticable cherubs a good turn, he frightened the grown ones so prodigiously, according to the authentic histories of Bob Southey, and that unfortunate victim of a liver complaint and then un-congenial spouse, Mrs. Heman's.*

*Bad weeds grow apace, and the Cid illustrated the philosophy if not the letter of the axiom; for the abomination is at this moment in the harbor of New Bern, N. C., and advertises for freight and passengers with as much audacity as if it was a fit craft to carry a load of Brazilian hides.

Chapter XIII

I plainly foresee that this chapter is going to run into statistics, as I have had a reasonable core of mathematics from the blessed days when every application of my mind to figures was followed by the application to my shoulders of something else, I will be excused for invoking the patience of the reader, assuring him—a favorite lie with four-legged Tory parents while horsing their heirs—that the pain I inflict causes me more suffering than it can be possibly occasion him.

For more than a year before our arrival, Elmira was the site of the rendezvous for the drafted men of Western New York. Here the gushing Patriots were received and housed, trained to turn out their toes and survived "hard-tack," and otherwise qualified to patch the rents in a certain lacerated Anaconda, which has been prowling around the continent tobacco country with varying fortunes these four years back. These gay volunteers required three camps, which were severely denominated "barracks, one, two, and three," and here they were Till they graduated in the manual of arms, and squandered their bounty money, when they were incontinently bundled off to the front, and a performance which, according to the most authentic averments, resulted in the absconding of about 25%, of the Patriots before the ever came in sight of a camp sample of "the old flag."

Now it came to pass, that Mr. Stanton began to feel some apprehension that the "secesh" were getting too numerous at Point Lookout, and offered to tempting a prize to the profane general then meandering the sourkrout and smear-case (?) of the honest Deutschers in rule Pennsylvania, so he ordained and established by imperial ukase a prison in the hyperborean regions of New York, where for at least four months of every year, anything short of a polar bear would find locomotion impracticable, and where therefore, no apprehension need to be felt of trouble within, or assault without, for the same interval. Early in July, therefore, the "Yanks" were ousted from Barracks no. 3, and preparations made for receiving the first installment of prisoners, who arrived on 6 July, numbering 399, the 400th men have been escaped on the way. (The 400th men will always escape.) On the 11th, 249 arrived, and the next day we were added to the list.

We were escorted to the "Penn," by a large concourse of admiring citizens, a number of whom were the gentler sex, in every stage of development, curiosity being, in Elmira, a feeling of the sex. A margin of about a mile brought us to our prison. We file in, were counted, divided into companies of 100, the roll call, and we were led off to our quarters. These consisted of wooden buildings, about one hundred feet long, by sixteen in width, and high enough for two rows of bunks. There were about thirty-five of these buildings in the enclosure, standing side-by-side, in a line parallel to the front of the pen, and about midway the ground. I soon asserted a pre-emption claim to a top bunk in No. 21, the quarter of most of my Petersburg friends, and having deposited my very modest pack, started out to view my promises.

I found a level plain of about thirty acres of land, situated, as I have said, a mile or so west of Elmira, and immediately on the bank of the Chemung. The ground is unequally divided by a long narrow lake or lagoon, which runs parallel to the river, into two sections, the one furthest from the entrance gate being dominated by the Trans-Mississippi Department, in the vernacular of camp. This lake starts within 20 feet of the fence on one side of the pen, and flows under the opposite fence, and the ground beyond the lake is a sandy bottom, indicating what I found, on inquiry, to be the case, that the unruly Chemung occasionally gets uproarious, overflows its banks, and floods the adjacent grounds.

The whole site is a basin surrounded by hills which rise several hundred feet, and are covered richly and thickly with the luxurious foliage of the Hemlock, ash, poplar, and pine. This was the most grateful relief from our Point Look out experience, where nothing met the eye, in any direction, except the sky, water, and prison fence. But a more available and practical improvement was in the water, which was here pure cool, and abundant, and the newcomers luxuriated in the delicious beverage with the gusto of a lost traveler in Sahara, or a repentant legislator after a nocturnal spree.

In the general arrangement of the guard detail there was little difference from Point Lookout, except in the absence of the colored guards, and in the presence of the officers, all of whom spent a portion of each day within the "pen." A roll of tents running parallel with the front fence of the "pen" was assigned to these gentlemen, and until the approach of winter drove them into certain barracks outside, where ventilating arrangements were not so extensive, they continued to occupy them.

Back of the thirty-four or thirty-five barracks, already referred to, is a row of wooden buildings, containing the adjutant's office, dispensary, various rooms of the Yankee sergeants, store-rooms, and the like, and back again of these, the mess rooms and cook houses, which extend to the lagoon. These, with one or two other buildings, constituted all the appliances of the prison at that time, nor was any change made until the miasma from the lagoon sowed the seeds of febrile disease so widely, that eight or ten hospitals had to be built, and the advent of prisoners by the thousand exhausted the sleeping capacity of the barracks.

The government of this prison was in the hands of Major Henry V. Colt, One Hundred and Fourth New York Volunteers, a gentleman, fair in fact, if not quite forty, 5 ½ feet high, with the florid complexion, a comfortable *embonpoint,* a very prepossessing appearance and manner, a jaunty way of cocking his head on the side of his head, and a chronic attack of smoking cigars, which he invariably holds in his mouth at about the angle at which mortars are ordinarily fired.

I perform a very grateful duty, in here bearing testimony to the various admirable qualities of this gentleman, as an officer and a man. Uniformly urban and courteous in his demeanor, he discharged the varied, and often times annoying, offices of his post with a degree of justice to his position and to the men under his charge, a patience, fidelity, and humanity, that could not be surpassed, and, I fancy, were seldom equaled, either side of the line, in similar positions. There was none of the slipshod indifference of Point Lookout regime. Major Colt either discharged in person or superintended the execution of every duty respecting the prison, which appropriately claimed his attention, doing all with the thoroughness of a trained man of business; and although charged with duties whose performance demanded almost every moment of his time, he was always ready to hear and redress any just complaints that were made to him, if they were of a character that justified him in interfering, or that he had the power to remedy, and to afford any information or assistance, consistently with his position, to the humblest prisoner. It is a pleasant office to do this justice to an enemy, and to record this offset to the many cruelties which are charged, no doubt justly, to other officers in charge of our unfortunate prisoners.

The major's adjutant was Captain C. C. Barton, an active, smart, and rather consequential young gentlemen, as adjutants are want to be— and here I call attention to the fact that these officers constitute a class, *sui generis*, in every army; but, upon the whole, Barton was a good fellow, notwithstanding he considered Abe Lincoln a Chesterfield, and accounted Grant a compound, in about equal proportions, of King Solomon and Alexander the Great. Captain B. was assisted by a young sergeant, H., who was promoted to an adjutants place shortly after our arrival, but did not exchange his comfortable quarters for "the front" till the summer was over; and a youth, Frank E., who, in a fit of spasmodic patriotism, joined a heavy artillery company, before he was out of his teens, and straightaway periled his invaluable life for his beloved country, as an adjutants clerk, in the dangerous "Department of the Chemung."

In the executive duties of his office, Major Colt was assisted by fifteen or twenty officers, and as many noncommissioned officers, chiefly of the militia or the veteran reserves. Among them were some characters which are worth a paragraph.

There was a long-nosed, long-faced, long-jawed, long-bearded, long-bodied, long-legged, and was-endless-footed, and long-skirted curiosity. Captain Peck ostensibly simply engaged in taking charge of certain companies of "rebs," but really employed in turning a penny by huckstering during the various products of prisoners skills--an occupation very profitable to Peck, but generally unsatisfactory, in a pecuniary way, to the "Rebs." Many of them have told me of the impossibility of getting there just dues from the prying, round-shouldered captain, who had a snarl and an oath for everyone out of whom he was not, at that instant, making money.

Page 134

Another rarity of the pen was Lieutenant John McC., a braw chiel frae the land o' cakes, who was a queer compound of good-nature and brutality. To some of us he was uniformly polite, but he had his pistol out on any occasion when dealing with the majority of the "Johnnies," and would fly into a passion over the merest nothing, that would have been exceedingly amusing, but for a wicked habit he had of laying about him with a stick, a tentpole— anything that fell into his hands. He was opening a trench one day, through the camp, when, for the crime of stepping across it, he forced the poor, sick boy, who was on his way to the dispensary for medicine, to leap backwards and forwards over it till he fell from exhaustion amid the voluble oath's of the Valiant Lieutenant. One Lieutenant R. kept McC. and countenance by following closely his example. He is a little compound of fice and weasel, and having charge of the cleaning up of the camp, has abundant opportunities to bully and insult, but being, fortunately, very far short of the Grenadier size, he does not use his boot or fist as freely as his great exemplar. No one, however, was safe from either of them, who, however accidentally and innocently, fell in their way, physically or metaphorically.

Of the same block Captain Borden was a chip: a fair-haired light-mustached, Saxon-faced "Yank"—far the worst type of man, let me tell you, yet discovered— whose whole intercourse with the prisoners was of the essence of brutality. An illustration will paint them more thoroughly than a philippic. A prisoner named Hale, belonging to the old Stonewall brigade, was discovered one day rather less sober than was allowable to any but the loyal, and Borden being officer of the guard, arrested him and demanded where he got his liquor. This he refused to tell, as it would compromise others, and anyone but a Yankee would have put them in the guardhouse, compelled him to where he barrel shirt, or inflicted some punishment proportionate to his offense.

All this would have been very natural, but not Bordenish, so this is Valorous Parolles determined to apply the torture to force a confession! Hale was accordingly tied up by the thumbs—that is, his thumbs were fastened securely together behind his back, and a rope been attached to the cord uniting them, it was passed over a crossbar over his head and hauled down, until it raised the sufferer so nearly off the ground that the entire weight of his body was sustained by his thumbs, strained in an unnatural position, his toes merely touching the ground. The torture of this at the wrists and shoulder joints is exquisite, but Hale persisted in refusing to peach, and called on his fellow-prisoners, many of whom were witnesses of this refined villany, to remember this when they get home. Borden grew exasperated as his victim's fortitude, and determined to gag him. This he essayed to accomplish by fastening a heavy oak tent-pin in his mouth; and when he could not open his mouth sufficiently—not an easy operation—he struck him in the face with the oaken billet, a blow which broke several of his teeth and covered his mouth with blood!

On the other hand, some of the officers were as humane and merciful as these wretches were brutal and cowardly, and all who were my fellow-prisoners will recall, with grateful remembrance, Captain Benjamin Munger, Lieutenant Dalgleish, Sergeant-Major Rudd, Lieutenant McKee, Lieutenant Haverty, commissary of one of the regiments guarding us, a whole-souled Fenian, formerly in the book-business in New York, and still they were probably, and one or two others.

These officers were assigned in the proportion of one to every company at first, but to every three hundred or four hundred men afterwards, and were charged with the duty of superintending roll calls, inspecting quarters, and seen that the men under their charge got their rations; and the system was excellent.

During the month of July, four thousand three hundred and twenty-three prisoners were entered on the records of Elmira prison, and by 29 August, the date of the last arrivals, nine thousand six hundred and seven.

The barrack accommodations did not suffice for quite half of them, and the remainder were provided with A-tents, in which they continued to be housed when I left the prison in the middle of the following October, although the weather was piercingly cold. Thinly clad as they came from the summer's campaign, many of them without blankets, and without even a handful of straw between them and the frozen earth, it will surprise no one that the suffering, even at that early day, was considerable.

As I left, however, the contributions of the Confederate Government, which, despairing of procuring and exchange, was taxing its exhausted energies to aid the prisoners, began to come in.

An agent was in New York selling cotton for the purpose, and many boxes of blankets and coarse clothing were furnished from the proceeds of the sale.

This tender regard was a happy contrast to the barbarity of Washington management, which seem to feel the utmost indifference to the sufferings of the soldiers, and embarrassed their exchange by every device of delay in every suggestion of stubbornness.

185

Chapter XIV

As I have spoken of the military government of Elmira prison, it may not be inappropriate to pursue the statistical view, now that I am in it, a brief chapter on the Medical and Commissary Departments, before I resume the thread of the more personal portion of my narrative.

The chief of the former department was a club-afforded little gentlemen, with an abnormal head and a snaky look in his eyes, named Major E. L. Sanger. On our arrival in Elmira, another surgeon, remarkable chiefly for his unaffected simplicity and virgin ignorance of everything appertaining to medicine, played doctor there. But as the prisoners increased in numbers, a more formal and formidable staff was organized, with Sanger at the head.

Sanger was simply a brute, as we found when we learned the whole truth about him from his own people. If he had not avoided a court-martial by resigning his position, it is likely that even a military commission would have found it impossible to screen his brutality to the sick, although the fact that the United States hanged no one for the massacre of Indian women and sucking infants during the year 1865, inspires the fear that this systematic * * * * * * * *of Confederate prisoners would have been commended for his patriotism.

He was assisted by Doctor Rider, of Rochester, one of the few "copperheads" whom I met in any office, great or small, at the North. My association was rather more intimate with him than with any of the others, and I believe him to have been a competent and faithful officer. Personally, I acknowledge many kindnesses with gratitude. The rest of the "meds" were, in truth, a motley crew in the main, most of them being selected from the impossibility, it would seem, of doing anything else with them. I remember one of the worthies, whose miraculous length of leg and neck suggested "crane" to all the observers, whose innocence of medicine was quite refreshing. On being sent for to prescribe for prisoner, who is said to have bilious fever, he asked the druggist, a "reb" in the most naïve manner, what was the usual treatment for that disease! Fortunately, during his stay in Elmira, which was not long, there were no drugs in the dispensary, or I shudder to picture the consequences. This department was constantly undergoing changes, and I suspect that the whole system was intended as part of the education of the young doctors assigned to us, for as soon as they learn to distinguish between quinine and magnesia they were removed to another field of labor.

The whole camp was divided into wards, to which physicians were assigned, among whom were three "rebel" prisoners, Doctor Lynch of Baltimore, Doctor Martin, of South Carolina, and Doctor Graham, formerly of Stonewall Jackson's staff, and the fellow-townsman of the lamented hero. These ward physicians treated the simplest cases and their patient's barrack, and transferred the more dangerous ones to the hospital's, of which there were ten or twelve, capable of accommodating about eighty patients each. Here every arrangement was made that carpenters could make to ensure the patients against unnecessary mortality, and, indeed, a system was professed which would have delighted the heart of the Sisters of Charity; but, alas! The practice was quite another thing. The most scandalous neglect prevailed even in so simple a matter as providing food for the sick, and I do not doubt that many of those who died perished from actual starvation.

One of the Petersburg prisoners having become so sick as to be sent to the hospital, he complained to his friends who visited him that he could get nothing to eat, and was dying in consequence, when they made application for leave to buy him some potatoes and roast them for him. Doctor Sanger not being consulted, the request was granted, and when, a few hours afterwards, roasted potatoes were brought in, the poor invalids on the neighboring cots crawled from their beds and begged the peelings to satisfy the hunger that was gnawing them.

When complaint was made of this brutality to the sick, there was always a convenient official excuse. Sometimes the fault would be, that a lazy doctor would not make out his provision return in time, in which case the whole ward must go without food, or with an inadequate supply till the next day. Another time there would be a difficulty between the chief surgeon and the commissary, whose general relations were of the stripe characterized by S. P. Andrews as "cat and dogamy," which would result in the latter refusing to furnish the former with bread for the sick! In almost all cases the "spiritus frumenti" fail to get to the patient's, or in so small a quantity after the various tolls, that it would not quicken the circulation of a canary.

But the great fault, next to the scant supply of nourishment, was the inexcusable deficiency of medicine. During several weeks, in which dysentery and inflammation of the bowels were the prevalent diseases in prison, there was not a grain of any preparation of opium in the dispensary, and many a poor fellow died for the want of a common medicine, which no family is ordinarily without— that is, if men ever die for want of drugs.

There would be, and is much excuse for such deficiencies in the South—and this is a matter which the Yankees studiously ignore—inasmuch as the blockade renders it impossible to procure any luxuries even for our own sick, and curtails and renders enormously expensive the supply of drugs, of the simplest kind, providing they are exotics; but in a nation, whose boast is that they do not feel the war, with the world open to them, and supplies of all sorts wonderfully abundant, it is simply infamous to starve the sick as they did there, and equally discreditable to deny them medicines—indispensable according to Esculapian traditions. The results of the ignorance of the doctors, and the sparseness of these supplies, was soon apparent in the shocking mortality of this camp, notwithstanding the healthfulness claimed for the situation. These exceeded even the reported mortality of Andersonville, great as that was, and disgraceful as it was to our government, if it resulted from causes which were within its control.

I know the reader, if a Northern man, will deny this, and points to the record of the Wirz trial. I object to the testimony. There never was, in all time, such a mass of lies as that evidence, for the most part, could have been proved to be, if it had been possible to sift the testimony, or examine, before a jury, the witnesses. I take, as the basis of my comparison, the published report made by four Andersonville prisoners, who were allowed to come North, on their representation that they could induce their humane government to assent to an exchange. Edwin M. Stanton would have seen the whole of them die before he would give General Lee one able-bodied soldier.

These prisoners alleged (I quote from memory), that out of a population of about thirty-six thousand at that pen, six thousand, or one sixth of the whole, died between the first of February and the first of August, 1864. Now at Elmira, the quota was not made up till the last of August, so that September was the first month during which any fair estimate of the mortality of the camp could be made. Now, out of less than nine thousand five hundred prisoners, on 1st of September, three hundred and eighty-six died that month.

At Andersonville, the mortality averaged a thousand a month, out of thirty-six thousand, or one thirty-six. At Elmira, it was three hundred and eighty-six out of nine thousand five hundred or one and 25th of the whole. At Elmira, it was four percent; at Andersonville, less than three percent. If the mortality at Andersonville had been as great as at Elmira, the deaths should've been one thousand four hundred and forty per month or 50 percent more than they were.

I speak by the card representing these matters, having kept the morning return of the deaths for the last month and a half of my life at Elmira, and transferred the figures to my diary, which lies before me. And this, be it remembered, in a country where food was cheap and abundant; where all the appliances of the remedial art were to be had on mere requisition; where there was no military necessity requiring the government to sacrifice almost every consideration to the inaccessibility of the prison, and the securing of the prisoners, and where Nature had furnished every possible requisite for salubrity.

And now that I am speaking of the death-record, I will jot down two singular facts in connection therewith.

The first was the unusual mortality among the prisoners from North Carolina. In my diary, I find several entries like the following:

Monday, October 3rd--Deaths yesterday, 16, of whom 11 were from North Carolina.

Tuesday, October 14th--Deaths yesterday, 14, of whom 7 were from North Carolina.

Now, the proportion of North Carolinians was nothing even approximating what might have been expected from this record. I commit the fact to Mr. Gradgrind. Can it be explained by the great attachment the people of that state have for their homes?

Now, I know well that many of the sick died from this, and kindred diseases produced by the miasma of the stagnant lake in our camp; but the reports, which I consolidated every morning, contained no reference to them. I inquired at the dispensary, where the reports were first handed in, the cause of this anomaly; and learned that Dr. Sanger *would sign no report, which ascribed to any of these diseases is the death of the patient!* I concluded that he must have committed himself to the harmlessness of the lagoon in question, and determined to preserve his consistency at the expense of our lives,--very much after the fashion of that illustrious ornament of the profession, Dr. Sangrado, who continued his warm water and phlebotomy, merely because he had written a book in praise of that practice, although "in six weeks he made more widows and orphans than the siege of Troy."

I could hardly help visiting on Doctor Sanger the reproaches his predecessor received at the hands of the persecuted people of Valladolid, and call the doctor a Gil Blas no more euphonious name then "ignorant assassins."

Any post in the medical department in a Yankee prison-camp is quite valuable on account of the opportunities of plunder it affords, and many of the virtuous "meds" made extensive use of their advantages. Vast quantities of opium were prescribed they were never taken, the price (eight dollars an ounce) tempting the cupidity of the physicians beyond all resistance; but the grand speculation was in whiskey, which was supplied to the dispensary in large quantities, and could be obtained for a consideration in any reasonable amount from a "steward" who pervaded that establishment.

I ought not to dismiss this portion of my manuscript of matters medical without adding that the better class of officers in the pen were loud and indignant in their reproaches of

Sanger's systematic inhumanity to the sick, and that they affirmed that he vowed his determination to stand those poor helpless creatures in retaliation for alleged neglect on the part of our authorities! And when at last, on 21 September, I carried my report up to the major's tent, with the ghastly record of TWENTY-NINE DEATHS YESTERDAY, the storm gathered which in a few weeks drove him from the pen, but which never would have had that effect, if he had not by his rudeness attained the ill well of nearly every officer about the pen whose goodwill was worth having.

I ascend from pills to provender.

The commissary department was under the charge of a cute, active ex-bank officer, Captain G. C. Whitton. The ration of bread was usually full pound, forty-five barrels of flour being converted daily into loaves in the bakeshop On the Premises. The meat ration, on the other hand, was invariably scanty; and I learned, on inquiry, that the fresh beef sent to the prison usually fell short from one thousand to twelve hundred pounds in each consignment. Of course, when this happened, many had to lose a large portion of their allowance; and sometimes it happened that the same man got bones only for several successive days. The expedience resorted to by the men to supply this want of animal food were disgusting. Many found an acceptable substitute in rats, with which the place abounded; and these Chinese delicacies commanded in average price of about four cents apiece—in greenbacks. I have seen scores of them in various states of preparation, and have been assured by those who indulged in them there were worse things could have been eaten— an estimate of their value that I took on trust.

Others found in the barrels of refuse fat, which were accumulated at the cookhouse, and in the pickings of the bones, which were cut out of the meat and thrown out in a dirty heap back of the kitchen, to be removed once a week, the means of satisfying the cravings for meat, which rations would not satisfy. I have seen a mob of hungry "rebs" besieged the bone cart, and beg from the driver fragments on which an August sun had been burning for several days, until the impenetrable nose of a Congo could hardly have endured them.

Twice a day the camp poured its thousands into the mess rooms, where each man's ration was assigned him; and twice a day the aforesaid rations were characterized by disappointed "rebs" in language not to be found in a prayer book. Those whose appetite was stronger than their apprehensions frequently contrived to supply their wants by "flanking"—a performance which consisted in joining two or more companies as they successively went to the mess-rooms, or and quietly sweeping up a ration as the company filed down the table. As every ration so flanked was, however, obtained at the expense of some helpless fellow prisoner, who must lose that meal, the practice was almost universally frowned upon; and the criminal, when discovered, which was frequently the case, was subjected to instant punishment.

This was either confinement in the guardhouse, solitary confinement on bread and water, the "sweat-box," or the barrel-shirt. The war has made all these terms familiar, except the third, perhaps; buy it I mean a wooden box, about seven feet high, twenty inches wide, and twelve deep, which was placed on end in front of the major's tent. Few could stand in this without elevating the shoulders considerably; and when the door was fastened all motion was out of the question. The prisoner had to stand with his limbs rigid and in movable until the jailer opened the door, and it was by far the most dreaded of the *peines fortes et dures* of the pen. In midsummer, I can fancy that a couple of hours and such a coffin would

189

inspire Tartuffe himself with virtuous thoughts, especially of his avoirdupois was at all respectable.

Chapter XV
Authors note: The first page of this chapter has nothing to do with Elmira prison camp or the army. Therefore, I feel justified in excluding it from this text.

My only purpose was to claim credence for an averment I am about to make, by showing that my experience was not exceptional, and that there is nothing absolutely without parallel, in the declaration that I owe whatever of particular advantage I enjoyed, throughout my whole stay at Elmira, to a sudden attack of that undignified disorder which is treated with copious libations of extract of anise-seed, in infantile victims, and Jamaica ginger and paregoric when the patient gets well out of long clothes, but which the mature wisdom of adult age finds most certain relief from in Otard or Hennessey "straight."

As Napoleon is said to have been a constant victim of this complaint, I need not blush to own that I was similarly affected on my arrival at Elmira, and soon wended my way to the drugstore to seek a remedy. Such are the wiles of temperance people, that it will not do to ask, under certain circumstances, for a dram, the subterfuge is of the Maine Law men having destroyed human confidence to an alarming degree, so I suggested "ginger" to a mild looking descendent—longe intervallo—of Esculapius, whom I found the presiding genius of the dispensary. I must have made my request in a super professional tone, for he straightaway inquired whether I was a practitioner of medicine. Being among enemies, I exhibited none of the indignation proper to such an imputation, and commanding my feelings, merely returned a decided "No," but the doctor evidently doubted me still, and seem to infer that I must needs have a diploma, because I knew the *quant. Suf.* of Brown's essence; so he insisted that I should consent to come and aid him in the daily augmenting duties of his new post. As, however, I did not have quite impudence enough to undertake the bolus business, I Stoutly really resisted, to the mingled amazement and grief with the surgeon.

He was kind enough to say that he was very sorry for it, as he would've been glad to have had me with him. I instantly conceived a high respect for the doctor's discernment, and told him that I would be glad to obtain some clerical duties to keep me from insanity.

The doctor intimated that I might obtain employment at headquarters by making application; whereupon, I framed, in immaculate calligraphy, a note to Major Colt, requesting him to assign me to some duty, which, without compromising my position as a hopeless "rebel," would give me employment--something to eke out the monotonous days of durance. This, the doctor, in whose eyes I had evidently found favor—I do not suppose he meant an insult by suspecting me of medicine—undertook to deliver.

Night soon came, and on a French bedstead, composed of a couple of planks, with no bed clothing of any description, I stretched myself for a nap. By about 3 o'clock, I found it necessary to turn out to the wood pile, and seek, in diligent chopping, the means of restoring the circulation, and, thereupon, I find the following entry:

"Elmira, July 13th—Chopping wood, disgusting. If I had been that "Woodsman," it would've been required deuced little singing to have induced me to "spare that tree," or any other tree."

Day broke at last—and by at last, I essay to express the fact, that it seemed about as hard to break as Colonel N.'s passion for wearing clothes that won't fit him—and shortly after roll call I received a summons to the major's tent. He offered me a cigar, which, having no small vices, I declined, and soon entered into a free conversation on matters military, political, and personal, including by handing me a note, which I found to be an assignment to duty in the office of his adjutant. I reported at once, and was soon at work transferring a large "Dooms-day Book" the record of the name, Regiment, company, place and time of capture, ward and number of each prisoner, a volume which finally swelled to colossal portions. I subsequently found that my position entitled me to a couple cups of coffee, and a fee of--$.10 *per diem*! The coffee was in anomalous production, made by a suspending a bag of ground coffee (?) in a boiler, holding, I presume, a hundred gallons, the water in which was renewed for three days, when the bag was taken out, emptied, and refilled. The first days boiling was fair, the second unfair, the third a mockery and a delusion; but such as it was, I accepted it very thankfully, and considered myself entitled to make no complaint, as the Yankee sergeants, in the pen, were furnished with the same.

In the course of a few days, the finances of the prisoners required attention, as money began to be sent them, and the ledger was entrusted to my keeping, and air along this business became so onerous that a reorganization of the department took place; three professional bookkeepers were employed, and the miscellaneous role of duty was assigned to me— making out the morning death report, answering letters sent to the major, making various inquiries respecting the camp, keeping the sutlers daily account straight, and thrice a month making out the "detail accounts" of the prison. As to the latter matter, Elmira formed an exception, I believe, to other Yankee prisons. All duty performed by prisoners, except the police of the quarters— that is, the daily cleaning of the camp— was paid for at the rate of five cents a day for mere laborers, and ten cents for clerks and artificers. These workmen were divided into four heads, according as they report to the adjutant, the commissary, the surgeon, or the officer commanding the labor detail; and as many as four hundred men and all were thus provided with employment, which relieved them of the horrible *ennui* of imprisonment, and furnish them with the means of securing a moderate supply of tobacco—the Universal Consolation of *Lee's Miserables*.

I may add that the wages thus earned were, in all cases, as far as I had the opportunity of knowing, honestly paid. I have one thousand times entered the credits on the ledger to various prisoners, and have seen them draw out their deposits in the form of orders.

In the course of the various changes in my line of duty, I gradually acquired possession of a comfortable room, in which I soon rigged up a bunk, and, greatest blessing of all, formed, through the partiality of Captain Whitton, an alimentary association with the sergeant of the cookhouse, the chief baker (resembling the good patriarch Joseph in my prison association, if in nothing else) and a pair of "rebs" engaged in those establishments, which secured me then, and thenceforth against any apprehensions on the subject of rations, or any interest in the rise of rats.

My association with the officers commanding the prison gave me, of course, many opportunities of assisting my fellow confederates, and I had the happiness of being the means of making the state of many of them less irksome, and their restraints less grievous to bear, without any compromise of their or my principles or position, which were known to be those of a rebel, *sans reproche*.

191

Chapter XV

I resume my extracts from my diary, occasionally anticipating events of subsequent dates referring to subjects treated of also under a preceding one, to avoid repetition.

Tuesday, July 12th—Having staked out my sleeping premises, I indulged in the luxury of a good scrubbing, for myself and my inside clothing and the sun being warm, I spread both—the close in their where—on the grass to dry. At 4 PM dinner was announced— deuced fashionable clothes up here—tin-plates, knives and forks, plenty of soup and bread, and beneficent gentleman in blue clothes politely inviting us to "ask for more," if we had not had enough. We all asked. Not that we were hungry, but merely to satisfy ourselves that the thing was real.

All this over, our captain benignly informs us that at 5 o'clock he would take us to the Chemung to bathe! Some unregenerate rebel, prepared to expect anything after his experiences so far, asks him dubiously, "if they furnish Windsor soap and towels," and affects much indignation at the laugh he provokes, and a little disappointment at the negative response.

One by one, and that speedily, all these little luxuries vanished. Gone were our tin-plates; gone the knives and forks; gone the seats at the table; gone the encouragement to cry out for more; gone the ablutions in the placid Chemung.

Saturday, July 16th--An ugly rumor prevails in camp that a fearful accident occurred yesterday on the Erie Railroad— the train bringing prisoners here colliding with a coal train going east, near a place called, I think, Shohola. The deaths, it is said, number sixty-seven, and among them are seventeen of the Yankee guards. Tonight, we were roused about midnight, with a request that we would come and help the wounded in, the train having arrived with the surviving victims of the catastrophe. Many of them were in horrible condition, and when I went to the hospital the following Monday I found the wounds of many still undressed, even the blood not washed from their limbs, to which, in many instances, the clothing adhered, glued by the clotted gore; still, the Advertiser, the administration paper in Elmira, of this morning, proclaims to the world that the poor fellows were humanely cared for! Lieutenant H., who visited them on Tuesday, and who expressed to me his indignation, in no measured terms, at the neglect, could tell a different story. An attempt was made to court-martial this officer for acts of kindness to the prisoners, but he put a stop to all proceedings at once, by intimating to the authorities, that in the event of a trial, he had a story to tell the Herald of the inhumanity of those hospital treatments at Elmira, which a trial would certainly force them to print. *He was not molested.*

For many weeks afterwards, friends and relatives try to obtain admission to the prison to see and administer aid to the sufferers, but were denied the privilege. In one case a very near female relative made a trip of hundreds of miles to see a prisoner, and the only indulgence she received was a permission to ascend an observatory near the "pen," on a certain hour in the afternoon, when her kinsmen was allowed to post himself under a tree in the enclosure, with a white handkerchief around his arm, and thus, at a distance too great to for any communication, they were allowed *to gaze at each other* for an hour! While I was at Elmira, I remember but two or three instances in which anyone was allowed to visit a prisoner. A lady, by dint of great exertions, obtained from the authorities at Washington permission to visit her son, who was badly wounded; and a clergyman, by officiating in the "pen" (a little arrangement of which Major Colt deserves the credit), got the opportunity of a brief conversation with his son. One or two similar cases finished the chapter.

I must not forget to record here the humanity with which the maimed and mangled prisoners were treated by the "Copperheads," near the scene of the disaster, many of whom, as the prisoners informed me, urged upon those who were unhurt, or not too badly wounded to travel, to seize the chance then offered them to escape. Without money, and with hundreds of miles of an enemy's country between them and freedom, there was little encouragement to accept this well meant consul. Not more than four escaped.

Friday, July 22nd—Major Colt placed in my hands today, for reply, a letter from Mrs. D. G. M., Making inquiries concerning certain members of the fourth South Carolina cavalry. I had the good fortune to be able to answer her question; and I noticed the fact, since it gives me the occasion to speak of the exceeding kindness of hundreds of northern ladies to prisoners. There was a society in Baltimore, composed of the noblest women of that noble city, some of whom denied themselves every luxury becoming their education and position in life, that they might contribute what was thus gained to soothe the sorrows of the gallant boys would lost their liberty in a cause, which, however proscribed and overmatched, was inexpressibly dear to these good women.

That God blessed the pro-offered cup of water cannot pass unheeded such noble and devoted benefactors.

Our curiosity had been excited for some days past, by noticing a wooden structure, consisting of two large platforms, one above the other, which has been going up across the road that bounds one face of our prison. I learned, today, that it is an observatory where the sightseeing penchant of the Yanks is to be made available, to put money in the purse of an enterprising partnership, which proposes to turn our pen into a menagerie, and exhibit the inmates to the refined and valorous people of the Chemung Valley, at the modest fee of $.15 a head! *"Refreshments provided below."*

The event justified the wisdom of the venture, for one of the proprietors, who was part of the management in our pen, assured me that the concern paid for itself in two weeks. I am surprised that Barnum has not taken the prisoners off the hands of Abe, divided them into companies, and carried them in caravans through the country, after the manner of Sesostris, and other antique heroes, turning an honest penny by the show.

So profitable was this peculiarly Yankee "institooshion," that a week or two thereafter a rival establishment, taller by a score of feet, sprang up, and the grand "sightseeing and spruce beer" warfare began, which shook Elmira to its uttermost depths. One building was Radical, the other Copperhead; one was taller, the other older and more original—qualifications considered important by Doctor Sands, and quite apropos to sightseeing as sarsaparilla. Heaven knows where it all would have ended, but that the government confiscated the "Democratic platform," under the plea of military necessity, and its Abolition brother remained master of the situation.

Here, every summer afternoon, the population of Elmira— chiefly of the female persuasion— congregated to feast their eyes on their enemies, Much after the fashion that the worshipers of Dagon the mighty son of manoah; and until the days became so cold that exposure in so high a position was unpleasant, the shin plasters rolled in, and the lemon pop and ginger cakes rolled out of the orthodox observatory, to the great pecuniary comfort of the true believers who owned it.

Patriotism is spelled with a "y" at the end of the first syllable up here.

Sunday, July 24th— Major Colt suggested, yesterday, that it might be desired by some of the prisoners to have divine service regularly on Sunday; and added, that if an application were made out, he would forward it to Colonel Eastman, who commanded the post, and who would doubtless approve it. This was done, and the clergymen of the city readily assented to the proposition to visit the prison alternately. Under this arrangement we had service this evening, and almost every Sunday afternoon thereafter. The abolition editor of Elmira complained very bitterly of the alacrity with which the clerical gentlemen accepted the proposal, and intimated that it was due to their curiosity, not their zeal,--a little quarrel I do not pretend to adjust.

The first minister who visited us was Reverend Thomas Beecher, a brother (he had a dozen or so, all preachers) of the notorious Henry Ward, who cultivates politics, preaching, and potatoes, to much temporal advantage, as the world knows. "Tom" is not as "sound on the crow" as Ward, and gave us a very practical, sensible, and liberal talk. During his sermon, six twenty-five more prisoners arrived, and, indeed, they began to come in pretty rapidly now—three hundred on the 25th, seven hundred and thirty-five on the 29th and so on.

I saw a man today, a "reb," asking Negro to give him the quid of tobacco he was chewing when he was done with it, that he might dry it and then smoke it, and the incident furnished me with as much food for reflection as did the little prison flower to the poor prisoner of Saintine's beautiful story. We hear a great deal of the ignorant Irish, the stolid Dutch, etc., but it is my deliberate conviction that the French Academy, if would on thin soup in prison regimen, and deprived of books, papers, etc., for three months, would relapse into Hottentotish heathenism.

A Flagstaff was raised today, and our drum corps, a "rebel band," brought out to salute the "astral" with hail Columbia. It is a beautiful manner, unquestionably. Got a peep today at the July number of the Atlantic Monthly, which contains an account of Grant's doings so far, illustrated by a diagram curiously illustrating the fact that he has been beaten every time he has met Lee. It consists of the routes of the respective armies from Orange Courthouse to the James. Grant's route is described by a series of arcs, of which Lee's forms the cords. Starting from Orange Courthouse, they met in the Wilderness, when Grant is driven off into space, and curves back to Spotsylvania Courthouse, when, again repulsed, he flies off on a larger curve to meet Lee at North Anna, and again makes a comet leap, crossing the James. Yet, alas, the struggle cannot last forever. The last regiments have come to the gallant old Knight of Arlington, and he who gloried in the past two years to meet McClellan, Burnside, and Hooker on the plain, fights now "always behind breast works." You must husband his little handful that they may last as long as possible against the fresh legions which the draft and the emigrant ships are pouring into the camp of his adversary.

Chapter XVII

Sunday, 14th—Had two sermons today. One in front of the observatory, by Reverend Father Kavanagh, a Catholic priest—a Christian discourse; the other by a Reverend Bainvi

194

bridge, a freedom schrieker, in front of the major's tent. Bainbridge's speech was one long insult to the prisoners. Indeed, his conduct was so disgusting that Lieutenant Richmond, heretofore in this chronicle honorably mentioned, presented the worthy with ten dollars, and testimony of his appreciation! The joke was on that Bainbridge was full enough to publish Richmond's letter in the Elmira B. R. organ— a gratuitous advertisement of a full and a knave.

During the delivery of B.'s harangue, some of his auditory quietly rose and left the presence of his abolitionship; whereupon Richmond arrested the nonconformist, and but for the intervention of another officer, would have clapped them in the guardhouse, for the unpardonable sin of unwillingness to receive gratuitous insults. The clerical world in Puritandom has not changed altogether from the happy days of Quaker whipping and Papist hanging, where of the annals of Connecticut orthodoxy are rife.

I should be glad to be able to present the reader with the correspondence between Bainbridge and Richmond, but I have lost it.

R. being a negrophilist to the extent of his very limited capacity, greatly belauded the Africanism of B.s harangue, while B. replied with an unction that nothing but a ten dollar note could inspire in such a soul.

While on the subject of the disposition of parties unconnected with us officially, I take occasion to make grateful acknowledgments to the mayor of Elmira, John Arnot, Esquire, and his most estimable sister. They were noble representatives of a class neither few in numbers nor unimportant in influence throughout the North, with whom charity to an unfortunate people fighting for the right of self-government against far greater odds than their forefathers encountered in the same battle ninety years before, was not considered inconsistent with the obligations of good citizenship.

Thursday, August 18th—An order was received here today from Colonel Hoffman, the commissary general of prisoners (but emanating from the vindictive breast of Stanton no doubt), prohibiting the settlers from selling any more food or clothing to the prisoners; prohibiting all eatables from being sent into the camp by any party whatsoever; and also forbidding any clothing from being furnished by any person, "except one change of underclothing, and one suit of course grade material" to each prisoner.

A dozen or two of the prisoners were getting blankets and overcoats in anticipation of the coming winter, whose rigors will far exceed anything to which most of them are custom, that dire suffering must result. Stanton could not endure that.

I obtained today several of what they call "family papers"—newspapers published weekly for circulation in the families of the good loyal people of the North-- and was very much struck with a novelty which has been introduced into them since the war began,-- advertisements of obscene pictures, and what are called among men "fancy" articles. These papers teem with them, and nothing could more forcibly illustrate the debauchery of the people. Its effect is visible among the officers and men around us, the daily conversation of many of whom would disgrace a brothel. The hearts must be extremely corrupt which could inspire such foul utterances.

In this respect, as well as in the matter of profanity, there was no comparison between the two armies. I heard more oats, and far more vulgarity of speech, from Federal soldiers during the five months of my captivity, then I heard in Dixie during the 2 ¾ years of my connection with Lee's army; and the evidence is overwhelming, that the immorality, of which there were many examples, tainted much of the Northern life. More than one of the officers of the post-assured me that there were 1000 prostitutes in Elmira, while I continued a depot for drafted men; and from more than one surgeon I heard statements of the proportion of their soldiers who suffered from venereal taint, which surpassed anything in the recorded military statistics of the world. The developments on this head with which the Northern press has teamed since hostilities have ceased, the appalling lists of divorces for adultery, the crimes of violence traceable to lust, are too well known to need recital here. I found in the May number of Harper's Magazine an article deploring this horrible corruption among the young, referable in great part to this source; and since my return I have seen one thousand evidences in Northern papers of the almost universality of this particular form of vice.

Friday, August 19th--Today another batch of prisoners arrived. They were brought through by land, to avoid falling in with the Tallahassee, which is playing the devil with Yankee shipping, almost within sight of New York Harbor. The greatest panic prevails in Gotham thereanent.

Saturday, August 20th—A heavy mail from Dixie, which we can't get, because some villainous "reb" made away with the bulletin board last night! The adjutant vows that, until the plank comes back, the letters must lie in his desk, and great is our grief thereat.

Sunday, August 21th--This morning the missing plank came back, ornamented with a well-executed checkerboard, whereby some enterprising Confederate, disgusted with prison monotony, doubtless supposed he would be allowed in peace to regale himself.

One painful episode mars the record of this month. On 21st August, one of our comrades, a young man of irreproachable character, of intelligence, and of gentleness of manner which won all hearts, even among the enemy, sank under an attack of intermittent fever, and died. Major Colt, who had been as considerate as possible during his illness, and who had permitted us to procure anything the town afforded that he needed, ordered a metallic coffin for him, and allowed a hearse to enter the gates for the convenience of the body to the potter's field, where the prisoners are recorded Their stinted share of "God's Acre." Reverend Arthur Edey, a Confederate chaplain, of one of the Texas regiments, and a decided rebel, though a native of New York, read the impressive service of the Episcopal Church over the remains; while a little group of bareheaded men stood together around the dead-house, in whose front the body lay. This over, we formed in procession behind the hearse, and marched as far as the prison gate— all the indulgence we could procure— with heavier hearts, I ween, and far more of genuine respect, then has often marked the obsequies of King or Kaiser.

How many of us might make our exit from our prison bars on this wise, and who should be the next thus followed, were questions that did not fail to suggest themselves to all, and questions which kept some faces solemn for days thereafter.

The last three mails have brought three envelopes to me, each one containing only the signature of the writer. The letters were probably a line or two over the orthodox length, and therefore contraband.

I do not know that I shall have a more appropriate occasion than the present to give place to a colored patriot who performed orderly duties in the pen for the major. His name was Bonus, and he belonged, as he informed me, to a Mister Posey, of Hendersonville,

Kentucky, from whom he was taken by some passing officers, who wanted the servant and did not care to pay for one.

Bonus was an exceedingly good-natured fellow, and had been evidently a well-trained servant, but the Army had spoiled him pretty effectually. He did me a good many services, for which I compensated him as well as I could, but his work for me had the unction of a labor of love, and he did not hesitate to express his preference for "Southern gentlemen."

I went down to the cookhouse one evening for my dinner, and found Bonus getting himself up with an extreme elaborateness. His boots were as glossy as his cheeks—and this exhausts praise— he sported a brilliant paper collar, a crimson scarf, and a uniform almost new.

Of course I desired to know the cause of all this preparation, a surmise crossing my mind that he was about to enlighten the dullness of Republican minds in Elmira by a speech, after the manner of his brother Douglas. So I asked:

"What's the matter, Bonus?"

"Gwine to be married, sir!"

"Married! The mischief! You told me you had a wife in Kentucky, and another in Cincinnati, already."

"Oh yes, sir, but I ain't got none in Elmiry!"

Bonus evidently thought this concluded the argument, as he delivered himself of the self-satisfied guffaw, while he completed a "miwaculuos tie."

I asked him next morning what he thought when the parson made him promise to cleave to his present wife and forsake all others, inasmuch as he declared he loved his first wife best?

"Oh," said Bonus, "I didn't say nuffin, but I had my 'pinion 'bout dat."

August 28th—The regulations of the pen are growing more strict. No food is permitted to be sold to us by the sutler. That which is sent to us from outside is confiscated, ostensibly for the use of the hospital's, but when Major Colt's back is turned the officers do the confiscating on their own private account. Today I was at the major's tent when a box was open containing pears for one of the prisoners. Of course he was not permitted to have them, and the Yankee officers began eating them before the boy's face—he could not have been more than seventeen. One of the Yanks remarked with a sneer, "I wish they would send better fruit!"

This was rather too much for the "rebel" temper, and the boy retorted instantly—

"My sister did not suppose she was putting them up for the Federal officers, I reckon exclamation point"

The pear thief almost blushed.

Last night two prisoners were captured in a tunnel under one of the hospitals. They had almost completed their labor, when they were found out and locked up in solitary confinement.

Monday, 29th—Some clothing arrived today. Major Colt been absent on leave, Peck, the purloined or of rings in chains, is in command.

Anticipating the early approach of cold weather, I thought I would apply for a jacket. The ring thief refused. Said I was "not ragged enough yet."

Wednesday, 31st—An order received today prohibiting the officers from reading newspapers to prisoners.

Cannon firing tonight in Elmira—a salute over the nomination of McClellan by the Chicago Convention. Sentinels ordered to carry to the guardhouse everyone who speaks to them.

Sunday, September 4th—Bishop Timon, Catholic Bishop of Buffalo, preached today in surplice and cape on the sublime and suggestive text, "I thought of the ancient days. The eternal years were in my mind."

Sunday, 11th—The restricting of the prisoners to a uniform diet of bread and meat, and denying them the privilege of purchasing other food, are showing their affection an epidemic, almost, of scurvy.

A thorough examination of the camp has been made during the past week, and the surgeons consolidated report, as a clerk at the dispensary has just informed me, announces eighteen hundred and seventy scorbutic cases out of nine thousand three hundred prisoners.

Last evening the boys, to the number of a hundred, were holding a debating society, one Lieutenant McC. passed by. The president, seeing him eyeing the crowd, invited him to come and take a seat. He was hunting an affront at all times, and took this for one. "No," said he, "damn you, I'll move on, and if I get any impudence from you, I'll disburse ye damn quick—the whole of ye."

He would listen to no explanations, and the meeting waited in solemn silence until the great man passed.

The authorities have for peremptorily refused permission to establish a school here. A number of us who had assurances the books would be furnished us, requested permission to organize elementary schools for those who could not read or write, and seeing no possible objection, made application for leave, without a doubt of success. Major Colt approved the request, but higher authority forbade.

In order to furnish light to the sentinels at night, and prevent efforts to escape, a number of kerosene lamps are hung up around the enclosure, which are extinguished every morning at dawn by a detail of prisoners. This morning, while engaged in this duty, one of them was hailed by the nearest sentry with a low whistle, and when he stopped, the soldier threw a note to him and passed on. Picking it up, he found it was addressed to me. Contraband, of course. How it got to the sentinel, I have not been able to surmise.

One of the men who died today in the room where our comrade B. is lying, told his brother, almost with his last breath, to tell his family he died of *starvation*. I told this to Captain Munger, who made this characteristic reply:

"It takes all the surgeons time and capacity to do justice to this camp, and if his brain is seven × nine, he wants help."

The daily death list is increasing rapidly, and although they are building hospitals continually, there is never room enough.

Wednesday, 21st—The deaths yesterday were *twenty-nine.* Air pure, location healthy, no epidemic. The men are being deliberately murdered by the surgeon, especially by either the ignorance or the malice of the chief.

Dr. Graham assured me that he had stopped one of the attendants today who was carrying to the dispensary the prescriptions for sixty-five beds, and he had but two. The other sixty-three the surgeon in attendance only looked at.

Of fourteen men in one of Dr. Martin's sections, twelve were dead; and seventeen and another, fourteen had died, and two more certain to die, from the want of food and medicines. He illustrated to me the ignorance of one of the doctors, by declaring that, for a clear case of inflammation of the bowels, he prescribed a styptic so powerful that it is used to stop hemorrhage! Both of these gentlemen have refused to send any more patients from their rewards to the hospital, as death is almost certain to supervene. As I went over to the first hospital this morning early, there were eighteen dead bodies lying naked on the bare earth. Eleven more were added to the list by half past eight o'clock!

And thus the weeks rolled by. With the outside world we had little in common—cities were surrendered, States overrun, conventions held, battles won, the immortal roll of glory received the names of Polk, Chambliss, Morgan, Rhodes, Greg, into the vast record of the unnamed heroes were added thousands is worthy of memory as the noblest of these. A new throne was set up on this continent—another turn in that great kaleidoscope which never changes the nature of one bead or bit of glass, be the changes in combinations of position ever so radical and numerous. But to us the book of the events were sealed. Occasionally, by a bribe, we would achieve the reading of a newspaper, and near, and such a partial phrase is prejudice affords, the story of the great tragedy our comrades were playing; but the last details, the points of personal interest—who was wounded, who was promoted, who dead among those with whom we had shared march and camp, bivouac and battle-field—above all, what individual havoc the battering of our little city has occasioned—whom those sweet harbingers of union in Amity, the shells of Grant, had sought out and destroyed, these were unanswered questions, big with import to all.

Yet a fairer summer never blessed the eye, and as we lolled on the grass in the long, dreamy autumn evenings, indulging *les delices du far niente*, nature seemed to whisper in every passing cloud and sighing breeze, a protest against the fatal strife that was desolating the land.

Early in September an addition was made to our comforts in the shape of a contribution on the part of some benevolent persons in New York, of two hundred or three hundred volumes, wherewith a prison library was formed, and the rush for reading was boundless. Of course these volumes were as diligently expurgated as though the official "let it be printed" adorn the title page; still, in our circumstances, a playbill or a price current would have been interesting, and the shelves were soon denuded of everything, down to infantile toy books and dilapidated geographies. Surely these beautiful words were never written in a prison.

About this time, two attempts at escape by tunneling were made—the first a failure, the Second successful. By the latter, eleven enterprising beavers made their escape on the night of 6th of October. They commenced digging in the middle of their tent, which was near an angle of the pen, and conveying the earthen blankets to the lagoon in the night, they avoided detection until a hole about thirty feet long and three feet in diameter was completed, under the fence, and on the first moonless and cloudy night offered, they escaped.

Captain Munger, Lieutenant McConnell, and Sergeant Major Rudd were at once dispatched after the fugitives, but they returned on the third day without having found a trace of them.

The weather now grew very cold, and the men, especially the thousands who were lying on the ground in tents, began to suffer severely, many of them being almost, if not quite, destitute of necessary clothing.

Many of the men have been vaccinated also with virus from patients with venereal disease, and are suffering from the most loathsome sores produced in consequence. I will not suspect any human being of the infamy of thus deliberately poisoning innocent and helpless prisoners by the hundred, but the effect to the poor rebels is the same, whatever the intent of the poisons. Several have entirely lost the use of their arms from this cause.

Chapter XVIII

October 1st—For several days past, the rumor has been current in camp that an exchange of the sick and wounded on both sides is on the carpet, and the knowing ones are rubbing up their old complaints, getting their asthmas, rheumatism's, lame legs, etc. in working order for the examination about to take place. What wonder is that many a paling eye flashes up now with unusual fire, and many a poor, feeble pulse, that for weeks past has been fighting an unequal battle with fever, starvation, memory, and despair, bounds now with the fresh impetus, as in the distance, not very remote, there looms up the enchanting vision of wife and child, mother, sister--home. Many, alas! Who are indulging themselves with this fair prospect, will turn their trembling, tottering feet towards another home ere the light of the earthly one can answer their longings.

Today the rumor takes definite shape as the surgeons make the rounds through the wards examining the sick, and excluding from the role all but those whose convalescence is apparent, and those who will never get better here; and it leaks out that the order from Washington is that a list must be made of those only who will be *unfit for duty for sixty days*. Having beat up England, Ireland, Scotland, France, Germany, Switzerland, Asia and Africa for recruits, these invincible twenty millions of Yanks admit they are still not a match for the five millions of Southerners, and they cling with the tenacity of death to every able-bodied "reb" they can clutch, lest he may again enter the Southern army. The Negro question, which they played as their excuse for declining a general exchange, is all bosh of the first water. The Northern people, and I speak from a long acquaintance with them, care much less for Negroes than we. The instinctive aversion with which all white races regard the blacks—an aversion which begins with the traditions of infancy, when "the big black man" is the bugaboo wherewith rebellious babyhood who it is terrified into obedience—is in the South modified, if not conquered, by constant association and the interchange of mutually serviceable offices. In the North, and wherever the white and Negro live together in the ordinary condition of society as rivals and labor, competitors for employment, claimants for equality of privilege, or contestants for a share of public patronage of any kind, the interest and instincts of the whites coalesce to intensify instinctive repulsion into interested hate, and a degree of intolerance exists, of which we in these South have no conception. It is the free states which have made the most odiously lead discriminating laws against the free blacks; and it is only in a free state that such bloody outbreaks against the Negroes as have characterized Chicago and New York could possibly occur. It is not, therefore, black love but white fear, which is interposing difficulties in the way of a general barter of prisoners; and so controlling is this latter motive that the prisoners at Andersonville might forever have sung their sorrows to deaf ears, but for the advent of that crucible of parties and policies—election day. The McClellan men have proclaimed the general exchange as a plank in her platform, and Humanitarianism—sorry I can't use a shorter word, but the difference between that and inhumanity is as great as between Homousion and Homoiousion, which kept Christendom in hot water for generations—Humanitarianism, I therefore say, must have its sop. So the ingenious Yankees make a compromise between justice and expediency by exchanging only those who will not be fit for fighting until the present campaign is over! And thus take the wind out of the Democratic sails, without sending a man to that army which the veracious Grant affirms is deserting to him at the rate of a regiment a day!

Individually, my case is pitiable indeed. Full rations of beef, a quiet conscience, and a good digestion, have left me in an awkward exuberance of health which precludes all hope of discharge on the ground of unfitness for duty for sixty days. Indeed, I am afraid that protracted residence here may induce a physical condition which even the example of Louis le Gros, Sobieski, and Dixon H. Lewis could not reconcile me to, and I am forced, therefore, to seek an occasion of deliverance on grounds not hygienic. It occurs to me that it is incredible that so many miserabels will be sent on a voyage south without attendance as nurses, and I am resolved to try the effect of an appeal for permission to accompany the sick in that capacity.

October 3rd—The hospital examinations completed, the search for unavailable's began today in the wards. At 10 o'clock, the camp was mustered by companies, and Major Colt, accompanied by the medical staff and clerk to record the names, made a careful inspection. The prisoners, by company, being in line, Major Colt gave notice that all who desire to be examined must step three paces to the front. Each man thus presenting himself was examined, and those found unfit by reason of age, or sickness, or wounds were recorded, while the rest were sent back sorrowing. This operation, and the making out of the roles, occupied several days, and nothing else was talked of or thought of in camp. At last, on the 8th, the list were completed, some fifteen hundred were found "unfit for duty for sixty days"—one-sixth of the whole—and on the morning of the 9th, notice was given that the paroles would be taken that day.

I speak in all reverence when I say, that I do not believe a spectacle was ever seen before on earth, since the sick, and the maimed, and the afflicted of every sort crowded for help and healing around the Saviors feet. Four or five officers took the paroles on the long porch which ran along the front of the hospitals, and having nothing better to do, I spent an hour or two watching the scene.

As soon as the announcement was made in the various hospitals that the parole list were ready, those who had been notified that they had been entered for exchange began to crawl from their cots, and turn their faces towards the door. On they came, a ghastly tide, with skeleton bodies and lusterless eyes, and brains bereft of but one thought, and hearts purged of all feelings but one—the thought of freedom, the love of home. On they came on their crutches, on their cots, born in the arms of their friends, creeping, some of them, on hands and knees, pale, gaunt, emaciated; some with the seal of death already stamped on their wasted cheeks and shriveled limbs, yet fearing less death the added agony of death in the hands of enemies, when no kindred hand should give them reassuring grasp, as they tottered forth into the dark valley, and their bones should lie in unhonored graves amid aliens and foemen.

Such haggard, helpless, homeless wretches I never saw, and I saw more than one consignment of Federal prisoners on their way home. Several died between the signings of the paroles and the date fixed for their departure—paroled by an authority that permits no official perfidy to go behind the record.

No news head, up to this type, reach me as to the results of my application for detail as a nurse; and my hopes of deliverance received Sunday rude shocks during the week from the announcement, confidently made by one or two of the Yankee officers, that I should be "the last sash that should leave that pen;" an honorable distinction, for which I was indebted to the circumstance that I was considered the worst rebel in camp.

I should say it (now at least), with the strongest self-reproach it is impossible for me to get up even a respectful counterfeit of penitence, while I confess that the name of rebel has no terrors whatever for me.

October 9th—A knock at my door 10 minutes after nine; my friend D. Calls me out with the gravity of the Lord-Chancellor, and, announces, "Major Colt has just put your name down on the list." Unfortunately, the regulations of the pen preclude the Orthodox American fashion of expressing unlimited gratification, so I content myself with feeling as much joy as his consistent with sanity, and straightaway go about disposing of my various on portable chattels among less favored friends—the Universal commitment of emigration.

Little was now done or talked of by anyone except the approaching hegira of the lucky candidates for exchange. Many a brawny fellow with the thews of Alcides would gladly exchange his exuberant health and perfect strength, for the most helpless frame in the puniest limbs in the hospital, and numberless expedience to exclude the vigilance, or corrupt the integrity of the examiners were practiced, and with very encouraging success.

One prisoner assured and examining surgeon that he was wounded in the arm, so as to make it impossible to carry a musket for more than 60 days. Slyly turning up his sleeve, he exposed to the doctor's eyes alone, a five dollar greenback rolled up. The Emile goal doctored text areas Lee removed it, and told the clerk to "enter Mister B., Gunshot wound in the left arm."

I was much amused, after my return, with a story told me by the Confederate Commissioner of exchange. A stalwart prisoner called to see him on one of those vein hunts after money, which green rebs occasionally wasted their time about, when Colonel O. asked him how he managed to get off.

"Oh, I had fits, sir."

"Fits! You don't look much like it."

"Oh, yes, sir. I had 'em a half dozen times a day, towards the last."

"Do you have them, now?"

"Well, no, sir. There is no occasion."

"Indeed. You could have them, then?"

"Yes, certainly. Would you like to see one?"

The Colonel expressed his desire for that phenomenon, and in a second his visitor was sprawling on the floor, kicking things about generally, and foaming at the mouth after the most epileptic fashion. In the course of a few minutes his limbs grew rigid, he began to breathe painfully, and he finally stretched himself out as though utterly exhausted—the only part of the performance that was not feigned.

After lying a moment or two, he jumped up, and saluted the astonished Commissioner with:

"Don't you call that a pretty fair fit, sir, on short notice? Well, that ain't a first-class one, by no means"

Thus the poor ones had to rely on their wits, while the better off ones bribed.

Bonus, my colored friend, is in great grief today notwithstanding the moral and Christianizing influences of several months in the Federal Army, Bonus, alas! Will steal, and unfortunately does not discriminate enough. Yesterday Lieutenant McConnell lost one of his revolvers; today, Bonus is proved the thief, and he is tied up for. Tomorrow, he is to go to the front—the rod held perpetually in terror is him over patriots with little moral idiosyncrasies, like the one referred to.

By the way, Bonus had some companions and misfortune. To rebels were brought in before the major, on charge of fighting. The fact was proved, and the punishment was of immediately pronounced. They were tied, back-to-back, and forced to walk up and down the major's tent two hours every morning, and to every afternoon, until amiable relations were restored. It did not take long. He has just come in to tell me that H. gets off. The reason is that he is a Mason!

This order was has spread wonderfully over the country and so war began, and especially in the North. The material advantages which incontestability secures, have contributed largely to this; but I am persuaded that there is a deeper reason, which I will merely indicate. The course of many of the churches before and during the war, especially in the Northern states, almost destroyed popular reverence for religion, and Masonry, which proposes as high a morality as these churches, offered at the same time indubitably superior worldly advantages. In a word, it was as much of a religion as most of the churches, and much more of a benefit. No wonder it spread. The vilest men make use of it. About the brightest Mason in New England is Ben Butler, which, of course, ends the argument. And while in prison at Elmira, I found the worst and most worthless man could outstrip the best in a contest for the "good places" about camp, if they were only Masons. All this, however, is only incidental to my purpose, which is to note the omnipotence of the order, and its gigantic influence for the good or evil, according as it is well or improperly directed.

Almost all of my Petersburg comrades being old men, easily obtained the entry of their names on the coveted role, since it was manifest they would be fit for no active duty in the field; and a was the greatest of my delights to anticipate our return and company to the city which had so long mourned our absence, and made so many efforts to procure our special release.

On the morning of the 11th, all being in readiness, the 1400 for exchange were called out alphabetically, and in three squads, at different hours of the day, marched through the city from the pen to the Erie Railroad depot, were two trains of boxcars stood waiting.

I took leave of my companions with the regret with which intimate association, such as that of prison, is sure to tinge the parting of the most callous, and from none with more than the excellent officer and gentlemen who commanded the prison. His eyes filled as he bade me goodbye at parting, and I fear my own or not altogether dry, as for the last time I rung the hand of the true man, and humane, courteous official, Major Colt. He handed me a memorandum as we parted, asking my kind offices for Lieutenant-Colonel John R. Strang, of his regiment; and I almost felt regret at hearing, subsequently, of Colonel Strang's release, as it prevented me from reciprocating on my return home, in some slight degree, attentions and courtesies which I, in common with all my Petersburg comrades, had constantly received at the hands of this excellent officer.

Chapter XIX

Our passage through Elmira did not quite excite the attention which marked our journey through the same streets three months before, the curiosity of the Chemung Athenians having become satiated with such sites. Many citizens who dared to approach us with expressions of sympathy accompanied us to the cars, administered as they were able to the comforts of the most needy, but there was none of the obtrusive following and staring, with which we were honored on our first appearance.

It was nearly nightfall when we were "all aboard." A worthy and influential citizen of the town, to whom I was introduced, loaded me down with sandwiches and a bottle of Monongahela as I stepped into my box car—may the Angels make his bed in glory, for that same—the engine screamed, and off we started for Dixie. We would scarcely have felt this much exhilaration had we known that the trip would take a full month.

The events of the next forty hours consist in the dismal items of a creeping ride over the Northern Central Pennsylvania Railroad, which leaves the Erie Road at Southport, and traverses the most barren and uninteresting region of the Keystone State, through Harrisburg to the Maryland line, and on to Baltimore. I remember nothing particularly of this trip, except that whenever the train stopped, the guards robbed the nearest orchards; that I slept the first night in the space of 3' x 6"; that I consumed fabulous quantities of crackers; that when I got into Maryland, we found various flags flying in honor of the vote for emancipation, given the delay before; that for slowness of movement, I'll match that ride against even the traditions of the "old City Point" road, in my own state—a comparison which exhausts the resources of her reproach.

The condition of the long train of box cars, filled with such a number of helpless sick, confined in the same spot, and crowded unnecessarily during the ride of some 260 miles, at the rate of less than seven miles an hour, can easily be imagined.

Finally, however, we arrived in Baltimore at 10 o'clock on the morning of the 13th, with seven dead men on the train, the first toll of the dreaded Reaper on our journey home.

A few ladies and children were at the depot—those who dared to brave the fines and dungeons, the imprisonment, and insult, and exile, with which humanity and the natural yearning of kinship are crushed out in loyal Baltimore; but, I doubt that, there were thousands of hearts in that fair town that day, who would have thought it the highest honor to have been allowed to minister to the sick and dying in our long trains, and were only restrained from coming by their unwillingness to witness sufferings that they could not alleviate, while the mere effort would compromise them, without aiding us. The train had hurriedly stopped, when a gorgeously caparisoned horse and major dashed into the little crowd of ladies who were pressing around the car nearest the street, with inquiries about their relatives, and the less noble animal force them back with a brutal sneer, and then intimidation in decided terms, that a renewal of the experience of speaking to us would infallibly result in their being sent to the common guardhouse!

I was particularly sorry for this, as I desired to send a message to a friend in the city, and I resolved to evade the order prohibiting intercourse. Tearing a leaf from my notebook, I jotted down a few lines, and rolling the letter in as small a compass as possible, I watched my opportunity when the guards were not looking in my direction, to hold it up with a gesture that attracted one of the ladies. As soon as a fair opportunity offered, I shot the paper pellet towards her, and much gratified to observe the diplomatic nonchalance with which she put her foot on the missive, quietly continuing her conversation with a female friend meanwhile. A moment or two afterword's she accidentally let fall her hanker-chief, and stooping to recover it, picked up my note with it, and conveyed both to a pocket—all this without a look towards me. It was several minutes before she honored me with a glance of intelligence, which satisfied me my communication was in safer hands than any mail system in Christendom them could furnish.

During the day, for it required all day to get us from the depot to the dock, several ladies remained near us; by stratagem, and treaty—any means, and every means—conveying to the wretched inmates of our train, coffee, bread, cakes, fruit, tobacco—anything in short that money could buy, or woman's kindness of hearts suggest. Among these, if you were conspicuous in their zeal to serve us; and I remember best a courageous woman, with a true Baltimore face, dark eyes, a Southern complexion, lithe, graceful form, and features radiant in mobile with intelligence and beauty, and the divine glory of Charity, who spent the long day in these ministrations, unawed by frowns, undismayed is made by threats, and conquering her native womanly disgust at the vulgar hirelings, that outstripped even heathen heartlessness in the cruelty and brutality with which they repulsed all efforts at communication with us. Her name in two hemispheres is the synonym of all that is noble, true, and good, and from Pope's day to our own, has formed a proud antithesis to "-----knaves and fools and cowards."

The sun was setting as I jumped on an ambulance well filled with hospital equipment, and rattled off to the wharf, where three steamers were awaiting us—the Thames, the Tappahannock, propellers, and the side-wheeler whose name I have forgotten.

I was a long time getting there, not so much because of the distance as because of the company I was in.

This consisted of the driver (drunk), a Federal guard (drunk), and three rebs, one drunk, the other two merry. All besides myself being familiar with the city of monuments, they amiably concluded to see a little of the town before going aboard ship, and if visiting barrooms and other attractive places is seeing the town, they saw it as Artemis Ward would express it, "Slightly, if not more so."

Five bells struck aboard a vessel near us, as our well loaded steamer, with this ghastly freight of the sick, wounded, and dying slowly move from the dock. We left behind us, in Baltimore, several of our companions, whose condition was such that their future progress would have been certain death, one of them a gray-haired old man of our own city, who died shortly after, in a Federal hospital in that city—one of the many "unfit for duty in 60 days."

It was nearly dawn when I awoke to find our craft hard aground off Point Lookout; but soon the tide rose, and we steamed up to the dock, a heavy sea running.

Now commenced the troublesome and dangerous operation of getting the helpless sick of shore. A gangway was stretched from one side of the ship to two flour-barrels standing on the dock, and down this chute the poor helpless, maimed creatures were slid like coal into a vault. Those of us who were able spent our time in alleviating the roughness of this original process of debarkation, and assisted in placing the sick and wounded in the ambulances which conveyed them to the hospital, a quarter of a mile distant.

Between the arrival of the first ship and the second, I walked to the hospital, and deposited in the storage room of No. 8 my pack, expecting to return and get it when my duties on the wharf were over.

These occupied me, as well as the rest of us, until late in the afternoon, when those of us who did not need immediate hospital treatment (about one half of the whole number) were ordered to fall in line, and marched to the old "officers pen," the enclosure in which we were temporarily placed prior to starting for Elmira in the preceding July. As the steward of hospital No. 8 had taken charge of my pack, and promise to keep it for me, I had little apprehension respecting its contents, but, inasmuch as the nights were already becoming cold, I felt some solicitude about the immediate recovery of my blanket, and asked Captain Munger, one of the officers who had accompanied us from Elmira, to state the case to Major Brady, the commandant, who was standing within a few feet of us, and asked permission for me to go get my clothing. He was refused so curtly and insolently, that he had once told me, "You need not expect to get your goods, you see."

I bade him goodbye, and have not seen them since, nor, perchance ever will again. Wherever he is, and whatever he does, however, Captain Ben Munger has the goodwill of every prisoner whoever drew rations at Barracks No. 3, on the banks of the Chemung.

I may as well say here, that I made several efforts to obtain my satchel, without avail he did pretty good I guess, for two days, and when I did recover it, everything valuable was stolen. This petty larceny was committed by a smooth faced innocent, with the downy upper lip, who at that time acted as orderly for Dr. Thompson, the chief surgeon of the post. Three weeks afterwards, Dr. Thompson returned me one or two of the article stolen, but allowed (I presume) his underlying to keep the rest. This, at least, I know, that I furnished Dr. Thompson with a full description of the stolen goods, some of which I saw his orderly wearing the day I finally left the Point, but never received any except a trifling portion of the whole. All this I regretted, mainly, because I lost there several beautiful specimens of prison work that I was bringing home to my friends; and the only comfort I received from my comrades, was a sneer at my gullibility leaving anything valuable out of my sight when Yankee soldiers were about.

When we were turned into the pen, Brady, whom the tenants of Point Lookout prison were disloyal enough to accuse of superior skill in confiscating their property, and in general roughness of demeanor, facetiously conjured us to make ourselves as comfortable as possible.

This was a rather grim joke. The appliances for comfort consisted of a scant supply of tents, to which, after a few days, was added a more scant supply of straw, then the water was scant, the ration scant, and everything else was a scant pattern. When it is remembered that these prisoners were, for the most part, sick men, many of whom had just come out of hospitals, our chance of comfort in open tents, sleeping on the ground, in the cold humidity of Point Lookout, was about as slim as LL. D. Butler's prospect of paradise, or his various subjects' chances for the recovery of their missing silver. Apropos of Ben, I think I have discovered a trace of his revolutionary ancestry in a letter written by Washington to General Lee, which describes, in its final paragraph, that peculiar virtue which has flowered out in such consummate perfection in the Duke of Spoons.

Wednesday, 26th—Our numbers have been largely increased by arrivals from the other pen of prisoners ordered thence because of unfitness for duty for sixty days, or for the better reason that they had the wherewithal to bribe out. We have also been receiving additions from General Early, who, according to Sheridan, has been thrice beaten, with exceeding spoil of war in the Valley of Virginia. Sheridan boasts, with a ferocity which will forever blacken his name and the judgment of impartial history, of the devastation he has inflicted upon the noncombatant population. I have never before read an official report in civilized war in which so great a parade is made of vandalism. The Barns and stacks of grain destroyed afford him obviously far more pleasure than his captures either of men or munitions of war. What a crop of hate this conqueror of grist-mills is sowing!

Chapter XX

Revenons! The days drag very wearily here. As we were all nominally sick men, the fastidious Yankees put us on a sick diet or half rations, and as there was no sutler, and no chance, therefore, of eking out our allowance, we began to fear our enemies were in a fair way of unfitting us for active service for the balance of the war. It seems that we are to be kept here until 5,000 are accumulated, and then deported. Having no other occupation, I undertook some duties in connection with the hospital—for we had a hospital within the pen—and thus managed to endure the tedium of my cage by pious exercises in the shape of administering hospital slops and allopathic boluses.

In the midst of the pen was a vile pile of logs which the prisoners used as an observatory to get the earliest information on the arrival of the "New York," the truce boat of Colonel Mulford, United States commissioner of exchange, whose coming, it was thought, would ensure a speedy exit: but the Yankees took it into their sapient heads that there was something irregular in this, and our logs were pulled down and all spying put under the ban.

October 28th—An order came to diagnose us today, and it became necessary that everyone should have a disease forthwith—at least on paper. We were accordingly called up and asked our various complaints: being still in a vulgar condition of health, it became necessary for me to catch a disease suddenly; accordingly, I soon became painfully afflicted, and when called on by the doctor, I drawled out a disease with a name as long as Nantucket "sea sarpint" and was passed. This looks as though we were about to move, and Dixie stock is rising.

Sunday, October 30th—Saturday we had a false alarm. We were ordered out, inspected, examined, and marched down to the dock where, in the offing, the Arctic, Baltic, and Northern Light are lying, and then marched back again, to our measureless and unspeakable disgust. But today we are off in earnest. About 11 AM we were summoned into line, our names called, and all our blankets stolen from us, by order of the incomparable Brady, unless they were so worthless as to not to be an object. I objected to giving up mine, as I had bought and paid for it, and as it was obvious, on inspection, that it never could have been an army blanket; but the amiable Brady assured me that "If it was not an army blanket it should soon be," and instructed his under-thief to take it.

Having been stripped of these and any contraband articles of clothing, such as an extra coat or pair of pants, we were conducted to the wharf, where a small steamer received us in lots, and conveyed us to the "Northern Light", which, with steam up, was lying about a half-mile out. The other transports were already laden with the most helpless of the prisoners—those who, in the first instance, had been taken to the hospitals.

We scrambled up the side of the fine steamer, formerly a mail and passenger ship in the California trade, then a government transport in the employment of Uncle Abe, at $1,000 a day besides her coal, and were marched in various directions to the two lower decks of the ship, where hammocks of canvas had been slung in sufficient number to accommodate 900 men. Some twenty or thirty were separated by the surgeon, and kept on deck; for what purpose, we never knew, and our little tug steamed ashore for another load. It was near nightfall when she returned; and, as many of the prisoners were victims of night blindness, I asked and obtain permission to assist them aboard, the dangerous footing of the ladder inspiring them with uncomfortable apprehension of a plunge overboard.

I had helped the last one aboard, when a handsome, frank-looking sailor with as genial a face as ever bent over a binnacle, tapped me on the shoulder, and informed me that he wanted to see me forward. My military habit of obedience, I presume it must of been that induced my instant compliance, and under the guide of Samuel H. Rich, first officer of the ship, I soon found myself in his cabin, scrutinizing the pattern of his furniture through an excellent glass, not a magnifier much—cubical contents one point; whose make, I never knew. From this time I, and, with all my fellow prisoners who had any intercourse with him, had occasion to bless the day we fell into the hand of so clever a gentleman and the capital officer. A young man, but an old seaman, he had circumnavigated the globe a half-dozen times, be the same more or less, knew every foot of sea from Fulton Ferry to Van Diemen's Land, and possessed that ease of manner, that cosmopolitan heart in large fund of information and anecdote which, with thorough professional knowledge, forms the highest type of sailor—almost the highest type of the social man.

Devolved on Mister Rich, during our stay aboard, the captain being very sick; and I thereby occasion to observe the universal respect and goodwill which he commanded from the whole crew. These, by the way, were an exceptional party. There was not a Yankee among them, as far as I discovered, and a more liberal set of enemies would be hard to find. As I have spoken to the captain, I may mention that he was the officer who commanded the Vanderbilt when she was down in Hampton Roads, threatening destruction on our Merrimac. When the Merrimac threw all Yankeedom into such confusion early in 1862, Lincoln sent for Commodore Vanderbilt, to advise with him as to what was to be done with the monster. The Commodore informed him that there was no use trying to fight her, and the only chance was to run her down; but, as the United States possessed no vessel of sufficient tonnage for that achievement, he presented Lincoln with the Vanderbilt, a magnificent steamer of 6,000 tons, and hurried to New York to put her in order for the great work. She had her upper works at once taken off, a formidable battery of heavy timber and cotton bales put in, enforcing her bows with thirty solid feet of structure, and a heavy casing of cotton bales put around her boilers. In this trim she was sent down to Hampton Roads, and there lay for sixty days; but as the Merrimac challenge the whole Yankee fleet for two days after her arrival, in vain, I presume the Naval commandant at Fortress Monroe did not have as much faith as Vanderbilt in the success of the running down project.

Monday, October 31st—Arrived off Old Point this morning. The harbor is filled with vessels of war; among which, I recognize the Minnesota, Susquehanna, Wabash, Shenandoah, Ironsides, and any number of ironclads, double-enders, etc.; the whole floating, I understand, two thousand guns!

Commodore Lee has been superseded, on account, it is said, of too much love for the rebels, and Porter reigns in his stead. On each side, the war seems to have eliminated natives of the other from its service, until it has become a war of race rather than of institutions. Porter's vessel, the Malvern, lies a mile west of us.

We remained in Hampton Roads until Tuesday, the 8th. The Atlantic and Baltic lay near us, and every morning we saw coffins going over the side and numbers which suggested uncomfortable reflections on the uncertain tenor of life on the prison ship. On the Atlantic alone, there were forty deaths during our stay in the harbor—a stay obviously unnecessary, and therefore, shamefully cruel, since it compelled the confinement of hundreds of sick man in the filthy and unventilated holds of large ships without proper food, medicine, or attendance—the second great toll of the reaper. Captain Gray, of the Atlantic, protested loudly against the inhumanity of the procedure, circumlocution must have time. On the 2nd and 3rd, we were visited by a furious storm, during which Commodore Porter steamed up to Portsmouth, out of the reach of danger, and there remained until Saturday. On the 4th, Butler left for New York, where he goes to keep the peace! The crew of our ship are from New York, principally, and all McClellan men—their friends of "the Bloody Sixth" is quite refreshing, and they freely promised him a merry time if he interferes. They are mistaken—no race ever bowed the knee to bayonets with such edifying humility as our Northern brethren. If Mister Davis, under any conceivable pretext, had dared to make use of military intimidation in any one of his scores of cases in which Mister Lincoln successfully tried it, he would have been impeached in twenty-four hours, and yet the world has been, and will be, filled with terrible stories of the despotism of the "Slaveholders Rebellion." Lions no more write books than they paint pictures.

Saturday, 5th—The New York, Colonel Mulford's exchange boat, is alongside the wharf today, and any number of rumors filled the ship, of speedy departure. These are confirmed somewhat by the arrival of Mister Beebee, agent of the Sanitary Commission, with large supplies for the Yankee prisoners, who will be received in exchange for us. Some of these supplies fail to reach Savannah, as the guards broke into the treasure tonight, and all got gloriously drunk on the liquid contributions of the Commission.

Sunday, 6th—A prize steamer loaded with cotton came in today, and two more during the week. These vessels with their cargoes are sold after condemnation by a prize court, and half the proceeds turned over to the government. One-twentieth of the remaining half goes to the commandant of the North Atlantic squadron, and the rest is divided among the officers and crew of the capturing vessel. Under this rule, it is estimated that Porter's share of prize money, while on duty here up to this time—about 25 days—will amount to twenty thousand dollars. Last night we were aroused by an indiscriminate firing throughout the fleet, and getting on deck, found the harbor ablaze with colored lights, and guns going off in every direction—a sham naval battle at night. This, and the constant drilling of the guns, with the daily practice of launch drill, indicate an early and vigorous naval attack in some direction—probably Wilmington; and as an armada is accumulating here, already more powerful than any ever set afloat from the days of the Argonauts, we may look for a powerful blow, when it is delivered. Boatloads of soldiers are constantly passing down the river.

These are patriots of the right political stripe, who are being furloughed to go home to vote—no other need apply.

At half-past four on the evening of Tuesday, the 8th, we weighed anchor, and in company with the Atlantic, Baltic, Illinois, Herman Livingstone, and two or three empty transports, we started for Hilton Head, where we arrived about 9 o'clock, Thursday night. This, as the world knows, is the point of the military operations of the enemy in South Carolina.

We lay in this roadstead until Saturday, when orders came to proceed as near as possible to Fort Pulasky; in a few hours we were safely moored alongside the single Yankee gunboat which kept watch and ward over the entrance to the Savanna River, in which, by the way, was covered to the tops with a strong netting to prevent enterprising rebels from boarding and capturing her, by one of those "horse marine" movements, which have been among the most amusing and most successful feats of the war.

We remained here all night—a soft, summery night, though late in the fall; and many of us lounged on the deck till morning, too much exhilarated by the safe termination of our captivity, and the near approach of home, to waste our hours in a prosaic Stupidity of Sleep. Major Abrams, the officer in charge of us, and Lieutenant Gordon, both of the 85th Pennsylvania, I met frequently while pacing the deck, and found them quite is anxious to deliver us as we were to be delivered. Their terms of service had expired, and they had been pressed into the service by a piece of military smartness—which is not wisdom either side of the line—in order that some duty might be extorted from them after the legal claim of the Government had expired. Early next morning, the exchange boat "New York," with Colonel John E. Mulford, Commissioner, board, came alongside; we were hurried aboard, and with three rousing cheers for the "Northern Light" and her officers and crew, steamed up stream to the truce ground, some ten miles up the river. Here we were met by a deputation of citizens and a squad of that excellent society of Good Samaritans, who secured the soldiers of both armies on every field and under all circumstances, from the spring of 1862 to the end of the war, the Richmond Ambulance Committee, and transferring ourselves with commendable speed—for invalids—to an aboriginal craft composed of a railroad shed mortised into a flat boat, we were soon puffing at a safe speed to Savannah.

It was near midday when we arrived here, amid the enthusiastic shouts of the people, and the enlivening music of a genuine Southern band, vocal with "Dixie."

Anthony M. Keiley

Private John R. King

Account of King's Stay at Elmira Prison

Copied from United Daughters of the Confederacy, 1917

The prison at Elmira consisted of thirty-six acres enclosed by a wall constructed in the same way as Point Lookout Prison. It was located a short distance from the Chemung River in Chemung County, New York. The river made a bend in front of the prison, but everything indicated that perhaps a hundred or more years before the prison was there the river had run straight and later a beaver dam had changed its course. In our pen there was a body of water within banks very much like a river which occasionally became high. The North side of this body of water had a much higher bank than the South side. Next to the river it became stagnated in the warm season and was not healthful. Elmira was located on the west and near the prison; there were hills on the east which kept our minds on the beautiful and majesty of nature. The Elmira prison looked much cleaner and healthier than Point Lookout, and the water was good. It was a pleasant summer prison for the southern soldiers, but an excellent place for them to find their graves in the winter. The plan was different from the prison at Point Lookout. All our quarters were built on the north side of the water, it being higher than the south side which was a blue grass sod and used for small pox hospitals.

We arrived on Aug. 1st, crossing the water by means of bridges. Our camp was situated in the north east quarter of the pen. The regular prison hospital was in the northeast quarter, the big entrance of the big gate, a cross street leading to the cookhouse; all other of the streets ran east and west. They were ditched and thrown up in the center. The hospital grounds contained frame buildings of medium size, tents and smaller buildings for carpenter shops where coffins were made and other houses for the use of the sergeants, and those who were compelled to be in the prison for various purposes. An undesirable building was erected in the middle of the camp for a guard. We lived in low tents for the first three months, there being no houses and we often suffered with cold.

The manager arranged the building of the houses two months after our arrival and they were completed near Christmas. They were 100 feet long by 25 feet wide; material rough lumber, sawed blocks were set on end and on these sills and lower joists were placed, then a double floor of rough planks was made sided up with ten foot siding, they were stripped roughly and a few binders used, the roof was very flat made by sheeting the rafters with plank this was prepared and covered with pitch gravel. There was no ceiling over head, a large door was arranged at each end and two windows in the sides, three rows of bunks, one above the other, were built on the sides of the building, they were 6 by 4 feet with bottom made of rough plank and six inch boards were railed on the outside, to prevent our rolling out, shavings or bedding of any kind was not permitted as the authorities said they produced vermin, but it mattered little to us for we were already well supplied. Two ventilators were placed in each roof which provided for two stoves. At first we had wooden stoves, but they were not satisfactory and were replaced by Burnside Coal stoves.

211

The management was somewhat like that at Point Lookout. The head man inside was a major called Provost Marshall, two captains, assistant Provost Marshall, Lieutenants and Sergeants, assisted him. Our first Provost Marshall was Major Colt, his assistants were Captain Mungery and Captain Peck, they were good men and treated us well, but these officers had nothing to do with feeding, clothing and housing us. This was done by contractors, whose ambition was to make money, they were cruel and caused much suffering. In the tent one night three of us, myself and two boys from Alabama, Burd Messer and Jerry Dingler were sitting on our blankets talking, and suddenly someone in front called out sharply, "Halt" two shots followed tearing through our tent just above my head. The three of us threw ourselves on our backs instantly, and the next morning revealed that the man who fired the shots was an over bearing Lieutenant whom we disliked. At another time Jerry Paugh, one of our companions discovered that some of the boys in our ward planned to escape. Our row of tents was the nearest to the wall and these fellows dug a hole in the bottom of the tent extending to the outside of the prison, a distance of 25 or 30 feet, by means of haversacks they emptied the dirt in the water without being detected. When all was in readiness a few whistles served as a signal for those who desired to exit. Five escaped, two of these later were caught. Others would have ventured the following night, had not the officers been informed.

Our rations were better after we arrived at Elmira, but they soon decreased. We entered the cookhouse by wards, being 42 in all. Soup was placed on long tables in mess pans. Bread and meat was served in the morning, bread and soup in the evening. Marching to the tables two ranks deep, the head of one column stopped at the first place, then the column separated half of them going on each side of the table, each man stopping at the next place and so on down the line. By the time the last man reached his place the first one was leaving, each man was obligated to furnish a vessel in which to carry his soup it being hot and we were given no time to let it cool. Those who could not carry it with them did without soup. Many kinds of vessels were used some had canteens with the neck broken off, others had old tin cans, coffee pots, tin buckets or often a very small wooden bucket which a prisoner by the name of Morgan made to sell and frequently some shiftless fellow had nothing so punished himself trying to swallow the hot soup.

In winter on very cold mornings what a sight we were starting to the cook house for our food; Each ward had a head man called a ward sergeant, he went to the cook house morning and evening to learn when to bring his ward, usually about 200 or 240 men. After securing the information he called out, "Fall in 39 and get your rations." We went in a trot, canteens, buckets, tin cans, coffee pots, rattling, old rags and strings and long unkempt hair, dirt and grey backs, cheek bones projecting for there was very little of us except skin and bones. Our legs were spindling and weak. Here we went over the frozen ground and in crossing ditches some poor fellow frequently fell. We were obliged to leave him struggling to gain his position as our time was limited. This is only a few of the facts. It has often been said that the northern people treated and fed their prisoners well. I wish it were true, but during my imprisonment which was more than a year, I never saw any of the good treatment, except from the old veterans, the men who had been to the front and had seen service in the army were kind.

Tainted meat appeared more frequently and our pieces of bread were perceptibly smaller. The size and weight of our rations, as told heretofore is exactly correct, for many times I measured my piece of bread both in width and thickness. It was very uniform in size, exactly as thick as the distance from the end of middle finger to the first joint inside and just as wide both ways as the length of a table knife blade, this being 5 1\2 inches wide and 1 1\2 inches thick. Our meat ration was very little smaller and often we could see through the soup to the bottom of the pan. At times the officers discovered some dirt or misbehavior near one of our wards, then all the ward was given small rations as a punishment for what one or two had done. We called these morsels of bread detailed rations because men, who were put on detail at cleaning streets or something of the kind, were given small pieces of bread and this was all they had to eat while working. While they were being punished we nearly starved. In the later part of the winter crackers were used in place of soft bread, we enjoyed them but for some reason they were not healthful, causing a stubborn diarrhea and many deaths resulted.

I was in the hospital myself a month with the disease. Weakness and starvation had caused me to lose my sight, consequently often times when wandering some distance from our ward spots appeared before my eyes and I was dependent upon some kind comrade to lead me home. The blindness left me as I grew stronger. Others suffered the same way. Many times a poor fellow staggered along until his old shaky legs failed to support him then he staggered until he was on his feet again with a ghastly smile trying to bear it bravely. It was touching to see the poor, ragged gaunt, half famished, much abused, noble fellows trying to be cheerful through it all. Dear old comrades in misery, how often do I remember you and our friendship. Had all been conducted as well as the government of the prisons, we could have had no cause to complain.

The best treatment came from the citizens, those at home and the contractors. In addition to the other officers there were ward sergeants, who were our prisoners. One of their duties was to examine all letters coming to or going from the prison; also every cent of money sent to the prisoners was credited in a big book and should we find by reading our letters that money had been sent we secured a written order for everything we intended to buy. We never saw any money but there was a Sutler store inside the pen where we made our purchases. First, we ascertained how much to our credit by examining the big book, then a clerk filled out an order blank something like this: "This was the Stutler's name." Demorest, Let J. R. King have 15 cts in apples, 10 cts cabbage, 20c onions, 10 cts on flour, and so on. After receiving the articles we balanced the account to see how much was left to our credit. We had but little money and prices were high; flour five cents per pound, meal the same, onions 15 cents a pound, cabbage 10 cents, small apples one cent each, tobacco 15 cents for a small thin plug, and the man charged to suit himself. Money letters were cried in a public place and it was necessary to answer several questions before it was considered safe to deliver the letter. The people at home never knew how we suffered in prison. If we attempted to tell it in our letters, the Censor saw that they were not mailed. The assistant Provost Marshalls Captain Munger and Captain Peck, and several under officers looked after the inside of the prison. They were responsible for the sanitary condition and the management of the hospitals, cookhouse, the wards, the dead house, burrying the dead and other things. The ward sergeant's duties were to conduct his men to their meals, call the roll, give reports to headquarters concerning his ward, make out requisitions for clothing, coal, etc.

There were nearly 10,000 prisoners at Elmira one time; sometimes less and sometimes more. During the winter those who came from the South felt the cold exceedingly and died from pneumonia. Our clothes poor. The pants I had when arriving at Elmira were in such a bad condition that for a long time I wore nothing but my underwear. However, when the cold weather appeared I was glad to welcome old pants again and after much patching they were a great comfort. In the late winter, out-of-date government coats were presented to us for overcoats: for some reason unknown to us the tails had been cut unevenly, one side being a foot long and others extending only a few inches below the waist line. They helped to keep us warm but should we have been out in the world in such costume, one might have mistaken us for scarecrows eloping from the neighboring cornfield. Oilcloth and two blankets was the covering in our bunks, with a big snow outside and the bitter wind raging around the plank building and whistling in at the cracks. We didn't dream of comforts and many of us had very poor shoes. Mine were ready to be cast aside and did not get a new pair until the last day of February. While in the house I wrapped my feet in old rags which kept them warm, but in the late winter we were compelled to stand in the snow every morning for roll call, consequently my feet and shins were badly frozen. In the spring they had the appearance of a gobbler's legs and it was many years after I returned home before they were entirely cured. Many besides myself had frozen feet.

The man who looked after the fires made only two fires in 24 hours. Each ward had two stoves. The first fire was made at 8:00 in the morning, the other at 8 p.m. Near noon and midnight we were comfortable, but during the twelve hours between fires when the temperature of the stoves lowered we often suffered with the cold. A dead line nailed to the floor three feet in circumference surrounded the stoves. Of course we could not cross the dead lines and often a petty officer entering on a cold evening found some of the ragged shivering men standing too near the fast cooling stove, would become enraged and would run cursing, striking right and left through the crowd, little caring who received the blows or what he did. One day a poor fellow was standing near the stove with an old blanket thrown about his shoulders, held at the throat by an enormous safety pin made from a piece of large wire. The long sharp point of a pin extended through the hook which held it in place. The man of authority struck a swinging blow at the poor fellow when his hand came in contact with the point of that big pin which tore his fingers unmercifully. But it cured him of his fighting propensities. Punishment often resulted from trifling offences and of course we dared not defend ourselves. Some of the men in our ward were powerful men. One was a very tall sergeant who lived in Elmira. His duties kept him inside the prison continually and we called him Long Tom. It gives me pleasure to speak of him for he had a kind heart and was a favorite of every one. He was called our coal sergeant, often when the weather was intensely cold and our fires were low upon request our big friend would get us coal if possible.

Much sickness prevailed among the prisoners In the latter part of the winter many came from near Mobile Bay and brought with them small pox. There were more than forty cases in our ward, and many died. When seven years of age I was vaccinated and although surrounded with it I escaped, there were also many cases of pneumonia, measles and thousands of us were afflicted with the stubborn diarrhea. The poor fellows died rapidly, despondent, homesick, hungry and wretched, I have stood day after day watching the wagons carry the dead outside to be buried and each day for several weeks 16 men were taken through the gate. While the prison was occupied by us which was about one year it was estimated that 3,000 men died. The physicians were very good but it was impossible to save all. At one time scurvy was among us. There were not many deaths, but it caused much suffering. I was among the victims. It frequently attacked the mouth and gums, become so spongy and sore that portions could be removed with the fingers. Others were afflicted in their limbs, the flesh became spotted and the pains were almost unbearable. The remedy was raw vegetables and a medicine called chalk mixture.

Our dead were buried outside by a detail of 16 or 17 prisoners. The name of the company and Regiment of the dead were written on a piece of paper and put in a tightly corked bottle and burried with the corpse, all were buried in that way. Their caskets were made in the pen by prisoners detailed for that purpose. During the early spring the 40th, 41st and 42nd wards were converted into hospitals. We all decided beds made of shavings would be a luxury, so every fellow that was able procured a sharp knife and a pine board and I doubt if the world ever saw such a universal whittling in so short a time. All tried to possess a comfortable bed, but in a few days the Provost Marshall inspected our quarters and ordered every shaving burned. They advocating that the shavings would breed vermin, but we had already been made very uncomfortable by their presence. Near the cook-house there were vessels for heating water, but few of us could get soap and consequently the few clothes we had never were washed.

The prisoners passed the time making trinkets. Capt. Munger and Capt. Peck, secured the material and after the articles were completed they sold them in the city for the best price possible, always remitting the money. In passing through the prison one would see a boisterous lot playing cards or some other game, numbers making rings out of Gutta-percha buttons and riveting sets on to them of real silver which the captains had purchased, others were making pretty trinkets out of bone, such as tooth picks and seals for watch chains, with birds, squirrels and other figures designed on them Some made watch chains out of horsehair with single links, with two links interlocked and others with three links interlocked making a round chain. This was done with horsehairs and two common needles. We took a board 18 inches wide, near one end a small hole was made into which a flat post a foot in length with a little pole near the top was placed, in that hole was a little round tapered stick running almost to a point. The stick was as large around as we desired the links of the chain inside, after taking the coarse hair from the horses' tails, we placed a small board on a chair and sat on it with the post between our knees, the little stick pointing to us, threaded the needles on both ends of the horse hairs, then make the little links around the stick, slide the needles each way under the link across the hair, and worked the bottom hole stitch around the center of the link, and then interlocked as many links as we wanted. With little practice very pretty chains could be made. Others in our pen made fans out of white pine wood, the board was cut in the shape of a paddle with a fancy handle, then the part which formed the paddle was notched and cut into thin slices with a very sharp knife. The wood was softened with warm water and then the slices bended like a fan. Different colored ribbons were worked through the notches and the ends tied in a bow around the handle. They were very pretty, but frail. One man made a small parasol on the same plan. I saw Capt. Peck, carrying it around one day. I suppose he found a purchaser for it. Another man made a rude engine. One day I gave him a cracker to see it run, that was the admittance.

Many wore green shades over their eyes on account of the blazing sun on the sand, tents and water, some of the managers sowed patches of oats which was restful to the eyes.

I will tell you something of the many punishments inflicted on the soldiers; one was wearing the barrel shirt, the big pork barrel with wooden hoops was used, one end was out, a round hole was cut in the other end large enough for a man's head to pass through. The barrel was put over the body by two men leaving the head sticking out through the hole in the end. This he would have to wear two hours before noon and two hours afternoon with a guard behind to keep him in action. Then crosses were nailed on the sides of the barrel on which the man's offense was painted in big black letters. Sometimes it was a lie; other times theft, so here promenaded the man, the barrel, the crosses and the guard; one cross said: "I am a liar." Another said: "I am a thief." This continued day after day. Capt. Whiton, the boss of the cookhouse, had a fat dog which was very friendly and one day was missing. So the Captain found upon investigation that two hungry fellows had killed his dog. Enraged with anger he had the two men taken to headquarters, barrel shirt put on them and dog eater painted on the cross. The prisoners ate every rat they could find and it is well for the rat I didn't find any. They smelt very good while frying. Sometimes men were bucked and gagged or tied up by the thumb for punishment, which was the most cruel of all punishments. I would not punish a dog in that way.

Some enterprising fellow built a large frame work outside near the big gate and not more than fifty feet from the wall. The building had three floors besides the ground floor and was called the observatory. There was no roof and it was built for the sole purpose of observation. One on the upper floor had a fine view of our prison and prices were regulated according to the floor on which they stood. The building was forty feet in height. When the weather was pleasant a great many went to the top to look at us. On a beautiful late spring day there was a number of nicely dressed ladies and gentlemen on the top floor. Our provost marshall was sitting on the floor below when presently there came a big Negro among the ladies. He shoved them aside and squared himself to get a good look at us. He was finely dressed and apparently thought himself a very important character. We did not like his attitude so a number of the men groaned at him, hissed, hooted making all sorts of expressions about his impudence but he stood reared back and paid little attention to them. Then the Major got up immediately, went upstairs, took the negro by the shoulders, drew his sword, turned him around and marched him down and out. The negro wanted to argue with the Major but it was useless. Of course we gave the Major a big cheer which seemed to please him. I never saw but one negro who stood guard sometimes in our pen. He behaved like a gentleman.

After warm weather came we had many visitors, often ladies. Some of them spoke pleasantly and were well behaved, while others were impudent and insulting. I remember one day Colonel Moore's son came in our pen with a few young girls, (Colonel Moore was commander of the post), his son was a foppish young fellow and one of the girls over-dressed and attracted him. While passing through our ward, with her dainty fingers she tipped up her rustling silken skirts and passed along with an effected air and a disdainful look on her countenance, saying, "Oh, the nasty, dirty, ignorant, beastly Rebels, how filthy they are," and on she continued with a peculiar air, while some of the girls gave us kindly words and looks and were embarrassed by her rudeness; but she was punished for being so unlady like. One of our number, Bish Fletcher, a daredevil, took the opportunity as the girl passed by him to present her with some body lice, 'Grey Backs", we called them. Two sisters of charity visited the prison leaving each a religious tract published by the American Tract Society, and as they passed they treated us with a smile and a kind word. They were real ladies.

I do not want to leave the impression that every prisoner was sick, poor, ragged and weak like the majority of us, for there were many who escaped sickness and numbers who were kept at detail work. Those who worked were fed much better, but of course the majority of us had to work. We had a ray of sunshine occasionally; in the latter part of the winter my good sister, Elizabeth, and my kind parents sent me a box containing biscuits, butter, a piece of bacon, dried apples and a cake. It was all very nice, but unfortunately just before the box arrived I was sick and had no appetite. I ate very little of the contents of my box which was a curiosity to the prisoners. When it came they gathered in a great circle about my bunk and Mr. Breen, a rich iron merchant from Georgia, made a speech to the crowd regarding my dear sister's hands which had prepared it and how my dear parents had remembered their boy in the far away prison. Jaco L. Hale, a large robust man, a Virginian, and one of the "Gray Devils", a company belonging to one of the regiments in the Stonewall Brigade, used the bunk under mine. He was kind to me and was always hungry. I said to Mr. Hale: "Don't you want some butter and bread?" "Yes, sirree," the big fellow answered, and it did me good to watch him sit on the edge of my bunk and eat biscuits and butter. He was a big bony man and a biscuit soon disappeared between those massive jaws. I gave him much of my precious box. He was always my powerful protector and was the last man to whom I spoke in the prison before leaving. Dear old fellow, he had a wife and children at home and was ever the protector of the weak.

Prisoners whose homes were within the Yankee lines could receive money at different times and I always got credit in the big book at the headquarters. Everything was so high at the Sutler store we could not get much but it helped to keep the wolf from the door. Some of the prisoners bought and made much for sale so for five cents one could be satisfied for a while. A market place was located near one end of the cookhouse where the prisoners congregated on certain days and tried to sell numberless things to one and another. They sold rings, watch charms and many other trinkets made by the prisoners and besides these men would cry their articles on the market. Some tried to sell eatables. We called a piece of the loaf, cut off the crust end, a "Keno-ration", by reason of a game of chance some of the men played called "Keno". In the game when a certain number was called out the lucky one would cry out: "Keno-o-o". So at the cookhouse when one got a heel ration he called in a loud voice: "Keno-o-o". In the market some would cry: "Here is your keno ration with five chew of tobacco on it for five cents." Still another, "Here's your two rations of meat and ten chews of tobacco on it all for ten cents," and so on. It was a strange medley of things in progress that could never have been seen elsewhere, but little buying was done. Many traded rations. Money was too scarce with which to make purchases. Hunger often caused people to do desperate things. I myself often watched for the bones, after the meat had been eaten off. I got up many times in my bunk with a bone and after knawing the soft ends, sucked at the bone for hours at a time. I wasn't the only one. No bones went to waste as long as there was any substance left on them. One morning while we were eating our beef ration, Dan Singleton, who occupied one of the top bunks, cried out while holding a small rib in his hand, "Look here boys, here's a fine piece of mule meat." The ribs we were eating were all alike, being round and smaller than the ribs of cattle; the cow's ribs are flat as everyone knows. The meat was good and we could have relished several more mules had the opportunity been presented.

A few of the under officers were quartered in a little house on a steep bank of a creek. They cooked and ate in front of the house, and here the cook emptied his dishwater which sometimes contained a little meat and bread and I often saw two men on either side of the greasy place scrambling for the crumbs as the dishwater rushed down the bank. It was pitiful. Many men, once strong, would cry for something to eat. I know from experience. A few more of us could have worked in the carpenter shop had we agreed to take the oath of allegiance to the United States, but we refused. Our wages would have been 5 and 10 cents per day according to our capabilities; this didn't tempt me. A day or two after the lamentable death of our President, Abraham Lincoln, the inside officers approached us with a paper telling us that all who would say they were sorry for the President's death would be released first. Not many said they were sorry and those who did stayed there as long as anybody else. I did not say I was sorry and when I came out I left thousands in; yet of course the whole nation was grieved over his death, but we did not care to express our sorrow in that way. However, it was sad to hear the bells tolling in the city when the news came that the President was dead. When Gen. McClellan and Abraham Lincoln ran for president, the majority of the prisoners favored McClellan. They cheered for Little Mac, and one fellow drew the picture of Abraham Lincoln mauling rails and McClellan marching to the White House. Little Mac. was very popular in New York.

Then a flood came in the Chemung, or Gioga River as some called it. There had been much snow during the winter and early in March the thaw caused high water. The snow melted rapidly and soon the little Chemung was raging. The water came into our prison higher and higher, and in a short time the small pox hospital across the creek had to be abandoned. The water increased and in a few hours it reached nearly every house in the prison. The lower bunks were submerged and the second row was threatened. We were surrounded by a wilderness of water. A great part of the prison wall was gone and we could see about half of the cookhouse extending above the water. In every direction men could be seen hustling around in boats trying to save things. The hospitals were flooded and all the sick had to be taken into the city. The dead house was on a little higher ground therefore the dead were not washed away. We were confined in the higher bunks for a day or two with nothing to eat or drink but the dirty river water. After the water receded men came into our wards through the doors in row boats, passing near where we were "roosting". They gave us something to eat. My, but it tasted good! In transferring the sick from the hospitals to the boat, often they fell into the cold water. A poor fellow came out of the hospital next to our ward. He tried to walk a short plank which had been placed from the hospital to the boat, carrying his blanket and some old ragged clothes which belonged to him. Trembling and tottering with weakness, as he stepped on the plank, the boat vacillated and the poor fellow staggered, threw up his arms and went headlong into the water. I feared he would drown, but he was rescued and shivering was taken away in the boat. I have no doubt it caused the man's death.

As soon as we could with safety we waded out to the highest pump in the prison, which was near the dead house, to get some water. On my way to the pump I noticed several old blankets near my feet. Looking closer I discovered a number of dead men concealed under them. The high water had prevented the people from taking them to the graveyard. The walls were rebuilt and in a week or so our old prison was in its natural condition. After the overflow I noticed several extremely large ells lying dead in the water. One day while the cleaning was in progress a petty officer of some sort had four or five men under him working at a crossing. Just as the little platform or little crossing had been nearly placed I happened along and this petty officer was bossing, puffing and swearing at the men. He issued a mighty order to the prison that no man should cross the platform until it was completed. Ignoring the order I crossed and as I was landing on the other side this great man caught me by the shoulders, shoved me roughly towards a Yankee guard who happened to be near and said: "Here, take this man to the guard house and put a barrel shirt on him." The guard asked no questions but conducted me to the guard house and in the afternoon I was wearing the barrel shirt. The Yankee guard at headquarters said in a low voice to me "If I were you I would saw wood for the cookhouse and you will not have to wear the barrel longer." Next morning I told them that I wanted to saw wood, so the old measly pork barrel and I parted company forever. I sawed wood a few hours every day for nearly a week. Major Beall came to the guard house to take the place of Major Colts as Provost Marshall. When I was brought before him he said: "What are you here for?" I said: "For nothing at all." He turned to the jailor and said: "What are the charges against this man?" The jailor after looking at his book said: "No charges." Looking at him sternly the Major said: "Let this man out. What is he here for?" I made my departure never to return.

As the spring passed the number in our wards decreased. At roll call there was no answer to nearly a third of the names. Many had died but early in the spring about 300 of the sick had been sent south to be exchanged. I think the government had intended to send the most of us back to Dixie in the spring had the war not closed, but when Gen. Lee surrendered we then knew that those who lived would return to Dixie. There was great rejoicing and ringing bells at Elmira when the news came that Lee had surrendered. After that we received better treatment from the Yankees and were not guarded so closely. Of course we felt badly when we heard that our beloved Gen. Lee had surrendered, for we knew our noble Army of Northern Virginia would hereafter be only a memory. I am proud to say that I once belonged to the Army of Northern Virginia and marched and fought under the illustrious Robert E. Lee, who, when he had to go down, went down bravely. We started out for what we thought was right and stayed with it faithfully to the bitter end.

I want to speak of some of the characters in our prison who were very interesting. One fellow whom we called Shocky, seemed to have a mysterious influence over the Yankees. He was always well dressed and apparently loyal to the South, but it was always a mystery to us how he could go over the wall at a certain place at anytime he desired and always be respected by the guards. We thought it possible that some free masonry was connected with it. Five of the young Virginians also seemed to be more favored than the rest of us. Among them was Bill McGruder, Bill Hale and a Georgian called Nick Carnochan; the latter pronounced his name Conahan. These young fellows enjoyed many privileges denied the others. Then there was "Old Buttons", a man who sewed buttons on promiscuously to show every battle or skirmish in which he had been. I saw the old fellow die while he and I were in the hospital. We had "Old Blue Ridge" too, a man of gigantic size who wore a homemade blue coat trimmed in various places with fringes, who with all his eccentricities was very kind. Old Pickett, the Florida fisherman, watched from morning till night for the

219

chews of tobacco others had thrown away. He threw them into his mouth as though his life depended upon it. There were many remarkable men with us, of whom I would like to speak but time will not permit.

As the summer drew near we all became restless and were longing for home. Parnell from South Carolina had been employed around headquarters as a messenger boy. As I sat in my bunk despondent and hungry one evening early in June, Parnell appeared, saying in a low voice: "King, you are going out on the next load. I heard your name called today at headquarters. Be still and do not tell anybody but get ready." I asked who also was going from our ward. He said only four: myself, Hoy Reger, Andrew Winster Reger, who was one of my own company in Dixie, and himself. Elated over the news I commenced to get ready. My pants were ragged and dirty. I had an old U. S. blanket and ten cents in money. I went to Bill Goans, who was handy with the needle, and asked him if he would make me a pair of pants out of the blanket. He wanted 25 cents for the job, but I told him I had but 10 cents in the world and that I was to start home on the next load. He hesitated, then said: "All right. I will do it, as you are going home." They were better than the ones I wore but I believe Wanamaker would have made a better fit. All our comrades were soon informed that we were going home and we did not try to keep it a secret. As soon as Mr. Hale, a friend of mine, knew we were going he said: "come and sit down. I want to give you a shave before you leave. He fixed me up the best he could. Then in a day or two we were taken out, measured and our complexion taken down on paper.

The next morning 300 of us were taken to the cookhouse and while standing together with our right hands raised, the oath of allegiance to the U. S. was administered. Then we were given two days rations, our paroles handed to us and we were ready for the journey. I will never forget the march from the cookhouse to the big gate. All the prisoners who were left behind congregated near the street as we went out. No battle scarred veterans ever marched to victory prouder than that ragged, poorly fed, miserable 300 which passed through the big gate never to return. Many of the poor fellows left behind waved us fare-wells, for but few ever met again. The last familiar face I remember as I went out was that of Mr. Hale, my best friend. He waved his hand and said: "Good-bye, King" This was the tenderessed goodbye for me of all. As I write today the memories of that prison, our suffering, many old comrades I knew well, all rush to my memory so vividly that I seem to live it all over again. It brings a sadness to my heart that I can hardly shake off at times.

We waited in the city until afternoon before taking the train for Baltimore and while there I sold an old blanket I had left for 40 cents and that was all the money with which I had to buy anything to eat on the journey. My two days rations I drew before leaving the prison were so small that I ate all before I passed through the gate, so after getting 40 cents for the blanket I spent 20 cents of it for bread and cheese and ate the most of that before taking the train. The U. S. government gave us free transportation home as far as we could travel by rail or water. In the evening we started for Baltimore on the Pennsylvania North Central R. R. We went through Williamsport, Sunburg, Harrisburg and several other towns and passed long trains of Yankee soldiers going to New York to be discharged. They cheered us as they passed and our train stopped outside of Baltimore for a few minutes. Above us were some women in a garden which had fine onions in it and upon asking for some a Negro girl threw us a few. They were what we called clove onions and were fearfully hot. We ate one or two of them and kept the others.

In Baltimore while waiting at the Band (circled in ink) Depot all day before getting through to West Virginia, I was sitting in the Camden Street station eating one of my hot onions when I noticed some ladies looking at me. I thought probably they were admiring the fit of my new pants, but later one said kindly: "Poor fellow, he looks pitiful." Then I discovered that they thought I was crying and were sympathizing with me. I concluded I would eat more onions, as it was comforting for someone to look at me kindly. I ate my supper that evening at the Soldier's home near the station and I can assure you that I did not leave that table hungry. We took the train in the evening for Grafton, W. Va., and reached there the next day. I spent that night with my Uncle, my Father's brother, John M. King. The next day I went to Clarksburg and from Clarksburg home. I walked 36 miles that night, Hoy Reger and myself. Being timid to approach the house, we slept in a pasture field. The next day we went by way of Buckhannon and parted at the mouth of Turkey Run. I crossed the river at Hyer's Mill and arrived home in the evening, finding all alive and well. I will not try to tell about our happy reunion. There will never be another so happy until we shall meet up there where God will never let us part.

Brother Cyrus is sitting in front of me as I write. I have a beautiful home, children and grandchildren who are tall big men. In a few weeks I will be seventy-four and am hale and hearty and I thank our good master for it all.

In conclusion I will say the war is over. We have peace and prosperity. The North and South are united, but the South is our South. I love it. My heart is with the South and nobler women never lived than our women of the South and there never was in any country nobler women banded together than the Daughters of the Confederacy for the work which they have undertaken. Dear Children of the South, U. D. C.'s, may the kind hand that led me through battles and prisons safely lead everyone securely through the battle of life to a happy old age. To you all I send a greeting. This imperfect sketch was written near Roanoke, W. Va., Feb. 23, 1916.
JOHN R. KING

Private Lewis Leon

Company C, 1st North Carolina Regiment

On April 25, 1861, Lewis Leon joined the Charlotte Grays, Company C, 1st North Carolina Regiment. He began his diary when he joined the Confederate Army and continued to make entries throughout his imprisonment at Point Lookout and Elmira prisons. Because his diary is so extensive I have limited its presentation to cover the time he was captured and sent to prison.

Diary of a Tar Heel Confederate Soldier

May 5 - Moved this morning, feeling for the enemy, and came up to them at noon, five miles from the Run, in the Wilderness. It certainly is a wilderness; it is almost im-possible for a man to walk, as the woods are thick with an underbrush growth and all kinds of shrubbery, old logs, grape-vines, and goodness knows what. My corps of sharp-shooters was ordered to the front. We formed in line and advanced to the enemy. We fought them very hard for three hours, they falling back all the time. Our sharpshooters' line got mixed up with Gordon's Brigade, and fought with them. In one charge we got to the most elevated place in the Wilderness. We looked back for our brigade, but saw it not. Just then a Yankee officer came up and we took him prison-er. Some of Gordon's men took him to the rear. Six of our regiment, sharpshooters, myself included, went to the right to join our regiment, but were picked up by the Yankees and made prisoners. We were run back in their line on the double quick. When we got to their rear we found about 300 of our men were already prisoners. The Yankees lost very heavily in this fight, more than we did. Although we lost heavy enough, but, my Heavens! What an army they have got. It seems to me that there is ten of them to one of us. It looks strange that we could deliver such fearful blows when, in fact, if numbers counted, they should have killed us two years ago. In going to their rear we passed through four lines of battle and reinforcements still coming up, while we are satisfied with, or at least have no more than one line of battle.

May 6 - Fighting commenced at daylight, and lasted all day. So did it last with their everlasting reinforcements. If General Lee only had half their men, and those men were rebels, we would go to Washington in two weeks. When he has fought such an army for four years it certainly shows we have the generals and the fighting-stock on our side, and they have the hirelings. Look at our army, and you will see them in rags and barefooted. But among the Yankees I see nothing but an abundance of everything. Still, they haven't whipped the rebels. Several of our boys came in as prisoners to-day, with them Engle of our company. They think I was killed, so does my brother, but as yet the bullet has not done its last work for your humble servant.

May 7 - We are still penned up as prisoners in the rear of the army, close by General Grant's headquarters. A great many prisoners came in to-day. From some of them I heard that my brother was well.

May 8 - We left this place at dark last night, but only got a distance of two miles, and it took us until 9 in the morning of the 9th.

May 9 - Started again this morning, and passed over the Chancellorsville battlefield. Marched twelve miles today. We passed a brigade of Negro troops. They gave us a terrible cursing, and hollered "Fort Pillow" at us. I am only sorry that this brigade of Negroes was not there, then they certainly would not curse us now. We halted at dark on the plank road seven miles from Fredericksburg.

May 10 - Fighting to-day at Spotsylvania Court House. Prisoners still coming in, two more from my company.

May 11 - This morning about 800 more prisoners came in. Most of them were from my brigade, as well as from Dole's Georgians. I was surprised to see my brother with them. He was taken yesterday, but before he surrendered he sent two of the enemy to their long home with his bayonet.

May 12 - Raining hard all day, and fighting all last night. About 2 o'clock this after-noon about 2,000 prisoners came in, with them Major-General Johnson and Brigadier-General Stewart. We have moved four miles nearer to Fredericksburg. I suppose they think we are too close to our own lines, and they are afraid we will be recaptured, as it was a few days ago. We heard our boys', or, as the Yankees call it, the Rebel yell. We prisoners also gave the Rebel yell. A few minutes after that they brought cannon to bear on us, and we were told to stop, or they would open on us. We stopped.

May 13 - Left here this morning and passed through Fredericksburg. Crossed the Rappahannock on pontoon bridges, and got to Belle Plain on the Potomac at 3 o'clock - nineteen miles to-day. It rained all day, and it is very muddy.

May 14 - We are still camped here. Have been prisoners since the 5th of this month, and have drawn three and a half days' rations. On that kind of a diet I am not getting very fat. We certainly would have suffered a great deal, but our Yankee guard gave us quite a lot of their own rations.

May 15 - Still here. They are fighting very hard on the front.

May 16 - Left this morning at 11 in a tugboat, and from here packed into the Steamer S. R. Spaulding. We are now on our way to a regular prison. We got there at 8 o'clock to-night, and found it to be Point Lookout, Md., fifty miles from Belle Plain. It is in St. Mary's County. We were drawn up in line, searched for valuables, and they taken from us, and marched to prison, one mile from the landing. There are sixteen men in each tent.

May 17 - Saw Mack Sample, Will Stone and several of our company to-day that have been prisoners since the battle of Gettysburg. We get two meals a day.

May 18 - We are divided in divisions and companies. There is a thousand in each division and one hundred in each company. A sergeant commands each company. We get light bread one day and crackers the other.

May 19 - Saw Darnell, of my company, to-day. He was just from the front. He brings us very bad news. Our General Daniels was killed, which is certainly a great loss to us, for he was a good and brave man, also our major of the 53rd, Iredell, and my captain, White, all killed. Colonel Owens, my colonel, was mortally wounded, and quite a number of my company were killed and wounded. He says there is only seven of our company left, and that our Lieutenant-Colonel Morehead is commanding Daniels' Brigade.

May 20 - Three years ago to-day the Old North State left the Union, and we went to the front full of hopes to speedily show the Yankee Government that the South had a right to leave the Union; but to-day, how dark it looks!

May 21 - I heard to-day that my brother Morris was a prisoner at Fort Delaware, Pa. I asked for a parole to-day to go and see my parents in New York, but they could not see it.

May 22 - Nothing new from the front.

May 23 - We are guarded by Negro troops, who are as mean as hell. At each meal there is a guard placed over 500 prisoners, who go to their meals in ranks of four. We are not allowed to cross a certain line, called the "Dead Line," but as 500 men go at one time to meals, of course near the door there is always a rush. To-day one of our men accidentally crossed the line. He was pushed over by the crowd, when a black devil shot and killed him, and wounded two others.

May 24 - One of yesterday's wounded died today. This negro company was taken away to-day, as there is no telling what even men without arms will do to such devils, although they have got guns.

May 25 - Engle received a letter from his father today, who told him they had seen my parents, and I would hear from them soon. This is the first time that I have heard about my parents since the commencement of the war. Thank God, my parents, as well as my sisters and brothers, are well.

May 26 - Received two letters to-day, one from home and one from my brother Pincus, who went to Washington on his way to visit Morris and myself, as he has to get a pass from headquarters before he can see us. He was refused and returned home. Our daily labor as prisoners is that at 5 in the morning we have roll call; 6, breakfast, 500 at a time, as one lot gets through another takes its place, until four lots have eaten; we then stroll about the prison until 1 o'clock, when we eat dinner in the same style as breakfast, then loaf about again until sundown. Roll is called again, thus ending the day. We get for breakfast five crackers with worms in them; as a substitute for butter, a small piece of pork, and a tin cup full of coffee; dinner, four of the above crackers, a quarter of a pound mule meat and a cup of bean soup, and every fourth day an eight-ounce loaf of white bread. Nothing more this month.

June 8 - There is nothing new up to to-day, when I received a box of eatables, one or two shirts, and one pair of pants from home. The only way we can pass our time off is playing cards and chess. Six hundred prisoners came in to-day, with them a lady, who is an artillery sergeant. Being questioned by the provost marshal, she said she could straddle a horse, jump a fence and kill a Yankee as well as any rebel. As time in prison is very dull and always the same thing as the day preceding, I shall not mention each day, but only those days upon which something happened.

June 11 - Five hundred more prisoners came in to-day.

June 12 - To-day, as the Negro guard was relieved, two of them commenced playing with their guns and bayonets, sticking at one another. Fortunately one of their guns, by accident, went off and made a hole in the other one's body, which killed him instantly. The other one kicked at him several times, telling him to get up as the rebels were laughing at him, but in a very short time he found out that he had killed his comrade and that we were laughing sure enough.

June 27 - Received money to-day from home, but they gave me sutler's checks for it, as we were not allowed any money, for fear we would bribe the sentinels and make our escape.

July 4 - Four hundred prisoners left here for some other prison, as there were too many here.

July 8 - Engle, Riter and myself received boxes from New York to-day, but as Riter has gone to the other prison with the 400 we have made away with his box.

July 23 - Three hundred more were sent from here to the new prison, which is in Elmira, N. Y., myself with them.

July 25 - Left Point Lookout at 8 o'clock this evening in the frigate Victor for New York. There are 700 prisoners on board.

July 26 - To-day on the ocean a great many of our boys were seasick, but not I. I was promised a guard to take me to see my parents in New York for thirty minutes.

July 27 - We see the Jersey shore this morning. Our vessel was racing with another. We had too much steam up; the consequence was a fire on board, but we soon had it out. We landed at Jersey City at 12 M., and were immediately put in cars, and the officer that promised to send me to my parents refused to do so. We left here at 1, got to Elmira at 8 in the evening.

July 28 - We were treated very good on the road, and especially at Goshen, N. Y. The ladies gave us eatables and the men gave us tobacco.

July 29 - There are at present some 3,000 prisoners here. I like this place better than Point Lookout. We are fenced in by a high fence, in, I judge, a 200-acre lot. There is an observatory out-side, and some Yankee is making money, as he charges ten cents for every one that wishes to see the rebels.

August - Nothing worth recording this month, except that the fare is the same as at Point Lookout.

September - It is very cold, worse than I have seen it in the South in the dead of winter.

October - We have got the smallpox in prison, and from six to twelve are taken out dead daily. We can buy from prisoner's rats, 25 cents each, killed and dressed. Quite a number of our boys have gone into the rat business. On the 11th of this month there were 800 sick prisoners sent South on parole.

November and December - Nothing, only bitter cold. We dance every night at some of our quarters. Some of the men put a white handkerchief around one of their arms, and these act as the ladies. We have a jolly good time.

THE YEAR 1865

January - Nothing, only that I fear that our cause is lost, as we are losing heavily, and have no more men at home to come to the army. Our resources in everything are at an end, while the enemy are seemingly stronger than ever. All the prisoners in Northern prisons, it seems, will have to stay until the end of the war, as Grant would rather feed than fight us.

February - The smallpox is frightful. There is not a day that at least twenty men are taken out dead. Cold is no name for the weather now. They have given most of us Yankee overcoats, but have cut the skirts off. The reason of this is that the skirts are long and if they left them on we might pass out as Yankee soldiers.

March - Nothing new. It is the same gloomy and discouraging news from the South, and gloomy and discouraging in prison.

April - I suppose the end is near, for there is no more hope for the South to gain her independence. On the 10th of this month we were told by an officer that all those who wished to get out of prison by taking the oath of allegiance to the United States could do so in a very few days. There was quite a consultation among the prisoners. On the morning of the 12th we heard that Lee had surrendered on the 9th, and about 400, myself with them, took the cursed oath and were given transportation to wherever we wanted to go. I took mine to New York City to my parents, whom I have not seen since 1858. Our cause is lost; our comrades who have given their lives for the independence of the South have died in vain; that is, the cause for which they gave their lives is lost, but they positively did not give their lives in vain. They gave it for a most righteous cause, even if the Cause was lost. Those that remain to see the end for which they fought - what have we left? Our sufferings and privations would be nothing had the end been otherwise, for we have suffered hunger, been without sufficient clothing, barefooted, lousy, and have suffered more than anyone can believe, except soldiers of the Southern Confederacy. And the end of all is a desolated home to go to. When I commenced this diary of my life as a Confederate soldier I was full of hope for the speedy termination of the war, and our independence. I was not quite nineteen years old. I am now twenty-three. The four years that I have given to my country I do not regret, nor am I sorry for one day that I have given - my only regret is that we have lost that for which we fought. Nor do I for one moment think that we lost it by any other way than by being outnumbered at least five if not ten to one. The world was open to the enemy, but shut out to us. I shall now close this diary in sorrow, but to the last I will say that, although but a private, I still say our Cause was just, nor do I regret one thing that I have done to cripple the North.

Private Miles Sherill

A SOLDIER'S STORY: PRISON LIFE AND OTHER INCIDENTS

I have been requested to write some incidents, experiences and observations of prison life during the war of 1861-65. After thirty-eight or thirty-nine years it is somewhat difficult to recall anything like all that transpired in those dark days. Some people say it is time to stop talking about that war. Now, that would be a hard thing for those who lived in those days to do: stop talking about that war. The men, women and children at home had almost as hard a time as those at the front-not quite so dangerous, yet it required courage and true patriotism to stand in their places. Furthermore, it seems necessary, in order to keep history straight, that those who lived and participated in that part of our history should occasionally be heard from, otherwise those who write so much, who live north of the Mason and Dixon's line, would make our rising generation believe what is false. So I say to all such: "Nothing in the past is dead to the man who would learn how the present came to be what it is." Much has been written and said by our Northern friends as to the

Miles Sherrill. Source: Unknown.

suffering of the Union soldiers in Southern prisons-Andersonville, Salisbury and other places-during the war. They draw an awful picture of their poor soldiers suffering and dying in Southern prisons. In some respects this was true. To be in prison of itself was bad enough, but to be there without proper food or medicine was very bad indeed. The South did not have the means, neither the medicine, but the prisoners in our care were put on the same footing as our own poor soldiers. The question is: Who was to blame for this state of things? The Confederate authorities made proposition after proposition for exchange of prisoners, but the Government at Washington positively declined. It is said that General Grant said: "It was hard, and a great sacrifice, to leave the Union soldiers in Southern prisons, but it must be made; that the Confederates could not afford to leave their men in prison for want of men to take their place, but the United States could; to exchange the prisoners the Confederates would return to the army and go to fighting again." So here is the key to the responsibility for all to suffering and deaths on both sides in the prisons. The Confederate Government offered to let them send medicine South for their sick prisoners, but they

228

declined to do that. It must be remembered the Confederate Government was shut in from the outside world, and could not secure necessary medicine, etc. Now, as to Andersonville, it was under the command of Wirtz, and since men have had time to cool off it has long since been decided that the hanging of that poor man was simply murder. He did the best he could for the poor prisoners there. General Dick Taylor in his book, "Destruction and Reconstruction," gives the following account of meeting with Wirtz, as his troops were passing Andersonville, during the march of Sherman through Georgia, in 1864: "In this journey through Georgia, at Andersonville, we passed in sight of a large stockade inclosing prisoners of war. The train stopped for a few moments and there entered the carriage to speak to me a man who said his name was Wirtz, and that he was in charge of the prisoners nearby. He complained of the inadequacy of his guard and the want of supplies, as the adjacent country was sterile and thinly populated. He also said that the prisoners were suffering from cold, were destitute of blankets, and that he had not wagons to supply fuel. He showed me duplicates of requisitions and appeals for relief that he had made to different authorities, and these I endorsed in the strongest terms possible, hoping to accomplish some good. I know nothing of this (man) Wirtz, whom I then met for the first and only time, but he appeared to be in earnest in his desire to mitigate the condition of his prisoners. There can be but little doubt that his execution was a 'sop' to the passions of the 'many-headed.'" So, then, poor Wirtz was made a scapegoat to cover the sins of those who could have had those poor prisoners released at anytime but would not. The sacrifice was made to quiet the poor prisoners and their friends. Many things will be settled at the great Assize, when the Judge of all shall sit in judgment.

I was shot in the first charge that was made at Spotsylvania Court House, Virginia, early on the morning of the 9th day of May, 1864. The charge was made by our brigade, composed of the Fifth, Twelfth and Twenty-third N.C., Regiments, led by General R.D. Johnston. The charge was a success so far as the enemy in our front were concerned, but our lines were overlapped by Burnside's troops. Our regiment (the Twelfth) and our company (A), being on the extreme right, were exposed to an enfilading fire clear across an open field; so we were exposed to a fire from front and from the right. The enemy had torn down a rail fence and made temporary breastworks in our front, from which our men drove them, but could not hold the position because Burnside's whole army corps was on hand, and could easily have cut off our little brigade; so General Johnston gave the command to fall back. As our troops fell back, Sergeant Silas Smyre (now county commissioner of Catawba) and Corporal E. G. Bost endeavored to carry me from the battlefield. They were so exhausted from marching and fighting that they could not hold me up so as to prevent the crushed leg from dragging on the ground. To prevent their being captured, I begged them to leave me to my fate. (May I never forget this act of kindness by these brave men, who risked so much for me.) I was in the broiling hot sun, without water, my canteen having been shot in the fight, and the water all run out.

I was concealed from the enemy by some shrubbery. Late in the afternoon I realized that I could not live without water. The loss of blood, together with the burning rays of the sun, made me feel that life was about to ebb out; so I called to the enemy and surrendered. Here I commenced the life of a prisoner, which lasted ten months. Besides the suffering from wounds, the humility, the loss of liberty, the absence of all friends and loved ones, no face but that of enemies, was just about as much as I could bear up under in my condition. In that hour home and friends would have been "a haven of rest" sure enough.

The day following, May 10, 1864, when I was laid on the slaughter table, my eyes caught the sight of arms and legs piled on the ground-an indication of what I might expect. Dr. Cox, of Ohio, examined my leg. The only conversation that passed between us was this: I said, "Doctor, can you save my leg?" He replied, "I fear not, Johnny." Chloroform was applied, and when restored to consciousness I was minus one limb. I lay there in what was designated "a field hospital" for two or three days without further attention to the wound, and the result was the flies "blowed" the amputated limb, and when I reached Alexandria City, some days later, the nurse who dressed the wound found that I was being eat up by the vermin. Just here I will state that on the last day spent at the field hospital there was a great rush in gathering us up in ambulances. Under great excitement, I said to the doctor who was supervising the movement: "Doctor, what is the matter?" He replied that "Burnside was falling back to get a better position." I had been in the army long enough to know that was an evasive answer. The fact was that our troops were driving Burnside back, and the Federals were not willing to lose any of their prisoners though maimed for life. The roads from this place were cut to pieces by the artillery and wagon trains of the Union army going to the front. Those of us who were badly wounded cried for mercy. No mercy came until we reached the boat-landing, where we (those living) were transferred from ambulance to the boat. I do not know how many died en route from the battlefield to the boat-landing. I do know that Charles P. Powell, Adjutant of the Twenty-third North Carolina Regiment, who had lost his leg just as I had, died on this trip, and they stopped on the roadside and covered him up. This young man Powell was from Richmond County, N.C. He was a private soldier at Malvern Hill, July, 1862. When in line of battle, in front of the artillery, a shell fell in the ranks. The men could not leave the line of battle. There lay the shell, sputtering, ready to explode. Young Powell sprang up, grappled the shell and "soused" it into a pool of water nearby. What a risk was that! Yet that heroic act may have saved the lives of several men. Later that day he was wounded, and again at the battle of Gettysburg in July, 1863, and died as above stated. On page 189 of Volume II, North Carolina Regimental Histories, it is stated that C.P. Powell, Adjutant, was killed on the 9th of May, 1864, whereas the truth is he was shot on the 9th and his leg was amputated, and about the 11th or 12th of May he was jolted to death between Spotsylvania Court House and Bell Plains. I venture the assertion that he was not buried two and a half feet deep; and the place is unknown to his people, who think he was buried on the battlefield. We were shipped to Alexandria City, where I spent three months in the "Marshall House," where the proprietor, Jackson, shot and killed Colonel Ellsworth, who tore down his Confederate flag in April, 1861, and Jackson was killed by Frank Brownwell, of Colonel Ellsworth's regiment. This hotel was used as a prison hospital for those who were permanently disabled. For awhile the patriotic women of Alexandria were permitted to visit us, and often when they would bid us good-bye a "green-back" bill or something else was left in our hand. However, before we were removed from there the good women were prohibited from coming to see us.

While a prisoner here our troops, under General Early came down near Washington City, and there was great excitement in Washington and Alexandria, for it did seem that the Confederates were going into Washington. We prisoners were expecting to be released and get home, but our expectations were soon blasted by the Confederates having to retreat back to the south side of the Potomac, and did not come via Alexandria. My next move was to the Lincoln Hospital in Washington City. Here I spent about two months. After I could walk with crutches I was transferred to the old Capitol prison. I was honored with a seat in the old Capitol, but had to look through iron bars.

In November, 1864, I (with others) was shipped off to Elmyra, N.Y. We reached Elmyra on Sunday morning. Being in the mountains, the ground was covered with snow. Arriving at the barracks, we were lined up (I was on my crutches, and had to stand there on one foot for what seemed to me a very long time) just inside the gate, Negro soldiers on guard. The commanding officer, Major Beal, greeted us with the most bitter oaths that I ever heard. He swore that he was going to send us out and have us shot; said he had no room for us, and that we (meaning the Confederate soldiers) had no mercy on their colored soldiers or prisoners. He was half drunk, and I was not sure but that we might be dealt with then and there. Then we were searched and robbed of knives, cash, etc., and sent into our various wards. While we were standing in the snow, hearing the abuse of Major Beal, some poor ragged Confederate prisoners were marched by with what was designated as barrel shirts, with the word "thief" written in large letters pasted on the back of each barrel, and a squad of little drummer boys following beating the drums. The mode of wearing the barrel shirts was to take an ordinary flour barrel, cut a hole through the bottom large enough for the head to go through, with arm-holes on the right and left, through which the arms were to be placed. This was put on the poor fellow, resting on his shoulders, his head and arms coming through as indicated above; thus they were made to march around for so many hours and some many days. Now, what do you suppose they had stolen? Why, something to eat. Yes, they had stolen cabbage leaves and other things from slop barrels, which was a violation of the rules of the prison. One large, robust prisoner from Virginia was brought into the surgical ward where I was, having been seriously wounded by one of the guards. On inquiry, I learned that the poor fellow was caught fishing out scraps from a slop barrel and was shot for it. A small, very thin piece of light-bread with a tin pint cup full of what purported to be soup twice a day was the rations for the prisoners. I heard the men say: "My soup has only three eyes on it." meaning there was no grease in it-only hot water. Now, this fare was not enough to sustain life in healthy, able-bodied men. The result was that where they could not make something-make rings, etc.-and thus secure something from the sutlers, many, yes hundreds of the poor fellows would be attacked with dysentery-so common and often so fatal in camp, and especially in prison life. The food they had seemed to be only enough to feed the disease; the result was that scores and hundreds died. Speaking of the light-bread, the Confederates would sometimes hold it up and declare "that it was so thin that they could read *The New York Herald* through it"; then they would grab it and squeeze it up in one hand till it looked about like a small biscuit. Men died there for the want of food. I do not know, it may be that the Government issued enough rations, but it had to pass through too many hands before reaching the soldiers.

The truth is that there was a great deal of speculation and swindling carried on in the prisons; and I am ashamed to say it, yet it is true that sometimes some of our own men were engaged in the conspiracy to cheat and defraud their fellow-prisoners. It was in this way: those in charge of the prison would take Confederates and make ward-masters, etc., of them (like in prisons now a few are made "trusties"); and a little authority, even of that kind, would ruin some men. Some prisoners, like Jeshrun, grew fat, but others starved for want of suitable food and enough of it. Well, to go back a little, while standing there, receiving the profane blessing from Major Beal, I was drawing near as he dared to venture and old fellow-prisoner that I had met in Washington, who had preceded me to this place. I do not remember his name. I had at Washington nicknamed him "softy." He recognized me, and as Beal closed his eloquent abuse, and we were ordered to march into the barracks, "Softy" ventured in a low tone to speak to me. His greeting was: "Sherill, you have come to hell at last. Did you see those four-horse wagons going out? They were full of dead men, who died last night. They are dying by hundreds here with small-pox and other diseases." He was discovered by one of the guards (standing too near us). He hollowed at him: "Get away from there!" He got away immediately, if not sooner. When I reflected on the situation-the cursing major, the colored guards, the robbing us of our little stock of valuables, the barrel shirts, the wagons with the dead, the appearance of some of the living, the earth covered with snow-I thought, "Well, 'Softy' has given a true bill."

When I was located, I found I had kinsfolk there: J.U. Long (now chairman of the board of county commissioners), Nicholas Sherrill and W.P. Sherrill. There may have been others, but I do not recall them now. My haversack had been supplied with rations on leaving Washington. When I was located in the ward, "Nick" Sherrill came to see me. Of course we were glad to see each other, for it had been many moons since we had met. We were not in the same command in the army. "Nick" asked me if I had anything to eat. I replied, "Yes." He said: "I want to trade you a cup, spoon, etc., for some bread; I am about perished." Poor fellow, he looked the picture of despair. I said: "Nick, I do not want you cup and spoons, but you are welcome to what I have." He devoured in short order all that I had, and wanted more. Poor fellow, he soon died, as did W.P. Sherrill; died away from home and loved ones, buried by their enemies.

I had to spend several days in the barracks before I was transferred to the surgical or hospital ward. I was there long enough to know why Cousin Nicholas was so anxious for my bread. After I was placed in the surgical ward of the hospital I fared fairly well-a great improvement over the fare out in the wards of the regular prison. After a few weeks I was taken with small-pox, and of course was transferred over S. Creek to the small-pox camp. I was carried over on a cot, or "stretcher," with a blanket thrown over my face. When I reached the place, and the blanket was removed, I found myself in a large "wall tent," with several cots, or "bunks," about two and a half feet wide, with two Confederates on each "bunk," in reverse order, i.e., A's head at one end and B's at the other-so your bed-fellow's feet were in very close proximity to your face. They were all sandwiched in this way, because the bed was too narrow to admit of the two to lay shoulder to shoulder. On waking up on a morning one of these poor fellows would be dead and the other alive; this, of course, occurred day after day, and night after night. Well might those poor fellows, who had spent at least a part of the night with a corpse for a bed-fellow, have exclaimed with St. Paul, "Who shall deliver me from the body of this death?" When I took in the situation, I told the man who was going to place me on a bunk by the side of a poor fellow bad off with that awful disease (and who finally died) "that he could not put me on there." He replied "that he would show me whether he could or not." I stuck to it that I would not be put there. The fellow went and brought in the ward-master, and when he appeared it was Jack Redman, from Cleveland County, Company E, my regiment. Redman said, "Why, hello, Sherrill, was it you that was raising such a racket?" I told him it was. He wanted to know what was the matter. I explained that with my amputated limb it would never do to put me on a bunk with another fellow, and he finally consented to arrange for me to gave one to myself. I said: "Redman, you must grant me another favor." He wished to know what it was. I replied: "I want you to let me keep my blanket that came over from the surgical ward." "Why so, Sherrill?" I said: "Jack, you see those blankets that you fellows have been using on these men-there are five 'army lice' to every hair on the blanket." Redman took a hearty laugh. He knew there was more truth in it than poetry, so he granted my request. Redman had had small-pox and was an "immune," hence was made a ward-master. He was especially kind and considerate towards me. When I got well and was carried away, I never knew what became of him. Some of our men, who felt that the thing was gone, and that we could not succeed, never came back South. I am inclined to think that Redman did that thing. After the doctor had declared me well, and directed that I should be removed back to the hospital ward from whence I came, this was indeed glorious news; for all of the diseases that flesh is heir to, small-pox is the filthiest. The small-pox such as we had there was "sure enough" small-pox. Such as we have in North Carolina these days, in comparison with that, is only make-believe. I don't think it an exaggeration to say that seven out of ten who had it died. I was carried over into what was called a bath-house, where I was placed in a large bath-tub of water, almost too hot to bear. The Yankee soldier who had charge went out to look after something else or to loiter around, and I waited and waited for his return (the water was beginning to get cold) so I could get out and get clothing to put on. The atmosphere of the room was colder, if anything, than the water. I was in great distress, and it seemed that I could make no one hear me; so I had to wait the return of the villain, who finally came when the water in the bath-tub seemed to me to be nearly to the freezing point. He came, bringing a full Yankee suit, and when I gave him a piece of my mind he apologized and begged me not to speak of it-said he had actually forgotten me. When I reached the hospital ward I was a blue man in feelings and in appearance. I was dressed in a Yankee suit, even to a cap. I felt humiliated, and my skin was blue from cold. But for the kindness of my comrades there, giving me of their allowance of spirits that night, I don't know but what I would have gone hence.

It is indeed wonderful how the prisoners would work to make a little money. One of the most common occupations was to make finger rings; they did some real nice work. Some of the men would secure a few cents, and on that little capital build up quite a business. Some had teachers and attended school. The teachers were, of course, fellow-prisoners with the pupils. As before stated, I was in the surgical ward while in New York, and had no personal experience in the traffic and trading above alluded to, for it was not allowed in the hospital wards. I am reminded that General Lee says in his memoirs that he used every effort and means at his command to effect an exchange of prisoners, but General Grant refused.

Along toward the close of February, 1865, I with others, was marched to the train and shipped to Richmond. I think that was the happiest day that I ever experienced in my life. To get out of that death-hole was enough to make one happy; and to add to it the prospect of getting home to friends and loved ones, from whom I had been so long separated, not having heard from them in ten months, was indeed a treat. Many and great changes had taken place since I had left Dixie. I never did doubt that we would eventually succeed. I presume I was cheered up and was kept optimistic from the many rumors all the time in circulation that France and England would soon recognize our independence; which, of course, never took place. The air was filled with that and other rumors, not only in the Confederate army, but even in prison. Such rumors of great victories for the Confederate arms were all the time circulating among the poor fellows. As I came on from New York it looked to me as if the whole world was being uniformed in blue and moving toward General Grant's army. As we came up the James River, both sides were lined with soldiers dressed in blue. When we came to the Confederate lines, seeing such few ragged men confronting all that blue host, my courage came near failing me. In fact, I could not see how this little thin line of Confederates could hold at bay such a multitude of well-fed, well-equipped men. The patriotic women of Richmond tried to be cheerful, but I could see plainly enough that they were depressed. While they were just as kind in their attention to the returning soldiers as in former days, yet it was evident that the cheerful hope of former days was gone. When I reached home I soon learned that many who were living on the 9th of May, 1864, when we made that charge, had been numbered with the dead.

There never was any trouble between true soldiers, whether they wore the blue of the gray. It was the warlike civilians who did not fight and the soldiers who were mere hangers-on and camp followers that made the trouble. But for the influence of General Grant and other army officers we would have fared much worse in the South after the close of the war than we did; they, as conquerors, became our protectors. The true soldiers could be seen exchanging coffee for tobacco, going in bathing at the same time, in the same river; and when the enemy fell into his hands as a prisoner he would empty his own haversack and the canteen to relieve his prisoner. When there was no fighting going on, the soldiers of the two armies were on the best of terms. The outrages committed on either side during the war were not attributable to the true soldier; neither can the outrages perpetrated on the South after the war be charged up to the United States Army proper, but to the "bummers," who were no good in the army or at home. The storm has long since gone by. The true soldier has no prejudice against the soldier who fought on the other side.

Private G. T. Taylor

Reprinted from *The Confederate Veteran Magazine*, July, 1912.

PRISON EXPERIENCE IN ELMIRA, N.Y.

I belonged to Company C, 1st Alabama Battalion of Heavy Artillery, and served on the Gulf Coast most of the war of 1861-65. I was captured August 23, 1864, at Fort Morgan and was taken to New Orleans and placed in Cotton Press No. 3 on September 18, (?). About 300 of us were sent on board a ship for New York City and placed in Castle Williams, on Governor's Island. We were kept there until December 4, when we were sent to Elmira (N.Y.) Prison. While in New Orleans we fared fairly well under the circumstances. While on Governor's Island a corporal (I think his name was Toby) stole our rations, and we suffered hunger until Colonel Bumford, in command of the prison, removed the man, who was making money while we were starving. While there I took smallpox, as did several others, and we carried the disease to Elmira, where a number died of it.

Talk about Camp Chase, Rock Island, or any other prison as you please, but Elmira was nearer Hades than I thought any place could be made by human cruelty. It was in a bend of the small river, surrounded by a high board inclosure, with sentinels walking on a platform near the top outside, with a dead line some fifteen or twenty feet on the inside; and if prisoners went near the line, a wound or death was the invariable result. Snow and ice several feet thick covered the place from December 6 to March 15, 1865. We were in shacks some seventy or eighty feet long, and they were very open, with but one stove to a house. We had bunks three tiers high, with only two men to a bunk, while we were allowed only one blanket to a man. Our quarters were searched every day, and any extra blankets were taken from us. For the least infraction we were sent to the guardhouse and made to wear a "barrel shirt" or were tied up by the thumbs for hours at a time. There was one Major Beal who, I believe, was the meanest man I ever knew. Our rations were very scant. About eight or nine in the morning we were furnished a small piece of loaf bread and a small piece of salt pork or pickled beef each, and in the afternoon a small piece of bread and a tin plate of soup, with sometimes a little rice or Irish potato in the soup where the pork or beef had been boiled. We were not allowed to have any money, but could make rings or pins or buttons and sell them for sutler tickets and buy tobacco or apples; but we were not allowed to buy rations. After the surrender of General Lee, we thought it would be better, but were mistaken.

In May they commenced to liberate prisoners, sending three hundred every other day. I got out on July 7, 1865, and started for my home in Alabama. Upon arrival in New York City I secured my first "square meal" in over ten months.

My experience was that when you met a Western man you met a gentleman and a soldier; but when you met a "down Easterner" or a Southern renegade, you met the other fellow.

If any of the 1st Battalion of Heavy Artillery of Alabama or any of the 1st Tennessee Heavy Artillery or any of Captain Butt's company, 21st Alabama Infantry sees this, please write me.

Private Washington B. Traweek

Recollections of Escaping Elmira

About the 1st of July the prisoners were being transferred to Elmira, N.Y., and Zeke Melton and I were among the first to be transported to Baltimore, where we took a train for Elmira.

We were placed in boxcars, with three sentinels at each door. About eleven o'clock that night, it being very dark, Zeke Melton tapped me on the shoulder and said: "Wash, let's go." I said to him that it was impossible then. The train was going at forty miles an hour, and I told him to look at the guards. He took me by the hand, bid me good-bye, and said: "Watch me."

As I turned he squared himself and rushed through the door knocking two of the guards off into the darkness, and made his escape. The train had gone about fifty yards before it could be stopped, and when it backed to the place of escape no one was found but one crippled guard. Melton made his escape, and went back to his company.

A few days after reaching the prison at Elmira, N.Y., Sergeant John Fox Maull, John P. Putegnat and I, all of whom were members of the Jeff Davis Artillery, held a consultation and determined to dig a tunnel from the second row of tents, on the north side of the prison next to the city streets. The tunneling was actually begun in a vacant tent next to ours ... (missing text) ... decided to tunnel from that. The ground within the prison walls was covered with a thick sod of grass. Our first work was to remove this sod in a solid mass that it might be used to conceal our work, during its progress, when needed. A circle about three feet in diameter was cut in the sod, and the latter was removed in a solid sheet and laid aside for future use.

To prosecute our work it was necessary to know the distance from the tent to the wall. To ascertain this without arousing the suspicion of the guard whose beat was twelve feet inside the wall, we threw stones at the wall, apparently as a pastime. After watching us for three hours the guard became careless, and Putegnat attached a stone to a thread and threw the stone to the wall. It was then drawn to the tent and the thread measured, when the distance to be tunneled was found to be sixty-eight feet.

Having no tools, we began the work with pocket knives, working at night. Finding we could not do much work after "Tatoo", we decided to work during the day. The dirt could not be carried away and concealed at night.

To carry away the dirt, during the day without arousing suspicion, little sacks, holding about a quart, were made from an extra shirt owned by Putegnat. These filled with dirt could be easily secreted about the person. The prison walls extended sufficiently out to enclose a part of the river nearby. Over this enclosed water (actually a pond which stretched

236

the length of the enclosure) were prison privies, and into this part of the water, from the privies, the little sacks of dirt were emptied.

After working at the tunnel for a few days we decided that we needed more help, and so took in a man by the name of Frank E. Saurine of the Third Alabama Infantry, and not long after another man named S.C. "Cyclops" Malone of the Ninth Alabama Infantry. These additions, with the first three names, made five. Each of these five men took a solemn oath, with his right hand on the Bible, pledging not to reveal the character of the work going on, and to aid in putting to death any one guilty of revealing the existence of the tunnel. To this number others were added at different times in the following order: Gilmer G. Jackson and William H. Templin, members of the Jeff Davis Artillery; J.P. Scruggs, South Carolina; Glenn Shelton, Mississippi; Barry Benson, First South Carolina; and James W. Crawford, Sixth Virginia Cavalry. Every man who joined the party took the solemn oath not to divulge the scheme, under penalty of death.

After removal the circle of sod (ground originally broken on August 24th, nine days after their arrival) we dug straight downward for six feet, and at this depth we dug the tunnel, horizontally, in direct line toward a stairway on the outside of the wall, in use by the prison guard. Receiving information that there would be an inspection the succeeding day, when we would be required to stack tents, we prepared for it be taking pieces of plank from the sidewalk and placing them over the hole three feet below the surface, filling the vacancy with dirt, and placing the circle of sod over the fresh dirt, and pressing it down so that there were no signs indicating the work being done. We passed the inspection safely.

We found, after doing our work for a short time, that our clothing was beginning to show the color of the dirt clay, that we were working in, and consequently would like arouse the suspicion of the prison authorities. To prevent this, after working in the tunnel, each would turn his clothing, the stained side in, and the inside out, before leaving the tent for roll call.

The food we received, not being sufficient to sustain us to perform the work we were doing, we took in Parson Scruggs, sick sergeant of our ward. As he had free access to the cook room, he supplied us with the necessary additional food.

I owned a large Confederate overcoat, and could carry two of the quart sacks of dirt in each tail pocket. That these sacks of dirt might not attract attention by their bulk, when we carried them off to empty them in the pool, I walked so that the coat tails would swing from side to side, which caused me to be called a "dude."

About this time the prison authorities began building seventeen new hospitals, for sick prisoners near the prison wall in another part of the prison. They were designated by numbers from 1 to 17.

After discussing and considering the matter, Putegnat and I concluded we could dig out in a shorter time under one of these hospitals. Accordingly we began work under hospital No. 2.

We secured a spade, and by its use succeeded in digging out on the second night after beginning the work. As the others in our party, who were engaged with us digging the first tunnel, knew nothing of the work being done by Putegnat and me, under the hospital, we decided not to go out that night, that we might inform our associates of our success and give them an opportunity to get out with us.

After notifying our associates in my tent the next morning, we prepared ourselves and went down in front of hospital No. 1. About twilight we saw a man pass and go under hospital No. 1. It proved to be James W. Crawford (not yet a member of Traweek's tunnel organization). The prison authorities threw a guard around the hospitals, 17 in number, and captured Crawford, took him out and court-martialed him, sentenced him to a dungeon during his imprisonment.

Afterwards our tunnel was also discovered and we went back to work at our first tunnel. Putegnat and I worked in the back of the tunnel, the others carrying the dirt off. About four o'clock in the afternoon I became tired, and came out to the mouth of the tunnel and changed my clothes by turning them wrong side out. About this time five Yankee guards, with bayonets and guns, asked if my name was Traweek. I said it was and they said Major (Henry V.) Colt wanted to see me at his headquarters. I became very uneasy and asked if there was a letter for me. One of the Yankees winked at the other and replied that the major would explain that to me, come on, and I was marched down to Major colt's headquarters.

After we arrived Colt greeted me by saying, "Good morning, my young tunneler, they tell me you are engaged in tunneling." I replied that I didn't know what a tunnel was.

He replied by stating, "We have a way here of making you know what a tunnel is."

At this time the members of my tent not knowing where I had gone, made inquiry, and Maull and one or two of others came to where I was at headquarters and stood around to ascertain what I was carried there for. In the meantime Major Colt ordered me to a sweatbox. I was placed in it and the crank turned on me, and had my breath squeezed out. They claimed to have kept me there three quarters of a minute, but it seemed to me to be three hours and a half.

After I got my breath Major Colt said, "Now you have to state where you are tunneling and who was with you." I still told him I didn't know, and he ordered me back to the sweatbox and carried me through the same process.

After the second time...I saw it was my death anyway, and pointed my finger at Colt I told him I would see him in hell as far as a blue bird could fly in a year before I would tell him and that I would rather he would kill me; that he and his comrades were too damn cowardly to do it. He ordered his guards to come around, which they did, and I told him that no brave soldier would treat a man as he had me, with my hands behind my back.

At this time Fox Maull pushed me two or three times and showed me his pocket knife in his sleeve. At about the same instant a man came up, who was afterward known to me as Captain (Bennett) Munger, the officer of the day, and said, "Major Colt, I know this boy, and if you will turn him over to me, he will tell me all about this tunneling, etc." Major Colt replied: "All right Captain, but he is a sassy son of a bitch and ought to be shot."

Following the headquarters episode, Captain Munger took me to the front of the Federal tents, and said to me, "Wash, they have you, and you might as well tell it all." I said to him: "Who are you?" He responded by saying, "I am Captain Munger, the officer of the day here, and I heard you lie to Colt about the tunnel, saying that you didn't know what a tunnel is, and I know that you do know what a tunnel is, because you went to school to me. You remember I taught school, at Summerfield, near Selma, Alabama, before this war began, ...and what I have said to you, Wash, is for your own good."

I said, "Thank you Captain Munger, I know who you are, and I thank you for your kind intercession, but do not know what tunnel you are talking about."

He said, "You know, Wash, that you are engaged in tunneling under hospital No. 2," and pulled out a list of names who were engaged in that effort. I then acknowledged to tunneling under No. 2, then realizing that he had not discovered the one under the tent. He said, "You should have told Colt this," and I said: "This was not a tunnel but a ditch."

After confessing that I had been a participant, the captain marched me back to Major Colt's headquarters, and told Colt that I had acknowledged, and showed me the list of tunnellers. Major Colt asked me who was engaged in this tunneling with me, and I replied that it was done at night, and I could not tell who they were, except that I knew I was there myself. Then he ordered Captain Munger to take me before the court, which was composed of several Federal officers, who, after making some inquiries, sentenced me to the dungeon, which was in an old military barracks.

Munger carried me, and on reaching it, some twenty or thirty yards off, Captain Munger ordered the diamond holes to the cells opened so that I might see faces of the prisoners, as he had agreed to allow me to go in with some of the other prisoners. As I went down the line I asked each man what he was in there for. Some said for stealing rations, others for fighting, and asked me what I was in for. I told them for tunneling, and a man from the extreme end calling, "I am a tunneler on No. 1, come in with me." I told him I would take a look at him, and if his face looked all right I would go in with him. The cell door was opened, and I was placed in with him. Captain Munger then ordered all the diamond holes closed. He left my hole open, and in talking with me said they were going to have a general inspection and break up all the tunneling. He further stated that he would be off the next day, but would see me the day following.

In the meantime, no one in my tent knew what I was imprisoned for, but suspected it. After getting the information from Munger that there was going to be an inspection, about dark they sent my rations to be by Scruggs, one of my tent mates. He handed it to me through the hole. It consisted of soup and light bread. I took a piece of candle out of my pocket, that I had used in tunneling and lighted it, and took a memorandum out of my pocket and wrote on it that Captain Munger informed me that an inspection would be made the next day to ascertain who was tunneling, and to close down the tunnel. I folded this up, and put it down in the bottom of the soup, crumbled my bread in it and handed it back to the guard, explaining that I was sick and wished either Scruggs or Maull to have my rations, that I knew they were hearty eaters and would want it. The guard gave Scruggs the rations, who soon found the note and delivered it to Maull. They immediately proceeded to close down work on the tunnel.

The next morning, when my ration came in, I received a note from Maull saying that everything had been closed down. I ate about half of the soup and sent Maull another note, saying that I would let him know the next day how everything went.

The next day, when Captain Munger came in, he stated to me that they had gotten them corralled at last, and that they had found 28 tunnels. I asked him how No. 2, my tent, had come out, and he replied that they had been complemented on being kept so clean. I then wrote Maull a note that he could proceed with the work.

They went on with it for about a week. By this time Crawford became very inquisitive, wanting to know what I was writing so much about. In holding the candle for me he had seen the work tunnel, and told me he knew we were tunneling somewhere, and wanted to know about it. I told him I would let him know in due time.

About this time Maull wrote me that he was making fine progress with the tunnel, and it would be only a few days before it would be completed. I then wrote Maull of Crawford's suspicions, and explained that I could not make my escape without his assistance, and wanted to know if I could swear him into the organization individually. He replied that it would be all right, and knowing that I could not swear Crawford in without a Bible, I asked Captain Munger if he could get me one. He said: "My God, boy, what use have you for a Bible there, where you can't see your hands before your face, and particularly after giving Major Colt the cussing you gave him." I replied that if he was in my fix he would be glad to have a Bible to put his head to sleep on. He said "Well, as there is no harm in the Bible, I will step out and try to get you one." He brought in a small gilt-edged Bible. I then swore Crawford in, and made him a member of the tunnel organization.

After examining the cell overhead, I found two rods with taps on the ends, and in order to get the taps off I had to have a file. I notified Maull of this, and he went out to where the prisoners were making rings of buttons and bones, and sat around awhile, and slipped one of the files and sent this to me in a loaf of bread, at the same time telling the guard that inasmuch as I had divided my rations with him when I was sick, he would divide his with me now that he was sick.

240

About that time a downpour of rain fell, which was in our favor. I got astride Crawford's neck and filed off the taps. About eleven o'clock I got one of the rods loose, and filed on until four o'clock, when I finished the other rod. After taking the rods loose, I raised the trap door and went into the upper story. On that floor there were glass windows through which I could see the tunnelers at work on the tunnel. Maull also looked and saw me, and I notified him that I was ready, and he replied that he was also ready.

As this was Captain Munger's day on duty, I told Crawford that I would make one more effort through him to get out. I told Captain Munger to see Major Colt and tell that I thought he had punished me enough for what he would have done under similar circumstances. Captain Munger took the message to Major Colt, and about a half hour after returned saying that he would take us to Major Colt's headquarters. I insisted on Crawford's talking to Coly when we arrived there as I thought Colt would be prejudiced against me for the way I had spoken to him before sent to the dungeon. Crawford refused and I had to talk to Colt myself.

I commenced by apologizing to him, as what I said was in the heat of passion, and told him I thought I out to be released as I did not consider myself any more dangerous than the other 45,000 men in prison, not even having a pocket knife. He studied awhile and finally agreed to release us, but wanted to give advice. I told him if ever a man needed advice, I needed it then, and would appreciate any advice he could give me. He began by saying, "My lad, you were too hasty. If you had been more cautious and taken more time, you would have made your escape. Next time don't be so hasty and you may get out." I told him that at that time I felt too despondent to undertake tunneling again, that I had enough of it. I thanked him for the advice and bid him good-bye, and went to my tent. We had been confined three weeks in the dungeon before being released.

On reaching the tent and making a careful inspection of the tunnel, I discovered that a bend had been made in it. We went to work and corrected this. That part of the tunnel already dug, which could not be used for depositing the newly dug dirt resulting from further work to complete the tunnel. This relieved us from having to carry the dirt so far, in small quantities, to conceal it. In two nights after I got out of the dungeon, our tunnel was ready to be opened outside the wall.

A question arose as to who should go out first. I volunteered to go out first, with J.W. Crawford, my cellmate in the dungeon, and J.F. Maull agreed to go next. As I broke the dirt on the outside the sentinel called, "Half past three o'clock and all is well." As I crawled out and stepped into the streets of Elmira, Crawford followed immediately.

Before leaving the prison, we had all agreed to meet at a church in the city, whose steeple we had seen from the prison, and there it separate into pairs. But as it was almost daylight, Crawford and I did not wait long. We waded across the river and went into the mountains. From our elevated position we could see inside the prison walls. Our vision was aided by a little glass. We saw the confusion in the camp resulting from the discovery of the tunnel and the escape. We also saw the cavalry in its movements clearly indicating that it was searching for the escapees.

We traveled about nine miles the first day, sleeping in a barn at night. The next morning we went to a house nearby and asked the lady for food and directions. She gave us both but accused us of being escaped Confederates. We, in turn, acknowledged that we were. She then showed us the morning paper telling of the escape of the others. This is the first information we had received concerning the others.

We traveled in the mountains along the Harrisburg and Pennsylvania Railroad until our feet were sore and tired. We then stole a skiff and floated down the river. After getting in the boat and floating for about four miles, we heard what we thought to be a storm coming, but it proved to be a roar of water falling over a factory dam. To our right was a small village. We got over the dam with the loss of one oar. We then traveled down the Susquehanna River and came in contact with several dams, going through the mill race of each of these. After going about 75 miles down the river, we left the skiff and went up into the mountains and rested that day.

While resting we discovered a little village of about two or three hundred people at the foot of the mountain. About twilight we saw two men leave the village and come up to a house at the foot of the mountain. We moved up close to this house and camped for the night. Next morning the men went back down to the village. Two ladies from the same house, went to their right, about two hundred yards to a cow lot and went to milking cows. We then went back down by the back way to the house, and went in and found two suits of clothes. One was a fine dress suit with a velvet cap and a pair of shoes. In a dresser drawer I found a pistol, what is known as a pepper-box revolving pistol. We took these and went back to the mountains the route we came. There we took off our Confederate uniforms, and I put on my suit. We traveled some five or six miles and concluded to stop for the night.

After dark, we found a large horse and a good buggy and harnessed it up and drove out on the turnpike. We continued to drive until the horse gave out, when we left him standing in the road and returned to the mountains, where we lay over all that day.

We discovered another house next morning and entered it as we had done before, and secured an overcoat apiece. Walking about eight or nine miles, we came to a barn where we found a pair of horses and a double buggy, but could only find one bridle, and I was harnessing the horses, Crawford was attacked by a bull dog, which tore off the entire tail of his overcoat. We went on down the road on foot, and I laughed at Crawford until he got mad.

Next we came to a lot where there were two or three horses. I took the bridle I still held in my hands and bridled one of the horses. We both mounted this horse and rode him as far as he could go and left him standing in the road. We traveled from here on foot for about a mile, when we took another turn in the turnpike road and soon came to another house where we found a pair of horses and an apparently new buggy. We took these and traveled about seventy-five miles before they both gave out, and we left them standing in the road as we had left the others. We then went back into the mountains and traveled about a mile.

We had gone some distance and still did not find anything else to ride, but just after the point of discouragement, we came upon a hut where we found a horse tied to a tree. We mounted this horse and rode about two or three miles when we met two old citizens who asked, "What in the name of God are you boys doing with old Blaze?" I replied, "Blaze, hell, you get out of the way," and at the same moment pointed my old pepper-box pistol at them.

They took to their heels. After proceeding about half a mile the old men called from our rear and at the same time were ordered by Federal guards to halt. We jumped off old Blaze, and ran across a small steam wading, over which a railroad crossed. As we ran they fired and killed old Blaze. We went into the mountains, built a fire, dried our clothes, and remained there for the night.

The next morning it commended snowing a little before daylight. We moved on for a mile or so and discovered a nice farm, and concluded to stay in the barn. We went into the wheat loft and slept all night until about nine o'clock next morning, when we were aroused by voices below.

The father was telling the sons that they had better thrash the wheat that morning. They came up and commenced throwing out the wheat, and I cautioned Crawford if they stepped on us not to speak/ However, when they stuck us with their pitch forks we decided to get out. I got up and pointed my pepper-box pistol at them. The old man wanted to know if we intended to murder them, and I replied that we did not, but were citizens traveling from Canada to join Grant's army. We claimed to have formerly lived in Berlin, Md., but had been in Canada, and were on our way back to join Grant's army. He gave us our dinner and a full supply of rations, and laid out a diagram in the yard of the position of both Grant's and Lee's armies and stated that we could have to hurry or grant would have captured Lee's army and we would miss the fun.

We traveled only a short distance in the mountains, and got a two horse buggy and traveled some seventy-five miles. We then went back unto the mountains and lay over until night when we got another horse and went another twenty-five miles.

We went again in the mountains, and next morning walked some eight or ten miles when we arrived at Mr. Rodes' place, to which we had been directed by his brother-in-law. When we arrived there Rodes gave us dinner and a drink of whiskey and told us the way was clear as his son had come from Edward's Ferry that day, and said there were no Yankees there. We went on towards the Ferry as he had directed us.

That evening, about sundown, we met several federal cavalry men at the mouth of the lane, and as we passed them, one of the cavalry men said, "Damned if those are not rebels."

Crawford and I ran when the commended firing at us. We ran unto the ravine and escaped. We then went on and finally saw a light described to us by Rodes as being at the ferry. There we looked through the window and saw a man waiting on someone apparently sick. We called, and he came to the door, and I asked him if his name was Edwards. He replied, "No, are you Edwards' sons?" I replied that we were, and he said, "Your father's yard is heavily guarded by Yankees; don't go there." He then wanted to know how we got across the river, and we replied that we didn't know as it was so dark when we crossed. He then directed us back to the river, and we struck out.

We hadn't gone more than half a mile when I fell over a sleeping Yankee. When I realized that we had gotten into a Yankee camp, I said, "Hello, where is the water?" The sleeping man mumbled something in his sleep, and we crawled from there about fifty yards where we butted up against some saddles, and also were some horses were picketed. There I found, on one of the saddles, two army pistols. I appropriated one and handed the other to Crawford. We then turned and crawled about one hundred yards and struck a corn field. We went out in the field about seventy-five yards and nestled up in a corn shock.

At daylight the bugle sounded the feed call and the Yankees came pouring over the fence into the corn field and got their corn from all around us without disturbing us. While they were getting the corn, I told Crawford if they disturbed us to fire into them and we would run into the briar thicket. As they crossed the fence with the corn, we got out of our shock and ran into a ravine and escaped. We lay over all day in that ravine, climbed up a tree, and with our spy glass located their lines of pickets on the canal and their canal boats.

We came near the canal where the boats were passing about every five minutes. The two path was picketed to that as each boat passes, a picket would follow the boar, talking to the boatman until he met the next boat, when he would follow it. Thus we discovered that to make it across the canal we must proceed cautiously. At the proper time we approached the canal and I said to Crawford, "We must swim this." He said, "I can't swim." I replied by saying, "You must swim or be captured." I swam it and Crawford joined in, and the splash was so great that the boatman hollered "Man overboard!"

While this was going on, Crawford and I, having reach the opposite side of the canal, ran down the river bank of the Potomac, Crawford hiding in the brush at the river's edge. I took to the river, swimming and watching. They were standing all around Crawford, and I heard someone say, "That's some of Mosby's men, hungry devils, hunting something to eat." I swam across the river, a mile distant. After getting across the river, Crawford gave me a distress whistle which meant that I must help him. I answered his whistle, and succeeded in finding a log on the river bank. I got the log over the river to where Crawford was waiting, and we got astride it and paddled across. We were now on Jenkin's Island.

After getting back to the island with Crawford, we built a fire out of some river weeds with some matches we had in a bottle. As the fire began to burn, a squadron of Federal cavalry begin firing on us, supposing us to be Mosby's men. We moved off some 250 yards, and scratched a hold in the sand and made another fire. We were entirely without clothing, and

244

the weather was intensely cold, as it had been sleeting this afternoon. Crawford then took off a little jersey jacket he had on and gave it to me.

We remained there all night until daylight, when we crossed the other prong of the river a mile in width, wading across waist deep, and went up to Jenkins' house. Crawford insisted that I stay behind and let him go ahead. I told him that I would freeze if I remained at the gate. We met two young ladies and I told them I was an escaped prisoner, to give way to me. They broke and ran, and I went on to the house, and the old man came out and said , "Come on boys." I ran into the house, where there was a bog log fire. The old man handed us his brandy bottle and told us to drink.

In fifteen minutes I had another $75.00 cloth suit, which was presented to me by one of the young ladies, Miss Jenkins, stating that it belonged to a brother of hers, a captain in the Confederate army, who had been killed and that she was satisfied for me to wear it. They also gave Crawford a suit of clothes. Then two of Mosby's men came in and we joined them and succeeded in getting to Winchester, Virginia, our main Confederate lines. Herte Crawford and I separated, he going to his Virginia home, and I to Greenville, Alabama.

John J. Van Allen

Reprinted from the *Southern Historical Society Papers*, Volume I, page 294-295.

Late in the fall of 1864, and when the bitter sleets and biting frosts of winter had commenced, a relief organization was improvised by some of the generous ladies and gentleman of the city of Baltimore for the purpose of alleviating the wants of those confined in the Elmira Prison, where there were then several thousand prisoners.

I had the honor to be appointed by that organization to ascertain the needs of the prisoners, to distribute clothing, money, etc., as they might require. I had formerly lived at Elmira, where I studied my profession, but then (as now) I resided at this place, twenty miles distant from Elmira, where I resided for nearly twenty-five years and was well known at Elmira.

As soon as appointed I journeyed to that delightful paradise for Confederate prisoners (according to Walker, Tracy and Platt), and stated the object of my visit to the commanding officer, and asked to be permitted to go through the prison in order to ascertain the wants of the prisoners, with the request that I might distribute necessary blankets, clothing, money, medicines, etc.

He treated me with consideration and kindness, and informed me that they were very destitute of clothing and blankets; that not one-half of them had even a single blanket; and that many were nearly naked, the most of them having been captured during the hot summer months with no other than thin cotton clothes, which in most instances were in tatters. Yet he stated that he could not allow me to enter the prison gate or administer relief, as an order of the War Department rendered him powerless. I then asked him to telegraph the facts to the War Department and ask a revocation of the order, which he did; and two or three days were thus consumed by me in a fruitless endeavor to procure the poor privilege of carrying out the designs of the good Samaritans at Baltimore who were seeking to alleviate in a measure the wants of the poor sufferers, who were there dying off like rotten sheep from cold and exposure. The officer in command was an army officer, and his heart nearly bled for those poor sufferers; and I know he did all in his power to aid me, but his efforts were fruitless to assist me to put a single coat on the back of a sufferer. The brutal Stanton was inexorable to all my entreaties, and turned a deaf ear to the tale of their sufferings. The only proposition that could be entertained was this: If I could fetch clothing only of a grey color (Confederate uniforms) I could place it in the hands of some understrappers of the *loyal persuasion*, as well as such moneys as I might wish to leave in the same hands, and they would distribute the same as they liked.

This could not be allowed to be done by the commanding officer, but must be done by any one of the *loyal* (?) gentry, who I became satisfied would absorb it before any poor Confederate soldier would even catch a glimpse at its shadow; and I was actually forced to give the matter up in despair.

The nearest I could get to the poor skeletons confined in that prison, was a tower built by some speculator in an adjoining field across the way from the prison pen, for which privilege a money consideration was exacted and paid. On taking a position upon this tower what a sight of misery and squalor was presented! My heart was sick, and I blushed for my country—more because of the inhumanity there depicted. Nearly all of the many thousands there were in dirty rags. The rain was pouring, and thousands were without shelter, standing in the mud in their bare feet, with clothes in tatters, of the most unsubstantial material, without blankets. I tell the truth, and Mr. Charles C. B. Watkins dare not deny it, when I say these men suffered bitterly for the want of clothing, blankets and other necessaries. I was denied the privilege of covering their nakedness.

Private F. S. Wade

Getting Out of Prison

Getting Out of Prison is a reprint from *The Confederate Veteran Magazine,* 1926, October.

If there ever was a hell on earth, Elmira prison was that hell, but it was not a hot one, for the thermometer was often 40 degrees below zero. There were about six thousand Confederate prisoners, mostly from Georgia and the Carolinas. We were housed in long prison buildings, say one hundred and twenty feet long and forty feet wide, three tiers of bunks against each wall. A big coal stove every thirty feet was always kept red hot; but for these stoves, the most of us would have frozen. Around each stove was a chalk mark, five feet from the stove, marking the distance we should keep, so that all could be warm. We were thinly clad and not half of us had even one blanket. Our rations were ten ounces of bread and two ounces of meat per day. My weight fell from 180 to 160 in a month. We invented all kinds of traps and deadfalls to catch rats. Every day Northern ladies came in the prison, some of them followed by dogs or cats, which the boys would slip aside and choke to death. The ribs of a stewed dog were delicious, and broiled rat was superb.

One day I was at the guardhouse when about thirty-five of our boys had on barreled shirts, guards marching them around. A barreled shirt was made by knocking out the head of a barrel the cutting a hole in the other head and putting it on the body. On these barreled shirts was written in big letters, "Stole dog," "Stole cat," "Stole ration," "Stole a fur," etc. If a ladies fur was not fastened on, the boys would grab it off, and some of them had been caught.

All the Yankee soldiers were not cruel. The chalk marks were drawn around the stoves so that all could get some of the heat. One day a poor sick boy lay down near the chalk line and went to sleep. In his sleep he threw his leg over the chalk line. A big guard caught him by the shoulder and threw him against the wall, making his nose bleed. I popped my big fist against the guard's jaw, knocking him heels over head. He ran out cursing me. Of course I was scared. In a few minutes, a captain came in with a file of soldiers, having the guard I assaulted in the party, and asked, "Where is the man who knocked this soldier down?" I stepped out and said: "I am the man." Then I called up the sick boy and made him lie down, and I told the captain it made me so mad to see this poor boy so brutally treated that I could not help punishing the bully. He said to our men: Has this man told the truth?" A dozen of our men stepped forward and said that they would swear that I had related the scene correctly. The captain slapped me on the shoulder and said to the brute: "I will put you in the guardhouse." I was called before a court-martial, and, being sworn, related the whole matter as it occurred. The Judge Advocate said to the bully: "You will wear a ball and chain for thirty days and forfeit your pay for a month for brutality to a prisoner."

Good luck came to me after I had been in this prison, say, a month. Some Yankee ladies got up a lot of old schoolbooks and established a prison school, and I was appointed one of the teachers, the pay was an extra ration. I soon got back my twenty pounds of flesh. This was the best pay I ever got for a job in my life.

My father and mother lived in Illinois. I wrote them my starving condition, and they sent me a big box of grub, and told me in their letter that my Uncle Jones lived in Utica, N.Y. I at once wrote him. He sent me a splendid suit of clothes and a pair of boots, and said that he would come to see me. He was what was called a "Copperhead," as he was opposed to the war, and could not get a pass. Then he smuggled a letter to me, asking me to be at the corner of a certain ward at sunset that day, and he would climb up on the observatory, a building outside the prison walls. At sundown, I saw a large old man slowly climb to the top of the observatory. On reaching the top, he faced me. We took off our hats and saluted. He slowly climbed down, with his handkerchief to his eyes. That was the only time I ever saw my dear uncle.

My dear comrade, Jimmie Jones, took the smallpox and was sent to the smallpox hospital. I was immune and got permission to help nurse him. A young Chinese physician, by the name of Sin Lu, had just been put in charge of the ward. The doctor had just become a Mason. Jim and I were very proficient in the work. All the doctor's spare time he spent in Jim's room learning the work. We became great friends. One day the doctor went over to Lake Erie, a few miles away. The next day he told me to go to Jim's room. To my great surprise, Jim was sitting in a coffin with a white sheet around him. He handed me a paper of flour and said: "Sprinkle my face and hands with flour, then slightly fasten the coffin lid down, and when the dead wagon comes around, be sure to put my coffin on top of the other dead." Soon the dead wagon, driven by a Negro, came up. I got help and put Jim's coffin on top. It was forty years before I saw Jim again at a reunion of Green's Brigade at Cuero, Texas.; but a day or two after, I got a letter from him telling me about his experiences. He said when the dead wagon got out of the prison walls, he raised up the coffin lid rapped on it, and said in a sepulchral voice: "Come to judgment." The darky looked around, jumped off the wagon, eyes like saucers, yelling: "Ghosties! Ghosties! Ghosties!" As soon as the darky was out of sight, he stripped off his sheet, wiped the flour off his face and hands, took one of the horses out of the wagon, mounted, and galloped to lake Erie, where he found a boat awaiting him, and was soon in Canada.

Soon after, an order was issued for all prisoners from the subjugated States of Missouri, Kentucky, West Virginia, and Louisiana, to report for parole. All that night I rolled over in my bunk and wished that I was from one of those states. Just before daylight, I had another inspiration. I slipped on my clothes, ran to the office where the prison rolls were kept, and asked the officer in charge to turn to the entry of a certain date. I ran my finger down the list till I came to the name, "F.S. Wade, sergeant of McNeill's Texas Scouts." I said to the officer: "I will give you $10 to erase Texas and substitute Louisiana." Said he: "Show me the money." I started to take it out of my vest pocket, but he put his hand over mine and saw the "X." Then he made the change, and I walked out with my parole.

Soon an officer came in my ward and called my name for parole. I stepped out and fell in line. The boys in the prison kept saying: "He always said he was from Texas." But I kept mum.

Federal Soldier's Statements

Lieutenant Frank Wilkeson

The fact that this statement was given voluntarily by a Federal officer guarding Elmira Prison makes it unique and worthy of note.

Chapter XIII is reprinted from the book: *Turned Inside Out:*

Recollections of a Private Soldier in the Army of the Potomac

Chapter XIII: The Military Prison at Elmira

Captain Frank Wilkeson, 4th US Artillery

After General Early had withdrawn his soldiers from the front of Washington, Battery A Fourth United States Artillery joined the artillery reserve then lying in Camp Barry, near Washington. Life in Camp Barry was exceedingly monotonous, and enlisted men and officers alike were impatient to be ordered to active service. There was joy in the camp one afternoon in late fall, when an order came, directing the commanding officer of Battery A to go at once to Elmira, New York, with a section of artillery, and to report for duty to the commanding officer, of that post. The senior lieutenant, Rufus King, was absent on leave. Lieutenant Cushing, eager to get out of Washington, ordered me to get a section in marching order. I did so, and we marched to the railroad station, and loaded guns, caissons, and horses on the cars, and left Washington in less than two hours after receiving the order.

We had heard that the Confederate soldiers who were confined in the military prison at Elmira were somewhat unruly, and next day, then we reported for duty to a 100-day colonel, we were not surprised to hear that the prisoners were insubordinate, and that an outbreak was imminent. We marched the battery to the military prison. There we found about twelve thousand Confederate prisoners, who were confined in a large stockade, inside of which were many barracks, and through which the Chemung River flowed. The stockade, made of logs set deeply in the ground on end and standing side by side, was about twelve feet high. About four feet below the top of the stockade, on the outside, was a platform, guarded by a handrail, which extended around the prison. This platform was studded by sentry boxes at short intervals. On it sentinels walked to and fro, day and night, and watched the prisoners. During the night they, at half hour intervals, loudly called the number to their post, and announced that all was well. It was almost dark when we arrived at the prison, and we parked the guns in an open space near the stockade. Around us were many camps, which were occupied by disorderly, undrilled 100-day men. We speedily discovered that there was a lack of discipline in the prison. The Confederates were ugly-tempered and rebellious. That night that gathered in mobs, and the Confederate charging-yell rang out clearly. They threw stones at the sentinels. They refused to go into their barracks. Evidently they knew that the men who guarded them were no soldiers. The uproar increased in volume. I was confident that the prisoners intended to break out that night. Our guns were placed in battery, and the ammunition chests opened. We waited, and waited, and waited, and finally I rode over to an infantry camp in search of information, and there found a 100-day colonel, who was playing cribbage with a sergeant. I asked the meaning of the uproar in the prison, and the colonel said, indifferently: "Oh, that is nothing! They generally make twice as much noise," and he continued to move his pegs up and down the cribbage-board. I returned to camp greatly disgusted.

The next day Cushing and I went into the prison, and after carefully examining it concluded that if an attempt to break guard was made it would be directed against the point where the river left the stockade. As we walked slowly around the prison, groups of Confederates looked curiously at us and talked insultingly about us. One crowd of men followed us to the riverbank and jeered us as we inspected the stockade there. Cushing lost his temper and turned savagely to face them, and said, in a low, clear voice: "See here, ---- ---- ----! I am just up from the front, where I have been killing such infernal wretches as you are. I have met you in twenty battles. I never lost a gun to you. You never drove a battery I served with from its position. You are a crowd of insolent, cowardly scoundrels, and if I had command of this prison I would discipline you, or kill you, and I should much prefer to kill you. I have brought a battery of United States artillery to this pen, and if you will give me occasion I will be glad to dam that river," pointing to the Chemung, "with your worthless carcasses, and silence your insolent tongues forever. I fully understand that you are presuming on your position as prisoners of war when you talk to me as you have: but," and here his hand shook warningly in the faces of the group, "you have reached the end of your rope with me. I will kill the first man of you who again speaks insultingly to me while I am in this pen, and I shall be here daily. Now, go to your quarters." And they went. We returned to camp, moved the guns to a position, which commanded the river, and then rearranged the ammunition, putting all the canister in the chests of the gun limbers. And we waited for the expected outbreak.

A military prison is not a place where life is enjoyed. The prisoners are enemies, and their keepers care but little for their lives and comfort. It is probable that we fed the Confederates better than they fed Union prisoners. Personally I know nothing of life in Confederate military prisons, as I was not captured. I saw many thousands of our soldiers shortly after they were exchanged. By far the larger portion of these men were in good condition and fit for service. It is true than many of them were diseased and almost dead when they were delivered to us, and these soldiers were grouped and photographed, very unfairly I think, and the illustrated papers which reproduced these photographs were widely circulated throughout the Northern States. I met no Union soldier who had been confined in a Confederate military prison, who thought it to be a pleasant retreat; and I know that the military at good taste. The prisoners, it was alleged, were allowed the same rations, excepting coffee and sugar, that their guards received. They did not get it. I repeatedly saw the Confederate prisoners draw their provisions, and they never got more than two thirds rations. Many of them were diseased, many were slightly wounded, many were feeble and worn out with campaigning in Virginia, and many more were home-sick; and these men died as sheep with the rot. Almost daily a wagon piled high with pine coffins entered the stockade, and these coffins were filled with dead Confederates. The sound men, the men of vigorous constitution, and those possessing aggressive minds, endured prison life without suffering greatly; and this I suspect was true of Union soldiers confined in Confederate prisons. The winter of 1864-65 was exceedingly cold. The Confederate prisoners, thinly clad, enfeebled by campaigning, and further weakened by insufficient supplies of food, were unable to endure the cold of a Northern winter. They died by the hundred. They were mentally depressed, and the inevitable result followed. Their wounds became gangrenous and they died; they were home-sick and they died; Fever stalked among them and struck hundreds down. Bowel disorders carried off other hundreds. I have seen groups of battle-worn, home-sick Confederates, their thin blankets drawn tightly around their shoulders, stand in the lee of a barrack for hours without speaking to one another. They stood motion-less and gazed into one another's haggard faces with despairing eyes. There was no need to talk, as all topics of conversation had long since been exhausted.

The majority of the prisoners were exceedingly ignorant. Many of them could not read or write. I often admired the military skill displayed by the Confederate officers in forging these ignorant men into the almost perfect soldiers they were. The discipline in the Con-federate armies must have been exceedingly severe to have enabled their officers to control these reckless, savage-tempered men. The prisoners at Elmira were exclusively Americans. I did not see a foreign-born citizen in that prison. These soldiers were penniless. They could not buy clothing or articles of prime necessity. They were eager to work, to earn money to buy tobacco. On pleasant days a few hundred of them were employed outside the stockade in digging ditches and trenches. For this work they were paid about twenty-five cents per day, which sum they promptly invested in tobacco. And they worked faithfully and honestly, and earned their scanty pay. Thinly clad, with blankets wound around them instead of overcoats, poorly fed, hopeless, these unfortunate soldiers swung heavy picks, and bent low over their shovels, as the cold wind swept through their emaciated frames as through a sieve. It was pitiful to see the poverty-stricken Confederates breaking the hard, frost-bound earth, while armed sentinels passed to and fro about them, and a battery of ar-tillery moved swiftly over the frozen plain in menacing drill.

Outside the stockade, and on the other side of the road, two tall wooden towers had been built by some enterprising Yankees. The owners of these buildings made a profitable show of the Confederate prisoners. Daily their tops were thronged with curious spectators, who paid ten cents each to look into the prison pen. A few weeks after these towers were built, I noticed a young and handsome woman visiting one of them daily. It was evident to me that she was communicating with the prisoners, probably to her friends or relatives who were confined in the stockade. One night seven or eight Confederates escaped from the prison by crawling through a tunnel that they had dug, and were seen no more. I was exceedingly glad that these men had escaped. The young woman disappeared also. Then I reported what I had seen, and the towers were closed by military orders.

One night the uproar in the stockade was terrific. A rifle shot rang out clearly. I heard a sentinel on post call for the officer of the guard. The long roll sounded in the infantry camps. The noise of infantry falling into line hummed in the air. The night was intensely dark. I stood in the door of my tent listening to the uproar in the Confederate pen. I judged that the prisoners were divided into two groups; one standing by the river bank, the other near the gate. Both groups were yelling at the top of their voices. Some of the soldiers of the regular brigade, which had been sent from the Army of the Potomac to assist in guarding the prisoners, were on duty that night. And I heard these cool veterans caution the Confederates not to cross the dead-line, and to repeatedly tell them to stand back or they would fire on them. Another shot rang out clearly. My battery bugler, a Jew, names Samuels, came to me, bugle in hand. "Blow Boots and Saddles," I said. Instantly the artillery camp was alive. Half-dressed men sprang to the guns, horses were harnessed and saddled. I called an old sergeant to me and said: "Trane No. 2 gun on the stockade near the river, and if the prisoners break out, dose the head of the column with double canister until they run over your gun. Fire a blank cartridge to summon Lieutenant Cushing and the enlisted men, who are in town, to the battery. I will take No. 1 gun close to the stockade and smash the flank of the column to flinders if it comes out. I will burn a lantern by the gun so as to mark my position." The sergeant moved off in the darkness. I saw the flash of his gun, heard a shot scream close above my head, and then heard the crash of timber as the shot tore through a barrack. I heard the Confederates cry: "Look out, the artillery has opened!" Instantly the uproar ceased. The great prison was as silent as death, and instantly I knew I was in a scrape, and would probably be court-martialed for firing on the prisoners. Out of town came Cushing, his horse in a lather. I explained to him what had happened. He looked soberly at me for an instant, and then said: "You will be court-marshaled, sure. You must get to your own battery at once (I belonged to battery H), and get off before the 100-day officers prefer charges against you." An officer from headquarters rode up and complained bitterly of the outrage of firing on the prisoners. From him we learned that it was a stone instead of a shot that had been fired into the prison. Early the next morning I left Elmira, having been ordered by a speedily procured telegram to join Battery H, Forth United States Artillery, in the department of the Cumberland. I afterwards learned that a few Confederates were wounded by splinters when the stone struck the barrack, and that they never again made the night hideous by their yells and howls.

Statement of a United States Ex-Medical Officer

Article Reprinted From *The Southern Historical Society Papers,*
Vol. I. Richmond, VA, March, 1876, No. 4 April, Pages 296-298

To the Editor of the World:

Sir-I beg herewith (after having carefully gone through the various documents in my possession pertaining to the matter) to forward you the following statistics and facts of the mortality of the Rebel prisoners in the Northern prisons, more particularly at that of Elmira, New York, where I served as one of the medical officers for many months. I found, on commencement of my duties at Elmira, about 11,000 Rebel prisoners, fully one-third of whom were under medical treatment for diseases principally owing to an improper diet, a want of clothing, necessary shelter and bad surrounding; the diseases were consequently of the following nature: Scurvy, diarrhea, pneumonia, and the various branches of typhoid, all super induced by the causes, more or less, aforementioned.

The winter of 1864-65 was an unusually severe and frigid one, and the prisoners arriving from the Southern States during this season were mostly old men and lads, clothed in attire suitable only to the genial climate of the South. I need not state to you that this alone was ample cause for an unusual mortality amongst them. The surroundings were of the following nature: narrow, confined limits, but a few acres of ground in extent, and through which slowly flowed a turbid stream of water, carrying along with it all the excremental filth and debris of the camp; this stream of water, horrible to relate, was the only source of supply, for an extended period, that the prisoners could possibly use for the purpose of ablution, and to slack their thirst from day to day; the tents and other shelter allotted to the camp at Elmira were insufficient, and crowded to the utmost extent-hence, small pox and other skin diseases raged through the camp.

Here I may note that, owing to a general order from the Government to vaccinate the prisoners, my opportunities were ample to observe the effects of spurious and diseases matter, and there is no doubt in my mind but that syphilis was engrafted in many instances; ugly and horrible ulcers and eruptions of a characteristic nature were, alas, too frequent and obvious to be mistaken. Small pox cases were crowded in such a manner that it was a matter of impossibility for the surgeon to treat his patients individually; they actually laid so adjacent that the simple movement of one of them would cause his neighbor type prevailed to such an extent, and of such a nature, that the body would frequently be found one continuous scab.

The diet and other allowances by the Government for the use of the prisoners were ample, yet the poor unfortunates were allowed to starve; but why, is a query which I will allow your readers to infer, and to draw conclusions there from.

Out of the number of prisoners, as before mentioned, over three thousand of them now lay buried in the cemetery located near the camp for that purpose; a mortality equal, if not greater than that of any prison in the South. At Andersonville, as I am, well informed by brother officers who endured confinement there, as well as by the records at Washington, the mortality was twelve thousand out of say about forty thousand prisoners. Hence it is readily to be seen that range of mortality was no less at Elmira than at Andersonville.

At Andersonville there was actually nothing to feed or clothe the prisoners with, their own soldiers faring but little better than their prisoners; this, together with a torrid sun and an impossibility of exchange, was abundant cause for their mortality. With our prisoners at Elmira, no such necessity should honestly have existed, as our Government had actually, as I have stated, most bountifully made provision for the wants of all detained, both of officers and men. Soldiers who have been prisoners at Andersonville, and have done duty at Elmira, confirm this statement, and which is in nowise in one particular exaggerated; also, the same may be told of other prisons managed in a similarly terrible manner. I allude to Sandusky, Delaware and other. I do not say that all prisoners at the North suffered and endured the terrors and the cupidity of venal sub-officials; on the contrary, at the camps in the harbor of New York, and at Point Lookout, and at other camps where my official duties from time to time have called me, the prisoners in all respects have fared as our Government intended and designated they should. Throughout Texas, where food and the necessaries of life were plentiful, I found our own soldiers faring well, and to a certain extent contended, so far, at least, as prisoners of war could reasonably expect to be.

The sick in hospitals were curtailed in every respect (fresh vegetables and other anti-scorbutics were dropped from the list), the food scant, crude and unfit; medicine so badly dispensed that it was a farce for the medical man to prescribe. At large in the camp the prisoner fared still worse; a slice of bread and salt meat was given him for his breakfast, a poor hatch-up, concocted cup of soup, so called, and a slice of miserable bread, was all he could obtain for his coming meal; and hundreds of sick, who could in nowise obtain medical aid died, "unknelled, unconfined and unknown."

I have in nowise drawn on the imagination, and the facts as stated can be attested by the staff of medical officers who labored at the Elmira prison for Rebel soldiers.

Ex-medical officer United States Army

Chapter 9

Confederate States of America, Congress, Joint Select Committee to Investigate the Condition and Treatment of Prisoners of War

Text reprinted from The Southern Historical Society Papers, Vol. I, pages 132-149

HOUSE OF REPRESENTATIVES, MARCH 3, 1865, on table and ordered to be printed. [By Mr. PERKINS.]

Report of the Joint Select Committee appointed to investigate the Condition and Treatment of Prisoners of War.

The duties assigned to the committee under the several resolutions of Congress designating them, "to investigate and report upon the condition and treatment of the prisoners of war respectively held by the Confederate and United States governments; upon the causes of their detention, and the refusal to exchange; and also upon the violations by the enemy of the rules of civilized warfare in the conduct of the war." These subjects are broad in extent and importance; and in order fully to investigate and present them, the committee propose to continue their labors in obtaining evidence, and deducing from it a truthful report of facts illustrative of the spirit in which the war has been conducted.

Northern Publications

But we deem it proper at this time to make a preliminary report, founded upon evidence recently taken, relating to the treatment of prisoners of war by both belligerents. This report is rendered especially important, by reason of persistent efforts lately made by the Government of the United States, and by associations and individuals connected or co-operating with it, to asperse the honor of the Confederate authorities, and to charge them with deliberate and willful cruelty to prisoners of war. Two publications have been issued at the North within the past year, and have been circulated not only in the United States, but in some parts of the South, and in Europe. One of these is the report of the joint select committee of the Northern Congress on the conduct of the war, known as "Report No. 67." The other purports to be a "Narrative of the privations and sufferings of United States officers and soldiers while prisoners of war," and is issued as a report of a commission of enquiry appointed by "The United States sanitary commission."

This body is alleged to consist of Valentine Mott, M. D., Edward Delafield, M. D., Governor Morris Wilkins, Esquire, Ellerslie Wallace, M. D., Hon. J. J. Clarke Hare, and Rev. Treadwell Walden.

Although these persons are not of sufficient public importance and weight to give authority to their publication, yet your committee have deemed it proper to notice it in connection with the "Report No. 67," before mentioned, because the sanitary commission has been understood to have acted to a great extent under the control and by the authority of the United States government, and because their report claims to be founded on evidence taken in solemn form.

Their Spirit and Intent

A candid reader of these publications will not fail to discover that, whether the statements they make be true or not, their spirit is not adapted to promote a better feeling between the hostile powers. They are not intended for the humane purpose of ameliorating the condition of the unhappy prisoners held in captivity. They are designed to inflame the evil passions of the North; to keep up the war spirit among their own people; to represent the South as acting under the dominion of a spirit of cruelty, inhumanity and interested malice, and thus to vilify her people in the eyes of all on whom these publications can work. They are justly characterized by the Hon. James M. Mason as belonging to that class of literature called the "sensational,"—a style of writing prevalent for many years at the North, and which, beginning with the writers of newspaper narratives and cheap fiction, has gradually extended itself, until it is now the favored mode adopted by medical professors, judges of courts and reverend clergymen, and is even chosen as the proper style for a report by a committee of their Congress.

Photographs

Nothing can better illustrate the truth of this view than the "Report No. 67," and its appendages. It is accompanied by eight *pictures*, or *photographs*, alleged to represent United States prisoners of war, returned from Richmond, in a sad state of emaciation and suffering. Concerning these cases, your committee will have other remarks, to be presently submitted. They are only alluded to now to show that this report does really belong to the "sensational" class of literature, and that, "prima facie," it is open to the same criticism to which the yellow covered novels, the "narratives of noted highwaymen," and the "awful beacons" of the Northern book stalls should be subjected.

The intent and spirit of this report may be gathered from the following extract: "The evidence proves, beyond all manner of doubt, a determination on the part of the rebel authorities, deliberately and persistently practiced for a long time past, to subject those of our soldiers who have been so unfortunate as to fall in their hands, to a system of treatment which has resulted in reducing many of those who have survived and been permitted to return to us, to a condition both physically and mentally, which no language we can use can adequately describe." And they give also a letter from Edwin M. Stanton, the Northern Secretary of War, from which the following is an extract: "The enormity of the crime committed by the Rebels towards our prisoners for the last several months, is not known or realized by our people, and cannot but fill with horror the civilized world, when the facts

257

are fully revealed. There appears to have been a deliberate system of savage and barbarous treatment and starvation, the result of which will be that few (if any) of the prisoners that have been in their hands during the past winter, will ever again be in a condition to render any service, or even to enjoy life." Report, p. 4. And the sanitary commission, in their pamphlet, after picturing many scenes of privation and suffering, and bringing many charges of cruelty against the Confederate authorities, declare as follows: "The conclusion is unavoidable, therefore, that these privations and sufferings have been designedly inflicted by the military and other authorities of the Rebel government, and could not have been due to causes which such authorities could not control."

Truth to be Sought

After examining these publications, your committee approached the subject with an earnest desire to ascertain *the truth*. If their investigation should result in ascertaining that these charges (or any of them) were true, the committee desired, as far as might be in their power, and as far as they could influence the Congress, to remove the evils complained of, and to conform to the most humane spirit of civilization: and if these charges were unfounded and false, they deemed it a sacred duty, without delay, to present to the Confederate Congress and people, and to the public eye of the enlightened world, a vindication of their country, and to relieve her authorities from the injurious slanders brought against her by her enemies. With these views, we have taken a considerable amount of testimony bearing on the subject. We have sought to obtain witnesses whose position or duties made them familiar with the facts testified to, and whose characters entitled them to full credit. We have not hesitated to examine Northern prisoners of war upon points and experience specially within their knowledge. We now present the testimony taken by us, and submit a report of facts and inferences fairly deducible from the evidence, from the admissions of our enemies, and from public records of undoubted authority.

Facts as to Sick and Wounded Prisoners

First in order, your committee will notice the charge contained both in "Report No. 67," and in the "sanitary" publication, founded on the appearance and condition of the sick prisoners sent from Richmond to Annapolis and Baltimore about the last of April 1864. These are the men, some of whom form the subjects of the photographs with which the United States congressional committee have adorned their report. The disingenuous attempt is made in both these publications to produce the impression that these sick and emaciated men were fair representatives of the general state of the prisoners held by the South, and that all their prisoners were being rapidly reduced to the same state, by starvation and cruelty, and by neglect, ill treatment and denial of proper food, stimulants and medicines, in the Confederate hospitals. Your committee takes pleasure in saying that not only is this charge proved to be wholly false, but the evidence ascertains facts as to the Confederate hospitals, in which Northern prisoners of war are treated, highly creditable to the authorities which established them, and to the surgeons and their aides who have so humanely conducted them. The facts are simply these:

The Federal authorities, in violation of the cartel, having for a long time refused exchange of prisoners, finally consented to a partial exchange of the sick and wounded on both sides. Accordingly, a number of such prisoners were sent from the hospitals in Richmond. General directions had been given that none should be sent except those who might be expected to endure the removal and passage with safety to their lives; but in some cases the surgeons were induced to depart from this rule, by the entreaties of some officers and men in the last stages of emaciation, suffering not only with excessive debility, but with "nostalgia," or home sickness, whose cases were regarded as desperate, and who could not live if they remained, and might possibly improve if carried home. Thus it happened that some very sick and emaciated men were carried to Annapolis, but their illness was *not* the result of ill treatment or neglect. Such cases might be found in any large hospital, North or South. They might even be found in private families, where the sufferer would be surrounded by every comfort that love could bestow. Yet these are the cases which, with hideous violation of decency, the Northern committee has paraded in pictures and photographs. They have taken their own sick and enfeebled soldiers; have stripped them naked; have exposed them before a daguerreian apparatus; have pictured every shrunken limb and muscle—and all for the purpose, not of relieving their sufferings, but of bringing a false and slanderous charge against the South.

Confederate Sick and Wounded—Their Condition When Returned

The evidence is overwhelming that the illness of these prisoners was not the result of ill treatment or neglect. The testimony of Surgeons Semple and Spence; of Assistant Surgeons Tinsley, Marriott and Miller, and of the Federal prisoners, E. P. Dalrymple, Geo. Henry Brown and Freeman B. Teague, ascertains this to the satisfaction of every candid mind. But in refuting this charge, your committee is compelled by the evidence to bring a counter charge against the Northern authorities, which they fear will not be so easily refuted. In exchange, a number of Confederate sick and wounded prisoners have been at various times delivered at Richmond and at Savannah. The mortality among these on the passage and their condition when delivered were so deplorable as to justify the charge that they had been treated with inhuman neglect by the Northern authorities.

Assistant Surgeon Tinsley testifies: "I have seen many of our prisoners returned from the North, who were nothing but skin and bones. They were as emaciated as a man could be to retain life, and the photographs (appended to 'Report No. 67,') would not be exaggerated representations of our returned prisoners to whom I thus allude. I saw 250 of our sick brought in on litters from the steamer at Rocketts. Thirteen dead bodies were brought off the steamer the same night. At least thirty died in one night after they were received."

Surgeon Spence testifies: "I was at Savannah, and saw rather over three thousand prisoners re-ceived. The list showed that a large number had died on the passage from Baltimore to Savannah. The number sent from the Federal prisons was 3,500, and out of that number they delivered only 3,028, to the best of my recollection. Capt. Hatch can give you the exact number. Thus, about 472 died on the passage. I was told that 67 dead bodies had been taken from one train of cars between Elmira and Baltimore. After being received at Savannah, they had the best attention possible, yet many died in a few days"—"In carrying out the exchange of disabled, sick and wounded men, we delivered at Savannah and Charleston about 11,000 Federal prisoners, and their physical condition compared most favorably with those we received in exchange, although of course the worst cases among the Confederates had been removed by death during the passage."

Richard H. Dibrell, a merchant of Richmond, and a member of the "ambulance committee," whose labors in mitigating the sufferings of the wounded have been acknowledged both by Confederate and Northern men, thus testifies concerning our sick and wounded soldiers at Savannah, returned from Northern Prisons and hospitals: "I have never seen a set of men in worse condition. They were so enfeebled and emaciated that we lifted them like little children. Many of them were like living skeletons. Indeed, there was one poor boy about 17 years old, who presented the most distressing and deplorable appearance I ever saw. He was nothing but skin and bone, and besides this, he was literally eaten up with vermin. He died in the hospital in a few days after being removed thither, notwithstanding the kindest treatment and the use of the most judicious nourishment. Our men were in so reduced a condition that on more than one trip up on the short passage of ten miles from the transports to the city, as many as five died. The clothing of the privates was in a wretched state of tatters and filth."—The mortality on the passage from Maryland was very great as well as that on the passage from the prisons to the port from which they started. I cannot state the exact number, but I think I heard that 3,500 were started, and we only received about 3,027."—"I have looked at the photographs appended to 'Report No. 67' of the committee of the Federal Congress, and do not hesitate to declare that several of our men were worse cases of emaciation and sickness than any represented in these photographs."

The testimony of Mr. Dibrell is confirmed by that of Andrew Johnston, also a merchant of Rich-mond, and a member of the "ambulance committee."

Thus it appears that the sick and wounded Federal prisoners at Annapolis, whose condition has been made a subject of outcry and of wide spread complaint by the Northern Congress, were not in a worse state than were the Confederate prisoners returned from Northern hospitals and prisons, of which the humanity and superior management are made subjects of special boasting by the United States sanitary commission!

Confederate Hospitals for Prisoners

In connection with this subject, your committee takes pleasure in reporting the facts ascertained by their investigations concerning the Confederate hospitals for sick and wounded Federal prisoners. They have made personal examination, and have taken evidence specially in relation to "Hospital No. 21," in Richmond, because this has been made the subject of distinct charge in the publication last mentioned. It has been shown not only by the evidence of the surgeons and their assistants, but by that of Federal prisoners, that the treatment of the Northern prisoners in these hospitals has been everything that humanity could dictate; that their wards have been well ventilated and clean; their food the best that could be procured for them—and in fact, that no distinction has been made between their treatment and that of our own sick and wounded men. Moreover, it is proved that it has been the constant practice to supply to the patients, *out of the hospital funds*, such articles as milk, butter, eggs, tea and other delicacies, when they were required by the condition of the patient. This is proved by the testimony of E. P. Dalrymple of New York, George Henry Brown of Pennsylvania, and Freeman B. Teague of New Hampshire, whose depositions accompany this report.

Contrast

This humane and considerate usage was not adopted in the United States hospital on Johnson's Island, where Confederate sick and wounded officers were treated. Col. J. H. Holman thus testifies: "The Federal authorities did not furnish to the sick prisoners the nutriment and other articles which were prescribed by their own surgeons. All they would do was to permit the prisoners to buy the nutriment or stimulants needed; and if they had no money, they could not get them. I know this, for I was in the hospital sick myself, and I had to buy, myself, such articles as eggs, milk, flour, chickens and butter, after their doctors had prescribed them. And I know this was generally the case, for we had to get up a fund among ourselves for this purpose, to aid those who were not well supplied with money." This statement is confirmed by the testimony of acting assistant surgeon John J. Miller, who was at Johnson's Island for more than eight months. When it is remembered that such articles as eggs, milk and butter were very scarce and high priced in Richmond, and plentiful and cheap at the North, the contrast thus presented may well put to shame the "sanitary commission," and dissipate the self-complacency with which they have boasted of the superior humanity in the Northern prisons and hospitals.

Charge of Robbing Prisoners

Your committee now proceeds to notice other charges in these publications. It is said that their prisoners were habitually stripped of blankets and other property, on being captured. What pillage may have been committed on the battle field, after the excitement of combat, your committee cannot know. But they feel well assured that such pillage was never encouraged by the Confederate generals, and bore no comparison to the wholesale robbery and destitution to which the Federal armies have abandoned themselves, in possessing parts of our territory. It is certain that after the prisoners were brought to the Libby, and other prisons in Richmond, no such pillage was permitted. Only articles which came properly under the head of munitions of war, were taken from them.

Shooting Prisoners

The next charge noticed is, that the guards around the Libby prison were in the habit of recklessly and inhumanly shooting at the prisoners, upon the most frivolous pretexts, and that the Confederate officers, so far from forbidding this, rather encouraged it, and made it a subject of sportive remark. This charge is wholly false and baseless. The "Rules and Regulations" appended to the deposition of Maj. Thomas P. Turner, expressly provide, "Nor shall any prisoner be fired upon by a sentinel or other person, except in case of revolt or attempted escape." Five or six cases have occurred, in which prisoners have been fired on and killed or hurt: but every case has been made the subject of careful investigation and report, as will appear by the evidence. As a proper comment on this charge, your committee report that the practice of firing on our prisoners by the guards in the Northern prisons, appears to have been indulged in to a most brutal and atrocious extent. See the depositions of C. C. Herrington, Wm. F. Gordon, Jr., J. B. McCreary, Dr. Thomas P. Holloway, and John P. Fennell. At Fort Delaware, a cruel regulation as to the use of the "sinks," was made the pretext for firing on and murdering several of our men and officers—among them, Lieut. Col. Jones, who was lame, and was shot down by the sentinel while helpless and feeble, and while seeking to explain his condition. Yet this sentinel was not only not punished, but was promoted for his act. At Camp Douglas, as many as eighteen of our men are reported to have been shot in a single month. These facts may well produce a conviction in the candid observer, that it is the North and not the South that is open to the charge of deliberately and willfully destroying the lives of the prisoners held by her.

Means for securing Cleanliness

The next charge is, that the Libby and Belle Isle prisoners were habitually kept in a filthy condition, and that the officers and men confined there were prevented from keeping themselves sufficiently clean to avoid vermin and similar discomforts. The evidence clearly contradicts this charge. It is proved by the depositions of Maj. Turner, Lieut. Bossieux, Rev. Dr. McCabe, and others, that the prisons were kept constantly and systematically policed and cleansed; that in the Libby there was an ample supply of water conducted to each floor by the city pipes, and that the prisoners were not only not restricted in its use, but urged to keep themselves clean. At Belle Isle, for a brief season (about three weeks), in consequence of a sudden increase in the number of prisoners, the police was interrupted, but it was soon restored, and ample means for washing both themselves and their clothes, were at all times furnished to the prisoners. It is doubtless true, that notwith-standing these facilities, many of the prisoners were lousy and filthy; but it was the result of their own habits, and not of neglect in the discipline or arrangements of the prison. Many of the prisoners were captured and brought in while in this condition. The Federal General Neal Dow well expressed their character and habits. When he came to distribute clothing among them, he was met by profane abuse, and he said to the Confederate officer in charge, "You have here the *scrapings and rakings of Europe*." That such men should be filthy in their habits, might be expected.

Charge of Withholding and Pillaging Boxes

We next notice the charge that the boxes of provisions and clothing sent to the prisoners from the North, were not delivered to them, and were habitually robbed and plundered, by permission of the Confederate authorities. The evidence satisfies your committee that this charge is, in all substantial points, untrue. For a period of about one month there was a stoppage in the delivery of boxes, caused by a report that the Federal authorities were forbidding the delivery of similar supplies to our prisoners. But the boxes were put in a warehouse, and were afterwards delivered. For some time no search was made of boxes from the "sanitary committee," intended for the prisoners' hospitals. But a letter was intercepted, advising that money should be sent in these boxes, as they were never searched;" which money was to be used in bribing the guards, and thus releasing the prisoners. After this, it was deemed necessary to search every box, which necessarily produced some delay. Your committee is satisfied that if these boxes or their contents were robbed, the prison officials are not responsible therefore. Beyond doubt, robberies were often committed by prisoners themselves, to whom the contents were delivered for distribution to their owners. Notwithstanding all this alleged pillage, the supplies seem to have been sufficient to keep the quarters of the prisoners so well furnished that they frequently presented, in the language of a witness, "the appearance of a large grocery store."

The Federal Colonel Sanderson's Testimony

In connection with this point, your committee refers to the testimony of a Federal officer, Colonel James M. Sanderson, whose letter is annexed to the deposition of Major Turner. He testifies to the full delivery of the clothing and supplies from the North, and to the humanity and kindness of the Confederate officers—especially mentioning Lieut. Bossieux, commanding on Belle Isle. His letter was addressed to the president of the United States Sanitary Commission, and was beyond doubt received by them, having been forwarded by the regular flag of truce. Yet the scrupulous and honest gentlemen composing that commission have not found it convenient for their purposes to insert this letter in their publication! Had they been really searching for the *truth*, this letter would have aided them in finding it.

Mine Under the Libby Prison

Your committee proceed next to notice the allegation that the Confederate authorities had prepared a mine under the Libby prison, and placed in it a quantity of gunpowder for the purpose of blowing up the buildings, with their inmates, in case of an attempt to rescue them. After ascertaining all the facts bearing on this subject, your committee believe that what was done under the circumstances, will meet a verdict of approval from all whose prejudices do not blind them to the truth. The state of things was unprecedented in history, and must be judged of according to the motives at work, and the result accomplished. A large body of Northern raiders, under one Col. Dahlgren, was approaching Richmond. It was ascertained, by the reports of prisoners captured from them, and other evidence, that their design was to enter the city, to set fire to the buildings, public and private, for which purpose turpentine balls in great number had been prepared; to murder the President of the Confederate States, and other prominent men; to release the prisoners of war, then number-ing five or six thousand; to put arms into their hands, and to turn over the city to indiscrim-inate pillage, rape and slaughter. At the same time a plot was discovered among the prison-ers to co-operate in this scheme, and a large number of knives and slung-shot (made by put-ting stones into woolen stockings) were detected in places of concealment about their quar-ters. To defeat a plan so diabolical, assuredly the sternest means were justified. If it would have been right to put to death any one prisoner attempting to escape under such circum-stances, it seems logically certain that it would have been equally right to put to death any number making such attempt. But in truth the means adopted were those of humanity and *prevention*, rather than of execution. The Confederate authorities felt able to meet and re-pulse Dahlgren and his raiders, if they could prevent the escape of the prisoners.

The real object was to save their lives as well as those of our citizens. The guard force at the prisons was small, and all the local troops in and around Richmond were needed to meet the threat-ened attack. Had the prisoners escaped, the women and children of the city, as well as their homes, would have been at the mercy of five thousand outlaws. Humanity required that the most summary measures should be used to *deter* them from any attempt at escape.

A mine was prepared under the Libby prison; a sufficient quantity of gunpowder was put into it, and pains were taken to *inform the prisoners* that any attempt at escape made by them would be effectually defeated. The plan succeeded perfectly. The prisoners were awed and kept quiet. Dahlgren and his party were defeated and scattered. The danger passed away, and in a few weeks the gunpowder was removed. Such are the facts. Your committee does not hesitate to make them known; feeling assured that the conscience of the enlightened world and the great law of self-preservation will justify all that was done by our country and her officers.

Charge of Intentional Starvation and Cruelty

We now proceed to notice, under one head, the last and gravest charge made in these publications. They assert that the Northern prisoners in the hands of the Confederate au-thorities have been starved, frozen, inhumanly punished, often confined in foul and loath-some quarters, deprived of fresh air and exercise, and neglected and maltreated in sick-ness—and that all this was done upon a deliberate, willful and long conceived plan of the

Confederate government and officers, for the purpose of destroying the lives of these prisoners, or of rendering them forever incapable of military service. This charge accuses the Southern government of a crime so horrible and unnatural, that it could never have been made except by those ready to blacken with slander men whom they have long injured and hated. Your committee feel bound to reply to it calmly but emphatically. They pronounce it false in fact and in design; false in the basis on which it assumes to rest, and false in its estimate of the motives which have controlled the Southern authorities.

Humane Policy of the Confederate Government

At an early period in the present contest the Confederate government recognized their obligation to treat prisoners of war with humanity and consideration. Before any laws were passed on the subject, the Executive Department provided such prisoners as fell into their hands, with proper quarters and barracks to shelter them, and with rations the same in quantity and quality as those furnished to the Confederate soldiers who guarded these prisoners. They also showed an earnest wish to mitigate the sad condition of prisoners of war, by a system of fair and prompt exchange—and the Confederate Congress co-operated in these humane views. By their act, approved on the 21st day of May 1861, they provided that "all prisoners of war taken, whether on land or at sea, during the pending hostilities with the United States, shall be transferred by the captors from time to time, and as often as convenient to the Department of War; and it shall be the duty of the Secretary of War, with the approval of the President, to issue such instructions to the Quartermaster General and his subordinates, as shall provide for the safe custody and sustenance of prisoners of war; *and the rations furnished prisoners of war shall be the same in quantity and quality as those furnished to enlisted men in the army of the Confederacy.*" Such were the declared purpose and policy of the Confederate government towards prisoners of war—and amid all the privations and losses to which their enemies have subjected them, they have sought to carry them into effect.

Rations and General Treatment

Our investigations for this preliminary report have been confined chiefly to the rations and treatment of the prisoners of war at the Libby and other prisons in Richmond and on Belle Isle. This we have done, because the publications to which we have alluded refer chiefly to them, and because the "Report No. 67" of the Northern Congress plainly intimates the belief that the treatment in and around Richmond was worse than it was farther South. That report says: "It will be observed from the testimony, that all the witnesses who testify upon that point state that the treatment they received while confined at Columbia, South Carolina, Dalton, Georgia, and other places, *was far more humane* than that they received at Richmond, where the authorities of the so-called Confederacy were congregated." Report, p. 3.

The evidence proves that the rations furnished to prisoners of war in Richmond and on Belle Isle, have been *never* less than those furnished to the Confederate soldiers who guarded them, and have at some seasons been larger in quantity and better in quality than those furnished to Confederate troops in the field. This has been because until February 1864 the Quartermaster's Department furnished the prisoners, and often had provisions or funds, when the Commissary Department was not so well provided. Once and only once, for a few weeks, the prisoners were without meat; but a larger quantity of bread and vegetable food was in consequence supplied to them. How often the gallant men composing the Confederate army have been without meat, for even longer intervals, your committee does not deem it necessary to say. Not less than sixteen ounces of bread and four ounces of bacon, or six ounces of beef, together with beans and soup, have been furnished per day to the prisoners. During most of the time the quantity of meat furnished to them has been greater than these amounts; and even in times of the greatest scarcity, they have received as much as the Southern soldiers, who guarded them. The scarcity of meat and of bread stuffs in the South in certain places has been the result of the savage policy of our enemies in burning barns, filled with wheat or corn, destroying agricultural implements, and driving off or wantonly butchering hogs and cattle. Yet amid all these privations, we have given to their prisoners the rations above mentioned. It is well known that this quantity of food is sufficient to keep in health a man who does not labor hard. All the learned disquisitions of Dr. Ellerslie Wallace on the subject of starvation, might have been spared, for they are all founded on a false basis. It will be observed that few (if any) of the witnesses examined by the "sanitary commission" speak with any accuracy of the quantity (in weight) of the food actually furnished to them. Their statements are merely conjectural and comparative, and cannot weigh against the positive testimony of those who superintended the delivery of large quantities of food, cooked and distributed according to a fixed ratio, for the number of men to be fed.

Falsehoods published as to Prisoners Freezing on Belle Isle

The statements of the "sanitary commission" as to prisoners freezing to death on Belle Isle, are absurdly false. According to that statement it was common, during a cold spell in winter, to see several prisoners frozen to death every morning in the places in which they had slept. This picture, if correct, might well excite our horror; but unhappily for its sensational power, it is but a clumsy daub, founded on the fancy of the painter. The facts are, that tents were furnished sufficient to shelter all the prisoners; that the Confederate Commandant and soldiers on the Island were lodged in similar tents; that a fire was furnished in each of them; that the prisoners fared as well as their guards; and that only one of them was ever frozen to death, and he was frozen *by the cruelty of his own fellow-prisoners*, who thrust him out of the tent in a freezing night, because he was infested with vermin. The proof as to the healthiness of the prisoners on Belle Isle, and the small amount of mortality, is remarkable, and presents a fit comment on the lugubrious pictures drawn by the "sanitary com-mission," either from their own fancies, or from the fictions put forth by their false witnesses. Lieut. Bossieux proves, that from the establishment of the prison camp on Belle Isle in June 1862, to the 10th of February 1865, more than twenty thousand prisoners had been at various times there received, and yet that the whole number of deaths during this time, was only one hundred and sixty-four. And this is confirmed by the Federal Colonel Sanderson, who states that the average number of deaths per month on Belle Isle, was "from two to five; more frequently the lesser number." The sick were promptly removed from the Island to the hospitals in the city.

Character of the Northern Witnesses

Doubtless the "sanitary commission" have been to some extent led astray by their own witnesses, whose character has been portrayed by Gen. Neal Dow, and also by the Editor of the New York Times, who, in his issue of January 6th, 1865, describes the material for recruiting the Federal armies as "wretched vagabonds, of depraved morals, decrepit in body, without courage, self-respect or conscience. They are dirty, disorderly, thievish and incapable."

Cruelty to Confederate Prisoners at the North

In reviewing the charges of cruelty, harshness and starvation to prisoners, made by the North, your committee has taken testimony as to the treatment of our own officers and soldiers in the hands of the enemy. It gives us no pleasure to be compelled to speak of suffering inflicted upon our gallant men; but the self-laudatory style in which the "sanitary commission" have spoken of their prisons, makes it proper that the truth should be presented. Your committee gladly acknowledge that in many cases our prisoners experienced kind and considerate treatment; but we are equally assured that in nearly all the prison stations of the North—at Point Lookout, Fort McHenry, Fort Delaware, John-son's Island, Elmira, Camp Chase, Camp Douglas, Alton, Camp Morton, the Ohio Penitentiary, and the prisons of St. Louis, Missouri, our men have suffered from insufficient food, and have been subjected to ignominious, cruel and barbarous practices, of which there is no parallel in anything that has occurred in the South. The witnesses who were at Point Lookout, Fort Delaware, Camp Morton and Camp Douglas, testify that they have often seen our men picking up the scraps and refuse thrown out from the kitchens, with which to appease their hunger. Dr. Herrington proves that at Fort Delaware unwholesome bread and water produced diarrhea in numberless cases among our prisoners, and that "their sufferings were greatly aggravated by the regulation of the camp which forbade more than twenty men at a time at night to go to the sinks. I have seen as many as five hundred men in a row waiting their time. The consequence was that they were obliged to use the places where they were. This produced great want of cleanliness, and aggravated the disease." Our men were compelled to labor in unloading Federal vessels and in putting up buildings for Federal officers, and if they refused, were driven to the work with clubs.

The treatment of Brig. General J. H. Morgan and his officers was brutal and ignomini- ous in the extreme. It will be found stated in the depositions of Capt. M. D. Logan, Lieut. W. P. Crow, Lieut. Col. James B. McCreary and Capt. B. A. Tracy, that they were put in the Ohio Penitentiary, and compelled to submit to the treatment of felons. Their beards were shaved, and their hair was cut close to the head. They were confined in convicts' cells, and forbidden to speak to each other. For attempts to escape, and for other offences of a very light character, they were subjected to the horrible punishment of the dungeon. In midwinter, with the atmosphere many degrees below zero, without blanket or overcoat, they were confined in a cell without fire or light, with a fetid and poisonous air to breathe— and here they were kept until life was nearly extinct. Their condition on coming out was so deplorable as to draw tears from their comrades. The blood was oozing from their hands and faces. The treatment in the St. Louis prison was equally barbarous. Capt. Wm. H. Se- bring testifies: "Two of us, A. C. Grimes and myself, were carried out into the open air in the prison yard, on the 25th of December 1863, and handcuffed to a post. Here we were kept all night in sleet, snow and cold. We were relieved in the day time, but again brought to the post and handcuffed to it in the evening" and thus we were kept all night until the 2nd of January 1864. I was badly frost-bitten, and my health was much impaired. This cruel infliction was done by order of Capt. Byrnes, Commandant of Prisons in St. Louis. He was barbarous and insulting to the last degree."

Our Prisoners put into Camps infected with Smallpox

But even a greater inhumanity than any we have mentioned, was perpetrated upon our prisoners at Camp Douglas and Camp Chase. It is proved by the testimony of Thomas P. Holloway, John P. Fennell, H. H. Barlow, H. C. Barton, C. D. Bracken and J. S. Barlow, that our prisoners in large numbers were put into "condemned camps," where small-pox was prevailing, and speedily contract-ed this loathsome disease, and that as many as 40 new cases often appeared daily among them. Even the Federal officers who guarded them to the camp, protested against this unnatural atrocity; yet it was done. The men who con- tracted the disease were removed to a hospital about a mile off, but the plague was already introduced, and continued to prevail. For a period of more than twelve months, the disease was constantly in the camp; yet our prisoners during all this time were continually brought to it, and subjected to certain infection. Neither do we find evidences of amendment on the part of our enemies, notwithstanding the boasts of the "sanitary commission." At Nashville, prisoners recently captured from Gen. Hood's army, even when sick and wounded, have been cruelly deprived of all nourishment suited to their condition; and other prisoners from the same army have been carried into the infected Camps Douglas and Chase.

Many of the soldiers of Gen. Hood's army were frost-bitten by being kept day and night in an exposed condition before they were put into Camp Douglas. Their sufferings are truthfully depicted in the evidence. At Alton and Camp Morton the same inhuman practice of putting our prisoners into camps infected by small-pox, prevailed. It was equivalent to murdering many of them by the torture of a contagious disease. The insufficient rations at Camp Morton forced our men to appease their hunger by pounding up and boiling bones, picking up scraps of meat and cabbage from the hospital slop tubs, and even eating rats and dogs. The depositions of William Ayres and J. Chambers Brent prove these privations.

Barbarous Punishments

The punishments often inflicted on our men for slight offences, have been shameful and barbarous. They have been compelled to ride a plank only four inches wide, called "Morgan's horse;" to sit down with their naked bodies in the snow for ten or fifteen minutes, and have been subjected to the ignominy of stripes from the belts of their guards. The pretext has been used, that many of their acts of cruelty have been by way of retaliation. But no evidence has been found to prove such acts on the part of the Confederate authorities. It is remarkable that in the case of Col. Streight and his officers, they were subjected only to the ordinary confinement of prisoners of war. No special punishment was used except for specific offences; and then the greatest infliction was to confine Col. Streight for a few weeks in a basement room of the Libby prison, with a window, a plank floor, a stove, a fire, and plenty of fuel.

We do not deem it necessary to dwell further on these subjects. Enough has been proved to show that great privations and sufferings have been borne by the prisoners on both sides.

Why have not Prisoners of War been Exchanged

But the question forces itself upon us why have these sufferings been so long continued? Why have not the prisoners of war been exchanged, and thus some of the darkest pages of history spared to the world? In the answer to this question must be found the test of responsibility for all the sufferings, sickness and heart-broken sorrow that have visited more than eighty thousand prisoners within the past two years. On this question, your committee can only say that the Confederate authorities have always desired a prompt and fair exchange of prisoners. Even before the establishment of a cartel they urged such exchange, but could never effect it by agreement until the large preponderance of prisoners in our hands made it the interest of the Federal authorities to consent to the cartel of July 22nd, 1863. The 9th article of that agreement expressly provided, that in case any misunderstanding should arise, it *should not interrupt the release of prisoners on parole*, but should be made the subject of friendly explanation. Soon after this cartel was established, the policy of the enemy in seducing Negro slaves from their masters, arming them and putting white officers over them to lead them against us, gave rise to a few cases in which questions of crime under the internal laws of the Southern States appeared. Whether men who encouraged insurrection and murder could be held entitled to the privileges of prisoners of war under the cartel, was a grave question. But these cases were few in number, and ought never to have interrupted the general exchange. We were always ready and anxious to carry out the cartel in its true meaning, and it is certain that the 9th article required that the prisoners on both sides should be released, and that the few cases as to which misunderstanding occurred should be left for final decision. Doubtless if the preponderance of prisoners had continued with us, exchanges would have continued. But the fortunes of war threw the larger number into the hands of our enemies. Then they refused further exchanges—and for twenty-two months this policy has continued. Our Commissioner of Exchange has made constant efforts to renew them. In August 1864 he consented to a proposition which had been repeatedly made, to exchange officer for officer and man for man, leaving the surplus in captivity. Though this was a departure from the cartel, our anxiety for the exchange induced us to consent. Yet, the Federal authorities repudiated their previous offer, and refused even this partial compliance with the cartel. Secretary Stanton, who has unjustly charged the Confederate authorities with inhumanity, is open to the charge of having done all in his power to prevent a fair exchange, and thus to prolong the sufferings of which he speaks: and very recently, in a letter over his signature, Benjamin F. Butler has declared that in April 1864, the Federal Lieut. General Grant forbade him "to deliver to the Rebels a single able-bodied man:" and moreover, Gen. Butler acknowledges that in answer to Col. Ould's letter consenting to the exchange, officer for officer and man for man, he wrote a reply, "not diplomatically but obtrusively and demonstratively, not for the purpose of furthering exchange of prisoners, but for the purpose of preventing and stopping the exchange, and furnishing a ground on which we could fairly stand."

These facts abundantly show that the responsibility of refusing to exchange prisoners of war rests with the Government of the United States, and the people who have sustained that government; and every sigh of captivity, every groan of suffering, every heart broken by hope deferred among these eighty thousand prisoners, will accuse them in the judgment of the just.

With regard to the prison stations at Andersonville, Salisbury and other places south of Richmond, your committee have not made extended examination, for reasons which have already been stated. We are satisfied that privation, suffering and mortality, to an extent much to be regretted, did prevail among the prisoners there, but they were not the result of neglect, still less of design on the part of the Confederate government. Haste in preparation; crowded quarters, prepared only for a smaller number; want of transportation and scarcity of food, have all resulted from the pressure of the war, and the barbarous manner in which it has been conducted by our enemies. Upon these subjects your committee proposes to take further evidence, and to report more fully hereafter.

But even now enough is known to vindicate the South, and to furnish an overwhelming answer to all complaints on the part of the United States government or people, that their prisoners were stinted in food or supplies. Their own savage warfare has wrought all the evil. They have blockaded our ports; have excluded from us food, clothing and medicines; have even declared medicines contra-band of war, and have repeatedly destroyed the contents of drug stores and the supplies of private physicians in the country; have ravaged our country; burned our houses and destroyed growing crops and farming implements. One of their officers (General Sheridan) has boasted in his official report, that in the Shenandoah valley alone be burned two thousand barns filled with wheat and corn; that he burned all the mills in the whole tract of country; destroyed all the factories of cloth, and killed or drove off every animal, even to the poultry, that could contribute to human sustenance. These desolations have been repeated again and again in different parts of the South. Thousands of our families have been driven from their homes, as helpless and destitute refugees. Our enemies have destroyed the railroads and other means of transportation, by which food could be supplied from abundant districts to those without it. While thus desolating our country, in violation of the usages of civilized warfare, they have refused to exchange prisoners; have forced us to keep fifty thousand of their men in captivity—and yet have attempted to attribute to us the sufferings and privations caused by their own acts. We cannot doubt that in the view of civilization we shall stand acquitted, while they must be condemned.

In concluding this preliminary report, we will notice the strange perversity of interpretation which has induced the "sanitary commission" to affix as a motto to their pamphlet, the words of the compassionate Redeemer of mankind:

"For I was a hungered and ye gave me no meat: I was thirsty and ye gave me no drink: I was a stranger and ye took me not in: naked and ye clothed me not: sick and in prison and ye visited me not."

We have yet to learn on what principle the Federal mercenaries, sent with arms in their hands to destroy the lives of our people; to waste our land, burn our houses and barns, and drive us from our homes, can be regarded by us as the followers of the meek and lowly Redeemer, so as to claim the benefit of his words. Yet even these mercenaries, when taken captive by us, have been treated with proper humanity. The cruelties inflicted on our prisoners at the North may well justify us in applying to the "sanitary commission" the stern words of the Divine Teacher: "Thou hypocrite, first cast out the beam out of thine own eye, and then shalt thou see clearly to cast out the mote out of thy brother's eye."

We believe that there are many thousands of just, honorable and humane people in the United States, upon whom this subject, thus presented, will not be lost; that they will do all they can to mitigate the horrors, of war; to complete the exchange of prisoners, now happily in progress, and to prevent the recurrence of such sufferings as have been narrated. And we repeat the words of the Confederate Congress, in their Manifesto of the 14th of June 1864:

"We commit our cause to the enlightened judgment of the world; to the sober reflections of our adversaries themselves, and to the solemn and righteous arbitrament of Heaven."

Chapter 10

General Orders No. 100, The Lieber Code

Instructions for the Government of Armies of the United States in the Field

GENERAL ORDERS No. 100.

WAR DEPT., Adjutant General's Office,
Washington, April 24, 1863.

SECTION I--*Martial law--Military jurisdiction--Military necessity--Retaliation.*

1. A place, district, or country occupied by an enemy stands, in consequence of the occupation, under the martial law of the invading or occupying army, whether any proclamation declaring martial law, or any public warning to the inhabitants, has been issued or not. Martial law is the immediate and direct effect and consequence of occupation or conquest. The presence of a hostile army proclaims its martial law.

2. Martial law does not cease during the hostile occupation, except by special proclamation, ordered by the commander-in-chief, or by special mention in the treaty of peace concluding the war, when the occupation of a place or territory continues beyond the conclusion of peace as one of the conditions of the same.

Dr. Francis Lieber was asked by Lincoln write a code of conduct for the army during war.

3. Martial law in a hostile country consists in the suspension by the occupying military authority of the criminal and civil law, and of the domestic administration and government in the occupied place or territory, and in the substitution of military rule and force for the same, as well as in the dictation of general laws, as far as military necessity requires this suspension, substitution, or dictation.

The commander of the forces may proclaim that the administration of all civil and penal law shall continue either wholly or in part, as in times of peace, unless otherwise ordered by the military authority.

4. Martial law is simply military authority exercised in accordance with the laws and usages of war. Military oppression is not martial law; it is the abuse of the power which that law confers. As martial law is executed by military force, it is incumbent upon those

who administer it to be strictly guided by the principles of justice, honor, and humanity-- virtues adorning a soldier even more than other men, for the very reason that he possesses the power of his arms against the unarmed.

5. Martial law should be less stringent in places and countries fully occupied and fairly conquered. Much greater severity may be exercised in places or regions where actual hostilities exist or are expected and must be prepared for. Its most complete sway is allowed-- even in the commander's own country--when face to face with the enemy, because of the absolute necessities of the case, and of the paramount duty to defend the country against invasion.
To save the country is paramount to all other considerations.

6. All civil and penal law shall continue to take its usual course in the enemy's places and territories under martial law, unless interrupted or stopped by order of the occupying military power; but all the functions of the hostile government--legislative, executive, or administrative--whether of a general, provincial, or local character, cease under martial law, or continue only with the sanction, or, if deemed necessary, the participation of the occupier or invader.

7. Martial law extends to property, and to persons, whether they are subjects of the enemy or aliens to that government.

8. Consuls, among American and European nations, are not diplomatic agents. Nevertheless, their offices and persons will be subjected to martial law in cases of urgent necessity only; their property and business are not exempted. Any delinquency they commit against the established military rule may be punished as in the case of any other inhabitant, and such punishment furnishes no reasonable ground for international complaint.

9. The functions of ambassadors, ministers, or other diplomatic agents, accredited by neutral powers to the hostile government, cease, so far as regards the displaced government; but the conquering or occupying power usually recognizes them as temporarily accredited to itself.

10. Martial law affects chiefly the police and collection of public revenue and taxes, whether imposed by the expelled government or by the invader, and refers mainly to the support and efficiency of the Army, its safety, and the safety of its operations.

11. The law of war does not only disclaim all cruelty and bad faith concerning engagements concluded with the enemy during the war, but also the breaking of stipulations solemnly contracted by the belligerents in time of peace, and avowedly intended to remain in force in case of war between the contracting powers.

It disclaims all extortions and other transactions for individual gain; all acts of private revenge, or connivance at such acts.

Offenses to the contrary shall be severely punished, and especially so if committed by officers.

12. Whenever feasible, martial law is carried out in cases of individual offenders by military courts; but sentences of death shall be executed only with the approval of the chief executive, provided the urgency of the case does not require a speedier execution, and then only with the approval of the chief commander.

13. Military jurisdiction is of two kinds: First, that which is conferred and defined by statute; second, that which is derived from the common law of war. Military offenses under the statute law must be tried in the manner therein directed; but military offenses which do not come within the statute must be tried and punished under the common law of war. The character of the courts which exercise these jurisdictions depends upon the local laws of each particular country.

In the armies of the United States the first is exercised by courts-martial; while cases which do not come within the Rules and Articles of War, or the jurisdiction conferred by statute on courts-martial, are tried by military commissions.

14. Military necessity, as understood by modern civilized nations, consists in the necessity of those measures which are indispensable for securing the ends of the war, and which are lawful according to the modern law and usages of war.

15. Military necessity admits of all direct destruction of life or limb of armed enemies, and of other persons whose destruction is incidentally unavoidable in the armed contests of the war; it allows of the capturing of every armed enemy, and every enemy of importance to the hostile government, or of peculiar danger to the captor; it allows of all destruction of property, and obstruction of the ways and channels of traffic, travel, or communication, and of all withholding of sustenance or means of life from the enemy; of the appropriation of whatever an enemy's country affords necessary for the subsistence and safety of the Army, and of such deception as does not involve the breaking of good faith either positively pledged, regarding agreements entered into during the war, or supposed by the modern law of war to exist. Men who take up arms against one another in public war do not cease on this account to be moral beings, responsible to one another and to God.

16. Military necessity does not admit of cruelty—that is, the infliction of suffering for the sake of suffering or for revenge, nor of maiming or wounding except in fight, nor of torture to extort confessions. It does not admit of the use of poison in any way, nor of the wanton devastation of a district. It admits of deception, but disclaims acts of perfidy; and, in general, military necessity does not include any act of hostility which makes the return to peace unnecessarily difficult.

17. War is not carried on by arms alone. It is lawful to starve the hostile belligerent, armed or unarmed, so that it leads to the speedier subjection of the enemy.

18. When a commander of a besieged place expels the non-combatants, in order to lessen the number of those who consume his stock of provisions, it is lawful, though an extreme measure, to drive them back, so as to hasten on the surrender.

19. Commanders, whenever admissible, inform the enemy of their intention to bombard a place, so that the non-combatants, and especially the women and children, may be removed before the bombardment commences. But it is no infraction of the common law of war to omit thus to inform the enemy. Surprise may be a necessity.

20. Public war is a state of armed hostility between sovereign nations or governments. It is a law and requisite of civilized existence that men live in political, continuous societies, forming organized units, called states or nations, whose constituents bear, enjoy, and suffer, advance and retrograde together, in peace and in war.

21. The citizen or native of a hostile country is thus an enemy, as one of the constituents of the hostile state or nation, and as such is subjected to the hardships of the war.

22. Nevertheless, as civilization has advanced during the last centuries, so has likewise steadily advanced, especially in war on land, the distinction between the private individual belonging to a hostile country and the hostile country itself, with its men in arms. The principle has been more and more acknowledged that the unarmed citizen is to be spared in person, property, and honor as much as the exigencies of war will admit.

23. Private citizens are no longer murdered, enslaved, or carried off to distant parts, and the inoffensive individual is as little disturbed in his private relations as the commander of the hostile troops can afford to grant in the overruling demands of a vigorous war.

24. The almost universal rule in remote times was, and continues to be with barbarous armies, that the private individual of the hostile country is destined to suffer every privation of liberty and protection and every disruption of family ties. Protection was, and still is with uncivilized people, the exception.

25. In modern regular wars of the Europeans and their descendants in other portions of the globe, protection of the inoffensive citizen of the hostile country is the rule; privation and disturbance of private relations are the exceptions.

26. Commanding generals may cause the magistrates and civil officers of the hostile country to take the oath of temporary allegiance or an oath of fidelity to their own victorious government or rulers, and they may expel everyone who declines to do so. But whether they do so or not, the people and their civil officers owe strict obedience to them as long as they hold sway over the district or country, at the peril of their lives.

27. The law of war can no more wholly dispense with retaliation than can the law of nations, of which it is a branch. Yet civilized nations acknowledge retaliation as the sternest feature of war. A reckless enemy often leaves to his opponent no other means of securing himself against the repetition of barbarous outrage.

28. Retaliation will therefore never be resorted to as a measure of mere revenge, but only as a means of protective retribution, and moreover cautiously and unavoidably—that is to say, retaliation shall only be resorted to after careful inquiry into the real occurrence and the character of the misdeeds that may demand retribution.

Unjust or inconsiderate retaliation removes the belligerents farther and farther from the mitigating rules of regular war, and by rapid steps leads them nearer to the internecine wars of savages.

29. Modern times are distinguished from earlier ages by the existence at one and the same time of many nations and great governments related to one another in close intercourse.

Peace is their normal condition; war is the exception. The ultimate object of all modern war is a renewed state of peace.

The more vigorously wars are pursued the better it is for humanity. Sharp wars are brief.

30. Ever since the formation and coexistence of modern nations, and ever since wars have become great national wars, war has come to be acknowledged not to be its own end, but the means to obtain great ends of state, or to consist in defense against wrong; and no conventional restriction of the modes adopted to injure the enemy is any longer admitted; but the law of war imposes many limitations and restrictions on principles of justice, faith, and honor.

SECTION II.--*Public and private property of the enemy--Protection of persons, and especially of women; of religion, the arts and sciences--Punishment of crimes against the inhabitants of hostile countries.*

31. A victorious army appropriates all public money, seizes all public movable property until further direction by its government, and sequesters for its own benefit or of that of its government all the revenues of real property belonging to the hostile government or nation. The title to such real property remains in abeyance during military occupation, and until the conquest is made complete.

32. A victorious army, by the martial power inherent in the same, may suspend, change, or abolish, as far as the martial power extends, the relations which arise from the services due, according to the existing laws of the invaded country, from one citizen, subject, or native of the same to another.

The commander of the army must leave it to the ultimate treaty of peace to settle the permanency of this change.

33. It is no longer considered lawful-- on the contrary, it is held to be a serious breach of the law of war--to force the subjects of the enemy into the service of the victorious government, except the latter should proclaim, after a fair and complete conquest of the hostile country or district, that it is resolved to keep the country, district, or place permanently as its own and make it a portion of its own country.

34. As a general rule, the property belonging to churches, to hospitals, or other establishments of an exclusively charitable character, to establishments of education, or foundations for the promotion of knowledge, whether public schools, universities, academies of learning or observatories, museums of the fine arts, or of a scientific character-such property is not to be considered public property in the sense of paragraph 31; but it may be taxed or used when the public service may require it.

35. Classical works of art, libraries, scientific collections, or precious instruments, such as astronomical telescopes, as well as hospitals, must be secured against all avoidable injury, even when they are contained in fortified places whilst besieged or bombarded.

36. If such works of art, libraries, collections, or instruments belonging to a hostile nation or government, can be removed without injury, the ruler of the conquering state or nation may order them to be seized and removed for the benefit of the said nation. The ultimate ownership is to be settled by the ensuing treaty of peace.

In no case shall they be sold or given away, if captured by the armies of the United States, nor shall they ever be privately appropriated, or wantonly destroyed or injured.

37. The United States acknowledge and protect, in hostile countries occupied by them, religion and morality; strictly private property; the persons of the inhabitants, especially those of women; and the sacredness of domestic relations. Offenses to the contrary shall be rigorously punished.

This rule does not interfere with the right of the victorious invader to tax the people or their property, to levy forced loans, to billet soldiers, or to appropriate property, especially houses, lands, boats or ships, and the churches, for temporary and military uses.

38. Private property, unless forfeited by crimes or by offenses of the owner, can be seized only by way of military necessity, for the support or other benefit of the Army or of the United States.

If the owner has not fled, the commanding officer will cause receipts to be given, which may serve the spoliated owner to obtain indemnity.

39. The salaries of civil officers of the hostile government who remain in the invaded territory, and continue the work of their office, and can continue it according to the circumstances arising out of the war--such as judges, administrative or political officers, officers of city or communal governments--are paid from the public revenue of the invaded territory until the military government has reason wholly or partially to discontinue it. Salaries or incomes connected with purely honorary titles are always stopped.

40. There exists no law or body of authoritative rules of action between hostile armies, except that branch of the law of nature and nations which is called the law and usages of war on land.

41. All municipal law of the ground on which the armies stand, or of the countries to which they belong, is silent and of no effect between armies in the field.

42. Slavery, complicating and confounding the ideas of property (that is, of a thing),

and of personality (that is, of humanity), exists according to municipal or local law only. The law of nature and nations has never acknowledged it. The digest of the Roman law enacts the early dictum of the pagan jurist, that "so far as the law of nature is concerned, all men are equal." Fugitives escaping from a country in which they were slaves, villains, or serfs, into another country, have, for centuries past, been held free and acknowledged free by judicial decisions of European countries, even though the municipal law of the country in which the slave had taken refuge acknowledged slavery within its own dominions.

43. Therefore, in a war between the United States and a belligerent which admits of slavery, if a person held in bondage by that belligerent be captured by or come as a fugitive under the protection of the military forces of the United States, such person is immediately entitled to the rights and privileges of a freeman. To return such person into slavery would amount to enslaving a free person, and neither the United States nor any officer under their authority can enslave any human being. Moreover, a person so made free by the law of war is under the shield of the law of nations, and the former owner or State can have, by the law of postliminy, no belligerent lien or claim of service.

44. All wanton violence committed against persons in the invaded country, all destruction of property not commanded by the authorized officer, all robbery, all pillage or sacking, even after taking a place by main force, all rape, wounding, maiming, or killing of such inhabitants, are prohibited under the penalty of death, or such other severe punishment as may seem adequate for the gravity of the offense.

A soldier, officer, or private, in the act of committing such violence, and disobeying a superior ordering him to abstain from it, may be lawfully killed on the spot by such superior.

45. All captures and booty belong, according to the modern law of war, primarily to the government of the captor.

Prize money, whether on sea or land, can now only be claimed under local law.

46. Neither officers nor soldiers are allowed to make use of their position or power in the hostile country for private gain, not even for commercial transactions otherwise legitimate. Offenses to the contrary committed by commissioned officers will be punished with cashiering or such other punishment as the nature of the offense may require; if by soldiers, they shall be punished according to the nature of the offense.

47. Crimes punishable by all penal codes, such as arson, murder, maiming, assaults, highway robbery, theft, burglary, fraud, forgery, and rape, if committed by an American soldier in a hostile country against its inhabitants, are not only punishable as at home, but in all cases in which death is not inflicted the severer punishment shall be preferred.

SECTION III.--*Deserters--Prisoners of war--Hostages--Booty on the battle-field.*

48. Deserters from the American Army, having entered the service of the enemy, suffer death if they fall again into the hands of the United States, whether by capture or being delivered up to the American Army; and if a deserter from the enemy, having taken service in the Army of the United States, is captured by the enemy, and punished by them with death or otherwise, it is not a breach against the law and usages of war, requiring redress or retaliation.

49. A prisoner of war is a public enemy armed or attached to the hostile army for active aid, who has fallen into the hands of the captor, either fighting or wounded, on the field or in the hospital, by individual surrender or by capitulation.

All soldiers, of whatever species of arms; all men who belong to the rising *en masse* of the hostile country; all those who are attached to the Army for its efficiency and promote directly the object of the war, except such as are hereinafter provided for; all disabled men or officers on the field or elsewhere, if captured; all enemies who have thrown away their arms and ask for quarter, are prisoners of war, and as such exposed to the inconveniences as well as entitled to the privileges of a prisoner of war.

50. Moreover, citizens who accompany an army for whatever purpose, such as sutlers, editors, or reporters of journals, or contractors, if captured, may be made prisoners of war and be detained as such.

The monarch and members of the hostile reigning family, male or female, the chief, and chief officers of the hostile government, its diplomatic agents, and all persons who are of particular and singular use and benefit to the hostile army or its government, are, if captured on belligerent ground, and if unprovided with a safe-conduct granted by the captor's government, prisoners of war.

51. If the people of that portion of an invaded country which is not yet occupied by the enemy, or of the whole country, at the approach of a hostile army, rise, under a duly authorized levy, *en masse* to resist the invader, they are now treated as public enemies, and, if captured, are prisoners of war.

52. No belligerent has the right to declare that he will treat every captured man in arms of a levy *en masse* as a brigand or bandit.

If, however, the people of a country, or any portion of the same, already occupied by an army, rise against it, they are violators of the laws of war and are not entitled to their protection.

53. The enemy's chaplains, officers of the medical staff, apothecaries, hospital nurses, and servants, if they fall into the hands of the American Army, are not prisoners of war, unless the commander has reasons to retain them. In this latter case, or if, at their own desire, they are allowed to remain with their captured companions, they are treated as prisoners of war, and may be exchanged if the commander sees fit.

54. A hostage is a person accepted as a pledge for the fulfillment of an agreement concluded between belligerents during the war, or in consequence of a war. Hostages are rare in the present age.

55. If a hostage is accepted, he is treated like a prisoner of war, according to rank and condition, as circumstances may admit.

56. A prisoner of war is subject to no punishment for being a public enemy, nor is any revenge wreaked upon him by the intentional infliction of any suffering, or disgrace, by cruel imprisonment, want of food, by mutilation, death, or any other barbarity.

57. So soon as a man is armed by a sovereign government and takes the soldier's oath of fidelity he is a belligerent; his killing, wounding, or other warlike acts are no individual crimes or offenses. No belligerent has a right to declare that enemies of a certain class, color, or condition, when properly organized as soldiers, will not be treated by him as public enemies.

58. The law of nations knows of no distinction of color, and if an enemy of the United

States should enslave and sell any captured persons of their Army, it would be a case for the severest retaliation, if not redressed upon complaint.

The United States cannot retaliate by enslavement; therefore death must be the retaliation for this crime against the law of nations.

59. A prisoner of war remains answerable for his crimes committed against the captor's army or people, committed before he was captured, and for which he has not been punished by his own authorities.

All prisoners of war are liable to the infliction of retaliatory measures.

60. It is against the usage of modern war to resolve, in hatred and revenge, to give no quarter. No body of troops has the right to declare that it will not give, and therefore will not expect, quarter; but a commander is permitted to direct his troops to give no quarter, in great straits, when his own salvation makes it impossible to cumber himself with prisoners.

61. Troops that give no quarter have no right to kill enemies already disabled on the ground, or prisoners captured by other troops.

62. All troops of the enemy known or discovered to give no quarter in general, or to any portion of the Army, receive none.

63. Troops who fight in the uniform of their enemies, without any plain, striking, and uniform mark of distinction of their own, can expect no quarter.

64. If American troops capture a train containing uniforms of the enemy, and the commander considers it advisable to distribute them for use among his men, some striking mark or sign must be adopted to distinguish the American soldier from the enemy.

65. The use of the enemy's national standard, flag, or other emblem of nationality, for the purpose of deceiving the enemy in battle, is an act of perfidy by which they lose all claim to the protection of the laws of war.

66. Quarter having been given to an enemy by American troops, under a misapprehension of his true character, he may, nevertheless, be ordered to suffer death if, within three days after the battle, it be discovered that he belongs to a corps which gives no quarter.

67. The law of nations allows every sovereign government to make war upon another sovereign State, and, therefore, admits of no rules or laws different from those of regular warfare, regarding the treatment of prisoners of war, although they may belong to the army of a government which the captor may consider as a wanton and unjust assailant.

68. Modern wars are not internecine wars, in which the killing of the enemy is the object. The destruction of the enemy in modern war, and, indeed, modern war itself, are means to obtain that object of the belligerent which lies beyond the war.

Unnecessary or revengeful destruction of life is not lawful.

69. Outposts, sentinels, or pickets are not to be fired upon, except to drive them in, or when a positive order, special or general, has been issued to that effect.

70. The use of poison in any manner, be it to poison wells, or food, or arms, is wholly excluded from modern warfare. He that uses it puts himself out of the pale of the law and usages of war.

71. Whoever intentionally inflicts additional wounds on an enemy already wholly disabled, or kills such an enemy, or who orders or encourages soldiers to do so, shall suffer death, if duly convicted, whether he belongs to the Army of the United States, or is an enemy captured after having committed his misdeed.

72. Money and other valuables on the person of a prisoner, such as watches or jewelry,

as well as extra clothing, are regarded by the American Army as the private property of the prisoner, and the appropriation of such valuables or money is considered dishonorable, and is prohibited.

Nevertheless, if large sums are found upon the persons of prisoners, or in their possession, they shall be taken from them, and the surplus, after providing for their own support, appropriated for the use of the Army, under the direction of the commander, unless otherwise ordered by the Government. Nor can prisoners claim, as private property, large sums found and captured in their train, although they have been placed in the private luggage of the prisoners.

73. All officers, when captured, must surrender their side-arms to the captor. They may be restored to the prisoner in marked cases, by the commander, to signalize admiration of his distinguished bravery, or approbation of his humane treatment of prisoners before his capture. The captured officer to whom they may be restored cannot wear them during captivity.

74. A prisoner of war, being a public enemy, is the prisoner of the Government and not of the captor. No ransom can be paid by a prisoner of war to his individual captor, or to any officer in command. The Government alone releases captives, according to rules prescribed by itself.

75. Prisoners of war are subject to confinement or imprisonment such as may be deemed necessary on account of safety, but they are to be subjected to no other intentional suffering or indignity. The confinement and mode of treating a prisoner may be varied during his captivity according to the demands of safety.

76. Prisoners of war shall be fed upon plain and wholesome food, whenever practicable, and treated with humanity.

They may be required to work for the benefit of the captor's government, according to their rank and condition.

77. A prisoner of war who escapes may be shot, or otherwise killed, in his flight; but neither death nor any other punishment shall be inflicted upon him simply for his attempt to escape, which the law of war does not consider a crime. Stricter means of security shall be used after an unsuccessful attempt at escape.

If, however, a conspiracy is discovered, the purpose of which is a united or general escape, the conspirators may be rigorously punished, even with death; and capital punishment may also be inflicted upon prisoners of war discovered to have plotted rebellion against the authorities of the captors, whether in union with fellow-prisoners or other persons.

78. If prisoners of war, having given no pledge nor made any promise on their honor, forcibly or otherwise escape, and are captured again in battle, after having rejoined their own army, they shall not be punished for their escape, but shall be treated as simple prisoners of war, although they will be subjected to stricter confinement.

79. Every captured wounded enemy shall be medically treated, according to the ability of the medical staff.

80. Honorable men, when captured, will abstain from giving to the enemy information concerning their own army, and the modern law of war permits no longer the use of any violence against prisoners in order to extort the desired information, or to punish them for having given false information.

SECTION IV.--*Partisans--Armed enemies not belonging to the hostile army--Scouts--Armed prowlers-- War-rebels.*

81. Partisans are soldiers armed and wearing the uniform of their army, but belonging to a corps which acts detached from the main body for the purpose of making inroads into the territory occupied by the enemy. If captured they are entitled to all the privileges of the prisoner of war.

82. Men, or squads of men, who commit hostilities, whether by fighting, or inroads for destruction or plunder, or by raids of any kind, without commission, without being part and portion of the organized hostile army, and without sharing continuously in the war, but who do so with intermitting returns to their homes and avocations, or with the occasional assumption of the semblance of peaceful pursuits, divesting themselves of the character or appearance of soldiers--such men, or squads of men, are not public enemies, and therefore, if captured, are not entitled to the privileges of prisoners of war, but shall be treated summarily as highway robbers or pirates.

83. Scouts or single soldiers, if disguised in the dress of the country, or in the uniform of the army hostile to their own, employed in obtaining information, if found within or lurking about the lines of the captor, are treated as spies, and suffer death.

84. Armed prowlers, by whatever names they may be called, or persons of the enemy's territory, who steal within the lines of the hostile army for the purpose of robbing, killing, or of destroying bridges, roads, or canals, or of robbing or destroying the mail, or of cutting the telegraph wires, are not entitled to the privileges of the prisoner of war.

85. War-rebels are persons within an occupied territory who rise in arms against the occupying or conquering army, or against the authorities established by the same. If captured, they may suffer death, whether they rise singly, in small or large bands, and whether called upon to do so by their own, but expelled, government or not. They are not prisoners of war; nor are they if discovered and secured before their conspiracy has matured to an actual rising or to armed violence.

SECTION V.--*Safe-conduct--Spies-- War-traitors-- Captured messengers-Abuse of the flag of truce.*

86. All intercourse between the territories occupied by belligerent armies, whether by traffic, by letter, by travel, or in any other way, ceases. This is the general rule, to be observed without special proclamation.

Exceptions to this rule, whether by safe-conduct or permission to trade on a small or large scale, or by exchanging mails, or by travel from one territory into the other, can take place only according to agreement approved by the Government or by the highest military authority.

Contraventions of this rule are highly punishable.

87. Ambassadors, and all other diplomatic agents of neutral powers accredited to the enemy may receive safe-conducts through the territories occupied by the belligerents, unless there are military reasons to the contrary, and unless they may reach the place of their

destination conveniently by another route. It implies no international affront if the safe-conduct is declined. Such passes are usually given by the supreme authority of the state and not by subordinate officers.

88. A spy is a person who secretly, in disguise or under false pretense, seeks information with the intention of communicating it to the enemy.

The spy is punishable with death by hanging by the neck, whether or not he succeed in obtaining the information or in conveying it to the enemy.

89. If a citizen of the United States obtains information in a legitimate manner and betrays it to the enemy, be he a military or civil officer, or a private citizen, he shall suffer death.

90. A traitor under the law of war, or a war-traitor, is a person in a place or district under martial law who, unauthorized by the military commander, gives information of any kind to the enemy, or holds intercourse with him.

91. The war-traitor is always severely punished. If his offense consists in betraying to the enemy anything concerning the condition, safety, operations, or plans of the troops holding or occupying the place or district, his punishment is death.

92. If the citizen or subject of a country or place invaded or conquered gives information to his own government, from which he is separated by the hostile army, or to the army of his government, he is a war-traitor, and death is the penalty of his offense.

93. All armies in the field stand in need of guides, and impress them if they cannot obtain them otherwise.

94. No person having been forced by the enemy to serve as guide is punishable for having done so.

95. If a citizen of a hostile and invaded district voluntarily serves as a guide to the enemy, or offers to do so, he is deemed a war-traitor and shall suffer death.

96. A citizen serving voluntarily as a guide against his own country commits treason, and will be dealt with according to the law of his country.

97. Guides, when it is clearly proved that they have misled intentionally, may be put to death.

98. All unauthorized or secret communication with the enemy is considered treasonable by the law of war.

Foreign residents in an invaded or occupied territory or foreign visitors in the same can claim no immunity from this law. They may communicate with foreign parts or with the inhabitants of the hostile country, so far as the military authority permits, but no further. Instant expulsion from the occupied territory would be the very least punishment for the infraction of this rule.

99. A messenger carrying written dispatches or verbal messages from one portion of the army or from a besieged place to another portion of the same army or its government, if armed, and in the uniform of his army, and if captured while doing so in the territory occupied by the enemy, is treated by the captor as a prisoner of war. If not in uniform nor a soldier, the circumstances connected with his capture must determine the disposition that shall be made of him.

100. A messenger or agent who attempts to steal through the territory occupied by the enemy to further in any manner the interests of the enemy, if captured, is not entitled to the privileges of the prisoner of war, and may be dealt with according to the circumstances of

the case.

101. While deception in war is admitted as a just and necessary means of hostility, and is consistent with honorable warfare, the common law of war allows even capital punishment for clandestine or treacherous attempts to injure an enemy, because they are so dangerous, and it is so difficult to guard against them.

102. The law of war, like the criminal law regarding other offenses, makes no difference on account of the difference of sexes, concerning the spy, the war-traitor, or the war-rebel.

103. Spies, war-traitors, and war-rebels are not exchanged according to the common law of war. The exchange of such persons would require a special cartel, authorized by the Government, or, at a great distance from it, by the chief commander of the army in the field.

104. A successful spy or war-traitor, safely returned to his own army, and afterward captured as an enemy, is not subject to punishment for his acts as a spy or war-traitor, but he may be held in closer custody as a person individually dangerous.

SECTION VI.--*Exchange of prisoners--Flags of truce--Flags of protection.*

105. Exchanges of prisoners take place--number for number--rank for rank--wounded for wounded--with added condition for added condition--such, for instance, as not to serve for a certain period.

106. In exchanging prisoners of war, such numbers of persons of inferior rank may be substituted as an equivalent for one of superior rank as may be agreed upon by cartel, which requires the sanction of the Government, or of the commander of the army in the field.

107. A prisoner of war is in honor bound truly to state to the captor his rank; and he is not to assume a lower rank than belongs to him, in order to cause a more advantageous exchange, nor a higher rank, for the purpose of obtaining better treatment.

Offenses to the contrary have been justly punished by the commanders of released prisoners, and may be good cause for refusing to release such prisoners.

108. The surplus number of prisoners of war remaining after an exchange has taken place is sometimes released either for the payment of a stipulated sum of money, or, in urgent cases, of provision, clothing, or other necessaries.

Such arrangement, however, requires the sanction of the highest authority.

109. The exchange of prisoners of war is an act of convenience to both belligerents. If no general cartel has been concluded, it cannot be demanded by either of them. No belligerent is obliged to exchange prisoners of war.

A cartel is voidable as soon as either party has violated it.

110. No exchange of prisoners shall be made except after complete capture, and after an accurate account of them, and a list of the captured officers, has been taken.

111. The bearer of a flag of truce cannot insist upon being admitted. He must always be admitted with great caution. Unnecessary frequency is carefully to be avoided.

112. If the bearer of a flag of truce offer himself during an engagement, he can be admitted as a very rare exception only. It is no breach of good faith to retain such flag of

truce, if admitted during the engagement. Firing is not required to cease on the appearance of a flag of truce in battle.

113. If the bearer of a flag of truce, presenting himself during an engagement, is killed or wounded, it furnishes no ground of complaint whatever.

114. If it be discovered, and fairly proved, that a flag of truce has been abused for surreptitiously obtaining military knowledge, the bearer of the flag thus abusing his sacred character is deemed a spy.

So sacred is the character of a flag of truce, and so necessary is its sacredness, that while its abuse is an especially heinous offense, great caution is requisite, on the other hand, in convicting the bearer of a flag of truce as a spy.

115. It is customary to designate by certain flags (usually yellow) the hospitals in places which are shelled, so that the besieging enemy may avoid firing on them. The same has been done in battles when hospitals are situated within the field of the engagement.

116. Honorable belligerents often request that the hospitals within the territory of the enemy may be designated, so that they may be spared.

An honorable belligerent allows himself to be guided by flags or signals of protection as much as the contingencies and the necessities of the fight will permit.

117. It is justly considered an act of bad faith, of infamy or fiendishness, to deceive the enemy by flags of protection. Such act of bad faith may be good cause for refusing to respect such flags.

118. The besieging belligerent has sometimes requested the besieged to designate the buildings containing collections of works of art, scientific museums, astronomical observatories, or precious libraries, so that their destruction may be avoided as much as possible.

SECTION VII.--*The parole.*

119. Prisoners of war may be released from captivity by exchange, and, under certain circumstances, also by parole.

120. The term parole designates the pledge of individual good faith and honor to do, or to omit doing, certain acts after he who gives his parole shall have been dismissed, wholly or partially, from the power of the captor.

121. The pledge of the parole is always an individual, but not a private act.

122. The parole applies chiefly to prisoners of war whom the captor allows to return to their country, or to live in greater freedom within the captor's country or territory, on conditions stated in the parole.

123. Release of prisoners of war by exchange is the general rule; release by parole is the exception.

124. Breaking the parole is punished with death when the person breaking the parole is captured again.

Accurate lists, therefore, of the paroled persons must be kept by the belligerents.

125. When paroles are given and received there must be an exchange of two written documents, in which the name and rank of the paroled individuals are accurately and truthfully stated.

126. Commissioned officers only are allowed to give their parole, and they can give it

only with the permission of their superior, as long as a superior in rank is within reach.

127. No non-commissioned officer or private can give his parole except through an officer. Individual paroles not given through an officer are not only void, but subject the individuals giving them to the punishment of death as deserters. The only admissible exception is where individuals, properly separated from their commands, have suffered long confinement without the possibility of being paroled through an officer.

128. No paroling on the battle-field; no paroling of entire bodies of troops after a battle; and no dismissal of large numbers of prisoners, with a general declaration that they are paroled, is permitted, or of any value.

129. In capitulations for the surrender of strong places or fortified camps the commanding officer, in cases of urgent necessity, may agree that the troops under his command shall not fight again during the war unless exchanged.

130. The usual pledge given in the parole is not to serve during the existing war unless exchanged.

This pledge refers only to the active service in the field against the paroling belligerent or his allies actively engaged in the same war. These cases of breaking the parole are patent acts, and can be visited with the punishment of death; but the pledge does not refer to internal service, such as recruiting or drilling the recruits, fortifying places not besieged, quelling civil commotions, fighting against belligerents unconnected with the paroling belligerents, or to civil or diplomatic service for which the paroled officer may be employed.

131. If the government does not approve of the parole, the paroled officer must return into captivity, and should the enemy refuse to receive him he is free of his parole.

132. A belligerent government may declare, by a general order, whether it will allow paroling and on what conditions it will allow it. Such order is communicated to the enemy.

133. No prisoner of war can be forced by the hostile government to parole himself, and no government is obliged to parole prisoners of war or to parole all captured officers, if it paroles any. As the pledging of the parole is an individual act, so is paroling, on the other hand, an act of choice on the part of the belligerent.

134. The commander of an occupying army may require of the civil officers of the enemy, and of its citizens, any pledge he may consider necessary for the safety or security of his army, and upon their failure to give it he may arrest, confine, or detain them.

SECTION VIII.--*Armistice--Capitulation.*

135. An armistice is the cessation of active hostilities for a period agreed between belligerents. It must be agreed upon in writing and duly ratified by the highest authorities of the contending parties.

136. If an armistice be declared without conditions it extends no further than to require a total cessation of hostilities along the front of both belligerents.

If conditions be agreed upon, they should be clearly expressed, and must be rigidly adhered to by both parties. If either party violates any express condition, the armistice may be declared null and void by the other.

137. An armistice may be general, and valid for all points and lines of the belligerents; or special--that is, referring to certain troops or certain localities only. An armistice may be

concluded for a definite time; or for an indefinite time, during which either belligerent may resume hostilities on giving the notice agreed upon to the other.

138. The motives which induce the one or the other belligerent to conclude an armistice, whether it be expected to be preliminary to a treaty of peace, or to prepare during the armistice for a more vigorous prosecution of the war, does in no way affect the character of the armistice itself.

139. An armistice is binding upon the belligerents from the day of the agreed commencement; but the officers of the armies are responsible from the day only when they receive official information of its existence.

140. Commanding officers have the right to conclude armistices binding on the district over which their command extends, but such armistice is subject to the ratification of the superior authority, and ceases so soon as it is made known to the enemy that the armistice is not ratified, even if a certain time for the elapsing between giving notice of cessation and the resumption of hostilities should have been stipulated for.

141. It is incumbent upon the contracting parties of an armistice to stipulate what intercourse of persons or traffic between the inhabitants of the territories occupied by the hostile armies shall be allowed, if any.

If nothing is stipulated the intercourse remains suspended, as during actual hostilities.

142. An armistice is not a partial or a temporary peace; it is only the suspension of military operations to the extent agreed upon by the parties.

143. When an armistice is concluded between a fortified place and the army besieging it, it is agreed by all the authorities on this subject that the besieger must cease all extension, perfection, or advance of his attacking works as much so as from attacks by main force.

But as there is a difference of opinion among martial jurists whether the besieged have a right to repair breaches or to erect new works of defense within the place during an armistice, this point should be determined by express agreement between the parties.

144. So soon as a capitulation is signed the capitulator has no right to demolish, destroy, or injure the works, arms, stores, or ammunition in his possession, during the time which elapses between the signing and the execution of the capitulation, unless otherwise stipulated in the same.

145. When an armistice is clearly broken by one of the parties the other party is released from all obligation to observe it.

146. Prisoners taken in the act of breaking an armistice must be treated as prisoners of war, the officer alone being responsible who gives the order for such a violation of an armistice. The highest authority of the belligerent aggrieved may demand redress for the infraction of an armistice.

147. Belligerents sometimes conclude an armistice while their plenipotentiaries are met to discuss the conditions of a treaty of peace; but plenipotentiaries may meet without a preliminary armistice; in the latter case the war is carried on without any abatement.

SECTION IX.--*Assassination.*

287

148. The law of war does not allow proclaiming either an individual belonging to the hostile army, or a citizen, or a subject of the hostile government an outlaw, who may be slain without trial by any captor, any more than the modern law of peace allows such international outlawry; on the contrary, it abhors such outrage. The sternest retaliation should follow the murder committed in consequence of such proclamation, made by whatever authority. Civilized nations look with horror upon offers of rewards for the assassination of enemies as relapses into barbarism.

SECTION X.--*Insurrection-- Civil war--Rebellion.*

149. Insurrection is the rising of people in arms against their government, or portion of it, or against one or more of its laws, or against an officer or officers of the government. It may be confined to mere armed resistance, or it may have greater ends in view.

150. Civil war is war between two or more portions of a country or state, each contending for the mastery of the whole, and each claiming to be the legitimate government. The term is also sometimes applied to war of rebellion, when the rebellious provinces or portions of the state are contiguous to those containing the seat of government.

151. The term rebellion is applied to an insurrection of large extent, and is usually a war between the legitimate government of a country and portions of provinces of the same who seek to throw off their allegiance to it and set up a government of their own.

152. When humanity induces the adoption of the rules of regular war toward rebels, whether the adoption is partial or entire, it does in no way whatever imply a partial or complete acknowledgment of their government, if they have set up one, or of them, as an independent or sovereign power. Neutrals have no right to make the adoption of the rules of war by the assailed government toward rebels the ground of their own acknowledgment of the revolted people as an independent power.

153. Treating captured rebels as prisoners of war, exchanging them, concluding of cartels, capitulations, or other warlike agreements with them; addressing officers of a rebel army by the rank they may have in the same; accepting flags of truce; or, on the other hand, proclaiming martial law in their territory, or levying war taxes or forced loans, or doing any other act sanctioned or demanded by the law and usages of public war between sovereign belligerents, neither proves nor establishes an acknowledgment of the rebellious people, or of the government which they may have erected, as a public or sovereign power. Nor does the adoption of the rules of war toward rebels imply an engagement with them extending beyond the limits of these rules. It is victory in the field that ends the strife and settles the future relations between the contending parties.

154. Treating in the field the rebellious enemy according to the law and usages of war has never prevented the legitimate government from trying the leaders of the rebellion or chief rebels for high treason, and from treating them accordingly, unless they are included in a general amnesty.

155. All enemies in regular war are divided into two general classes--that is to say, into combatants and non-combatants, or unarmed citizens of the hostile government.

The military commander of the legitimate government, in a war of rebellion, distinguishes between the loyal citizen in the revolted portion of the country and the disloyal citizen. The disloyal citizens may further be classified into those citizens known to sympathize with the rebellion without positively aiding it, and those who, without taking up arms, give positive aid and comfort to the rebellious enemy without being bodily forced thereto.

156. Common justice and plain expediency require that the military commander protect the manifestly loyal citizens in revolted territories against the hardships of the war as much as the common misfortune of all war admits.

The commander will throw the burden of the war, as much as lies within his power, on the disloyal citizens, of the revolted portion or province, subjecting them to a stricter police than the non-combatant enemies have to suffer in regular war; and if he deems it appropriate, or if his government demands of him that every citizen shall, by an oath of allegiance, or by some other manifest act, declare his fidelity to the legitimate government, he may expel, transfer, imprison, or fine the revolted citizens who refuse to pledge themselves anew as citizens obedient to the law and loyal to the government.

Whether it is expedient to do so, and whether reliance can be placed upon such oaths, the commander or his government have the right to decide.

157. Armed or unarmed resistance by citizens of the United States against the lawful movements of their troops is levying war against the United States, and is therefore treason.

Notes:

Chapter 1:

    Page 1-28

1. Official Records, Series I, Volume XXVIII, part 2, page 58-59; Lieber, Francis, *General Orders No. 100*, April 24, 1863;
2. Cisco, Walter Brian, War Crimes Against Southern Civilians, page 85-88;
3. Official Records, Series II, Volume VI, page 42-43; Lieber, Francis, *General Orders No. 100*, April 24, 1863;
4. Heatwole, John L., *The Burning: Sheridan's Devastation of the Shenandoah Valley,* pages 89-95;
5. Grant, Ulysses S., "*Personal Memoirs of U. S. Grant*";
6. Official Records, Series I, Volume XLIII, part 1, page 916-917; 5. Sheridan, Philip H., *Personal Memoirs of P. H. Sheridan*, volume 1, page 486, Ulysses S. Grant to Sheridan, August 26, 1864;
7. Grimsley, Mark, *Hard Hand of War, Union Policy Toward Southern Civilians, 1861-1865,* page 184;
8. Heatwole, John L., The Burning: Sheridan's Devastation of the Shenandoah Valley, Page 89-95;
9. Bovard, James, *Sheridan's Scorched Earth Campaign, Forgotten Civil War Atrocities Breed More Carnage,* http://antiwar.com/blog/2015/04/09/forgotten-civil-war-atrocities-breed-more-carnage/
10. Richards, Samuel, *Sam Richard's Civil War Diary: A Chronicle of the Atlanta Home Front,* edited by Wendy Hamand Venet, pages 229, 232;
11. Reed, Wallace Putnam, *The History of Atlanta, Georgia*, page 183-184;
12 Official Records, Series 1, Volume XXXVIII, page 572-573;
13 Official Records, Series I, Volume 38, part 5, page 193; Sherman, William T. *Memoirs,* page 444;
14. Official Records, Series I, Volume 38, part 5, pages 408-409;
15. Hoehling, A. A., *Last Train From Atlanta*, pages 280-281;
16. Mobile, Alabama, Evening News, August 12, 1864; McDonough, James Lee and Jones, James Pickett, *War So Terrible,* page 275;
17. Hoehling, A. A., *Last Train From Atlanta*, page 281;
18. Richards, Samuel, *Sam Richard's Civil War Diary: A Chronicle of the Atlanta Home Front,* edited by Wendy Hamand Venet, pages 229, 232;
19. Reed, Wallace Putnam, *The History of Atlanta, Georgia*, pages 183-184;
20. Reed, Wallace Putnam, *The History of Atlanta, Georgia*, page 191;

21. Watkins, Sam R., *Co. Aytch, Maury Grays, First Tennessee Regiment or, A Side Show to the Big Show*, page 179;
22. Official Records, Series I, Volume 38, part 5, pages 408-409, 452;
23. Official Records, Series I, Volume 39, part 2, pages 420, 419-421;
24. Davis, Stephen, *What the Yankees Did to Us,* page 255;
25. Official Records, Series I, Volume XLIV, page 799;
26. Jones, Katharine M., *When Sherman Came: and the Great March,* 1964, pages 114-121;
27. Grimsley, Mark, *Hard Hand of War, Union Policy Toward Southern Civilians, 1861-1865,* pages 142-143;
28. Lieber, Francis, General Orders No. 100, April 24, 1863; Halleck, Henry W., International Law; Or, Rules Regulating the Intercourse of States In Peace and War, 1861;
29. Lieber Code, Section II, Article 44;
30. Official Records, volume XVII, part II, page 81;
31. Official Records, XVII, part II, pages 390-391;
32. Official Records, XXXII, part II, page 427;
33. Official Records, XXXIX, part II, pages 131-132;
34. Official Records, XXXIX, part II, page 157;
35. Official Records, Volume 39, part III, page 494;
36. Official Records, XXXIX, part II, pages 308-309;
37. Official Records, Series I, Volume XLIV, page 741;
38. Official Records, Series I, Volume XLIV, page 799;
39. Kennett, Lee, Marching through Georgia: The Story of Soldiers and Civilians During Sherman's Campaign, 1995, Page 287, Harper Collins Publishers New York;

Chapter 2:

Page 29-39

1. Official Records, Series II, Volume VI, pages 523-524;
2. Official Records, Series II, Volume VII, pages 113-114, Official Records, Series II, Volume VII, pages 150-151;
3. *The Medical and Surgical History of the War of the Rebellion, (1861-65),* Volume I, Part 3, page 46; there is a later publication entitled *The Medical and Surgical History of the Civil War,* the same information can be found in Volume 5, page 46; Broadfoot Publishing Company, Wilmington, North Carolina, 1991;
4. Eugene F. Sanger Papers, Records of the Office of the Adjutant General, Regimental Correspondence, 1861-1865, Maine State Archives;
5. Keiley, Anthony M., *In Vinculis Or, The Prisoner of War: Being the Experience Of A Rebel in Two Federal Pens*, pages 144-145;
6. Official Records, Series II, Volume III, page 157;
7. Official Records, Series I, Volume X, part 2, page 531;

8. Official Records, Series II, Volume IV, pages 271, 329-330;

9. Official Records, Series II, Volume I, pages 818-819;

10. Official Records, Series II, Volume IV, pages 836-837;

11. Official Records, Series I, Volume XV, pages 906-908; Official Records, Series II, Volume V, pages 795-797; Official Records, Series II, Volume IV, pages 328-329, 770-771; Official Records, Series II, Volume V, pages 795-797; Butler, Benjamin Franklin, *Autobiography and Personal Reminiscences of Major-General Benjamin Franklin Butler,* pages 370, 376, 437, 443, 542-546, 547; Bland, T. A., *Life of Benjamin F. Butler,* pages 74-75, 96-100, 101-104; Marshall, Jessie Ames, *Private and Official Correspondence of Gen. Benjamin F. Butler During the Period of the Civil War, Volume II, June 1862-February, 1863,* pages 22, 72, 557, 562, 569;

12. Official Records, Series II, Volume V, page 669;

13. Official Records, Series II, Volume VII, page 914; General Robert E. Lee letter to General U. S. Grant;

14. Official Records, Series II, Volume 5, pages 940-941, Joint resolutions adopted by the Confederate Congress on the subject of retaliation April 30-May 1, 1863;

15. Speer, Lonnie R., *Portal of Hell, Military Prisons of the Civil War,* page 109; Glatharr, Joseph T., *Forged in Battle, The Civil War Alliance of Black Soldiers and White Officers,* page 160;

16. Fox, William F., *Regimental Losses in the Civil War*, pages 52-56;

17. Official Records, Series II, Volume VI, pages 17-18;

18. Official Records, Series II, Volume VII, pages 606-607;

19. Grigsby, Colonel Melvin, *The Smoked Yank,* page 137-138;

20. Page, James Madison, *The True Story of Andersonville Prison: A Defense of Major Henry Wirz,* pages 108-109;

Chapter 3:

Page 40-71

1. Official Records, Series II, Volume IV, page 68-70;

2. Official Records, Series II, Volume IV, page 70-73;

3. Official Records, Series II, Volume IV, page 67-69;

4. Official Records, Series II, Volume IV, page 72-75;

5. Official Records, Series II, Volume VII, page 146;

6. Official Records, Series II, Volume VII, page 152;

7. Official Records, Series II, Volume VII, page 156-157;

8. Official records, Series II, Volume 7, page 152;

9. Official records, Series II, Volume 7, page 157;

10. Official Records, Series II, Volume 7, page 394;

11. Official Records, Series II, Volume 7, page 152;

12. Official Records, Series II, Volume VII, pages 603-604;

13. Official Records, Series II, Volume VII, pages 604-605;

14. Official Records, Series II, Volume VII, page 1093;
15. Official Records, Series II, Volume VII, page 424;
16. Official Records, Series II, Volume VII, pages 450-451, 465-466;
17. Official Records, Series II, Volume VII, page 502;
18. Official Records, Series I, Volume XXXVI, 36, Part I, pages 133, 149, 164, 180, 188;
19. Official Records, Series II, Volume VII, page 424;
20. Addison Walter D., Southern Historical Collection of the University of North Carolina Library, Chapel Hill, North Carolina;
21. Keiley, Anthony M., *In Vinculis Or, The Prisoner Of War: Being The Experience Of A Rebel In Two Federal Pens,* page 117-120;
22. Benson, Berry, B*erry Benson's Civil War Book, Memoirs of a Confederate Scout and Sharpshooter,* page 126-127; Byrne, Thomas E., "*Elmira's Civil War Prison Camp: 1864-1865,*" *Chemung Historical Journal, volume 10, No. 1, (September 1964)*: page 1287;
23. Elmira Daily Advisor, July 7, 1864;
24. Official Records, Series II, Volume VII, page 489;
25. *Elmira Daily Advertiser*, July 18, 1864, *The Train Accident at Shohola*, page 2;
26. Holmes, Clay W., *The Elmira Prison Camp, A History of the Military Prison at Elmira, N. Y., July 6, 1864 to July 10, 1865,* pages 30-34;
27. New York Tribune, July 18, 1864;
28. *New York Evening Post*, August 24, 1864;
29. *Rochester Daily Union and Advertiser*, New York, reprinted in *Elmira Daily Advertiser*, August13, 1864;
30. Towner, Ashburn. *A History of the Chemung County, New York*, pages 269-270;
31. *Elmira Daily Advertiser*, August 30, 1864;
33. Rochester, New York, *Union Dailey and Advertiser*, September 13, 1864;
34. Porter, G. W. D, page 159, *Nine Months in a Northern Prison, Annals of the Army of Tennessee and Early Western History*, July, 1878;
35. Huffman, James, *Ups and Down of a Confederate Soldier*, page 105;
36. Towner, Ashburn, *A History of the Chemung County, New York*, page 270;
37. *Elmira Dailey Gazette*, September 3, 1864;
38. Keiley, Anthony, M., In Vinculis; Or the Prisoner of War, page 158;
39. Official Records, Series II, Volume VII, pages 80-81;   Letter of Sgt. Washington S. Toland, *New York Times*, April 23, 1864;
40. *Speer, Lonnie, Portals To Hell, Military Prisons of the Civil War,* page 332;
41. Official Records, Series II, Volume VII, pages 80- 81;
42. Official Records, Series II, Volume VII, pages 113-114;
43. Williams, T. Harry, *Lincoln and the Radicals,* pages 344-345;
44. http://memory.loc.gov/cgibin/ampage?collId=llsr&fileName=038/llsr038.db&recNum=105 ;
45. *New York Times*, October 2, 1864;
46. Current, Richard N., *The Lincoln Nobody Knows,* page 86;
47. Horigan, Michael, *Elmira: Death Camp of the North,* page 86;
48. Official Records, Series II, Vol. VII, pages 1260-1262;
49. Official Records, Series II, Vol. VII, page 1261;

50. Official Records, Series II, Vol. VII, page 1263

51. Official Records, Series II, Vol. VII, page 72-75; Speers, Lonnie, *War of Vengeance, Acts of Retaliation Against Civil War POWs,* page 117;

52. Official Records, Series II, Vol. VI, page 503-504;

53. Official Records, Series II, Vol. VI, page 489;

54. Official Records, Series II, Volume VII, pages 150-151, 183-184;

55. Crocker, James F., *Prison Reminiscences,* pages 43-44;

56. *Diagnostic and Statistical Manual of Mental Disorders*, 5th Edition, *Arlington: American Psychiatric Publishing,* pages 160–168; Richards, C. Steven, PhD, and O'Hara, Michael W., PhD, *The Oxford Handbook of Depression and Comorbidity,* pages 160-168,

57. King, John R., *My Experience in the Confederate Army and In Northern Prisons,* page 40;

58. Neese, George M., *Three Years in the Confederate Horse Artillery,* pages 344-345;

59. Holmes, Clay, *Elmira Prison Camp*, page 336;

60. Wilkeson, Frank, *Recollections of a Private Soldier in the Army of the Potomac,* page 226;

61. Keiley, Anthony M., *In Vinculis Or, The Prisoner of War: Being the Experience of a Rebel in Two Federal Pens,* 154-155;

62. Wyeth, John Allen, *Cold Cheer at Camp Morton, Century Magazine,* volume 41 no. 6, April 1891, page 848;

63. Huffman, James, *Ups and Downs of a Confederate Soldier,* page 100;

64. King, John R., *My Experience in the Confederate Army and in Northern Prisons,* page 40;

65. National Archives, *General and Special Orders*, Volume 3, page 287;

66. *Elmira Daily Advertiser,* December 14, 1878;

67. Keiley, Anthony M. *In Vinculis, or The Prisoner of War*, page 145-146;

68. Keiley, Anthony M. *In Vinculis, or The Prisoner of War*, page 141;

69. Benson, Berry, *Civil War Book,* page 134;

70. Benson, Berry, *Civil War Book,* page 134;

71. Toney, Marcus, *Privations of a Private*, pages 100-101;

72. Toney, Marcus, *Privations of a Private*, pages 100-101;

73. Addison, Walter D., *Recollections of a Confederate Soldier*, page 9;

74. Stamp, James B., *Ten Months Experience in Northern Prisons,* page 496;

75. Ewan, R. B., *Prison Life*, page 14; Holmes, Clay, *Elmira Prison Camp*, page 305;

76. Benson, Berry, *Berry Benson's Civil War Book,* page 94;

77. Elliott, James Carson, *The Southern Soldier Boy,* page 49;

78. Walker, Thad. J., *Reminiscences of Point Lookout,* page 2;

79. Neese, George M., *Three Years in the Confederate Horse Artillery,* page 350;

80. Holt, David, *A Mississippi Rebel in the Army of Northern Virginia,* pages 323-324;

81. Berry, Berry, *Berry Benson's Civil War Book,* page 94;

82. Holmes, Clay, *The Elmira Prison Camp*, page 338;

83. King, John R., *My Experience in the Confederate Army and in Northern Prisons,* page 42;

84. Kieley, Anthony M., *In Vinculis Or, The Prisoner of War: Being the Experience Of a*

Rebel In Two Federal Pens, pages 90-91;

85. Official Records, Series II, Volume VIII, pages 52-53;

86. Official Records, Series II, Volume VIII, pages 76-77;

87. Wilkeson, Frank, *Turned Inside Out: Recollection of a Private Soldier in the Army of the Potomac,* page 225;

88. Toney, Marcus B., *The Privations of a Private,* page 98;

89. Official Records, Series II, Volume VIII, pages 767-768;

90. Official Records, Series II, Volume VII, pages 1134-1136, Inspector Surgeon William Sloan's November 14, 1864, report to Medical Director's Office, Department of the East, Green Lumber mentioned on page 1136;

Chapter 4:

Page 72-114

1. Official Records, Series II, Volume VII, pages 604-605; Official Records, Series II, Volume VII, pages 1,092-1,094;

2. Horigan, Michael, Elmira: Death Camp of the North, page 67;

3. Wilkeson, Frank, *Turned Inside Out: Recollection of a Private Soldier in the Army of the Potomac,* page 4-5;

4. *Elmira Daily Advertiser,* January 19, 1864;

5. Opie, John N., *A Rebel Cavalryman with Lee, Stuart, and Jackson,* page 318;

6. King, John R., *My Experiences in the Confederate Army and in Northern Prisons,* page 38;

7. Huffman, James, *Prisoner of War,* page 548;

8. King, John R, *My Experiences in the Confederate Army and in Northern Prisons,* page 38;

9. Official Records, Series II, Volume VII, pages 676-677;

10. Keiley, Anthony M., *In Vinculis, or The Prisoner of War,* pages 172-173;

11. Official Records, Series II, Volume VII, page 878;

12. King, John R, United Daughters of the Confederacy, 1917, page 4;

13. Official Records, Series II, Vol. VII, 573-74;

14. Sergeant George W. D. Porter, *Nine Months In A Northern Prison;*

15. *The Treatment of Prisoners during the War, Southern Historical Society Paper 1,* no. 4, April 1876, page 294;

16. *The Treatment of Prisoners during the War, Southern Historical Society Paper 1,* no. 4, April 1876, page 294;

17. *Southern Historical Society Paper,* Volume 1, no. 4, April 1876, 295;

18. Official Records, Series II, Volume VII, Series II, page 1217; Official Records, Series II, Volume VIII, Series II, page 23-24;

19. Official Records, Series II, Volume VIII, Series II, page 23-24;

20. Official Records, Series II, Volume VII, page 891-892;

21. Keiley, Anthony *In Vinculis,* 181-182;

22. Official Records, Series II, Volume VII, page 892-93;

23. Official Records, Series II, Volume VII, page 894;

24. Official Records, Series II, Volume VII, page 894;

25. Official Records, Series II, Volume VII, page 894;

26. *Daily National Intelligencer,* Washington, D. C., October 19, 1864;

27. *Elmira Daily Advertiser,* New York, November 19, 1864;

28. *Elmira Daily Advertiser,* New York, November 21, 1864; Official Records, Series II, Volume VII, page 1159;

29. Official Records, Series II, Volume VIII, Pages 986-1003, 999;

30. Official Records, Series II, Volume VII, page 1091-1094, 1093;

31. Official Records, Series II, Volume VIII, Pages 986-1003, 999;

32. Dibrell, Richard H., *Confederate States of America, Congress, Joint Select Committee to Investigate the Condition and Treatment of Prisoners of War, The Southern Historical Society Papers,* Vol. I, pages 136-137;

33. Grambling, Wilbur W., Diary; https://www.floridamemory.com/collections/gramling/people.php;

34. Keiley, Anthony M., *In Vinculis; or, The Prisoner of War,* page 185;

35. Keiley, Anthony M., *In Vinculis; or, The Prisoner of War,* page 175;

36. Keiley, Anthony M., *In Vinculis; or, The Prisoner of War,* page 174;

37. Huffman, *Ups and Downs of a Confederate Soldier,* page 97;

38. Keiley, Anthony M., *In Vinculis; or, The Prisoner of War,* page 138;

39. Holmes, Clay, *Elmira Prison Camp,* page 117-18;

40. Holmes, Clay, *Elmira Prison Camp,* page 328;

41. Horigan, Michael, *Elmira: Death Camp of the North,* page 131;

42. Butler, Benjamin F., *Butler's Book: Autobiography and Personal Reminiscences of Major-General Benjamin F. Butler,* page 610-611;

43. Official Records, Series II, Volume VI, pages 647-649;

44. Official Records, Series II, Volume VII, page 152; May 23, 1864;

45. Official Records, Series II, Volume VII, page 152; Official Records, Series II, Volume VII, pages 1134-1136; May 19, 1864, letter from Colonel Eastman to Colonel Seth Eastman suggesting 10,000 prisoners could be accommodated at Elmira; Official Records, Series II, Volume VII, page 157;

46. Official Records, Series II, volume 7, pages 1272-1273;

47. Official Records, Series II, volume 8, page 25;

48. *The medical and Surgical History of the War of the Rebellion,* volume I, part III, page

49. Smart, Major and Surgeon Charles, *The medical and Surgical History of the War of the Rebellion,* volume I, part III, page 625;

50. Addison, Walter D., *Recollections of a Confederate Soldier of the Prison-Pens of Point Lookout, Maryland, and Elmira, New York,* pages 4-5;

51. Smart, Major and Surgeon Charles, *The medical and Surgical History of the War of the Rebellion,* volume I, part III, pages 647-648;

52. Toney, Marcus B., *The Privations of a Private,* Nashville, Tennessee, 1905, pages 110-112;

53. *The medical and Surgical History of the War of the Rebellion,* volume I, part III, pages 627, 629;

54. Lamb, William, *Colonel Lamb's Story of Fort Fisher,* pages 14-16, 18, 22-23;

55. Official Records, Navy, Series I, Volume II, page 253;

56. *The Medical and Surgical History of the War of the Rebellion, (1861-65),* Volume III, Part I, page 56-57, 63;

57. Triebe, Richard H., *Fort Fisher to Elmira,* page viii;

58. *The Medical and Surgical History of the War of the Rebellion, (1861-65),* Volume III, Part I, page 57;

59. Keiley, Anthony M., *In Vinculis; or, The Prisoner of War,* page 185;

60. Official Records, Series II, Volume VII, pages 1063, 1101, 1117;

61. Official Records, Series II, Volume VII, pages 117-1118, 1148-1149; O. R., Series II, Volume VII, pages 27-28;

62. Official Records, Series II, Volume 8, page 20;

63. Official Records, Series II, Volume VIII, page 27;

64. Official Records, Series II, Volume VIII, pages 67-68, 70;

65. Official Records, Series II, Volume VIII, page 123;

66. Official Records, Series II, Volume VIII, pages 748-749;

67. Triebe, Richard H., *Fort Fisher to Elmira, the Fatal Journey of 518 Confederate Soldiers,* page 101, 103, 105;

68. Inspection report, March 4, 1865;

69. Davis, Thaddeus C., *Confederate Veteran* Magazine, February, 1899, page 65;

70. Official Records, Series II, Volume VIII, page 209;

71. Official Records, Series II, Volume VII, page 1217;

72. *Lieber Code of 1863*, Section III, No. 49, 75, 81;

73. Official Records, Series II, Volume VII, page 1217;

74. Official Records, Series II, *Vol.* VIII, Series II, page 23-24; Official Records, Series II, Volume VIII, page 90;

75. Official Records, Series II, Volume VII, page 1185;

76. Official Records, Series II, Volume VIII, page 318;

77. Official Records, Series II, Volume VIII, page 215;

78. Major Daniel S. Printup letters, file 500-325, Chemung County, New York;

79. Official Records, Series II, Volume VI, pages 503-504;

80. Holmes, Clay W., *Elmira Prison Camp,* pages 89-91, 96-97;

81. Official Records, Volume VII, pages 1184-1185;

82. National Archives, "General and Special Orders", Volume 3, page 287;

83. Holmes, Clay W., *Elmira Prison Camp,* pages 68-69;

84. Keiley, Anthony M., *In Vinculis; or, The Prisoner of War,* page 130; Ottman, Walter H., *A History of the City of Elmira, New York*, page 170; *Elmira Daily Advertiser*, February 11, 1865; Holmes, Clay W., *Elmira Prison Camp,* pages 68-69;

85. Official Records, Volume 8, pages 419-420;

86. Holmes, Clay W., *Elmira Prison Camp,* page 124;

87. King, John A., *My Experience in the Confederate Army and in Northern Prisons,* page 47;

88. Holmes, Clay W., *Elmira Prison Camp,* page 124;

89. King, John A., *My Experience in the Confederate Army and in Northern Prisons,* page 47;

90. Elmira (N.Y.) Daily Advertiser, March 17, 1865;

91. Official Records, Volume 8, pages 419-420;

92. King, John A., *My Experience in the Confederate Army and in Northern Prisons*, page 47;

93. Huffman, James, *Ups and Downs*, page 103;

94. Inspection Reports 3/20/1865;

95. Holmes, Clay W., *Elmira Prison Camp*, page 295;

96. Official records, Volume 8, page 1001;

97. Lieber Code of 1863, section III, article number 77;

98. Holmes, Clay, page 161;

99. Holmes, Clay, page 162;

100. Holmes, Clay, page 162;

101. Holmes, Clay, *The Elmira Prison Camp*, page 151;

102. Holmes, Clay, *The Elmira Prison Camp*, page 171-172;

103. Holmes, Clay, *The Elmira Prison Camp*, page 172;

104. *Montgomery, Alabama, Advertiser,* June 22, 1902;

105. Maull, John F., *The Elmira Prison Camp*, page 172-173;

106. Benson, Berry, *Berry Benson's Civil War Book*, page 137; Holmes, Clay, *The Elmira Prison Camp*, page 174;

107. Benson Papers, page 445-446;

108. Maull, John F., Holmes, Clay, *The Elmira Prison Camp*, page 174;

109. Benson, Berry, *Berry Benson's Civil War Book*, page 139;

110. Benson, Berry, *Berry Benson's Civil War Book*, page 138;

111. Benson, Berry, *Berry Benson's Civil War Book*, page 140;

112. Benson, Berry, *Berry Benson's Civil War Book*, page 140;

113. Maull, John F., Holmes, Clay, *The Elmira Prison Camp,* page 175;

114. Maull, John F., Holmes, Clay, *The Elmira Prison Camp*, page 173; Benson, Berry, *Berry Benson's Civil War Book,* page 138;

115. Maull, John F., Holmes, Clay, *The Elmira Prison Camp*, page 108;

116. Benson, Berry, *Berry Benson's Civil War Book*, page 142;

117. Benson, Berry, *Berry Benson's Civil War Book*, page 143;

118. Benson, Berry, *Berry Benson's Civil War Book*, page 143;

119. Holmes, Clay, *The Elmira Prison Camp*, page 195;

120 Benson, Berry, *Berry Benson's Civil War Book*, page 144

121. Benson, Berry, *Berry Benson's Civil War Book*, page 145;

122. Benson, Berry, page 115;

123. Benson, Berry, page 148;

124. Wade, F. S., *Getting Out of Prison;* Holmes, Clay, *Elmira Prison Camp*, page 160; Gray, Michael P., *The Business of Captivity, Elmira and Its Civil War Prison,* page 115;

125. Benson, Berry, *Berry Benson's Civil War Book*, page 148-149;

126. Benson, Berry, *Berry Benson's Civil War Book*, page 149;

127. Toney, Marcus page 109-110;

128. *New York Sun*, August 13, 1880;

129. Holmes, Clay, *Elmira Prison Camp*, pages 145-150;

Chapter 5:

Pages 115-118

1. Boate, Edward Wellington, *Southern Historical Society Papers*, Volume X, 1882, No. 1, 31-32;
2. Urban, John W., *Battlefield and Prison Pen*, page 382;
3. Ould, Judge Robert, *Southern Historical Society Papers*, Volume I, No.3, March, 1876, pages 128-129;
4. Ould, Judge Robert, *Southern Historical Society Papers*, Volume I, No.3, March, 1876, pages 128-129;
5. Official Records, Series II, Volume VII, page 891-892;
6. *New York Times*, March 24, 1864;

Chapter 6:

Pages 119-122

1. Official Records, Series II, Volume III, page 157;
2. Official Records, Series II, Volume VIII, page 804; Official Records, Series II, Volume VII, page 606-607;
3. Official Records, Series II, Volume VIII, Section 7, page 800;
4. Official Records, Series II, Volume VII, pages 606-607;
5. Grigsby, Colonel Melvin, *The Smoked Yank,* pages 137-138;
6. Page, James Madison, *The True Story of Andersonville Prison: A Defense of Major Henry Wirz*, pages 108-109; Grigsby, Colonel Melvin, *The Smoked Yank,* pages 137-138;
7. Official Records, Series II, Volume VI, page 315;
8. Official Records, Series II, Volume VI, page 390;
9. Official Records, Series II, Volume VII, pages 150-151;
10. Official Records, Series II, Volume VII, pages 1003-1004;
11. Official Records, Series II, Volume VII, pages 1004-1005, 1025; Official Records, Series II, Volume VIII, page 4;
12. Official Records, Series II, Volume VII, pages 918-919;

Chapter 7:

Pages 123-132

1. *The Medical and Surgical History of the War of the Rebellion, (1861-65),* Volume III, part I, page 46, table XVIII:

2. Greer, William R., *Recollections of a Private Soldier of the Army of the Confederate States,* page 3;

3. Addison, Walter D., *Recollections of a Confederate Soldier of the Prison-Pens of Point Lookout, Maryland, and Elmira, New York*, pages 4-5;

4. *The Medical and Surgical History of the War of the Rebellion,* Volume III, part I, table XVIII, page 46; Miller-Keane, *Encyclopedia & Dictionary of Medicine, Nursing, & Allied Heath, Fifth Edition,* Page 420;

5. Handy, Reverend I. W. K., *Southern Historical Society Papers*, Volume 1, April, 1876, page 271;

6. King, John R., My Experience in The Confederate Army and in Northern Prisons, page 37, Roanoke, West Virginia, February 23, 1916;

7. King, John A., *My Experience in the Confederate Army and In Northern Prisons*, page 37; Keiley Anthony M., *In Vinculis Or, The Prisoner Of War,* page 86;

8. *The Medical and Surgical History of the War of the Rebellion,* Volume III, part I, table XVIII, page 46;

9. *The Medical and Surgical History of the War of the Rebellion,* Volume I, part III, table LIII, page 629, 662-675;

10. *The Medical and Surgical History of the War of the Rebellion,* Volume I, part III, page 73, 649-661;

11. *The Medical and Surgical History of the War of the Rebellion,* Volume I, part III, pages 649-661; Miller-Keane, *Encyclopedia & Dictionary of Medicine, Nursing, & Allied Heath, Fifth Edition*, Page 890;

12. *The Medical and Surgical History of the War of the Rebellion,* Volume III, part I, table XVIII, page 46, pages 751-752; Miller-Keane, *Encyclopedia & Dictionary of Medicine, Nursing, & Allied Heath, Fifth Edition*, Page 1,344;

13. The Medical and Surgical History of the War of the Rebellion, Volume I, part III, pages 74-77, 109-190; Miller-Keane, Encyclopedia & Dictionary of Medicine, Nursing, & Allied Heath, Fifth Edition, Page 1,344;

14. The Medical and Surgical History of the War of the Rebellion, Volume I, part III, pages 683-715; Volume III, part I, table XVIII, page 46;

15. Miller-Keane, *Encyclopedia & Dictionary of Medicine, Nursing, & Allied Heath, Fifth Edition*, Page 1,344;

16. Hopkins, Luther, *Prison life at Point Lookout*, page 88;

17. Bowden, the Reverend Malachi, *My Life as a Yankee Captive*, page 97;

18. Rose, Minnie Bowen, Editorial Director, *Diseases, Nursing Reference Library*, page 391; Rose, Minnie Bowen, Editorial Director, *Diseases, Nursing Reference Library*, pages 669-670;

19. *The Medical and Surgical History of the War of the Rebellion,* Volume I, part III, table LIII, pages 624-648, 629;

20. Miller-Keane, *Encyclopedia & Dictionary of Medicine, Nursing, & Allied Heath, Fifth Edition*, Page 1,545-1,546;

21. *The Medical and Surgical History of the War of the Rebellion,* Volume I, part III, table L, page 209, 273-323;

Chapter 8:

Page 133-255

Prisoner's Statements

Chapter 9:

Page: 256-271
1. Confederate States of America, Congress, Joint Select Committee to Investigate the Condition and Treatment of Prisoners of War

Chapter 10:

Page 272-289

The Lieber Code

Bibliography

Articles and Periodicals:

Davis, Thaddeus C., *Confederate Veteran* Magazine, February, 1899, page 65;

Dillon, Philip R., *Great Moments In War, Told by Living Generals,* November 16, 1911, *The Pittsburg Press*

Ewan, R.B., *Reminiscences of Prison Life at Elmira, N.Y.,* January 1908;

Harkness, Edson J, *The Expeditions Against Fort Fisher and Wilmington,* page 174, *Military Essays and Recollections; Papers Read Before the Commandery of the State of Illinois, Military Order of the Loyal Legion of the United States,* Volume II;

Huffman, James, *Prisoner of War, Atlantic Magazine* 163, no. 4, April 1939;

Jones, James P., *A Rebel's Diary of Elmira Prison Camp, Chemung Historical Journal* 20, no. 3, March 1975;

Leon, Lewis, *Diary of a Tar Heel Confederate Soldier,* Stone Publishing, Charlotte, NC;

Lamb, Colonel William, *Colonel Lamb's Story of Fort Fisher*, The Blockade Runner Museum, 1966;

Lamb, Colonel William, *The Battles of Fort Fisher*, The Southern Historical Society *Papers*, Volume XXI, page 284;

Moore, Robert, *Break Out*, Civil War Times Illustrated, 30, No. 5, November/December 1991;

Sherrill, Miles, *A Soldier's Story: Prison Life and Other Incidents,* University of North Carolina at Chapel Hill, 1998;

Stamp, James B., *Ten Months Experience in Northern Prisons, Alabama Historical Quarterly 18,* pages 486-498;

Taylor, G.T., *Prison Experience in Elmira, N.Y., Confederate Veteran* Magazine 20, no. 7, July 1912;

Terry, Adrian's letter to his wife, *The Task Before Them,* page 43, Longacre, Edward G., *Civil War Times Illustrated,* volume XXI, No. 10, February, 1983;

The Treatment of Prisoners during the War Between the States, Southern Historical Society Papers 1, no. 3, March 1876;

The Treatment of Prisoners during the War, Southern Historical Society Papers 1, no. 4, April 1876;

Turner, Henry M. *Civil War Times Illustrated,* 31 (October/November, 1980);

Wade, F.S., *Getting Out of Prison, Confederate Veteran* magazine 34, no. 10, October 1926;

Ward, John Shirley, *Responsibility for the Death of Prisoners, Confederate Veteran* magazine 4, no. 1, January 1896;

Wyeth, John Allan, *Cold Cheer at Camp Morton, Century Magazine* 41 no. 6 (April 1891) 848;

Books:

Badeau, Adam, *Military History of Ulysses S. Grant, From April, 1861, To April, 1865.,* Vol. III, New York: D. Appleton and Company, 1885;

Benson, Berry, Susan W. Benson, ed., *Berry Benson's Civil War Book: Memoirs of a Confederate Scout and Sharpshooter,* Athens, Ga.: University of Georgia Press, 1962;

Bland, T. A., *Life of Benjamin F. Butler,* Lee and Shepard, Publisher, New York, 1879;

Butler, Benjamin F., *Butler's Book: Autobiography and Personal Reminiscences of Major-General Benjamin F. Butler*, A. M. Thayer & Co. Publishers, 1892;

Canney, Donald L., *The Old Steam Navy, Frigates, Sloops, and Gunboats, 1815-1885,* Vol. 1, Naval Institute Press, Annapolis, Maryland, 1990;

Catton, Bruce, *The American Hertitage, Picture History of the Civil War,* 1960, American Hertitage Publishing Co., Inc., & Bonanza Books, New York;

Cisco, Walter Brian, *War Crimes Against Southern Civilians*, 2013, Pelican Publishing Company Inc., 1000 Burmaster Street, Gretna, Louisiana;

Current, Richard N., *The Lincoln Nobody Knows,* Hill and Wang, 1958;

Davis, Stephen, *Atlanta Will Fall, Sherman, Joe Johnston, and the Yankee Heavy Battalions,*1948, Scholarly Resources Inc., 104 Greenhill, Avenue, Wilmington, DE;

Davis, Stephen, *What the Yankees Did to Us*, Mercer University Press, Macon, Georgia, 2012;

Diagnostic and Statistical Manual of Mental Disorders, 5th Edition, *Arlington: American Psychiatric Publishing,* pages 160–168, American Psychiatric Publishing, May 27, 2013*;*

Fonvielle, Chris E., *The Wilmington Campaign: Last Rays of Departing Hope,* Savas Publishing, 1997;

Fox, Lt. Colonel William F., *Regimental Losses In the American Civil War, 1861-1865, Albany Publishing Company,* 1889;

Garrison, Webb, *Atlanta and the War,*1995, Rutledge Hill Press, 211 Seventh Avenue North, Nashville, Tennessee;

Glatharr, Joseph T., *Forged in Battle, The Civil War Alliance of Black Soldiers and White Officers,* The Free Press, A Division of Macmillan, Inc., New York, 1990;

Gragg, Rod, *Confederate Goliath: The Battle of Fort Fisher,* Harper Collins, 1991;

Gray, Michael P., *The Business of Captivity: Elmira and It's Civil War Prison,* The Kent State University Press, 2001;

Grigsby, Colonel Melvin, *The Smoked Yank*, Chicago: Regan Printing Company, 1891;

Grimsley, Mark, *The Hard Hand of War, Union Military Policy Toward Southern Civilians, 1861-1865*, 1995, Cambridge University Press, Cambridge, New York;

Halleck, Henry W., International Law; Or, Rules Regulating the Intercourse of States In Peace and War, 1861, New York, Published by D. Van Bancroft & Company, London: Sampson Low, Son & Co.

Hallock, Judith Lee, *Braxton Bragg and Confederate Defeat*, vol. II, University of Alabama Press, 1991;

Hampson, Helen (Wyeth), My Great-Great Grandfather Was a Prisoner of War . . . Libby Prison, 2002;

Heatwole, John L., *The Burning: Sheridan's Devastation of the Shenandoah Valley,* 1998, Rockbridge Publishing, an imprint of Howell Press, Inc., Charlottesville, Virginia;

Hoehling, A. A., *Last Train from Atlanta*, New York, Thomas Yoseloff, 1958;

Horigan, Michael, *Elmira: Death Camp of the North,* Stackpole Books, 2002;

Holmes, Clay W., *The Elmira Prison Camp: A History of the Military Prison at Elmira, N.Y. July 6, 1864, to July 10, 1865.* New York: Knickerbocker Press, 1912;

Huffman, James, *Ups and Downs of a Confederate Soldier,* New York: William E. Rudge's Sons, 1940;

Jones, James Pickett & McDonough, James Lee, *War So Terrible, Sherman and Atlanta,* 1987, W. W. Norton & Company, New York, London;

Jones, Katharine M., *When Sherman Came: Southern Women and the Great March,* 1964, The Bobbs-Merrill Company, INC., Indianapolis, IN, Kansas City, Kansas, New York, New York;

Keiley, Anthony M., *In Vinculis; or, The Prisoner of War: Being The Experience Of A Rebel In Two Federal Pens,* Blelock & Co., No. 19 Beekman Street, New York, 1866;

Kennett, Lee, Marching through Georgia: The Story of Soldiers and Civilians During Sherman's Campaign, 1995;

King, John A., *My Experience in the Confederate Army, and in Northern Prisons,* Roanoke, West Virginia, Stonewall Jackson Chapter No. 1333, United Daughters of the Confederacy, Clarksburg, West Virginia, 1917;

Leon, Louis, *Diary of a Tarheel Confederate Prisoner,* Charlotte, N.C.: Stone, 1913;

Levy, George, *To Die In Chicago, Confederate Prisoners at Camp Douglas 1862-65,* Pelican, 1999;

Manarin, Louis H. and Weymouth T. Jordan, eds., *North Carolina Troops1861-1865: A Roster,* 13 volumes, Raleigh, North Carolina: Division of Archives and History, 1966-1993;

Marshall, Jessie Ames, *Private and Official Correspondence of Gen. Benjamin F. Butler During the Period of the Civil War, Volume II, June 1862-February 1863,* The Plimpton Press, Norwood, Mass., 1917;

Mast, Greg, *State Troops and Volunteers*, *A Photographic Record Of North Carolina Civil War Soldiers,* North Carolina Department of Cultural Resources, Volume I, 1995;

McCaslin, Richard B., *The Last Stronghold: The Campaign For Fort Fisher,* McWhiney Foundation Press, 2003;

McDonough, James Lee & Jones, James Pickett, *War So Terrible, Sherman and Atlanta,* 1987, W. W. Norton & Company, New York, London;

McPherson, James M., *Brother against Brother, Time-Life books History of the Civil War,* 1990, The Time In, Book Company, Prentice Hall Press, 15 Columbus Circle, New York, New York;

Miller-Keane, *Encyclopedia & Dictionary of Medicine, Nursing, & Allied Heath, Fifth Edition*, W. B. Saunders Company, Philadelphia, PA, 1992;

Moore, Mark A., *The Wilmington Campaign and the Battles For Fort Fisher,* Savas, 1999;

Opie, John N., *A Rebel Cavalryman with Lee, Stuart, and Jackson,* Chicago: W.B. Conkey, 1899;

Ottman, Walter H., *A History of the City of Elmira, New York;*

Page, James Madison, *The True Story of Andersonville Prison: A Defense of Major Henry Wirz*, The Neil Publishing Company, New York and Washington, 1908;

Pickenpaugh, Roger, *Captives In Gray,* The University of Alabama Press, 2009;

Poe, Clarence, *True Tales of the South At War, How Soldiers Fought and Families Lived, 1861-1865,* Pratt, Fletcher, *Stanton: Lincoln's Secretary of War,* W. W. Norton &

Company Inc., 1953;

Richards, C. Steven, PhD, and O'Hara, Michael W., PhD, *The Oxford Handbook of Depression and Comorbidity,* pages 160-168, Oxford University Press, June 14, 2014;

Rogers, Henry Munroe, *Memories of Ninety Years,* Cambridge, Massachusetts: Houghton, Miflin, 1928;

Sheridan, Philip H., *Personal Memoirs of P. H. Sheridan, General, United States Army,* Volumes 1 & 2, New York, Webster, 1888;

Sherman, William T., *Memoirs of General William T. Sherman, Library of America, New York,* 1990;

Sherman, William T., *Memoirs of General William T. Sherman*, Volume 2, Bloomington, Indiana University Press, 1957;

Speer, Lonnie R., *Portals To Hell: Military Prisons of the Civil War,* Stackpole Books, 1997;

Speer, Lonnie R., *War of Vengeance: Acts of Retaliation against Civil War POWs,* Stackpole Books, 2002;

Stephens, Alexander H., *A Constitutional View of the Late War Between the States,* vol. II, Chicago: National Publishing Co. 1868;

Styple, William B. & Fitzpatrick, John J., *The Andersonville Diary & Memoirs of Charles Hopkins,* Belle Grove Publishing, 1988;

Thomas, Leonard R., *The Story of Fort Fisher*, page 16, *The United Service: A Monthly Review of Military and Naval Affairs,* vol. X, Philadelphia: L.R. Hamersly & Co., 1893;

Toney, Marcus B., *The Privations of a Private,* Nashville and Dallas: M.E. Church, South, Smith and Lamar, 1907;

Towner, Ausburn, *Our County and Its People - A History of the Valley and County of Chemung From the Closing years of the Eighteenth Century*, D. Mason & Publishers, 1892;

Triebe, Richard H., *Fort Fisher to Elmira, the Fatal Journey of 518 Confederate Soldiers,* Coastal Books, Wilmington, North Carolina, 2013;

Watkins, Sam R., *Co. Aytch, Maury Grays, First Tennessee Regiment or, A Side Show to the Big Show*, Chattanooga, Tennessee, Times Printing Company, 1900;

Wilkeson, Frank, *Turned Inside Out: Recollections of a Private Soldier in the Army of the Potomac,* New York and London: G.P. Putnam's Sons, 1887;

Williams, T. Harry, *Lincoln and the Radicals,* Madison: University of Wisconsin Press, 1960;

Internet:

American Civil War Research Database, Historical Data Systems
Chemung Valley History Museum
Footnotes.com

Manuscripts:

Addison Walter D., Southern Historical Collection of the University of North
Carolina Library, Chapel Hill, North Carolina;

Blair, B.F., letter *To Mother*, December 27, 1864, B.F. Blair Papers, Archives Division,
U.S.,

Braddy, Captain Kinchen, Kitchen Braddy letter to Z.T. Fulmore, March 25, 1901, misc.
Civil War papers, Division of Archives and History, Raleigh, North Carolina;

James J. Cleer papers, Manuscript Department, William R. Perkins Library, Duke
University; Seaman James J., James Cleer in a letter to his mother and father,
January 17, 1865;

Confederate Veterans' Talks, Lower Cape Fear Historical Society, Wilmington, North
Carolina,

McQueen, Corporal Henry Clay, Henry Clay McQueen papers, *Confederate Veterans'
Talks*, Lower Cape Fear Historical Society Archives;

Greer, William R. Papers, *Recollections of a Private Soldier of the Army of the
Confederate States,* Manuscript Department, William R. Perkins Library, Duke
University, North Carolina

Montgomery, James, James Montgomery papers, *Confederate Veterans' Talks*, Lower Cape
Fear Historical Society Archives;

Reilly, James, James Reilly's Account of Fort Fisher, W. L. DeRossett papers, North
Carolina Department of Archives and History;

Sanger, Eugene F., Eugene F. Sanger Papers, Records of the Office of the Adjutant
General, Regimental Correspondence, 1861-1865, Maine State Archives.

College of William and Mary, William Lamb Collection;

William M. Reaves Collection

Newspapers:

The Daily Constitutionalist, Augusta, Georgia,
Daily National Intelligencer, Washington, D. C.,
Elmira Daily Advertiser,
Elmira Daily Gazette,
Mobile, Alabama, Evening News,
New York Times,
New York Tribune,
New York World,
The Pittsburg Press,
The Syracuse Daily Courier and Union,
Wilmington Daily Journal,
Wilmington Messenger,

Official Publications:

Confederate States of America, Congress, *Joint Select Committee to Investigate the Condition and Treatment of Prisoners of War,* March, 1865;

The Medical and Surgical History of the Civil War, Broadfoot Publishing Company, Wilmington, North Carolina, 1991;

The Medical and Surgical History of the War of the Rebellion, (1861-65), Volumes I, II and III, *Prepared in Accordance Acts of Congress, Under the Direction of Surgeon General Joseph K .Barnes, United States Army,* Washington Government Printing Office, 1870-1888;

United States War Department, ed. *The War of the Rebellion: A Compilation of the Official Records of the Union and Confederate Armies,* 128 Volunteers Washington, D.C., Government Printing Office;

Official Records of the Union and Confederate Navies In the War of the Rebellion 1861-65, Published Under the Direction of the Honorable H.A. Herbert, Secretary of the Navy, by Lt. Commander Richard Rush, U.S. Navy;

Index

About The Author

Richard H. Triebe is a freelance writer and historian published in multiple periodicals. He is the author of several historical novels and has done extensive research work regarding the Fort Fisher prisoners. Two of his books, *Fort Fisher to Elmira* and *Point Lookout Prison Camp and Hospital,* were awarded the coveted Jefferson Davis Historical Gold Medal Award for out-standing achievement for a literary work. His ground-breaking research resulted in hundreds of names being added to the rolls of Confederate prisoners who died at both prisons. This list contains the names of the Confederate dead which include civilians, marines, sailors and soldiers.

Richard has an Associate's Degree in Marine Technology. He is a former Chicago police officer and was a Provost Marshal investigator in the United States Army. Richard is a member of the *Friends of Fort Fisher,* the *Friends of Elmira,* the *Cape Fear Civil War Round Table*, and has presented historical

Richard H. Triebe

overviews of the battles of Fort Fisher to many local organizations. Richard is also presenting a PowerPoint talks about the northern prisons at Elmira, New York, and Point Lookout, Maryland. He and his wife, Barbara, live in Wilmington, North Carolina.

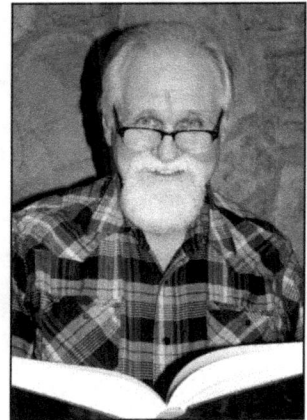

www.ingramcontent.com/pod-product-compliance
Lightning Source LLC
Chambersburg PA
CBHW050636150426
42811CB00052B/855